CHRISTOPHER COLUMBUS,
THE LAST TEMPLAR

CHRISTOPHER COLUMBUS,
THE LAST TEMPLAR

RUGGERO MARINO

TRANSLATED BY
ARIEL GODWIN

Destiny Books
Rochester, Vermont

Destiny Books
One Park Street
Rochester, Vermont 05767
www.DestinyBooks.com

Destiny Books is a division of Inner Traditions International

Originally published in Italian under the title *Cristoforo Colombo, l'ultimo dei templari*
    by Sperling and Kupfer Editori, Milano, Italy
First U.S. edition published in 2007 by Destiny Books

Library of Congress Cataloging-in-Publication Data
Marino, Ruggero, 1940–
  [Cristoforo Colombo, l'ultimo dei templari. English]
  Christopher Columbus, the last templar / Ruggero Marino ; translated by Ariel
Godwin.
     p. cm.
  Includes bibliographical references and index.
  ISBN-13: 978-1-59477-190-3 (pbk.)
  ISBN-10: 1-59477-190-1 (pbk.)
  1. Columbus, Christopher. 2. Columbus, Christopher—Relations with Templars.
3. Templars—History. 4. Explorers—America—Biography. 5. Explorers—Spain—
Biography. 6. America—Discovery and exploration—Spanish. I. Title.
  E112.M35413 2007
  970.01'5092—dc22
  [B]
                                                                    2007015037

Printed and bound in the United States by Lake Book Manufacturing

10 9 8 7 6 5 4 3 2 1

Text design by Priscilla Baker and text layout
This book was typeset in Garamond Premier Pro with Mason Alternate as the
display typeface

✠

To Gianni Letta, and to all men and
women able to dream

Contents

Charity, Truth, and Justice

Because the truth always triumphs
Let me not remain confounded forever.
Christopher Columbus

Christopher Columbus "discovered" America on October 12, 1492, the day the world changed, and the modern era began. Columbus, a mariner of humble birth and believed to be from Genoa, Italy, had left Palos, Spain, on August 3 of that same year. After years of persistence, Columbus had finally managed to convince the king and queen of Spain, Ferdinand of Aragon and Isabella of Castile, to support his undertaking. On the first voyage he sailed with three caravels, the *Niña*, the *Pinta*, and the *Santa Maria*, and crossed the Atlantic in a little more than two months. On his return, in January 1493, the pope, a Spaniard—Alexander VI, Rodrigo Borgia—placed the New World under Spanish sovereignty. Columbus made three more voyages to the Americas. He died in 1506 without ever truly knowing where he had landed, convinced that this territory was part of Asia. The name America was given to the New World in homage to the expeditions of the Florentine Amerigo Vespucci.

This story has been handed down for more than five hundred years. But the story has been corrupted, and now the time has come to set the record straight, to upturn it like an old hourglass—the instrument that navigators used to measure time.

In addition to my books published in 1991 and 1997, this book forms the main part of a new work, which took fifteen years to complete. The reconstruction of events is intended to confront the age-old question from various angles. The present part of the investigation takes a lengthy route through an amazing counterhistory, traversing past investigations (which waver between reality and legend), mysterious maps, the political panorama preceding Christopher Columbus's first official expedition, and the pontificate of Giovanni Battista Cybo (Pope Innocent VIII), the sponsor of the expeditions to the Americas. It also presents a crescendo of remarkable historical and geographical revelations. We have proceeded with the support of the two pillars of research: truth and justice, backed by actual facts. We shall move through a labyrinth and inevitably there will be a few errors—for which I ask the reader in advance for forgiveness.

It was truth and justice that Columbus invoked in his poignant letter, sent while he was stranded and ill in Jamaica:

The pure devotion which I have ever borne to the service of Your Highnesses, and the unmerited wrong that I have suffered, will not permit me to remain silent, although I would fain do so; I pray Your Highnesses to pardon me. I am so ruined as I have said; hitherto I have wept for others; now, heaven have mercy upon me, and may the earth weep for me. Of worldly goods I have not even a blanca for an offering in spiritual things. Here in the Indies I have become careless of the prescribed forms of religion. Alone in my trouble, sick, in daily expectation of death, and encompassed about by a million savages, full of cruelty and our foes, and so separated from the holy Sacraments of Holy Church, my soul will be forgotten if it here leaves my body. Weep for me, whoever has charity, truth, and justice.

I did not sail upon this voyage to gain honor or wealth; this is certain, for already all hope of that was dead. I came to Your Highnesses with true devotion and with ready zeal, and I do not lie. I humbly pray Your Highnesses that if it please God to bring me forth from this place, you will be pleased to permit me to go to Rome and to other places of pilgrimage. May the Holy Trinity preserve your life and high estate.

Done in the Indies in the island of Jamaica, on the
seventh of July, in the year one thousand five hundred and three.

CHRISTOPHER COLUMBUS

For the truth—which has been erased and concealed for a good five centuries, since the days when East and West, Islam and Christianity, were fighting for world domination just as they are today. History seems to repeat itself in a disquieting manner, and our present times are rooted more than ever in that past of which Christopher Columbus was the heroic protagonist. Because of his explorations, the West prevailed; the world was complete, and the course of humanity was forever altered.

Acknowledgments

A WORK SUCH as this, which took more than fifteen years, requires thanks to be given to many people: to those who generously brought me some detail or underlined some interesting passage, to those who contributed by sharing theories or hypotheses, and to those who, with their praise and encouragement, provided valuable psychological support—because doubt and discouragement, not to mention many attempts at pilfering my work, as well as premeditated opposition and downright calumny, were always lying in wait.

Thanks are therefore due, above all, to Piero Cesaretti, who aided me at some important junctions in my research. Thanks also to Alessandro Matteucci, self-styled Cybo of Anguillara, without whom my research would never have begun. Thanks also to my friend the writer Mario Farneto for his suggestions; he was the first to read my complete work. Special thanks to German Arciniegas (Colombia), Arnoldo Canclini (Argentina), Marina Como, Corrado Natalicchio, and Riccardo Tanturri, who in their books (respectively *America es otra cosa, La Fe del descubridor, Accadde solo per caso, Il vescovo di Molfetta diventa papa,* and *Carovana di lago*) dedicated a chapter, or at least ample space, to my research. Further thanks to: Ferdinando Adornato, Aldo Agosto, Francesc Llorens Albardaner, Bruno Alio, Fabio Andriola, Antonio Angelini, Donata Aphel, Stefano Ardito, Alberto Arecchi, Osvaldo

Baldacci, Raffaele Belvederi, Roberto Bencivenga, Marcella Bencivenni, Patrizia Bertolotti, Osvaldo Bevilacqua, Suzy Blady, Enrica Bonaccorti, Elio Cadelo, Marcello Calcagnini, Giuseppe Canessa, Lorenzo Capone, Memmo Caporilli, Angela Caracciolo Aricó, Luca Cardinalini, Franco Cardini, Giuseppe Carrisi, Giulio Castelli, Alessandro Cecchi Paone, Isabella Ceccopieri, Andrea Cecovi, Giorgio Celli, Francobaldo Chiocci, Maurizio Costanzo, Madel Crasta, Rosanna Cravenna, Walter de Gregorio, Pino dell'Orco, Michele del Vescovo, Isabella de Martini, Gennaro de Stefano, Vittorio di Cesare, Francesco di Maggio, Giovanni di Martino, Sandro Dini, Viviano Domenici, Barbara Farenholz, Claudio Farnetani, Mario Farneti, Vittorio Feltri, Giorgio Ferraresi, Maria Fiorelli, Publio Fiori, Roberto Fondi, Adriano Forgione, Agostino Gambino, Renzo Gente, Anna Gentilini, Roberto Giacobbo, Anna Giacomini, Paolo Granzotto, Brian Hammond, Roberto Iannone, Cardinal Pio Laghi, Marcello Lambertini, Gabriele La Porta, Don Lavagna, the Legion of Christ, Umberto Lo Faso, Rossella Lorenzi, Antonio Luciani, Luca Maccaferri, Carlo Maccallini, Luciana Marino, Luigi Mascheroni, Gaetano Massa, Enrico Massidda, Salvatore Mastruzzi, Claudio Matarrese, Enrico Messina, Alessandro Moriccioni, Giorgio Moser, Richard Owen, Antonio Patuelli, Susanna Pelle, Paolo Pelù, Francesco Perfetti, Arrigo Petacco, Paolo Picozzi, Roberto Pinotti, Geo Pistarino, Giorgio Radicati, Olga Raffo, Armando Ravaglioli, Claudio Robimarga, Gian Luigi Rondi, Carlo Rossella, Enrico Rossi, Enrico Rovai, Luigi Saitta, Paola Saluzzi, Luciano Santilli, Marco Sassano, Javier Sierra, Marina Silvestrini, Antonio Socci, Andrea Somma, Giuliano Soria, Emilio Spedicato, Romolo Augusto Staccioli, Cinzia Tani, Luigi Tasselli, Paolo Emilio Taviani, Franco Tosi, Giulio Vada, and Antonio Ventura. My apologies to any I have unintentionally omitted.

The list is long, but much longer would be the "infamous column" of the doors on which we have knocked, at all levels, without receiving the slightest answer, not even what courtesy would require.

ONE

THE FALL OF CONSTANTINOPLE

AUGUST 3, 1492: Three caravels[1] departed from Spain, three vessels with three masts like three crosses, held aloft in the name of the Holy Trinity, in the name of the *Santa Maria*. Thus the New World began in a golden dawn of hope. Like a bad omen, however, the red sky was a presage of the blood of innocent natives. The parable of the modern world began with this symbolic wound. The parable was embodied by a man named Christopher Columbus, and by the perfect number: 3, "the triad that leads to a new integration, one that does not negate the duality preceding it but rather, overcomes it, just as the child is a binding element that unites the male and female parents."[2]

A New World was born, and with it "the child." The birth was ordained under the banner of the kingdom of God in the Promised Land, in the crucible of the Great Work. On the wave of the Renaissance, tradition was wedded to remarkable innovation—in view of the new advent, the Resurrection.

The "discovery" of America was the dream most certain to unite East and West, sun and moon, physically and spiritually breaking the negative cycle of human events through the divine voice of the stars and by treasure not solely material. Humanity had grown, in past and present, like the twin hemispheres that were to be reunited in time and in space. It was not just the dream of a simple sailor or of a great navigator with the winds of Rome blowing in his sails. It was also the secret design of the Renaissance, of Christian Europe, of the eternal city, of the Vatican—and of a pope who was known as the sponsor pope, the disappeared pope, the betrayed pope: Giovanni Battista Cybo, Innocent VIII.[3]

A sixteenth-century chronicler, Francisco Lopez de Gòmara,[4] wrote the discovery of America represented the most important event for humanity in the course of history since the birth of Christ. In light of subsequent events and considering the present political and economic state of the world, we can only agree with this age-old statement.

Fifteen hundred years after the birth of Jesus, the winds of the church were blowing again. They steered the ship that bore the name of the Messiah's mother across the Stella Maris, the blue sea rippling like a Madonna's cloak. They steered a man marked by destiny and by his name. And yet, centuries-old tradition, which has codified the event of that fateful day, has left us with a view of the first and subsequent voyages of Christopher Columbus as the enterprise of a solitary visionary, a controversial master of the sea, a courageous adventurer blessed with good luck, despite his many errors.

The excellent planning and coordination of the project, its execution and perfect timing, given the particular moment in history, have been reduced by some sources to the rash perseverance of a Mr. Nobody, a calculation made entirely in error, an accidental discovery. But *discovery* is not even an appropriate term; nor is the Pharisaic and hypocritical *encounter,* coined in 1992 at the five hundredth anniversary of the voyage. We intend to avoid the debate of whether it was a *conquest.* The proper term is *revelation,* and Columbus was the revealer. The truth has been made official and is now considered tried and tested, and not just in the Christian world. In this geopolitical debate, Columbus forms the last link to the past—and the first link to the future, the definitive link. Was America, as has always been said, a phenomenon of serendipity?[5] Nothing in this enterprise, not even the smallest detail, was the result of chance.

The discovery of America was not exclusively a concern of the West, although it was the West that succeeded in making it. The indisputable fact remains that only as a result of Christopher Columbus's voyages did America become a fixed point in the consciousness of humanity, no longer restricted to existing in the imagination and in unconfessed and unconfessable secrets. It was Columbus who captured the moment of truth, drew back the veil, defeated the last resistance, and caused ignorance to crumble once and for all. He pitted the old world against all its responsibilities, confronting it with a world eager to be new. The discovery of America is the story of a man who proved himself much more capable in times of misfortune than in his brief and illusory moments of glory.

Lies and calumny have triumphed in a perfect crime, a "scientific" project of disinformation. As has been known all along, the surviving maps and documents lend themselves to all manner of interpretation.[6]

On the occasion of the five hundredth anniversary, the latest results of research came to an agreed conclusion, obviously reached irrespective of the facts and aiming to salvage the political aspect of the issue by a kind of compromise, stating: "Columbus was Italian, the enterprise was Spanish." Scholars are forever divided as to the authenticity of almost all the sources on which the reconstruction of events has been based. The prolific writings of Columbus have been discredited; his maps have mostly vanished. He studied many books, but almost nothing remains of his library. He continually found reasons to set things down in writing, yet gaps in the story are as large as they are mysterious.[7]

In short, Columbus is studied and judged without taking into account his words or the words of those who were near him. With the rise of nation-states, the first nationalisms were born. Spain was becoming a major power and would become greater still as a result of Columbus's discovery. It was through a fawning and subservient political press, and on the wave of pride and patriotism characteristic of the Iberian population even today, that these judgments were made. Italy, by contrast, was divided and torn by rivalries between nobles, and did not become a unified nation until the nineteenth century. The length of time the myth has been handed down represents the most successful press campaign in the history of humanity: a triumph of marketing, the fruit borne of a vision and encouraged by the Spanish crown, a distortion that humiliates Columbus and conceals his pope.

The event has been reconstructed to serve specific interests, answering to the eternal law of might makes right: the doctrine of reason of state. It has been reconstructed for the glorification of those who were the uncontested and incontestable victors in this game, this battle of Pope Cybo and the monarchs of Spain, albeit with due differentiation between Isabella of Castile and Ferdinand of Aragon. She, the pious queen, did her utmost to aid the Christian teller of tales; he, the astute and taciturn king, was disinclined to support this foreigner. In a series of entirely hagiographic meetings and anecdotes, the one paying the dues is always Columbus: petulant, cunning, begging, secretive, greedy, arrogant, sly, calculating, incapable, or ruthless.

Supposedly, Columbus was the man who appeared from nowhere, hiding the secret of his birth in order to conceal his plebeian origins. He was a Don Quixote, the man who would have met an inglorious and premature death on the endless seas had not America, of which he knew nothing, "arrived" to save him and make him a new Odysseus. He was the peddler of maps wreathed with the smoke of fantasy and ignorant of the truth; he was the jackal of the unknown pilots who preceded him, scavenging their knowledge from their deathbeds, and robbing them of their glory. He was the Admiral of the Land of Mosquitoes, as the area was called, the sailor with no fixed home or goal. He, who understood nothing of what had happened to him, was different from all the Spaniards. He was a madman, lost and insane among chimeras more powerful than he.

And yet it is enough to look through the few surviving maps[8] to see that the true identity of Christopher Columbus is far removed from what has been suggested—indeed, imposed—over the centuries. We can only hope that, sooner or later, some dusty archive, some moldering book, some surviving document, hidden map, covered-up wall painting, or sunken shipwreck—some lingering trace of evidence—may bring to light a lost truth.

The literature on Christopher Columbus has always been restricted to a few sources, and has ignored, overlooked, or interpreted in a distorted sense even the most significant aspects in a perfect example of censorship, manipulation, and forgery. It has been based on works considered classics and, as such, equivalent to dogma. The body of Italian historiography, meanwhile, has timidly followed suit.

Yet from those same maps, a totally opposite picture of Columbus is revealed. Emerging is an unknown Columbus, whose motivations were different from what we have been led to believe; a revolutionary Columbus, mystical and possibly even heretical, a mirror image of his Pope Innocent VIII. In light of this information we will seek to revise the view of that pope and of Columbus, of their lives and deeds—as if upending the hourglass. This will be a voyage back in time in search of the truth as we reweave the scattered and hidden threads of the magnificent tapestry depicting the origins of the great discovery. We seek to delve into that far-off and magical time, in order to understand the man who confronted the Ocean Sea, the boundary between all that was known and mysterious. It was a plan, a long-nurtured dream, for which he was the messenger of an ideal and of a faith not necessarily Christian, Catholic, and Roman: A faith with an ecumenical vision, wavering between orthodoxy and heresy and in tune with prophecy; faith balanced on a knife-edge, which could easily swing in either direction.

✠

Any peaceful attempts to reconcile Christianity with Judaism and Islam historically have appeared impossible, despite the efforts of altruistic idealists such as John Paul II. The labels applied to Columbus include, but are not limited to, esoteric, gnostic, kabbalistic, alchemical, and, if you wish, initiatory and are best summed up by two phrases to which insufficient attention has been paid. In these, Columbus states he has "had business and conversation with learned people, ecclesiastic and secular, Latins and Greeks, Jews and Moors, and with many others of different religions," and later writes "the Holy Spirit works in Christians, Jews, Moors, and in all others of every religion, and not only in the learned, more in the ignorant."[9] These phrases echo the *fiet unum ovile* (that they may be one flock) of St. John's Gospel.

These statements represent the most revealing insight into the five-century mystery of Columbus. People have burned at the stake for saying much less. This was the Spain of the Inquisition, where the terrible law of *limpieza de sangre* (purity of the blood) was devised. Muslims were betrayed, fought, and driven to surrender, and Jews were cheated, preyed upon, and expelled in the violent extermination and obliteration of what remained of the ancient and mythical Sepharad: the Spain of three (always the perfect number) sacred books, three religions. This was the Spain that would become mistress of the world by means of vicious and unscrupulous politics, destroying the memory of that universal Spain—the Spain that could have been an example for the world.

The eschatological yearnings with which the expedition was concerned increased. The whole second half of the fifteenth century was suffused with a Messianic atmosphere, fueled from the cloisters of the Franciscans. Christopher Columbus's enterprise originated in this climate. The war of Granada against the Moors had already been won. "This wish for power *(voluntad de imperio)* was escalated in the decade 1470–1480 by Friar Iñigo de Mendoza, who set Granada as the primary objective and, after that, Jerusalem—the highest ambition of the Crusades."[10]

The defeat of the Moors and the conversion of the Jews were among the events predicted to happen prior to the end of the world. Columbus believed in this sequence, based on the prophecies of the Calabrese abbot Joachim of Fiore, who predicted the coming of the Kingdom of God. These revelations were propagated particularly in the Franciscan spiritual circles that formed a silent background for the navigator's movements. Moreover, if it is possible Columbus concealed his origins because he was not proud of them, then the exact opposite also might be true: Namely, Columbus remained silent to conceal something he had to conceal. Perhaps he covered his tracks in both directions, through careful censorship, out of the necessity of hiding a connection that would have shed unwelcome light on the true nature of his role and mission.

The end of the world, St. John's Apocalypse, had opened the doors of revelation—the revelation of a New World, a providential outcome to fulfill both history and geography. There was little time left; less than a hundred and fifty years, according to the calculations of the Jews, which Columbus heeded. It was time to hurry up and break beyond the confines of Gog and Magog, as in the Apocalypse of St. John, to reach the wonder-filled Asia where the adventures of the legendary Alexander the Great had ended.

It was time to emulate Alexander and slash the Gordian knot holding fast the boundaries of the Macedonian conqueror's world; time to bring the word of Christ to all people; time to rediscover Ophir, the mythical Tarshish, the source of King Solomon's treasures; time to rebuild the Temple, to reunite the celestial Jerusalem with the terrestrial Jerusalem in a final crusade. With the gold of the Indies, the golden age, for which humanity—and particularly Christianity—had waited since the dawn of time, could finally begin. For this purpose Columbus made haste, toiling away at his voyages without pause. Nothing seemed to interest him other than his dream of circumnavigating the world and reaching the Holy Land as a new conqueror—and of heralding the new age and the return of a Christ upon earth, like a new John the Baptist, the forerunner of Christ.

It was no coincidence that Columbus signed his name Xpo Ferens, the bearer to Christ, the bearer of Christ, like John the Baptist, while the pope was Giovanni Battista (John Baptist). It was no coincidence that the navigator's name was Christo-pher, Christ-bearer, who was also the bearer of a New World, and of gold for that New World. It was a dream, a plan not to be nurtured in solitude, in an era that played upon the religious symbol, the allegory, the metaphor of splendid utopias, and that yearned for a better humanity.

The discovery of a new land posed a serious risk to accepted teachings and truths. The New World could no longer be tripartite, much less Trinitarian. It was a world deviating from the geographical dogma imposed over the course of centuries, a world in which the Christians would find their counterparts to be heathens immune to Original Sin, whose lineage was that of neither Adam nor Abraham, father of all the faithful. This was tantamount to unhinging the predictions of the church fathers and the words of the holy scriptures, restructuring reality based upon experience and nascent science. Only the Church could lead this "revolution," lest it undermine these foundations. Who would be the new Peter, the new rock on which to build a new church?

Only the pope, the builder of bridges, could create the connection leading to the New World. Only the pope possessed the keys—like the ones on his coat of arms—to open the gate to the Great Mystery and the hereafter. The lands to the East, where paradise lay, were still classified as *terra incognita* (unknown lands); the bountiful Indies were mystifying. Knowledge was controlled exclusively through the libraries and an inestimable treasury of books, but those in the majority were illiterate and ignorant. Although the invention of the printing press and the rise of the universities had shaken the balance of knowledge that had remained static for so many centuries, it tipped in the favor of the clerics.

In a world where those who came to power felt called to an absolute, universalistic task guided by the Lord, knowledge and information were now within the reach of all people. By now the so-called heresy of belief in the existence of new lands had been verified and could not be stamped out, but instead was becoming ever more prevalent. Inquisitions and the stake had accomplished nothing; this heresy was in full stride. A slow and meticulous preparation was underway, in anticipation of the most propitious moment of justice. It was necessary to concede the revolution, to reconcile the ever-widening gulf between faith and science. The prophetic return to Jerusalem finally occurred, in a Christian apotheosis and jubilation, in the year 1500—the date predicted for the Jubilee.

✠

Far-off movements spurred an epochal change. We can trace it back to the Council of Ferrara in 1438, which moved the following year to Florence. Rome and the "new Rome," Constantinople, were seeking a new path to follow. Christianity was battening down its hatches, facing an increasing threat from the infidels. It sought to move beyond the practical religious differences dividing the two main doctrinal fronts—including the dispute of whether secular priests should be allowed to marry.

Constantinople, "consciously a Greek city," had realized "only the Western Church could rally the West to [its] rescue"[11] in the face of danger from the Turks. Islam appeared more and more menacing, and the necessity of a new and final Crusade was more urgent every day. "Even in the great days of the Empire men had whispered of prophecies that it would not last forever. It was well-known that on stones throughout the city and in the books written by the ancient sages of the past the list of emperors was written, and it was drawing to an end. The reign of anti-Christ could not be long delayed."[12]

The prophecies would soon be made a cruel reality. The Antichrist assumed the face of a twenty-year-old youth, with a disquieting name: Mehmed. He heralded the sunset of the West at the Golden Horn, the closing of the Sublime Porte. Constantinople, the New Jerusalem, underwent a gentle decline as it drew near its final days, accompanied by an artistic and cultural effervescence, which had earlier characterized the Palaeologan era. (Palaeologus was the family name of the Byzantine rulers from 1259 to 1453.) Byzantium called, but Christendom, blind to the passage of events, in denial to the possibility of defeat, divided by political interests and economic conflicts, was unable to respond.

✠

On May 29, 1453, at the end of a lengthy and bloody siege and the death of four thousand victims, Mehmed II rode on his white steed to the Church of Holy Wisdom (Hagia Sophia). "Inside the shrine which Greeks considered 'the earthly heaven, throne of God's glory, the vehicle of the cherubim,' a Turk proclaimed: 'There is no God but Allah: Muhammad is his Prophet.'"[13]

The city founded by Constantine the Great should have become the new *caput mundi* (head of the world) but capitulated at the hands of the unfortunate Constantine XI, who died in combat. In the name of Constantine, from the Tiber to the Bosporus, Christianity had been born and now seemed dead; it could only be reborn. The greatest walls of

Europe crumbled beneath cannon fire, and the Ottoman power deployed a fearsome navy before the stunned eyes of the vanquished. No one had believed this could happen, but the signs and coincidences seemed to confirm the prophecies. The Turkish advance upon the European front was terrifying.[14]

The panic appeared justified. Mehmed's mother was a slave of Christian or Jewish origin[15]—a combination of ancestry that was common enough and might herald the possibility of negotiations. A Genoese wrote: ". . . [H]e has become so insolent after the capture of Constantinople that he sees himself soon becoming master of the whole world and swears publicly that before two years have passed he intends to reach Rome."[16] Holding Rome meant holding the whole world in his hands, and Mehmed knew it. No goal seemed unattainable to him, and his victories proved Allah was on his side.[17]

There were more signs. On his return to Naples from Constantinople in January 1454, Nicola Sagundino, a humanist friend of the Greek Cardinal Bessarion and a promoter of the Crusade, told King Alfonso of Aragon that the conqueror of Constantinople, inspired by ancient traditions, intended to make himself king of Italy and the city of Rome. Having taken possession of the "daughter," Byzantium, Mehmed believed he would likewise be able to conquer the "mother," Rome. "He said that the sultan was precisely informed of the disputes between Italian states, and that the passage from Durres to Brindisi could be easily taken."[18] Who would be Mehmed's counterpart in the Christian camp? Who would be the European version of Alexander the Great, forging the path to a united world in the name of the cross? To whom was the dominion of the world forthcoming? Who would become the king of the earth? Popes, emperors, monarchs, princes, and lords were all rivals for the scepter: a single dream, a single ambition. Men could have power over the earth, which at one time the popes had, and could make ready to defend their power with arms; but the pope also had power over the spirit. This set him above any other human being. His scepter was bestowed by God in a supremacy that the crowned heads recognized and bowed to—albeit in varying phases, in changing times and circumstances, and in the rotation of interests and personalities.

Rome under Pope Nicholas V received word of the fall of Constantinople from a messenger on July 8, 1453. The news was like a thunderclap out of a clear sky. Gone was the conviction that between "the beacon of Greco-Roman civilization in the East and the infrangibility of the Mediterranean unity established by Rome, God had created an unassailable covenant."[19]

On September 30 of the same year, the pope appealed in a bull to all the princes of the West, summoning them together for a holy crusade. All Christian kings must unite, all knightly orders must join forces, and a great deal of gold would be needed. The New World must shine brightly. It was the Ariadne's thread that led to Christopher Columbus and Innocent VIII. Among the lost relics were the lance of the Roman soldier Longinus, which pierced the side of Christ; a lost emerald with the "true profile" of Christ; the humerus and skull of St. John the Baptist; and the fingers of St. Thomas, the apostle of the East.

The supernatural (and not merely symbolic) power of these relics became part of the prerogative of Mehmed II, who showed a sincere interest in the Christian faith. It was therefore hoped he might embrace Christianity, and in 1465, a false claim was spread that he had indeed became a Christian.[20] This same cause had brought St. Francis of Assisi to the East centuries earlier, when he arrived at the sultan's court with the courageous intent of converting him. The Franciscans continued to walk the highways of the world as missionaries, and had not forgotten this—and they were always close to Columbus.

✠

A resounding attempt at this kind of conversion was subsequently made by Pius II (1405–1464), Enea Silvio Piccolomini, the humanist and geographer pope (whose book Columbus studied), in the form of a letter sent to Mehmed II, who did not reply. The pope addressed the conqueror and called for his submission in the name of the "consolation awaited by many people: peace" and the salvation of all people, "Greeks, Romans, Jews, Saracens" (the same list that appeared in Columbus's words).

Pius's words asserted the superiority of the Christian religion and its God compared to that of the Muslim faith.[21] He wrote that only the baptismal water could purify and redeem the "lost sinner."

> This is a matter of a little water, to baptize you and allow you to participate in the Christian rites and to put faith in the Gospels. With this done, no other prince on earth will surpass you in glory or equal you in power. We will call you emperor of Greece and of the East, and the territory that you presently occupy wrongfully and by violence will be yours by right. All Christians will revere you and make you the judge in their disputes . . . the Syrians, the Egyptians, the Libyans, the Arabs, and all other peoples who are outside the Christian fold will become your followers upon hearing this news, or else will submit with little difficulty to your weapons and to those of the Christians. And if they do not want to be allied to you under our laws, they will know you as master under their own. We will aid you, and with the help of Divine Grace, make you legitimate prince of them all.[22]

This was an unprecedented invitation, an offer of an unthinkable and perhaps impossible alliance; but no stone would remain unturned in the search for a peaceful solution to the conflict. Thus the Sienese humanist, now enthroned in St. Peter's Basilica, concluded his extreme attempt to save world peace: "The time of Augustus will return, what the poets call the Golden Age will be restored, the age of the lamb lying down with the lion, the calf with the lion; swords will be exchanged for sickles, all iron made into spades and hoes."[23]

The pope's epistle made references to Presbyter Giovanni (the legendary Prester John), Socrates, Plato, Aristotle (committed to the "system of the world"), Janus, Hercules, Alexander the Great, Moses, Aaron, and all the people of the Indies, Tartary, and Asia. (Many of these names will appear again in the labyrinth leading to Columbus.) It was an invective aspiring to show the inferiority of the Muslim prophet's morals compared to the spirituality of Catholicism; but it also represented an amazing openness toward Islam on Rome's part.

The world was changing: Currents of thought, in Rome and else-where, clashed between the desire for global renewal and the desire for conservative status quo. The splendor and pomp of the Vatican collided with mourning over the original Christian message in an unresolved disagreement. These were disputes not easily solved, even with the passage of time.[24] All of this colored Christopher Columbus's destiny and his voyage.

The church of the poor was tolerated in the papal eye as long as it was not opposed to the "regality" of the pope. Yet there were some who hoped for a return to a primitive church, penniless and pure—to the church of Eastern origin, which might have favored reconciliation. Thus there were two opposing ways of interpreting religion reflected in the development of future events and hanging in a delicate balance that would be overturned by the new discoveries. The pope's letter to Mehmed remains a mystery in many respects. It is not known how the entreaty was received—if it indeed ever reached its destination.

Had the pope's plea for Mehmed's submission been ill received, there would have been no recourse but the Crusade. This was the common denominator for Vatican politics up to the time of Innocent VIII—and after his time, until the final defeat of the Muslims at Lepanto. History has not taken note of this imperative, instead citing the lie that "No more Crusades were fought in the fifteenth century because people no longer believed in them. Pius II wanted to lead one because he lacked a sense of history."[25]

Pius II died in the name of holy war. Death overtook him as he watched the ships sail from the port of Ancona. He had intended to undertake and revive the great enterprise. What failed next to the cathedral of San Ciriaco was a trial run, not the grand design: One pope died, while another, given the right time, the need, and the same motives, might come to take the baton in the eternal relay of both good and bad, of the cross and the sword.

In those times, hope was placed in people to the East, who existed only in legends like those of the mythical Prester John. For centuries it was believed the Christian faith must have survived in areas that the word of Christ no longer permeated: beyond the boundary of the outward expansion of the Word. Prester John was a kind of permanent thorn in the side of the enemy, Islam. A Nestorian Christian,[26] he once sent a letter to Manuel I Komnenos, the emperor of Byzantium.[27]

A descendent of the Magi, with a scepter of green emerald, Prester John held Jerusalem as his goal. The figure of this mythical phantom wandered about in space and time. Despite the passing of decades, he remained an almost immortal constant, fueling the hope of a reunification of East and West.

Significantly, the name Presbyter Iaonnes was connected with a "persistent apocryphal tradition that the Apostle John did not die but was chosen by Jesus to wander [or sail] in the world as an immortal until the Second Coming of Christ. . . . People went on believing that the apostle had been exempted from mortality and roamed the earth unrecognized, awaiting the return of the Savior."[28]

The return of one named John was expected at a time when the recurrence and similarity of names bore a significance that was not only symbolic but also magical—a magic connected with a mysticism that might unite East and West. Nothing was omitted in the search for an ultimate solution for a new and improved humanity and world. To this flow of thought, however, there existed an opposing ebb that was perhaps even more susceptible to further variations and undercurrents. Such is always the case when societies are undergoing unstoppable global changes.

The Jews, for their part, were seeking the Lost Tribe of Israel; Prester John's letter mentions ten tribes of "servants and vassals" who live beyond a river in which precious stones can be found. Legend or not, Pope Alexander III (1159–1181), another Sienese like Piccolomini, sent a reply to this letter.

Meanwhile, the missionaries, with the Franciscans at the forefront and always on the verge of heresy, did their best to reestablish the lost harmony and gather the flocks. This began with Giovanni da Pian del Carpini, who traveled to the "Three Indies" and concluded an alliance with the Mongols in hope of defeating the Saracens. They took advantage of the fact that many of the Mongols' wives were Nestorian

Christians. The Genoese Sinibaldo Fieschi,[29] Innocent IV, relied on this type of pact, which was one—though not the only—reference point for Innocent VIII.

Pian del Carpini was followed by William of Rubruk and Bartolomeo di Cremona, then Giovanni da Monte Corvino, Odorico da Pordenone, Brother Giovanni di Marignolli (a Florentine noble), and many others. Each one, versed only in the ways of the habit, was seeking a Prester John for his own time: a Mongol king disposed to an alliance, and to the final conquest by Rome of those lost outposts in the East, especially Jerusalem. These men were part *homo viator*, part ambassador, and part spy in the service of the intelligence at which the Church excelled. This intelligence was also fueled by the reports of the merchants, such as the Venetian Niccolò da Conti. These men, who sought an alliance with the Tartars, can be considered as the pioneers of Christopher Columbus's venture.

China had a millenarian culture superior to that of Europe, with ships more like transatlantic vessels than the little boats sailing the Mediterranean. China, the mystery of the *extra Gangem* (the lands lying east of the Ganges), might have given information to emissaries sent by Rome. Was this mere surmise or legend? Believably, it was something more, considering that in Peru in recent times numerous traces of Chinese settlements have been found, predating Columbus's discovery of the Americas. Finally, seeking an alliance with Kublai Khan, Marco Polo (one of the writers that Columbus read most assiduously) was sent to China. Polo's *Travels* were written down by Rustichello da Pisa in a prison in Genoa. This same city, marked by the presence of Columbus and Innocent VIII, also saw the beginning of "the Ethiopian phase of the Prester John story," which "opens in 1306 with the arrival in Genoa of thirty Ethiopian envoys."[30]

Genoa then, somewhat like Rome, was a crossroads of news and initiative long before the time of Columbus and his papal patron. As the decades passed, Genghis Khan closed the gates to the exotic and the marvelous world of wonders; but the plan was not abandoned.

✠

The world of the Late Middle Ages and early Renaissance was a time ruled by the spirit, and ideas did not die out in the space of a decade. There were no sudden shifts or accelerations in the course of events, as there are today. Steadfast time was the guardian and the repository, safe and trusted. Faith was the glue of society. Tradition wove events into visions inscrutable to those who did not hold the keys of knowledge and power. Everything was interconnected; what was below was identical to what was above. Unpredicted events, when they happened, were always somehow traced back to some earlier prediction.

All roads led to Rome, as had been the case for the "golden" Rome. In the eternal caput mundi, the Church was divided into three great factions: First, there were the Christian and mystical followers of the kingdom of heaven, of the paradisal utopia to be formed on earth. Second, there were those determined to achieve this paradise by means of a holy war that superceded dialogue and conciliation, in opposition to which any compromise or syncretism with other faiths was unthinkable. These were forever ready to take up their swords to defend and vindicate the dominion of the Church of Christ. Finally, there was a third camp, the prelates, those who had chosen the House of God, either as required by their families or as motivated by politics, self-interest, or rank and social privilege. They were always ready to take a side, whichever one it might be, in exchange for deliciously temporal favors. Thus, despite all doctrine, Rome's foundations were built on eternally unstable ground.

The word of the Antichrist was proclaimed by the voices of the *muezzin* (chosen ones). The churches of the East were converted into mosques. This was necessary for the new prophecies to be fulfilled—prophecies stating the last emperor was not dead but had been turned into marble and "was sleeping in a subterranean cave beneath the Golden Gate, the traditional point of entry for victorious emperors, which Michael Palaeologus had used in 1261. One day he would hear a call from heaven: '[A]n angel will give him a sword, restore him to life and let him drive the Turks as far as the Red Apple on the Persian frontier.'"[31]

Christianity was severely mutilated, almost mortally wounded, by the fall of the "golden city," an event recorded by a scribe of the monastery of Agarathos: "There has never been, and never will be, a more terrible event." The New Rome had fallen, and another Rome, the seat of the *dominus orbis,* the "lord of the world," might fall next beneath the Muslim scimitar. "To Rome, to Rome!" resounded the threatening cry of the looming Turkish horde.

Mehmed II already considered himself the only true emperor of Europe, swearing publicly he would reach the capital of Christendom within two years. The gaze of the Lord's angels must have been turned in another direction: Perhaps "it is not God's will, God is no longer with us," *Deus vult, Deus non vult.* The hill of the Vatican, before which all of Europe bowed, hid its consternation. At the same time, the trade route known as the Spice Route and the routes for gold, pearls, and alum became impassable.

Not only did faith crumble; a whole economic structure shattered, especially for the Italian city-states. With the loss of their rich community, the Genoese suffered just as much as the Florentines and the Venetians.[32]

✠

1453, a date some consider as the beginning of the modern era, is one of those caesuras dear to interpretations seeking pigeonholes to fill and slogans to simplify. Instead, they often create imaginary barriers. Despite appearances, there was also a transverse relationship between the enemies, allowing both sides to send negotiators—sometimes sensitive and attentive, sometimes merely self-interested and eager to defect—into the enemy camp. The problem had become more pressing since the loss of Constantinople, and a whole system was at risk of collapsing now that the gates to the Orient were barred, beginning with the Sublime Porte. A frontier had closed; a new frontier must open.

Only a few Christian outposts remained in the East: Rhodes, Chios, and a few other Greek islands, with the heroic Knights of St. John at the forefront. These knights, defenders and paladins of the "true religion," knights of the sea, had faced the attacks of Mehmed II in 1469 and 1479. They also withstood a long siege in May 1480.[33]

The moment for counterattack had arrived for them, as for all knights—the time to join together into a single Christian army. All that was needed was the gold to set it in motion—gold that was known to be abundant in the "other world" (New World).

The nightmare worsened; the Turks could not be halted. The last funeral bell tolled at Otranto, the soft underbelly (as it still is today) of the Italian peninsula on the eastern front. The Turks had invaded Constantinople, the Balkans, and Greece, and had reached the gates of Vienna. Otranto is a miniature Byzantium in the province of Salento. The crypt of the cathedral is a perfect reproduction of the crypt of the Cisterna Basilica in Constantinople. In fact, the Byzantine Church of St. Peter is practically a replica of Hagia Sofia. On one column is inscribed: "Here St. Peter first preached Jesus Christ to the slaves of the West, and erected the altar for you."[34]

On the floor of the cathedral is a stupendous, mysterious mosaic, showing all the signs of the zodiac and a condensation of medieval symbolism: a gigantic tree, an enigmatic chessboard, Alexander the Great supported by two griffins, King Arthur, the Tower of Babel and the dispersion of the peoples, the two-faced figure of Janus, the gods of peace and of war, the Queen of Sheba and Solomon with the meeting of the peoples, a crowned devil, Noah's ark with the animals of the Flood, and a dove of peace heralding the Flood's end. Might this be a prediction? Is something foreseen in this work of art that, in view of subsequent events, appears as a prophecy conveyed and synthesized into an iconographic masterpiece?

St. Francis of Assisi once landed at Otranto, on his way to try to convert Sultan Malek-el-Kamil. Later, there was another Francis and another prophecy: St. Francis of Paola, founder of the Order of the Minims and "ruler of the sea," alarmed Ferrante, the king of Naples, who sent soldiers to silence him. "Go back," St. Francis warned, "go back to your king and tell him that the time has come to appease the wrath of the Lord, that God's right hand is raised to strike. The army of the Turks is threatening Italy, but is closest to your kingdom." And looking toward Otranto, he exclaimed: "Unhappy city . . . how many corpses will fill your streets! How much Christian blood will inundate you!"[35]

Events moved rapidly in the summer of 1480. There was a shower of cannonballs and the siege continued without respite, day after day. The disparity in forces was too great for the resistance. The last holdout, in the cathedral, collapsed when the door fell. A blow from a scimitar severed the archbishop's head: "It is no longer Christ but our Muhammad who reigns." A chronicle relates that the "Turk" "then took up [the archbishop's] miter and, wearing it on his head, walked through the city by way of derision. The others who were present were all bound and made into slaves."[36]

The Turks also wanted the Christians to convert to Islam. The ultimatum: either live for the Qur'an, or die for the Gospel. On August 14, eight hundred Christians who refused to convert were beheaded in groups of fifty by the seaside.

The popular epic poem about the martyrs is heartrending:

> *Until we meet in heaven,*
> *the weeping fathers and mothers bade*
> *farewell to their children,*
> *while the sea grew red with blood.*

"In Rome," narrates Sigismondo de' Conti, a member of Innocent VIII's court, "the consternation could not have been greater if the enemy had already been camped outside the walls of the city. Anxiety and terror had invaded all souls, so much so that even the pope was contemplating fleeing. . . . Sixtus had resolved to take refuge in France, should the state of things in Italy become any worse."[37]

The danger was so imminent the pope made ready to move to Avignon. Even the nightmare of flight to France seemed, at this juncture, a chance for salvation. A bull was issued on September 2: the umpteenth call to the Crusade. The ambassadors of all the Italian states were summoned to Rome. At this time, Sixtus IV's trusted confidant was the future Innocent VIII, from the Cybo family, who came from the East. Sacred vessels were melted down for silver. The Turks had arrived at the gates of Rome. Through treason at work in the Christian camp, Rome would be the next stage of the enemy advance. There were no more obstacles; the limit had been reached. The specters of the popes of the French "exile" seemed to be returning. Christianity had to retaliate or be lost. The fate of the world and of Rome must be redressed. This was the final battle for spiritual domination and now also for temporal rule of the world against the crescent of Islam that was beginning to stretch over the seas.

For a long time, too many clues and too many signs had foretold—almost as if knowledge and certainty were being carefully planted—that the known world was open for limitless expansion. In the wake of Henry the Navigator, the Portuguese continued to search for the route to the Indies. Rounding the coast of Africa ever farther south, they discovered new shores in those austral lands and found that life was actually possible there. The ocean of their nightmares did not have those fabled regions where the waters boiled with infernal heat. Since the time of the Phoenicians, the Pillars of Hercules had been an insurmountable threshold; the passage had been jealously guarded by the Carthaginians, and those who violated the proscription against crossing it had been condemned to death. It was considered impassable, and none would dare attempt it. Perhaps this was out of a desire to preserve the secrecy of this part of the world, which remained, or was meant to remain, hidden.

And yet, by the thirteenth century, Ramon Llull, the Catalan secular Franciscan, alchemist, and Templar, wrote:

> The principal cause of the ebb and flow of the Great Sea, or the Sea of England, is the arc of the waters of the sea which, to the West, is bordered or confined by a land across from England, France, Spain, and all of neighboring Africa, whereby our eyes see the ebb and flow of the waters because the arc formed by the water is like a spherical and natural body, which has supports (confines) on the opposite side on which it rests; because otherwise it could not be supported. Consequently, just as on this side it is supported by our continent,

as we see and know, so on the opposite side to the West it rests upon the other continent, which we do not see and do not know in our time; but by means of true philosophy, which recognizes and observes through the senses the sphericity of the water and the resulting ebb and flow, which necessarily requires two opposite shores to contain the water that is so lively, to be like the pillars of this arc, we may infer logically that on the western side there exists a continent on which the rough waves break, just as correspondingly they break upon our eastern side.[38]

It was a theory inviting no doubt and expressed with complete certainty—and it incorporated the roundness of the world. The phrase "upon the other continent, which we do not see and do not know in our time" was repeated almost verbatim by Columbus regarding the Land of Paria. The wording "we" and "in our time," an admission of lack of knowledge, indicates this world existed and implies a knowledge of it in the distant past—not to mention a confident assertion that, sooner or later, the gap in knowledge would again be filled. More than one scholar has supported a close connection between Llull and the Columbus family. Two Genoese merchants found—nearly dead—the Franciscan Llull, who sailed to Tunis to convert the Muslims. One of the merchants was named Stefano Colombo.

✠

The hypothesis of new worlds and new lands was lost in the mists of time and the voices of the prophets. Plato spoke of the mystic Atlantis in the *Timaeus* and *Critias*. Gomara, a Columbus scholar, states, without a shadow of doubt, that Columbus must have read Plato. The Greek philosopher placed Atlantis—an island greater than Libya and Asia Minor combined—beyond the Pillars of Hercules, among a multitude of other islands, concluding that "this sea which is within the Straits of Heracles is only a harbor . . . but that other is a real sea, and the surrounding land may be most truly called a boundless continent."[39]

In the history of humanity, the mythical Atlantis has never been identified with Asia. How could Columbus have become so confused? Atlantis, wiped off the map by an immense catastrophe, disappeared or was made to disappear from memory and remained only in the partial knowledge of an incomplete whole. It had been called an island—but this, in the Middle Ages, was also synonymous with peninsula, not to mention that even continents, floating in the great ocean, are fundamentally islands. Was the sinking of the ideal civilization a metaphor or a calculated submersion, a kind of prestidigitation that caused an entire continent to vanish? Perhaps it was an expedient to discourage those who might have had sufficient spirit of adventure to take a voyage into that nautical labyrinth, which must remain obscure. Perhaps the myth was propagated over time to protect the Netherworld, the place where people went to die; the place where the ancient Egyptians believed the souls of the dead sailed.

It was no coincidence that Plato's two dialogues dealt with the origins of the ideal state, a counterpart to the New World, in a narrative leading back to an ancestral time, to a mythical Golden Age forming one of the threads leading to Christopher Columbus and his pope. An idealization of the state was also composed by Cicero in his *Dream of Scipio*,[40] which echoes Plato's *Republic*.

Writing of the immortality of the soul, Cicero frequently makes astronomical references to "globed and round" planets, among them Earth, which "is girded and surrounded by belts, two of which—the farthest from each other, and each resting at one extremity on the very pole of the heavens—you see entirely frost-bound; while the middle and largest of them burns under the sun's intensest heat. Two of them are habitable, of which the southern, whose inhabitants are your antipodes, bears no relation to your people."[41]

We can also see the ancients knew the earth was round from the globes depicted on some Roman coins. The veneration of ancient Greek and Roman culture was very much alive in Columbus's time and even earlier; the fascination was fueled by (among other things) endless archaeological findings, which enriched the collections of the pope and the cardinals, the nobles and the lords. Proof that the earth was a sphere existed in countless writings of the "ecclesiastic and secular, Latins and Greeks, Jews and Moors." Some medieval writers, albeit only in limited circles, also shared this opinion.

One puzzle remains to be understood: how the false belief that the earth was flat could have been foisted on the populace over so many centuries, when divinity itself consisted of the spherical harmony of the celestial worlds. The flat earth was an immense mystification. Who aided the dissemination of the myth, and who was benefited by it? Was the spherical earth something that needed to be classified, covered up? Was it effectively kept secret through the passage of time and events? Yet with the same passage of time and with the expansion of travel and knowledge, it had to resurface eventually.

In Columbus's era geography was in the process of dispelling the Ptolemaic view that was sacred to the world, the common cause—or at least the geographic view that Ptolemy had left behind and made popular. At the time of Columbus, the ocean to the West was becoming more and more filled with known territories and islands. A plethora of landfalls dotted the waters extending to the north, but most of all to the south of those pillars formed by Hercules, the hero who had traveled to the far-off Atlantic in the course of his twelve labors, seeking the Garden of the Hesperides from which to steal the golden apples. "The admiral himself was the first to be convinced that the islands of the Indies were the Hesperides."[42]

✠

Eden, the earthly Paradise, the Garden of the Hesperides, the Fortunate Islands, the Blessed Isles, the Canaries, the Azores, the Isle of Antilya, Atlantis, Colchis, the island of the Seven Cities, St. Brendan's island, the island of Brazil, the Land of the Codfish, Ultima Thule, the Lost Tribes of Israel, the Land of Cockaigne: The mentality and scholarship of the High Middle Ages and the Renaissance resurrected, retraced, and proposed a multitude of routes to these places, though whether purely the fruit of fantasy or mixed with fantasy, we do not know. The time was ripe for new Argonauts, new heroes similar to Hercules, new Hesperides and new golden apples, new Solomons, princes or others in power—longing for a new ideal state. The time was ripe for a return to the primordial age of happiness.

Geniuses of classical times, the Latin and Greek authors, were translated and published, giving rise to the first great libraries. The fugitive culture of Constantinople landed on the banks of the Tiber, descending upon Italy. An interchange developed in which past and present culture and faith intermingled and overlapped in a syncretism of varying degrees in which it became difficult to determine at what point one was in hostile territory, faced with either mutual understanding or an inimical encounter.

Thus, the late fifteenth century was a mysterious jumble, an alchemical crucible from which strong characters and geniuses emerged, forming an unrepeatable era. In humanism, the fantasy of the reconciliation of opposites (of which Pius II was not the only proponent on St. Peter's throne), there was a return to paganism—not in a negative sense, as it is unfortunately often interpreted, but in a higher, more idealistic sense.

As we can read at the beginning of the pope's epistle to Mehmed II, "the ultimate hope of humanism was a unification of Earth and heaven, wisdom and revelation, East and West, peoples and religions, in a kind of Christian *plenitudo temporum* [plenitude of times]"—and therefore a *plenitudo gentium* (plenitude of peoples), an idea that Cardinal Nicholas Cusanus, the pope's inspiration for the letter sent to Mehmed II, identified with the *coincidentia oppositorum* (coincidence of opposites). For Pico della Mirandola, another of the great thinkers of the Renaissance, it was "an inimical friendship and a concordant discord," in search of universal harmony to emerge in one single peace, ennobling humankind. The goal was the same for many minds and many men, active or not—and the means for reaching it were numerous.

Thus flowed the mysterious waters of the Ocean of Serpents: between mysticism and universal judgment; from apocalypses to New Ages; from Moses and Noah to the oceans that were to be crossed; from St. John the Baptist and St. John the Evangelist to St. James and Prester John; amid legends of the True Cross, Sibyls, relics, Arthurian cycles, knightly orders, knights of the sea, and the prophetic and geographical ends of the world. From these waters, sometimes bathed in sunlight and brimming over like the Renaissance, sometimes restricted to subterranean passages, among an omnipresent fluttering of doves symbolizing peace, a submerged pontificate would resurface. These waters would baptize the birth and creation of a Christ-bearer Columbus, the man chosen to draw back the veil that too long covered the horizon of a New World, and chosen to show that the truth is not always as it seems.

TWO

THE GENOA-PADUA MATRIX

NOW THAT THE great ocean of silence[1] threatens to engulf the man who breached the limits of the great ocean of darkness, the moment has come to reconsider the navigator's destiny: to do our best to render unto Columbus that which is Columbus's. Now is the time to reconsider the puzzle of the Christ-bearer and his adventures, so peppered with contradictions, mysteries, and omissions. Let us begin with the pope.

There is—or at least there was, until my research began in 1990[2]—a conspicuous missing link in the lengthy mystery of the admiral's exploits. A key character, overlooked even by Italian scholars of Columbus, had slipped through the cracks just a few years after his death. His name was Giovanni Battista Cybo, Pope Innocent VIII. A Genoese man with origins in the East—in Greece, Rhodes, and Chios—he did not become caught in the tangled web of the New World's "revelation." Yet this pope was the true hidden and not so innocent weaver of this web. He was a forgotten pope, an erased pope, a disappeared pope leading a Church in pursuit of a universal dream. Cybo was a pope who could no longer protect and procrastinate over a centuries-old secret.

No eyes were upon the dome of St. Peter's in the time leading up to Columbus's departure from Palos. The pope always considered in view of Columbus's relationship to Rome is Innocent VIII's successor, Alexander VI, Rodrigo Borgia—a Spaniard. This pope's dubious fame culminated during his reign in his being identified, not without reason, with the feared and prophesied coming of the Antichrist.

The American operation was the brightest light of the Renaissance. The contributions of Rome and the Italian city-states—Genoa and Florence above all, as well as Umbria, St. Francis's homeland—were instrumental, as were the humble missionaries who walked the highways of the world while their representatives sat upon the Vatican throne. The contribution of the knowledge of the Dominicans, the Cistercians, and the knightly orders was fundamental. Many of the people in this complex intrigue were to be found in Padua, Venice, Naples, Siena, and in Spain, Portugal, and the Greek islands; and there was also the continued presence, either in the background or at center stage, of the Jews—converted or otherwise—and the Muslims. These characters, some Christian, sometimes of other origins and faiths, merged in a procession bordering on heresy.

Five hundred years after the most adventurous voyage of all time, after I've reread sources, interpreted acknowledged documents, and incorporated those newly emerged or reemerged, an incredible truth has irrevocably torn apart the accepted truth—all the more so considering that in Columbus's history a precarious patchwork has formed, stitching up obvious gaps in all reconstructions and the often incomprehensible passage of many events. And the missing link was the pope of Rome, the greatest leader of the known world, the *dominus orbis*.[3]

Innocent VIII had the last word on lands that had been or would be discovered. In those times, undertaking an expedition meant carrying the cross to a new place, evangelizing the idolaters and pagans with baptism during the endless search for the passage across the seas. It was a kind of eternal crusade in which chimeras, faiths, economic interests, science, exploration, and the desire for power and omnipotence all came together. In those times, the very survival of Europe and Rome was threatened, and since the year 1000, people had longed to reclaim the Holy Land.

Columbus sailed to discover new islands and continents and to bring the cross to new shores and new lands. His sights were set on the retaking of Jerusalem, the Holy Sepulchre. The pope could not have been ignorant of this; Rome had known it for a long time. Columbus's dreams and those of the pope coincided, and placing Giovanni Battista Cybo at the hub of these events fills a gap that remained inconceivably empty for the past five centuries. It must have been in someone's interest to obliterate the evidence leading to St. Peter's throne. In fact, if we study carefully the accepted facts surrounding Columbus, precious little is logical about them. Contradictions and unanswered questions arise at every step. Sometimes the threads are impossible to disentangle; the accounts—in the sense of narratives—do not add up properly and do not appear balanced according to logic and reason, but instead seem to arise out of a need to square the circle. This is even stranger given that the discovery of America was imagined and experienced in every sense as an extraordinary and providential triumph.

The chronicle of these events and of their protagonist should therefore be completely clear. The achievement was one to guarantee honor and rewards, both economic and spiritual—enough for all involved. Yet the atmosphere in which it took place was that of a murder mystery in which the killer still has not been identified. Reintroducing the Genoese pope into the plot line, so full of mysterious gaps, provides us with the material necessary to patch the myriad tears in Columbus's sails.[4]

✠

Constantinople had fallen. Pius II, the pope who studied geography so passionately, had died at Ancona and left the legacy of the holy war to his successors, Sixtus IV of Savona and the della Rovere family, a Ligurian dynasty of popes lasting for the second half of the fifteenth century. Genoa was a superb city in those days, with patrician palaces built of slate and Carrara marble, contrasting white and black, darkness and light, like the checkers on the Cybo escutcheon. It was a wealthy center of commerce, nestled between the mountains and the sea, between alpine peaks and boundless waters. There, escapism and the mirage of riches drove men to sail the seas.

A maritime power, it was a city-state rich in businessmen, bankers, navigators, merchants, geographers, knights, and Crusaders. It was cosmopolitan, a port for diverse religions, considering the remaining Jewish presence. Many Jews had fled to more tolerant nations, even before the Edict of Expulsion of 1492. "Genoa was just one such nation . . . in Genoa the presence of the displaced Sephardim was documented around 1449, in concomitance with pogroms against the Jews in Toledo."[5]

The city's destiny was entangled with its name, harking back to the god of peace and war. The Romans had stamped the two-faced head of Janus on the city's coins, and on the reverse, the profile of a ship. Where was it headed? In what directions, in the world of the reemerging Rome, was the pagan god looking? Janus is the guardian of the gates. Genoa is Janua (a gate), easily rearranged into Juana (the feminine John), the name Columbus gave to Cuba, like the name of Pope Giovanni (John). What gate was to be opened? Was it to usher in an age of peace and an end to the bloodshed that had ravaged Europe for so long?

The *Travels* of Marco Polo (1254–1324), the fascinating account of his voyage to the outer edges of the world, was written in Genoa. Columbus read this work voraciously and made notes in it. In Genoa, Bishop Jacobus de Voragine wrote his *Legenda aurea,* in which the figure of St. Christopher appears canonized for the first time: the holy ferryman steering to a New World. In Genoa, the Lanterna lighthouse—the workplace of Antonio Colombo, allegedly an uncle of Columbus—illuminated the gloom, enlightened the minds of the sailors, and, in the manner of its epoch, bore the same cross that would appear on the sails of the caravels.

In Genoa, a true icon of the face of Christ is preserved: the veil of Veronica, the sacred Mandylion with the holy face, given to John Palaeologus, emperor of Byzantium and the Greek lands he helped to liberate; lands now to be reconquered, to be brought back under the scepter of Christianity. The green emerald chalice was kept at Genoa, the cup held by Jesus at the Last Supper, used for washing hands and later for catching the blood of Christ. It was identified as the Holy Grail, sought in the never-ending quests of legendary knights.

St. Francis of Assisi passed through Genoa on his voyage from Rome to Spain. The intellectual Enea Silvio Piccolomini, the future Pope Pius II, came to Genoa in 1432. St. Francis of Paola, who had prophesied the capture of Otranto by the Turks, came to Genoa in 1483. He predicted an age of rebirth in which "there will no longer be any knight on earth who is not a member of the sacred army of the Holy Spirit." He also foretold the defeat of the "Mohammedan sect" by a new religion, "the last religion."[6]

In the cathedral, people have bowed before the ashes of St. John the Baptist, the messenger of Christ. John the Baptist is the patron saint of Genoa, of Florence, of the greatest knightly orders, and of Masonry. Over time, countless churches named after him have sprung up along the coast. In Genoa, people have prayed before the bones of St. James, the holy symbol of Spain and the prophet of the East. The precious ark that carried his remains was paid for by the Genoese of Chios, the Greek island known as "the right eye of Genoa"[7]—where the Cybo family was one of the noblest.[8]

The symbolic beast of Genoa is the griffin, the creature guarding the gold of Hyperborea in the unknown lands. This mythical creature, capable of flying, walking, and swimming, represents three elements: air, earth, and water—a zoomorphic existence somewhere between reality and metaphor. According to Dante, the griffin is even a symbol for the figure of Jesus and his double nature, human and divine.

The city's banner shows San Giorgio (St. George), the prince of knights, lance in hand, slaying the dragon of the enemies of Christendom, protecting himself with a shield bearing a red cross on a white background: "He holds the emblem of the Crusade in his hand: a banner that was used only in solemn ceremonies and sea battles."[9]

Significantly, this same cross appeared upon Columbus's sails as he battled the ocean. The same cross appeared on Innocent VIII's escutcheon, and the same red color appeared in one quarter of Columbus's first coat of arms.

Under William Embriaco (nicknamed Hammerhead), the Genoese were instrumental in the success of the First Crusade and the reconquest of Jerusalem. In one of the architraves of the Holy Sepulchre, letters in gold read *Praepotens genuensium praesidium* (the mighty Genoese garrison). By the seaside, on the site of the Church of the Holy Sepulchre, an eternal call to Jerusalem, stands the church of San Giovanni di Pré, still inhabited by the ghosts of the Templars and the knights of the Holy Sepulchre.[10] In their footsteps came the Knights of St. John of Jerusalem. In the church adjacent to the medieval hospital, Innocent IV, the pope from the Fieschi family, organized the Fourth Crusade.[11]

The Holy Spirit, religion, saints and knights, Crusades, the Grail . . . all these characters and relics are part history, part legend. Persons and deeds, memories and hypotheses, myths and traditions, places, books, and revealing literature together form a kind of enchanting fresco with so many symbols, so many signs in an age when symbols and signs were the keys to existence. These symbols and signs, in a mysterious and esoteric code, reflect the events of those times.

In this environment, encompassing the Genoese colonies to the East, a man whose name was a cipher, Christopher Columbus, and a pope beset by *damnatio memoriae* inhaled the salty air and felt the breeze that sped the faithful to meet and battle with Islam. Genoa's citizens and its vassals had this mission indelibly stamped in their very bones.

But who, really, was this pope, erased and liquidated from Columbus's story? Was not Columbus himself a kind of *ayatollah,* marking his ships and the places where he landed with crosses, bringing the natives evangelization and baptism? And was not his final destination the Holy Land? The very destinies of the two men were bound to intersect. In whose interest did it lie to suppress a connection, which, as we shall see, comes ever closer to culminating in a blood tie? A pope was needed who could force the Muslims to see reason or could fight and conquer them. What would be better than a pope who had known them and consorted with them? There is sometimes a subliminal capacity in Vatican politics to choose, in a moment of truth, the right man for the right time. The Muslims had to be converted or conquered. Someone must be found who knew how to deal with them—sometimes cajoling, sometimes threatening.

It is a process successfully repeated in modern times: Pope John Paul II, who came from behind the Iron Curtain, stood behind the fall of Communism. The same reasoning, the same intuition, must have been followed five hundred years earlier with the choice of Innocent VIII. Islam had to be fought and conquered, and for this the Cybo family had all the credentials. "This family had origins in Greece, and came to settle in Genoa at the time when the Palaeologi were emperors of Constantinople. . . . The Cybos indicated in their coat of arms that they had acquired the title of Campioni (Champions) and for a long period of time they styled themselves in this manner."[12]

They were a composite clan made up of not easily decipherable inter-connections, a puzzle to piece together requiring tremendous patience, a series of fascinating refractions. Once all the pieces of the mosaic are together, once the strangers are identified and those already known are put in their proper places, we see a completely different and unfamiliar portrait of Innocent VIII, the man whom historiography always dismisses contemptuously with a few denigratory and negligent words.

Even the name of the pope's father brings up a mass of implications. He was called Arano, Arrone, Aaron, Aronne, and Abramo, *equestri dignitate ornatus* (endowed with the dignity of a knight). He was a great knight, a great seaman, but little else is known about him. He was the son of Maurizio Cybo and Sarracina Marucella. His first marriage was to Teodorina di Montano de Mari, his second to Ginevra Giustiniani. De Mari and Giustiniani were two important surnames in aristocratic Genoa, so full of noble families. The de Mari family bragged about a long line of great seamen and admirals and owned castles and property in Corsica—today said to have been a port of call for Columbus, or perhaps even his birthplace.[13]

Aronne was born on the island of Rhodes, the eastern outpost of the defenders of Christianity, the knights of Jerusalem, heirs to the Templars, crusaders in an eternal order, *defensores fidei* (defenders of the faith).

Rhodes had weathered an Ottoman siege in 1480, and Christians, Jews, and Muslims lived there in harmony. This seemingly impossible coexistence continued peacefully. A Sufi colony also lived there, and the island was home to a settlement of Jews who spoke Greek and practiced the Byzantine rite. The participation of the Jews side by side with the Christians in the defense of Rhodes during the siege of 1480 has been neglected by Christian sources, but has been handed down from generation to generation by the small local Jewish community.[14]

Aronne and Abramo are names of Hebrew origin. Aaron was the brother of Moses, Abraham the "father of multitudes," the common ancestor of Christians, Muslims, and Jews. Sarracina, Aronne's mother, had a name of Muslim origin. Innocent VIII was the Christian, Catholic, and Roman pope: The three great monotheistic religions, divided and seemingly irreconcilable, were mingled in his blood. The vision of the Renaissance, in pursuit of "a new heaven and a new earth"—words spoken by Columbus—sought to reconcile the three as the end of time approached.

Aronne was made viceroy of Naples by René d'Anjou. Christopher Columbus wrote that in his youth, on a corsair ship bound for Tunis, he was in the service of an enigmatic and mysterious Frenchman who aspired to be King of Naples.[15]

René d'Anjou may have been the grand master of a knightly order that sought the Grail and held its secret. Thus the threads of the mystery and the sacred chalice begin to unravel. Aronne was René's man, but he had proved himself such an able diplomat and such an admirable knight after being wounded in combat that he was made viceroy of Naples amid public furor—by the same René who had previously been a rival but was now a staunch ally of the new conqueror, Alfonso of Aragon. The Cybo family had a talent for reconciling the irreconcilable. Crossing all boundaries, all divisions, despite war and cruelty, they were moved by the spirit of a timeless chivalry, inconceivable to us today—above all, a seafaring chivalry, afloat in tempests and calm alike.

The Cybo family produced more than one admiral. The waves of

the ocean led inevitably to Columbus; his clan had always had dealings with the sea. He even stated himself there were admirals among his
ancestors.[16]

Aronne was also a senator in Rome with Callixtus III, the Spanish
pope who was Alexander VI's uncle. After his time in Rome, he
returned to Naples and was buried at Capua. More is known of his
movements than of those of the young man who was to become pope.
Where had the Cybo family come from, if not from Rhodes? "This
family came to Italy also called Tomacelli, and under the name of
Cybo they always had most resplendent status. They became part of
the Venetian nobility."[17]

✠

Another important maritime republic now joins the puzzle through
monks and geographer-artists who measured the world, with its embas-
sies always open to the East. As with Genoa, it was urgent for Venice
to reopen the Silk Road in the interest of economy and commerce—
to remove the barrier raised by the Turks, with whom this city on the
lagoon still maintained relations. Such was the fluctuation of alliances
and rivalries, changing in the space of a day. The goal was the same,
as economic as it was spiritual, as temporal as it was eschatological: to
reopen the routes to the Levant, one way or another.

Giovanni Battista Cybo, Innocent VIII, was a noble and well-to-do
knight best known for his worldly qualities. He fathered a considerable
number of children, even for those times. His offspring, according to
some sources, numbered sixteen. They all vanished from history in suspicious fashion, except for two, Franceschetto and Teodorina.[18]

For a long time, Giovanni Battista Cybo had relations with a noblewoman in Naples (or elsewhere, according to others), in the court where
he had lived as a boy. Colón, besides meaning colonist, can also mean
colonna (column).[19] A Colonna family had settled in the Veneto and
Trevigiano. The Colonnas were powerful in both Rome and Naples.[20]

It is evident all the facts and legends surrounding Columbus's
birth—in Genoa, Savona and its surroundings, Cogoleto, Cuccaro,

Piacenza, Corsica, Chios, Spain, or Portugal—have contributed to a clouding of the navigator's true identity and origins. They form a series of conflicting and parochial stories and statements that may, in more than one case, lead to a single, all-embracing, complex truth. Here we must wonder: In those times, in the absence of a birth certificate, what nationality would be attributed to the illegitimate son of an unknown lady and a nobleman of Greek origin who was considered Genoese and who was destined to become pope?[21]

We know the future pope studied at the University of Padua in his youth. This was one of the most prestigious cultural centers of the time, particularly for the sciences. Religious tolerance was widespread there; Rome had not managed to impose its will completely.[22]

The four arts of the quadrivium were cultivated in Padua: arithmetic, astrology, astronomy, and geometry. Columbus's son Ferdinand wrote that his father "learned so many languages and sciences, as his writings show, especially in the four principal sciences that his work required—astronomy, geography, geometry, and navigation." Sixtus IV was educated at Padua, as were the poet Battista Mantovano,[23] the architect Leon Battista Alberti, and the humanists Ermolao Barbaro and Giovanni Pontano.

In Padua scholars were taught of Ptolemy, the acknowledged king of geographers, and learned all aspects of the Arabic astronomical tradition. They speculated upon the limits of the world and the universe. It was there Cardinal Nicholas of Cusa, one of the most brilliant and enlightened thinkers of the epoch—so brilliant he risked being accused of heresy—met with Paolo Fisico, forming a friendship only death could separate. Nicholas of Cusa stated, among other things, the earth was not at the center of the universe. Paolo Fisico was none other than Paolo Dal Pozzo Toscanelli, the Florentine scientist and one of the direct inspirers of Columbus's enterprise.[24]

In Padua, scholars discussed the Greek philosopher Aristotle and Averroes, the Muslim exemplar of tolerance. The Augustinian monk Paulus Venetus, who began teaching at Padua in 1395, introduced "into the environment of the Italian universities the subject of the description of the parts of the world, including those unknown,"[25] and also attempted a reconciliation of Averroism, Aristotelianism, and the Christian faith. He did not achieve this goal, but attracted the interest of Cardinal Bessarion, who acted as an intermediary between East and West among efforts toward reconciliation and the organization of a possible Crusade. After the fall of Constantinople, he brought precious collections of ancient texts, testimonies of lost knowledge, to Italy. The past was reemerging.

Bessarion's work formed part of the knowledge base of Copernicus, the scientist who toppled astronomical dogma. During his prolonged stay in Padua, Copernicus wrote: "finally, a long recipe, strange and almost magical."[26] This was sufficient to slip into the "pretense of having attained an ancient knowledge, always reserved for a few elite, and therefore 'divine' compared to all common science (like many alchemists)."[27]

In the dedication "To the most Magnificent Lord Signor Baliano di Fornari, Gioseppe Moleto," dated Venice, April 25, 1571 (in the publication of the *History of the Life and Deeds of the Admiral Don Christopher Columbus,* by his son), the navigator is described as a "truly divine man." Dante's comedy was also divine. Proportion was divine. It was an adjective used often in the Middle Ages and the Renaissance and was reserved, in those times, for the circles of the elite and privileged.

In this case, the thread leads us by way of geometry and astrology. Columbus cultivated these sciences, and was "led into an initiatory world of revelations and traditions, to the acquisition of astrological knowledge of an esoteric character (and therefore consistently of an aristocratic character),"[28] to a "scientific-theoretical" evaluation of astrology characteristic of Paduan studies.[29]

Thus Padua represented an academy of free thought, a melting pot in which the presence of astrological and occult interests was established even in disciplines such as botany and pharmacology.[30]

These were the subjects of many Templars. Columbus, like Copernicus, wrote "recipes." In one such recipe he wrote: "So that the parsley may grow, soak the seeds in vinegar for the space of three days.

For the third day, carry it in your armpit and, when you are ready, plant it; after an hour, it will sprout. And eat it."[31]

This remedy seems more like a recipe for an alembic. And this from a sailor said to be illiterate and of humble origins, a mere bloodhound of winds and waves? It is a baffling question, an anomaly accepted as a footnote of Columbian folklore.

The young philosopher Pico della Mirandola and the Florentine monk Girolamo Savonarola also studied at Padua. Savonarola predicted an imminent moral, political, and religious renewal. Many other influential persons passed through Padua, including Galileo Galilei. It was an academic crucible bordering on heresy in which the sensibilities and convictions of individuals and groups developed revolutionary currents of thought—currents heading in varying and sometimes opposite directions. Occasionally this would end in open fighting.

All in all, "[T]he Paduan education led to the preservation of the magical world together with the 'scientific' attitude, anchoring phenomena in a superior, immutable cause, in astral movements and with the corollary, equally full of interrogative potential, of the existence of a caste of 'priests' of the sciences, to whom the protection and interpretation of this world of traditions was assigned."[32]

Padua was not its only athenaeum; there was also Florence of the fourteenth century. If the Florentine Giotto's Scrovegni Chapel was the *Divine Comedy* of painting, then the baptistery of the cathedral, frescoed by the Florentine Giusto de' Menabuoi with the cycle of *Genesis,* was its *Decameron.* In the mid-fifteenth century, which saw the rise of two other splendid artists—Donatello and Mantegna—the city became a revolutionary center.[33]

In Padua, Donatello "braved the unthinkable in both the aesthetic and the technical realm," while Mantegna was "the greatest humanist of all, the most sensitive to the myth of antiquity." The present was renovated on the model of ancient times. Mantegna went to the court of Rome and was one of the favorite artists of Innocent VIII.

The young Giovanni Battista Cybo thus grew up admiring Giotto. The latter revolutionized art and is recognized as one of the great men of

Franciscanism, along with Dante and Columbus—a trio who, at the four hundredth anniversary of the discovery in 1892, were commemorated magnificently by the monument erected in Naples.[34]

Padua's golden age produced what has been described as the "greatest collection of fourteenth-century fresco cycles in Europe." Saints, gospel stories, Christ and Mary, the Christian and Hebrew scriptures together, the Apocalypse, and the Last Judgment, all were outlined in the Middle Ages and perfected in the Renaissance in an endless parable, exalting them in a new life, a new era, a New World.

Such views and ideas unfold in the Oratory of San Giorgio, where the holy warrior can be seen killing the dragon, the beast of the enemies of Christ. The Chapel of San Giacomo recalls St. James Matamoros (the Moor-Slayer), who fought the Moors in Spain. In the Ovetari Chapel, in the Church of the Hermits, fifteenth-century iconography once depicted the cycle of the story of St. James and St. Christopher. The saints, united for the triumph of Christianity, also bore the signature of Andrea Mantegna. The cycle is gone, destroyed by a bomb in 1944, but we can still admire the beautiful St. Christopher, resplendent on a gold background, painted by Giovanni da Bologna.

The arts of that time were not viewed as they are today. Pictorial cycles and paintings were illustrated texts and information for the eyes of the illiterate and painted images held infinite meaning for those who could interpret them. Art has never been more conceptual. The artist was closer than ever to the absolute; in a time when illiteracy ruled, his language resounded with storied images, with a series of theological and philosophical implications, allegories, and symbols. The people looked on in delight and in awe, but not necessarily with understanding.[35]

Padua still offers for veneration the remains of the only apostle whose body is complete: St. Luke the Evangelist, who, according to tradition, was born in Syria or Greece—Christopher Columbus's Suria, the Greece of the Cybos. Giovanni Battista Cybo came of age in this cultural humus, which we encounter again in Columbus and where perhaps Columbus even grew up. It sufficed to nourish the future pope's eyes and spirit in the light of what awaited him on St. Peter's throne.

Thus, in that city in the Veneto, disciplines, studies, men, minds, and religions intertwined in a manner analogous to the situation in Genoa, and in many ways more complex and fascinating. It was an anticipation of the Florentine, Neapolitan, and Roman academies, in a certainty, more than a hope, of molding a new being for a new era. The mission of the Renaissance was to send a kind of self-sufficient cyborg of the intellect, the perfect image of Leonardo da Vinci's *Vitruvian Man,* to the other side of the world by means of ships—just as today, in a new mission, spaceships are launched to seek contact with possible inhabitants of other worlds, in a new cosmos.

A close connection joined the many who, like Diogenes, carried the lantern of knowledge. They sought correspondences between microcosm and macrocosm. They sought the single universal harmony, which would be equal for all the peoples of the world. Such perilous and uncontrollable dreams could easily slip through their fingers or backfire, ending up in evil and despotic hands at the cost of the lives of multitudes. The Renaissance did not blossom spontaneously, independently from the past and detached from it. The Renaissance remained solidly joined to the legacy of the Middle Ages, an expansion of the latter, an ennobling of basic instincts.[36]

✠

Giovanni Battista Cybo abandoned the world, as St. Francis had done. He went to Rome, thanks to his friendship with Cardinal Calandrini, brother of Pope Nicholas V. So the future pope left behind his youth spent at the Aragonese court of Naples and was married to the rich and opulent Church.

A life of prayer and universal projects awaited him. The origins and wealth of his family went back to time immemorial—and had perhaps partly vanished—but the family was studded with "illustrious men, marked by the virtue that emerged among them at various times, decorated by honored sovereigns for the greatness of their merit and their outstanding deeds; and also by the splendor of the families of the princes and popes to whom they were frequently related, most ancient and most noble: and since that time, no lineage of Genoa has held such an honored place among the most illustrious and foremost families of Italy."[37]

By the year 1000, the Cybo family, some of whose origins we have already seen, was in service to the Church of Rome, and "to the empire in Italy and outside Italy."[38]

This list of personages culminates, after Innocent IV, in Pope Boniface IX (1355–1404), "[f]irst called, before ascending to that dignity, Pietro Tomasello Cibo [Cybo], descended, as was said, from a Tomaso Cibo [Cybo], a noble knight, also called Tomacello (Tomacelli), perhaps due to his short stature, 'who around the year of our salvation 1010 settled his family in Naples.'"[39]

From this family, lost in time, traces remain in the main Borgia room in the Vatican and in a marble statue of this pope in the basilica of San Paolo. In his hands he holds a book on which is inscribed "Boniface IX of the lineage *Thomacellus genere Cibo.*"

Panvinio (1530–1568), the Augustinian from Verona and successor to Platina in writing papal biographies, concludes it is impossible to catalog all the great persons in this family, and that "they ruled many lands and states in Greece, their ancient homeland, under the name of Cubi." The Cybos, then, over the centuries, were a dynasty of men of the Church, knights, Crusaders, and captains on sea and on land—just like Columbus. Their presence was continuous in the defense of Rome and in the courts of Europe. They cultivated a devotion to St. Francis and a love of the islands, Greece, Naples, and Genoa.

The dominant concept of the time was one of a pontifical seat capable of dazzling the world. For this it was not enough for the popes to sprinkle their heads with ashes or kiss the feet of the poor. They lived in a precarious and risky equilibrium. Not everyone thought of them in the same way; much depended on the character of the man and his more recondite inclinations. The pope, even with the tiara, remained an earthly being in spite of his divine investiture, particularly because vocations were often not very sincere. The ecclesiastical calling was a status symbol sought by noble families, and their business was outside the Church as much as it was within.

Even Giovanni Battista Cybo's course was part of a precise strategy, beginning in 1467 with his being made a bishop of Savona by Paolo II, the Venetian Pietro Barbo. Savona is the Ligurian city where records locate the young and obscure Columbus, who possibly lived there for about two years with his alleged father, Domenico Colombo. Both Columbus and Giovanni Battista therefore spent some time living in this part of Liguria.[40]

Giovanni Battista Cybo had by then formed a close friendship with Giuliano of the powerful della Rovere family, the future Pope Julius II. It is also certain he enjoyed, above all, the favor of another more important della Rovere: the Savonese Franciscan Sixtus IV, who conferred the diocese of Molfetta upon him in 1472, *Translatus ad Melphitanam ecclesiam, anno 1472*.[41]

This was a singular promotion. Savona was a prestigious seat, and had already produced one pope. Molfetta was a decentralized medieval town in Apulia.

Going to Apulia meant breathing the air of Magna Graecia and once again feeling the spirit of the struggle with the Turks at the crucial extremity of the Italian peninsula. From the ports of Apulia departed the warriors and the foolhardy army of pilgrims that had formed under Urban II: the first armed pilgrimage, which became a crusade.

At Molfetta, the monastery of Santa Maria and San Giovanni dei Padri di Banzi was, due to its proximity to the sea, the place most suited for the preparation and provisioning of the ships to sail overseas. There, in 1097, "were seen sailing in from all locations those cross-bearers known as Crusaders, who made up the elite ranks of volunteers fighting for the religion of Christ, with the cry: 'God wills it.' This was the first, truly real crusade."[42]

The hospital of St. John was built by the harbor for the recovery of pilgrims and warriors. It combined a monastery, church, and hospital: all reference points for those departing to or returning from the Holy Land. First the Templars established themselves in the town, and later the Knights of Jerusalem. Naturally, "even the fathers of the Abbey of Banzi at Molfetta had to leave their house of worship, because the Order of the Templars of Barletta and, in consequence, of Molfetta, was banned in March 1308."[43]

The Templars vanished, but their legacy remained. They passed into other orders, surviving in secret. They changed in the course of successive incorporations. Their presence, like that of other knights, is constantly encountered in the Grail-like quest for Columbus's story.

Yet another Genoese citizen, Giovanni Malvagio, occupied the Templar property at Molfetta while the order was still in existence in the early 1200s, in a presence that would solidify over the course of that century.[44]

In 1188 the image of a Madonna and Child miraculously appeared there. Giovanni Battista Cybo's veneration for the Madonna of the Martyrs of Molfetta—brought by sea from Jerusalem, purloined by pilgrims escaping from the Crusade—was immediate. As soon as he was elected cardinal in 1480 (the year in which a stunned Rome saw so much bloodshed at Otranto), he had it embellished by the construction of a niche of Leccese stone. Once he was pope, he encouraged its worship, issuing a bull that granted indulgences to those who went to visit the sacred image on Low Sunday and on the feast of September 8.[45]

The record of Frederick II of Swabia still survives in the Byzantine heel of Italy. He took an interest in Sufism and the East and obtained the crown of the king of Jerusalem, and in him the *regnum* and the *sacerdotium* were united by God. He surrounded himself with wise men, monks, and Templars. In death, he wore the gray habit of the Cistercians, the order of Citeaux. One legend tells of Averroes living at his imperial court.[46]

Even today, there is hope the crown of Jerusalem will rise again at the world's end. It is believed the West will join with the "promised emperor" to liberate the holy city without violence. Thus the final days will commence, and the Antichrist will come. According to another prophecy, "the 'emperor of the coming,' with the liberation of Jerusalem and before the end of the world, will give rise to a millenarian reign of peace."[47]

The octagonal structure of the Castel del Monte—designed to be a wonder of the world and built with the wise advice of Cistercians led by Bernard of Clairvaux, the monk who gave the Templar knights their rule—stands out against the sky, evoking the Temple of Solomon. There is an effusion of astronomical and astrological references. In one room stands the figure of the Baphomet, the idol venerated by the Templars and one of the reasons for their condemnation.

More celestial harmonies, esotericism, and arcane knowledge were lost and chased down. More Templars, more knights, and again the vision, sometimes of the pope sometimes of the king and emperor, would unite East and West. And always there were the Cistercians, who were also involved in the construction of one of the Apulian sanctuaries most frequented by pilgrims, Monte Gargano, dedicated to St. Michael, who fought to conquer the dragon of chaos. He is shown holding a lance, not only as the prince of angels, the divine messenger, like Hermes, but also as the prince of peace and guarantor of order since the days of Charlemagne.

Finally, on the facade of Bitonto, not far from Gargano and Castel del Monte, "on the lunette of the right door, we find a symbolic representation of Christ: To his right and left are plants, symbols of Islam and Christianity, twining together at the center. This is from the second half of the twelfth century. In that era there lived knights, Crusaders, and merchants who behaved as Christians in Europe and as Muslims in the Orient."[48]

Let us now return from Apulia to Tuscany, from Gargano and the lance to St. Galgano and the sword, to the calm Tuscan landscape of Pius II, Piccolomini. There, a lost map of the world, painted by Ambrogio Lorenzetti in 1344, once stood on a wall of the Palazzo Pubblico in Siena. It is gone now; only a circular mark remains on the wall. What world did it show? In the same building, the splendid cycle of the *Allegory of Good Government* divides black and white, like the squares of a chessboard, like the colors of the city of Siena and the arms of the Templars and the Cybo family. In a church not far from a Templar dwelling, objects from the New World, supposedly donated by Christopher Columbus, are still preserved today.[49]

In the countryside, where the atmosphere of the Piazza del Campo and the tower of Mangia dissolves into silence, in the solitary Gothic-Cistercian monument of St. Galgano, there is still the inexplicable mystery of the sword in the stone. Galgano's name naturally recalls that of Galvano (Gawain), the hero of the Arthurian cycle.[50]

The sword is embedded in the rock, impossible to remove without splitting it apart. Scholars have been vexed by the medieval mystery. The sword is not ready for use; it is sheathed, as in times of peace. The specter of chivalry continues to haunt the regions of the peninsula. The plot line, at this point no longer avoidable, repeats itself in a play sometimes too suggestive of reflection, of opposition, sometimes openly stated, sometimes concealed. It has been stated that Innocent VIII may never have come to Apulia. The opposite can be claimed just as well.[51]

At this time, the office did not imply the residence. No traces of the Cybo presence remain at Molfetta—except for a chronicle which states Giovanni Battista lived there, albeit for a brief time: "For a little time, the town was able to enjoy the presence of its prelate; then, the activity of such a man being known to the above-mentioned Pope Sixtus IV, he was sent in the office of legate to the Diet of Nuremberg, to establish peace between Hungary and the empire."[52]

No further proof exists either way but the Genoese and Greek pope must have been familiar with the "Greece of Italy," the southern part. It was the natural harbor for the knights coming from the Levant and from the sea. Thus, in the chosen land of the Crusaders, the Madonna of Martyrs, the Santa Maria, the Stella Maris of Pope Cybo, looked to the East from where she had come—toward the Holy Sepulchre to be reconquered, in one way or another. There could be no further delay.

THREE

✠

Columbus, Son of Innocent VIII

IT WAS LIKE waiting for the millennium. The Turks were advancing on all sides, menacing Europe. The pope, the sun of Rome, the head of the Christian body, was at risk of being beheaded by the Muslim scimitar. The resources of the Italian city-states, cut off from trade with the Indies, were in jeopardy. Upon the death of Sixtus IV, Rome had been partly sacked, shaken by internal discord. The threat of civil war was brewing in the air. "No Ligurian's property in Rome was safe any longer, and even the Genoese hospital was destroyed."[1] And yet, the chosen city would be in Liguria.

The cardinals, amid the popular terror, converted their palaces into fortresses. The streets were infested with bloodshed and crime. The alleys were often traps for those who ventured out at night, perfect places for ambushes. The capital of the world was a violent city, alliances were as unstable as they were intricate. Members of the Colonna and Orsini families fought each other; the great families were rivals both inside and outside Rome. Beyond its walls, discord reigned among princes, and Italy was a feudal land. Italians and foreigners alike aspired to the throne of St. Peter. The Spanish, working under the influence of Callixtus III's nephew, the ambitious and unscrupulous Rodrigo Borgia, began to "meddle ever more in the tangle of Italian politics."[2]

War was always on the doorstep, danger forever in the air. Rome and the world urgently needed a man of peace. Five hundred years later, another Giovanni, Pope John XXIII, dedicated an encyclical letter to *Pacem in terris*. Peace, justice, opulence, and the good of Rome were always the aims declared by Pope Innocent VIII: "who wished to attend to other matters with zeal and efficiency: to peace, justice, and prosperity."[3]

Giovanni Battista Cybo had given ample proof he was a man of peace. He had already shown himself able to reverse the downward spiral of instability and death that characterized the last decades of the century. His qualities had been evident since his first appearance on the stage. When Sixtus IV withdrew to Campagnano in 1476, fleeing a plague epidemic, he delegated the government of the Church to Cybo.

It was an act of extreme trust in cataclysmic times, when treachery was an everyday occurrence. Remaining with only a few of the faithful, Cybo did the best he could: "He succeeded in reconciling the remaining inhabitants, toned down profiteering, established rescue stations, did all things possible to alleviate the suffering of the more unfortunate, and took the time to dedicate himself to religious functions."[4]

These deeds confirmed the greatness of his gifts. In times of conflict and civil war, he had also been a legate in the Siena of the Piccolominis and St. Galgano. Thanks to him, peace was established between the pope, the king of Naples, the duke of Milan, and the Florentines. Cybo was also sent abroad as a peacemaker: "He made two voyages to the Levant to keep Turkish anger in check."[5] Those in his family before him, the thick web of his ancestors, were proof of this respect; their abilities and aptitude for personal relations compensated for any lack of education.

The office of pope was not a hereditary one. In a time when no one could be trusted, the nepotism prevalent since the thirteenth century represented, above all, a political expedient. The family, friends, and patrons and the appeal to any who owed gratitude were the most natural forms of defense for those with no lack of enemies who feared aggression from all sides: "It is prudent and praiseworthy," wrote the cleric Lambert de Huy, "for the pope to continue holding his relatives and friends dear, as in times past. As the proverb says, 'it is not well to tie strangers to your own navel.'"[6]

Even during attempts to curb corruption, it was emphasized he was "just and praiseworthy in providing to friends and relatives, especially if they were deserving and indigent."[7] The phenomenon, which could have been abused, constituted a necessity.[8]

The closeness and faithfulness of family was even more indispensable in the wielding of an anomalous power such as that of the pope. It was a kind of self-defense of the pontifical state, for which it was necessary to have a certain number of castles in the hands of devoted and loyal persons and a certain number of military and courtly appointments entrusted to relatives and friends.

True, the line grew ever thinner between lawful and illicit, between use and abuse, regarding which Guicciardini observed: "For no one did the pope have greater ambition than for himself." It was a progression that led, with Cesare Borgia, to the "triumph of the consolidation of the papal state, which bore its decline within itself."[9]

At carnivals, the princes of the Church paraded in disguise on horseback. They sometimes died from "excessive erotic activity." Many of them partook of all the pleasures of the world, especially when they had been forced, rather than called, to choose a life in the service of God. The aristocracy set up many of their children in a career that might reward the family fortune.

Roman opulence was part of the mentality of the Renaissance princes; in a contest no one could or wanted to escape—least of all the pope, who desired to affirm the universal supremacy of his office. It was equally obvious some people in the circles of the papal court thought themselves unjustly deprived of promotion and property, and there was ample opportunity for the more cutthroat among them to make a series of libelous accusations. Also, the families were not always in charge of the situation. Dissimulation, lies, and calumny formed part of the art of power.

The secular prelates were opposed, in equal measure, to those devoted to a life of the utmost spirituality, dedicated to the good of humanity, which could never be attained without peace. History is fond of exaggerating the most execrable aspects of the court of Rome. From the Protestant schism to the Enlightenment, positivism, and Masonry, for various reasons and motives, the popes were an expression of their times, and the times were exceptional—both in good and evil ways.

The pope was a transient, solitary, elective, and often elderly "monarch." His scepter clashed with the collective power of the cardinals, and his office generally lasted only a few years. Temporal power, as important as spiritual power, sometimes demanded an appeal to all the means used by the sovereign dynasties with which it was necessary to compete—and children and relatives were precious elements in this game.

Scandals, under these circumstances, were decidedly less influential than we might think today. The "cardinal nephew" was not seen as an institution merely proclaiming the dishonor of the Church's rules. He was one of the few possible means for fortifying the structure of the Church in a turbulent time shaken by continuous rebellions. Men of the sword and men of the faith were recruited from among the more influential relatives and dynasties. They formed an essential ingredient for survival.

The office of the senators of Rome had been created with the intent of better controlling the city through the involvement of the nobles— even if many risks were taken in this regard, for which a counterweight on the popular front was necessary to balance out the occasionally cumbersome bulk of the aristocracy. The present-day pejorative view of nepotism, in short, appears to be an invalid historical interpretation.

Even those who write, especially in this sense, that Innocent VIII was not a great pope—and the many who claim, without the slightest shadow of doubt, he was a bad pope—are forced to contradict themselves by recognizing some of his many merits. A halt had to be called to a situation whose control, more and more every day, risked being irremediably compromised. The cardinals, meeting after the death of Sixtus IV (whose passing was not mourned), were unanimous in wanting war waged against the infidels. They demanded a head-to-toe reform of the

Curia, as the court chronicler Johannes Burchard relates, the summoning of a council to defend the faith and organize a campaign against the Turks. The general reorganization of the Church would overturn "life and behavior." It would be "as much an affair of the secular and regular clergy as of the military orders, as much of princes as of nations, for all those loyal to justice and to the cause of the Church."[10]

✠

A genuine revolution was entrusted to the hands of the future elect, to be carried out in sight of the year 1500 and the new century, amid rising messianism.

The cardinals shut themselves in the conclave on August 26, 1484. The Venetian Marco Barbo and the Genoese Giovanni Battista Cybo were apparently in the running from the start. Both were great knights connected to the Order of St. John of Jerusalem. The overhauling of the Church must be given over to men such as these. The desire of Francesco della Rovere to put a stop to Rodrigo Borgia's scheming tipped the balance in favor of the second candidate.[11]

A mere three days after the beginning of the conclave, approximately twenty-five prelates had made their choice. In remembrance of the beheading of John the Baptist, to whom he dedicated his pontificate, and in the name of a diverse, evangelical, and prophetic Church, Giovanni Battista Cybo chose the name Innocent VIII. At a little more than fifty years of age, he was the chosen "rock" of Providence. He was pope number 213 (twice 3).

On a hot day in August, the dean of cardinals Francesco Todeschini Piccolomini appeared on the loggia of the piazza before the rejoicing crowds of Rome, optimistic of better times. His high voice resounded with the eagerly-awaited announcement: *Nuntio vobis gaudium magnum, habemus papam Reverendissimum Cardinalem Melphitensem Joannen Baptistam Cybo qui sibi nomen imposuit Innocentium* (I proclaim a great joy to you: We have a pope, the Most Reverend Cardinal of Molfetta, Giovanni Battista Cybo, who takes to himself the name of Innocent.) The crowd responded with shouts of joy.

The brevity of this conclave bears witness to the uncontested nature of the (almost) unanimous verdict reached by the judges—a highly unusual event in the fortunes of the Church and Christianity. There was no lack of the usual handouts and palpable promises, the simoniacal pacts that frequently occur in the course of an election, those underground agreements which even today are present in the political decisions on which the fate of humanity hinges. The balance of the world, in that moment more than ever, depended on the pope—all the more because Rome knew the announcement of a new geographic discovery was about to alter the course of the world and upend the current equilibrium.

Yet if we attentively read the *Diario* of Burchard—a German master of ceremonies objectively limiting himself to the recording of events, even though he sometimes risks saying who is good and who is bad—we will realize that in reality things proceeded very differently from how they have been reconstructed. Pacts were made preparatory to the election of a new pope that sought above all to restructure power: They foresaw a kind of immunity for the conclavists and were signed by all, obliging the future pope-elect to honor the agreements as a first condition of his appointment. "The monarchic constitution of the Church must be transformed into an aristocratic one, yet still providing, above all, for the personal benefit of the electors."[12]

Burchard was among those appointed to "gather all the goods belonging to the future supreme pontiff that are to be found at the conclave and distribute them fairly among the aforesaid conclavists."[13]

All things had been carefully considered. These were true and honest capitulations: dealings before which the meticulous pontifical diarist, always attentive to style, showed not the least embarrassment, even writing of a "fair" distribution. Did these agreements confirm a spreading corruption, or were they essential for a policy that could turn over a new leaf, leading to a more disciplined, more conciliatory, and less scandalous future? The preelectoral pacts even included a restriction on nepotism and a reorganization of the military orders—the branch of Rome armed against the infidels, ready to chase down the "dragon," or defend against it. The popes of the Renaissance certainly had their faults and were not wholly innocent; many were "children of their times," and many others became "stepchildren of their times" and of the historical interpretations that followed them.[14]

In the course of the brief conclave, the extremely wealthy Cardinal Rodrigo Borgia, a corpulent and worldly Spaniard, had given ample proof of his pride and perfidy. He was sure—more than sure—of being elected. Spain already had all its pawns moving, dealing in promises of "gold, real estate, and benefices" to the bitter end. The discovery of America, the gold, would be the guarantee, but the plan failed. The future Innocent then exercised what was considered normal practice before the beginning of the conclave of the College of Cardinals. Simony, in this light, was reduced to the granting of favors due in a precautionary electoral campaign in which the cardinals were willingly involved.

The phrase uttered by the cardinal of Siena therefore gained certain significance with regard to the eighth pope to choose the name Innocent. He had already gained the necessary quorum of seventeen votes. The Sienese Francesco Piccolomini, the future Pius III, was greatly renowned for his piety, honesty, discipline, order, and love of culture. Watching Giovanni Battista Cybo at the signing of petitions, he commented with a smile on the fact that the pope went down on his knees and leaned on a chest to sign the papers the cardinals presented to him: "This is an inversion of the right order of things; the pope is signing petitions on his knees, and we, the petitioners, stand upright." The pope took a stance of extreme humility—and the phrase has been used as a gavel in the judgment of Innocent VIII. Piccolomini presented his own petition in turn, like the rest of them. His words, spoken in front of the pope, were not offensive. In view of the smile accompanying the remark, they seem to have been a benevolent chiding on the part of a wise prelate in the presence of a pope-elect who had already shown he would be different from the others.

Giovanni Battista was installed on September 12, 1484. His Holiness, wearing the amice, alb, cincture, stole, red cope, and bejeweled miter, was carried on a litter to attend mass at St. Peter's. Bells chimed, fusiliers fired to mark the triumphal event, and all the canons knelt to kiss his foot. The cardinals kissed his hands, and the prelates his right foot. A piece of flax mounted on a reed was burned and the warning was recited: "Holy Father, thus passes the glory of this world." Then the procession headed toward the Lateran. The city was decked out for the festival, the palaces garlanded. The procession crossed the streets amid popular rejoicing, the pope riding on a white horse. Every now and again, coins were thrown to the crowds. At the top of the Castel Sant'Angelo, the procession ended and the Jews welcomed him, inviting him "to adore and honor their law and acclaiming him in Hebrew."[15]

The pope said he approved the law, but condemned the mode of interpreting it, because the Messiah had already come; he was "Our Lord Jesus Christ." The pontificate's relationship with the Jews was not hostile; the continuity between Judaism and Christianity was recognized, as confirmed by the great masterpieces of painting. The difference was a matter of interpretation of doctrine.[16]

At the time, the Jewish presence was increasing in the city. There was a migratory influx into Italy, and particularly into Rome, where an ecumenical spirit of tolerance reigned as never before, the legacy of the ancient caput mundi, a surge of universalism transcending race and faith.[17]

The pope made his entrance into the Church of Santi Giovanni, the Baptist and the Evangelist, upon the *sedia gestatoria*. No canopy was used, for fear of the crowd. The seat ended up in pieces, fought over by soldiers. Those bishops and ambassadors who approached Innocent VIII in the moments after his election have left an excellent impression of him: *"Honores mutant mores* [Honors alter customs]; surely his benevolence and affability are so innate and habitual that everyone firmly expects that we have a good pope." "He is described as a modest man, gentle and loved by all."[18]

He was always the picture of an "angelic pope," but his election was overshadowed by Cardinal Giuliano della Rovere, who had not favored choosing him, to the point that many saw him as a kind of figurehead. One ambassador wrote to Lorenzo the Magnificent: "Send a courteous letter to the cardinal of St. Peter's, for he is pope *et plusquam papam* [and more than pope]." Apparently, the Florentines also said "this pope sleeps with the eyes of this magnificent Lorenzo."[19]

Innocent, it is true, listened to the opinions of others and took advice with good grace, but he was never subordinate to anyone. Least of all was he complicit to injustice, exhibiting goodness and a morality that never descended into weakness. He immediately understood with whom he had to deal, including the king of Spain.[20]

Hasty opinions, gratuitous insinuations, and judgments progressively and deliberately distorted over the years forever damaged the reputation of Pope Innocent VIII, despite much documentation and many sources proving the absolute contrary. The truth was besmirched and mangled.

It is correct, however, that the prince of Florence was forced to complain to Innocent repeatedly regarding a lack of papal intervention on behalf of his son-in-law, the pope's son Franceschetto Cybo, who had married Maddalena de' Medici. After continued persistence Lorenzo succeeded in gaining some concessions. Their correspondence on this subject was lengthy: "Not without some blushing," wrote Lorenzo the Magnificent, "I remind Your Holiness of the matter of Sig. Francesco, this appearing to me a very absurd thing to have recall to Your Holiness, to whom he must naturally be more dear than to anyone else, nor should my letters and intercessions surely have more power than the natural relationship of Sig. Francesco to Your Holiness."[21]

The letter is from 1487, three years after the election of Innocent VIII, and Franceschetto's situation had not changed in the least. The pope, believed to be corrupt and nepotistic, had done nothing to support his son despite petitions and repeated requests from Lorenzo, acting as his mentor. Panvinio,[22] who punctiliously continued the work of writing the lives of the popes, which was begun by the Vatican librarian Platina, composed an informative portrait of Giovanni Battista Cybo a few years after his death, even writing of "an almost excessive coldness toward his relatives."

Lorenzo, who, in 1489, had acquired the rights to the alum industry—the precious substance indispensable for fabric dyes—wrote again, five years after Cybo's investiture, on behalf of his son-in-law and "many other servants," forever "fasting" and partaking only moderately "of such good fortune." He mentioned, yet again, "the bad condition of the poor Sig. Francesco, who in five years of Your Holiness's pontificate has only just begun to have anything substantial that he can absolutely call his own . . . that men are not immortal, and that a pope is only what he wants to be, and cannot leave the pontificate to any heir, and all that he can call his own is the glory and benevolence that he bestows on his family."[23]

✠

Pope Innocent's actions appear to have been characterized by rigor, honesty, and attentiveness to the problems of the fold rather than to personal or private concerns, his sincere reverence for blood ties notwithstanding. Considering that his transgressions were seen within the framework of the customs of the times, these transgressions were aimed toward the common good of Christianity. This was in keeping with a disposition of the spirit identified with *pietas* (duty; devotion), considered a virtue in moral theology, and also manifested "in an affection and devotion to his kin, his citizens, the nation, and God."[24]

These were the same criteria inspiring Columbus's behavior. The navigator, regardless of events, was always concerned with his friends, relatives (with the exception of the father and mother assigned to him by history), and progeny, as well as with the world's poorest people. Part of his legacy was willed "to persons in need and to charitable works."[25]

As for the pope, Panvinio praised his "infinite and merciful humanity toward the poor." It was a spirit of charity never lost to the Cybo tradition. Even today, in the church of San Marcellino in Genoa, which belongs to the Cybo family and was the place where Innocent VIII was baptized, a Mass for the poor is held on Sunday mornings, attended by the city's many homeless.[26]

When Innocent became pope, his family, although noble and illustrious, does not appear to have been particularly well off, according to some sources. Was he a "poor" cardinal?[27]

The adjective might refer to the conduct of a man who had chosen a life more appropriate to his new office: a voluntary return, in certain respects, to Sister Poverty, despite the occasionally unavoidable splendor of the Vatican court. Columbus is also said to have been of noble lineage that had momentarily fallen on bad times. In his *History,* Ferdinand Columbus writes that his father's parents "were persons of worth who had been reduced to poverty by wars and factions of Lombardy. I have not been able to find how or where they lived."

During his pontificate Innocent VIII's life was tumultuous and filled with unforeseen events. One day, a lightning bolt struck the pope's chamber. It was seen as a bad omen for him, all the more so because it was followed by his unexpected illness, prompting preparations for a new election. On this occasion, Franceschetto Cybo, who had gone to Castel Sant'Angelo, found about a million gold pieces they could mobilize with the aid of the king of France. These, then, were the funds Franceschetto, respecting his father's wishes, wished to reserve for carrying out the Crusade. This has passed into history as an attempt to pillage the funds of the Church.

The pope recovered as if by a miracle, but the incident "roused his relatives to secure their position for the future; and they entreated the pope to help them while he could. But he was of such constancy that he could never, by prayers nor by other means, do those honest and good things that appeared to him to twist a point. . . . [T]he pope, in dispensing the goods of the Church, always had his eyes more on Christ and on the sacred rules than on his family and kin; and he would often say that the revenues of the Holy Church were reserved for sacred use and for maintaining the authority and grandeur of that seat, not for worldly glory and splendor."[28]

To finally obtain a solid benefice, his son Franceschetto had to wait for the fiefdom of Anguillara to become vacant—"not, however, in times of great yield," according to Panvinio. This was not an imperious action; it was granted only after the Sacred College's approval. Innocent VIII did not act like a despot.

Franceschetto, often put to work in delicate diplomatic missions and military campaigns, ended up disgraced by the *damnatio* that would fall upon his family. Tradition has it that he was prone to gambling, that he committed rape and violence, and that his father had to use Church funds to pay his debts. Despite his bad reputation, Innocent's son in fact received rarely granted privileges from Emperor Frederick that were subsequently confirmed to him and his descendants by Leo X and Clement VII.

Meanwhile, Innocent tirelessly pursued his reformist politics: "With paternal solicitude, he lifted the heaviest burdens of the oppressed Roman people, bringing the useless pomp of profane ambition back within the confines of honest decorum. Indeed, in the hearts of the new subjects, the former resentment against the inadequate pope was replaced by a universal and lively sentiment of happy recognition of the successor."[29]

The love people felt for Innocent was demonstrated by what immediately happened each time he seemed at risk of premature death. The Curia and the Romans prayed for him, invoking the grace of the Lord. His rivals profited from it: Adversarial factions regained courage and cunningly spread the news, repeatedly, that the pope had died, heightening the disorder. The people were encouraged, without success, to rebel against the dominion of the "Genoese sailor."[30]

Innocent's strong constitution—a sailor's constitution—was fortunately always in the good care of Jewish physicians. Yet the pope's health was subject to mysterious recurring relapses, which continued up to 1492, as if something, or someone, was attacking him in a slow, insistent papicide.

His manner was characterized by extreme gentleness. "No one left him disconsolate," wrote his contemporary Sigismondo de Conti; "all were welcomed with truly paternal kindness and charm, and he was a friend of nobles and plebeians, of rich and poor."[31]

Innocent VIII also had a sister named Bianca, called Bianchinetta— and, interestingly, one of Columbus's sisters was also named Bianca and also went by Bianchinetta.

The Cybos, as we have seen, were descended from a long line of knights of land and sea, men on the cusp between East and West.

Throughout Innocent's life, all his actions seemed to bespeak this. His abilities were accompanied by wisdom, his nobility by loyalty, which inspired knights and Templars—and, on the opposing front, a section of the Muslim cavalry. "Loyalty above all" was his motto. Innocent was the jewel of a long dynasty. He was the great diplomat, the great strategist of this illustrious lineage, the heir who had finally conquered St. Peter's throne, crowning a dream that was also cultivated by the Templars: the vision of a universal synarchy.   *joint rule*

Panvinio also wrote of the pope that "he was gracious of manner, humane, and diligent and of a marvelous and sweet eloquence . . . and yet he stood by his motto *'Ego autem in Innocentia mea ingressus sum'* [For I have walked in my innocence—Psalms 26:11] and his deeds were truly always in keeping with his name." Panvinio relates that, having found the coffers of the Church exhausted, for which great works were in the making, the pope was constrained to create twenty-five officials for the leaden bulls, twenty-six secretaries, and thirty *presidenti di Ripa*.

The collection of funds, commonly indicating a sign of avarice, meant an influx of money that Innocent "did not spend in vain, because in the first two years of the pontificate, since the Turks were wreaking infinite damage upon the Christians, he spent 150,000 scudi to send an army against them to put down their violence."[32]

There is no inkling of his so-called squandering or the lack of funds to which Innocent condemned Rome in his immoderate desire for wealth. Panvinio's portrait proceeds in a laudatory crescendo. There appears none of the avarice of which some have accused Innocent VIII; he practiced the parsimony and discretion that he urged Mantegna, one of his favorite painters, to portray. Indeed, he promoted rigorous economic politics: "He relieved the Church, and with it the palace and his court, of superfluous spending." He favored the religious orders of St. Francis, St. Augustine, and St. Dominic.

Aside from the officially recognized Franceschetto and Teodorina, his other children were passed off by the Curia as nephews and nieces, in a situation toward which the pope showed no preoccupation, much less embarrassment. These children vanished mysteriously—too mysteriously—into thin air. Nothing is known of his supposedly unruly youth; no proof has been found to corroborate a mode of conduct and habits censured by many chroniclers.[33]

Pastor, the great historian of the popes, remarks, "It should be noted that from the moment Giovanni Battista entered the ecclesiastical state, there were no more unfavorable reports regarding his moral conduct." Incidentally, the story of his having pawned the tiara, the triple crown, several times, strains credulity—even though in one case the episode appears to be true.[34]

Perhaps this alienation had a predominantly metaphorical value, in the sense of a papacy doing its utmost for the renewal of the Church, holding nothing back, to the point where those not in favor of it interpreted this pawning as a clearance sale of tradition. The financial proceeds derived from the monopoly of the alum mines, the sale of offices, the collection of tithes, the selling of indulgences, the undertaking of public and architectural works, and the financing of the war in Spain against the Moors showed the Vatican had abundant resources, even sufficient to finance foreign sovereigns: "If not peace, at least money."[35]

Rigor and justice, within the limits allowed by the times, distinguished the pope's works, as is confirmed by the scant number of new cardinals chosen by Innocent: There were only two, apart from those who died. Among them were Lorenzo di Domenico, perhaps a de' Mari, who took the pope's surname (as was the custom at the time); Antonio Pallavicini Gentili (definitely from the family that also had branches in Spain) from Genoa; and Ardicino della Porta da Novara, a bishop from Corsica. He is presented as a person most respectful of all people, and "very well read."[36]

✠

The new vision of modernity, the attention paid by Innocent VIII to innovative and Neoplatonic cultural currents, is confirmed by his close friendship with the humanists Ermolao Barbaro and Pomponio Leto, as well as the great Angelo Poliziano, who translated numerous Greek classics for him. In one letter, the poet of the *dolce stil novo* even declared the pope *vicegiove*.[37] This was part of a return to ancient times, an essential component of a Renaissance finding its most fertile terrain in certain Roman and courtly settings, parallel to "Greek" Florence.

By now, everything about Innocent seemed to indicate the person foretold by the prophecies arising from the eschatological expectations so widespread with the approach of the year 1500. Peace in Rome, Italy, and all of Europe was the goal of an enormous and tireless activity,[38] and in order to find peace and harmony, the pope left no stone unturned.

It was a reformist vision, tackling daily life and the Vatican, battling both Catholic and Islamic fundamentalism. Thus, on St. Peter's throne, Pope Innocent VIII claimed "the innocence of Peter as if it were an inheritance." In a succession of disturbing events, in a time characterized by battles and prophecies, Rome continually searched its ranks for the desired *papa angelicus* who would restore the age of justice. The Franciscans saw it as their goal. By 1267, the learned Englishman Roger Bacon (1214–1293), known as Doctor Mirabilis, had written: "Forty years earlier, it was predicted that a pope would come who would reform the Church, heal the schism with the Greeks [the pope was also Greek], and convert the Tartars and the Saracens."[39]

A *papa angelicus* had been predicted for 1493—the same year in which the discovery of America was made official. The two events could not be coincidental. It was the beginning of the new golden age so widely foretold. In many ways, it seemed anything Innocent touched turned to gold. He had been born, it is said, in 1431, in the same city where Columbus was supposedly born in 1451 (according to the most recent research), but the navigator's birth tends to move around in time and space.

In order for the divided Church to be reunited, it had to change profoundly. Agostino Patrizi Piccolomini, who died in that fateful year, 1492, redefined the ceremonial at the order of Innocent VIII. The rituals always insisted on white, candor, and innocence.[40] White, black, and red, always the esoteric primary colors, the colors of the Cybo arms, became the colors of the celebrations.[41]

Innocent also applied himself to an urban renewal of the apostolic seat. He sought to reform the entire apparatus of the Church.[42] It was an extremely intense activity, in a progression that revamped Curial customs.[43] Order had to prevail in Rome; the city had to be the example for Christendom. It was an attempt to attain efficiency and control through a major organization of the Curia. "In good and in evil, bureaucracy represented one of the few elements of continuity in an institution subject to periodic crises of stability."[44]

In the pope's behavior sentiments of goodness, purity, and innocence—tempered with the strictness required by the times—alternated with an inflexibility, at the appropriate moments, equal to the lords of the Renaissance. For example, this can be seen in the execution of two forgers of papal bulls. It would be interesting to know who the instigators were, how many forgeries were subsequently passed off, and how many have survived as "documentation."

Innocent VIII's strength of character is confirmed by the vigor with which he managed the conflict with Ferrante (Ferdinand) of Naples[45] and the enmity between this king and the Neapolitan barons.[46] Confronted with the impossibility of reasoning with the quarrelsome and rebellious Ferrante, who refused to send taxes to Rome—setting a precedent that might have been extremely dangerous—the pope saw no recourse but armed battle and even excommunication. After many conflicts, he finally succeeded in reasoning with Ferrante and obtaining peace, though only after a lengthy standoff. Innocent was a steadfast but not vindictive man. The occasionally gratuitous cruelty of his times did not form part of his character, which was more disposed to forgiveness and justice: "He did not dwell on the memory of offenses made against his person, instead being often disposed to reward them with benefices."[47]

These identical words are found in a description of Christopher Columbus—as if the character of both had originated from a natural sympathy or an undeclared kinship.

In reference to Innocent VIII, a rising enmity with Genoa is recorded: A request for money made to the Ligurian city by the pope was received with much ill grace and resulted in a series of events not even "having to do with private merchants in danger of bankruptcy." The Turkish admiral Piri Reis, in a document we will examine later, writes of an offer made by Columbus at Genoa to take a voyage to obtain funds. It was rejected.

✠

The few existing biographies of Innocent VIII vary sensationally between scant elegies and numerous condemnations, between much severe criticism and little praise, an injustice that has lasted for centuries. It seems as if he had been two completely different people. Rebuilding the truth based on such conflicting reports is no easy task. Information on Innocent has been collected from the few remaining chronicles. In the absence of other documents, we can posit only a path of possible truth, in light of which the accepted truth appears impossible.

Even a pragmatist such as the Florentine writer Niccolò Machiavelli, author of *The Prince,* who could not have loved a personality such as Innocent if depictions of him are accurate, acknowledges in this pope the ability to make "the factions suddenly lay down their arms," as he writes in his *History of Florence,* "thanks to his being a humane and peaceful man."

On one point, however, all sources appear unanimous: Innocent VIII's unwavering commitment to carry the Crusade to fulfillment. "He sent delegates everywhere to urge the princes to forget their particular problems and unite against the common enemy, if by not sending troops, then at least with substantial contributions. He did not succeed in gaining peace, but he did gain money."[48]

That money would also allow him to aid Christopher Columbus, to speed his departure: "To the house of Spain, helping the Catholic king with money in gaining the kingdom of Granada . . . whence the Catholic monarchs should hold the house of Cybo in grateful memory"—which would not be the case.

Even today at St. Peter's there is a poster for sale, printed with the Vatican's approval, showing the portraits of "The Supreme Pontiffs of Rome" and summaries of their lives. For Innocent VIII, it reads: "Finished the great work of the pacification of the Catholic states. Cracked down unrelentingly on the slave market and aided Christopher Columbus in his voyage to discover America."

These few brief words on a poster may be of no value, but this poster was preceded by a publication printed after the death of John XXIII and entitled *Il papa umile e i suoi 261 predecessori* (The Humble Pope and His 261 Predecessors). Here we read that the chronology "has been composed based on the definitive list of popes and antipopes according to the most recent historical investigations of Mons. [signed] Angelo Mercati, prefect of the Vatican archives, officially accepted and published for the first time by the Holy See in the yearbook of 1947."[49]

Everything about Giovanni Battista Cybo points to a personality outside the norm in terms of those who had preceded him and those who immediately followed him on St. Peter's throne. In the turbulence of the late-fifteenth century, the foundations of the Church were crumbling and threatening to give way altogether to the force of movements demanding a change of direction on the part of Rome. Martin Luther achieved this soon enough in a schism anticipated by Columbus in his will, which the politics of Innocent VIII might have prevented.

With the exception of the obligations assumed at the moment of his election, Innocent's private and public actions show a course breaking the habits of Curial hypocrisy, probably opening the way for one of the charges made against him: that of favoring concubinage. Perhaps the pope had the potential to allow priests to marry.[50]

According to the customs of his time, he never gave up on politics that made use of children for securing alliances. He openly married his two heirs in St. Peter's; in 1488, Franceschetto's marriage to Maddalena de' Medici, daughter of Lorenzo the Magnificent, was celebrated. The bride, accompanied by her mother, Clarice Orsini, made a triumphal entrance into Rome in a sumptuous procession. Innocent was "the first pope to openly and ostentatiously celebrate the marriages of his sons and daughters."[51]

What other popes had concealed, Innocent revealed in broad daylight. The pope's daughter Teodorina was married to Gherardo Usodimare, a member of a great Genoese family and a merchant and treasurer to the pope. His family had evidently made its fortune at sea. Teodorina's daughter, the pope's granddaughter, married Alfonso del Carretto, marquis of Finale. Once widowed, she was remarried to a member of the Doria family, strengthening the bond joining the two great Ligurian families until the battle of Lepanto, which sealed the defeat of Islam. It is no coincidence the great corsair Andrea Doria, from the same family as Gian Andrea, victor in that epic sea battle of 1571, was sent from his parish to Rome in 1484 to join the pontifical guard.[52]

Even the pope's prolonged quarrel with the king of Naples ended in a marriage, helping to cement the new alliance. Battistina, the other daughter of Teodorina Cybo and Gherardo Usodimare, was married to Luigi, prince of Gerace, and uncle of King Ferrante of Naples. The bond extended to Aragon. Meanwhile, Spain, with Innocent's arrival, had become Columbus's preferred port of departure. The sequence unfolded like a domino effect.

The marriages of the "nephew" and "niece" were celebrated in the Vatican. The ceremony was held in St. Peter's. Burchard did not attend, and did not approve of it: "Nothing of it was kept secret: On the contrary, the news was spread throughout the whole city ahead of time." A procession of beautiful ladies was admitted into the rooms of the Vicar of Christ "in violation of the rule of our ceremonial, which expressly prohibits women from attending a banquet with the Pontiff." Rome looked on, flabbergasted. After Innocent's death, this marriage was soon annulled by Alexander VI, who arranged marriages more favorable to the Borgia family by offering up the hand of his daughter Lucrezia. Alexander would quickly undo all of Innocent's accomplishments, thus stifling truth and justice.

Lorenzo de' Medici passed into history as "the needle of the balance of peace in Italy." More than influencing the pope, as we have seen from the letters directed to his daughter's father-in-law, the pope may have influenced him; at least, the two appeared perfectly in tune. Harnessing Lorenzo to St. Peter's chariot was one of Innocent VIII's political triumphs.

Without the achievement of this concordance, more ambitious plans might have failed.

Another concession was made to Lorenzo: a cardinalate was granted at a tender age to his son Giovanni, who later became Leo X. Columbus recalls this episode in his writing, discovered only recently. Giovanni was called to Rome at the age of eighteen in late March 1492, after Granada had fallen to Spain and as Columbus's expedition was nearing departure. The Medici took on a debt of gratitude to Rome, and a banker from the family, Giannotto Berardi, became one of the major financers of Columbus's voyages.

The recommendation made by Lorenzo to his son in a letter, which may have been inspired by Franceschetto Cybo,[53] constitutes an example of wisdom, good sense, and Christian spirit. His words are admirable, even touching in their paternal affection, faith, and far-sightedness.

Lorenzo's wife was from the Orsini family. In a single move, the pope achieved two objectives: Florence and one of the greatest families in Rome remained indissolubly linked to his politics from the economic, religious, and political points of view. In Florence the Academy of Marsilio Ficino operated and in Rome that of Pomponio Leto operated. Together with Genoa and Venice, a matrix was formed, a framework of interests and ideas capable of spreading all over Europe.

✠

The marriages were part of the power play, the moves made in the game being played on the chessboard of Europe. Innocent had many children. It is impossible to think that none of them, whom the Curia hypocritically wished to pass off as nephews and nieces, managed to take part in the intricate struggle for a world that no longer had boundaries.

Furthermore, nothing is known of Columbus's youth; his visibility begins with his arrival in Portugal. Surely his relationship with his father must have been extremely important in the formation of his character. This is even revealed by the navigator's handwriting: polished, perfect, and ecclesiastic in style in a time when simple sailors did not know how to read or write.

Merely being such a good calligrapher would have been enough to allow Columbus to support himself, and if this fact is logically assessed, it is sufficient in itself to overturn hearsay. In his few remaining writings, "according to Freudian philosophy, the ideal of the ego stands out, exalting grandiose, idealistic choices, compensating for a conflicting sentiment toward the paternal image: a father to flee from or defy."[54]

This father certainly could not have been the unknown Domenico of Genoa. Columbus's provenance cannot be identified with the family to which he is attributed. We can presume that at best Columbus might have been entrusted to this familial nucleus for some period of time—hence certain political prizes, such as Domenico's appointment as gate warden of the Porta dell'Olivella, which would never have been assigned to a mere tavern keeper.

As for the navigator's upbringing and education, without a shadow of doubt it took place in a different house, a different lineage. The man whose perseverance resulted in the completion of four voyages fundamental to the path of humanity probably had the determination of a bastard—one who has a mission to complete, not only for the redemption of Jerusalem, but also for the redemption of his own blood.

At this point the investigation becomes even more intriguing. Merely taking a close look at the statue by Pollaiolo on the pope's tomb in St. Peter's and mentally superimposing his dark features upon those of Columbus produces a striking effect that cannot be simply the product of imagination. The resemblance between the two men is obvious—yet we do not have a definite record of the admiral's exact physiognomy. The many portraits of Columbus, so different from one another, render him "one, no one, and a hundred thousand."

Nevertheless, we do know some images are very faithful to the true face of Columbus. These are the ones most resembling the statue of Innocent VIII, even leading us to think they could have been the same person. It is a disturbing realization; Pollaiolo's red-pastel study of the pope's face, preserved at Florence, looks like a facsimile of some images of Columbus. If we look at Innocent VIII's profile on the aforementioned poster of the popes and compare it to the classic portrait of Columbus by

Ghirlandaio, it seems almost as if one image were traced from the other: the same face, the same cranial structure, the same Semitic nose. A rare portrait of Aronne Cybo, Innocent's father, resembles an engraving of Columbus by Aliprando Capriolo to a disturbing degree. The resemblance is equally strong in recently identified portraits of Columbus, such as the one by Pedro Berruguete. More similarities may arise.

The pope had so many unacknowledged children, so many "nephews" and "nieces." What became of them? *Nephew* was the term used by the Curia in their attempts to gloss over the frequent paternity of popes and cardinals. In a Roman edition of Ptolemy's *Geography* from 1508, in which mention is made for the first time of Christopher Columbus in a work "which humanist tradition deems untouchable," in a small treatise of fifteen chapters, "little known in Columbian literature today . . . the name of Columbus appears many times." A Columbus *primus* and a Columbus *nepos* are mentioned, as well as lands which either the Portuguese or Columbus discovered, and which were called the New World.[55]

Columbus had been dead for only a few months. The Celestine monk and mathematician Marco Beneventano must have been well-informed. "Columbus," he states, "discovered those lands in the company of the Portuguese and not the Spaniards." Here we see the definite possibility of voyages having taken place prior to 1492. More important, Columbus, whose accomplishments are exalted here, is identified as *nepos* (the Latin "nephew").[56]

It is said the surname Colombo was common in Jewish populations in the north of Italy, as was Esposito in the south. It was a reference to abandoned children who were often left in churchyards or to the foundlings placed in the rotating wooden containers designed for that purpose, the children whose birth was attributed to the Holy Spirit (symbolized by a dove, which is *colomba* in Italian) and whose parents' names remain unknown. Finally, Colombo and Colón are the translations of the Hebrew Jonah, "perhaps another name for John,"[57] the prophet who predicted the reconquest of the ancient lands of Israel.[58]

It is remarkable, furthermore, that considering his many affectionate family ties to his children as well as his siblings, Columbus never remembered the parents attributed to him, Domenico and Susanna. Susanna—the name means "lily"—was the Hebrew woman, chaste as a virgin. It signifies an unadulterated purity and a woman who has never been a mother in the carnal sense. Meanwhile, Domenico refers to *dominus,* the Lord *par excellence,* God himself. The adjective *dominicus* is equivalent to "belonging to the Lord," "dedicated, consecrated, and destined to the Lord."

These are highly significant names in this puzzle of which the Christ-bearer and those who surround him form the pieces: This man, a new Jesus, appears to have been the offspring of a virgin and a son of God, or a man consecrated to the Lord—like the men of the Church, and above all, the popes. Domenico, Susanna, and Christopher Columbus are equally symbolic names surrounding the birth of a man without a face, without parents, without a homeland, without a birthday: "From time to time his origin was Corsican, Catalan, French, Hebrew, [or he was] without origins (or rather, a foundling) or even a bastard of royal or papal blood."[59]

The hypothesis that Columbus was the son of Innocent VIII is extremely provocative.[60] It is also plausible enough in light of the words left by Columbus's son Ferdinand:

> The admiral was chosen for his great work by Our Lord, who . . . though his descent was from the blood royal of Jerusalem, yet was content to have his parentage from an obscure source. . . . Just as most of his affairs were directed by a secret Providence, so the variety of his name and surname was not without mystery. We could cite as examples many names, which a hidden cause assigned, as symbols of the parts that their bearers were to play. Just so, the admiral's name foretold the novel and wonderful deed he was to perform. If we consider the common surname of his forebears, we may say that he was truly Columbus or Dove, because he carried the grace of the Holy Ghost into that New World which he discovered, showing those people who knew Him not who was God's beloved son. As the Holy

Ghost did in the figure of a dove when St. John baptized Christ; and because over the waters of the ocean, like the dove of Noah's ark, he bore the olive branch and the oil of baptism, to signify that those people who had been shut up in the ark of darkness and confusion were to enjoy peace and union with the Church. So the surname of Colón, which he revived was a fitting one, because in Greek it means "member." [61]

These are revealing words. Everything returns to mystery, to the occult. The name and the surname, common enough in those times, were not depicted as random. They were an annunciation open to a variety of interpretations in the *summa* of a centuries-old vision—perhaps, indeed, that of the Templars. Meanwhile, the definition "member," in a language as familiar as Greek, appears to allude to a double meaning, including a physical one. Besides being a member of an ancient church, the primitive Church of Jerusalem was to merge with the new Church, to lead it back to its origins through the descendent of St. Peter and "his" Christo Ferens. It is an endless wordplay, with the final astonishing reference to "the royal blood of Jerusalem." The royal blood is *sang real,* the Holy Grail, the chalice whose guardians were the Templars. Innocent VIII, the pope who also had Jewish blood, was in turn a descendent of the lineage of Moses.

Were Columbus and Innocent united by the same lineage of divine blood, the blood of David and Jerusalem, from which Jesus is also supposed to be descended? It was a lineage anointed by the Lord in the circles of an enigmatic knightly order, perhaps Templars, knights of Jerusalem, knights of the Holy Sepulchre, or others . . . with the final destination of Jerusalem.

FOUR

An Epigraph in St. Peter's

INNOCENT VIII'S MOVEMENTS were bold and ingenious. One of the most important successes in his politics was accomplished with the arrival in Rome of Jem, the son of Mehmed II who had conquered Constantinople, mortally wounding Christianity. Jem's brother, Bayezid, in one of those fratricidal struggles that were typical of both the East and the West, had seized the throne in a *coup de main*. Jem, who had continually maintained relations with the Knights of St. John of Jerusalem, took refuge on the Greek island of Rhodes, which was simultaneously the bulwark of the Levant and the bridge to it. All the Christian sovereigns vied for the privilege of having this Turkish prince as a hostage in their courts. The pope prevailed, thanks to, among other things, his longstanding connection to Rhodes and the loyalty of the Knights of Jerusalem. The problem of the Turks had always been held in the highest importance; the prisoner might represent the keystone.

A letter from a pontifical ambassador reads: "As Pope Innocent, since the first day of his papacy, has thought of nothing more than of how aid may be given to the Christian republics that are exposed to so much danger, he is now offered a better opportunity than ever through having in his power the brother of the sultan, Prince Jem. This latter has promised that if, with the aid of the Christians, he can gain the caliphate, then he will withdraw the Turks from all of Europe, and even surrender Constantinople."[1]

The pope focused all his strategy upon the problem. His policies began with an encyclical of November 21, 1484, culminating in 1486 with the *Ortodoxei fidei propagationem*, generally known as the Bull of Granada. The Crusade had never been lost from view, and the incumbent threat of Islam, despite many failed attempts at negotiation, had never vanished. In 1485, an enemy attack was anticipated. Ambassadors from Rome were sent everywhere to gather support for the Holy War. From the farthest reaches of Russia the envoys of Grand Duke Ivan came to prostrate themselves before the pope, as Burchard relates. "The question of the Turks was probably also discussed with the ambassador of King Henry VII of England, who had excellent relations with Innocent VIII."[2]

Columbus's brother Bartolomeo was connected to the English court. Relations with the king of France were also good, and Columbus is said to have gone there after the last refusal of the monarchs of Spain to fund his voyage. Thus the two brothers, regardless of their humble origin (as has been the common belief for the last five centuries), moved at will among the royal courts of Europe.

Jem had initially been taken to France in 1482. The sultan's heir became the skeleton key to unlocking the enemy front. On the evening of March 13, 1489, the Grand Turk made his entry into Rome, having landed at Civitavecchia. He was escorted by the grand master of Rhodes, Pierre d'Aubusson, whose escutcheon also bore a red cross; d'Aubusson was later made a cardinal by Giovanni Battista Cybo, something that would occur only once more in the history of the order. On the other hand, an infidel prince being captured and held hostage in the Vatican was no novelty; it had happened before, under Pius II.[3]

The objective was to divide the enemy front. From Piccolomini to Cybo, history repeated itself, pursuing a new golden age now within reach for Christendom—thanks to the heralded geographical discoveries and the man who would "reveal" them.

Citizens of all ages and classes, some afraid, some joyful, lined the way for the Turk's passage. The appearance of a *giaour* (infidel) in the temple of Christ even presaged the end of the world. "The people could not get enough of this rare spectacle, and had the deep conviction that they had been saved from a great danger. All over Christendom, in fact, the prediction had spread that the sultan was to come to Rome and take his seat in the Vatican."[4]

This was indeed happening, but the terror of the prophecy, "by the grace of God," was being realized in a very different way. The noble Muslim entered the caput mundi with the honors due a sovereign.

The Turk rode impassively, like a statue, on the pope's white mule. He did not heed the homage or gifts rendered to him, remaining mute upon his steed with a melancholy expression. Only the next day, in a brief audience, did he meet with the pope. Jem made a slight bow with his head and, declining to genuflect, kissed the pope's right shoulder. He thought it a grace of God to be allowed to greet him. Through an interpreter he told the pope that in a private meeting he would communicate "other matters that would be to the advantage of Christianity."[5]

What did the "barbarian," as the Vatican artist, Mantegna, called him, have to tell the Vicar of Christ? What secrets would he reveal or confirm to him in the depths of the unfathomable mystery surrounding this event? Let us begin with names; his name recalls those of Alexander the Great, Solomon, and the magic power of the Grail,[6] the goblet of such mysterious significance. Now, on the Muslim front, the prophecy sought to manifest itself in the current protagonists of history.

Strange, secret meetings were said to be taking place in the chambers of the Vatican. These included a lesson in sacred history given to the Holy Father by Jem in which the events of the Roman Empire were interwoven with those of Christianity, with the names of the emperors altered and rendered unrecognizable. According to Jem, the story of Christ had been falsified by Christians, and the true Christians were therefore actually the Muslims: "For they were the ancient followers of Arius. According to Jem, the true gospel was that of Jesus, which we Christians did not know, only a few passages of which were included in our four gospels."[7]

A gospel written by Jesus himself! Such talk crossed the line into heresy. This confirmed the pope's desire to seek out unknown doctrinal paths or perhaps simply to return to ancient ones in a flood of spirituality from a time long past: the late twelfth century, when both the Christian and Muslim worlds had seen the burgeoning of mystic movements such as Sufism in Islam, the Kabbalah in Judaism, and the Cathar heresy in Christianity. This last had been extinguished with blood and arms, then reabsorbed into Franciscanism.[8]

It is certain that in Jem, Rome had an ally at the heart of the enemy empire and a thorn in Bayezid's side. In addition, Jem's mother was a Christian noblewoman, Cicek Khatun, Madonna Fiore. She had perhaps been born in the East or else was a Venetian captured by corsairs.[9] The prince's childhood, therefore, was also permeated by Christianity.

Jem was about thirty years old, tall and thickset with narrow eyes. Innocent allotted fifteen thousand ducats per annum for his upkeep. The papacy was pressured by many expenses, but Innocent "had it arranged for the good of Christendom."[10]

The Turk loved to hunt, and his apparel sparked an Eastern trend among some Roman nobles, who dressed themselves in his style. He entertained himself with music and banquets. His appearance was majestic, and he did not bare his head before the pope. A master of the saddle, he lived luxuriously in the Vatican and slept in his clothes. "He has a face which inspires fear, especially when he is under the influence of Bacchus."[11]

He also received ambassadors, holding banquets in the pontifical state. It is recorded that one day, the sky grew dark and a tempest burst forth: "Any ill-wishing Christian might surely look with dismay upon Peter's palace, where now—a spectacle unheard-of in all the history of the Church—a sultan and a pope were holding court side by side."[12]

Sinister prophecies began circulating, foretelling the collapse of the existing world and the end of the Church's power in 1493. Savonarola's voice rang out in Florence. He had arrived from the University of Padua and predicted the coming of a New Jerusalem and the abandonment of unbridled worldliness. The friar's fate, following his condemnation by the Spanish pope Alexander VI, would be torture and death—not from poison, but at the stake.

It was a pivotal time in the history of humanity. All people hoped for change, and at the same time were afraid of it—those in power above all. The most disparate, conflicting, and incredible voices spread their words in short order, in a genuine parallel war of information and disinformation. Among the vying factions, spies operated across the whole field with no lack of foul play. It is extremely difficult to discern the truth in hindsight. Perhaps we must remain satisfied with a single truth, or the closest thing possible to the truth.

The prince was educated and was particularly passionate about cosmography, like his father, Mehmed II. He was convinced the answer for humankind was written in the stars. Like all men in power, he was interested in the form of the earth's sphere. All people were curious about the vastness of the world and the universe, the islands and continents to be discovered. Jem asked to look at Ptolemy's *Geography,* put into verse by the Florentine Berlinghieri.[13]

Jem was the right man at the right time to bring Innocent VIII's plans to completion. He wanted to win back the throne, and he still had a host of faithful supporters who would aid his return. He might form the spear point of the Crusade.[14]

Bayezid, wishing to keep his scepter, offered the lance of Longinus, which had pierced the side of Christ upon the cross. He was ready to do anything to eliminate his rival brother. The pope had a finger in two pies. Both Innocent and Bayezid were willing to make large concessions for the benefit of Rome. The return of the relics most sacred to Christianity also entered into the game. John the Baptist's hand was sent to Rhodes, and was followed by the lance. The stakes even included the possible handing over of Constantinople, the Holy Land, Jerusalem, and the Holy Sepulchre. The promises made foresaw "perpetual friendship, peace, love, and harmony" and the restitution of "all the islands, along with the cities, the lands, castles, and places that my father took from the Christians."[15]

Bayezid, who was already paying a high tribute of forty thousand ducats a year to Rome in order to guarantee his brother's gilded exile, was required to raise the stakes, fearing "that the Western powers might make use of Jem in a common action against the empire."[16]

✠

Victory was approaching. The dream of universal submission beneath the cross was coming into view as the year 1500 drew near. It would be a triumphal Jubilee, with the *jabel* trumpet of the ancient celebration resounding in the New Eden, recovered and completed. And the mission of God's ambassador, Christopher Columbus, formed an indispensable part of the plan. Delegates were sent throughout Europe. Contacts back and forth among Venice, Florence, and the enemy Ottomans continued in a singular interplay. In 1487, a giraffe arrived from Cairo as a gift for Lorenzo, and Poliziano wrote a poem about it. Violins played the music of the Sufis and the dances of the dervishes. Were they heralding a celestial music?

The year 1489 was crucial, and July was the most important month. Two Franciscans from the Holy Sepulchre in Jerusalem presented themselves at the court of the Catholic monarchs Isabella and Ferdinand. Were they monks of the Order of the Holy Sepulchre? The great sultan of Egypt had sent them to the pope, and Innocent VIII had sent them on as ambassadors to Spain. They brought a message from the sultan threatening the Christian people of Palestine unless the war against the Moors was ended. The two brothers met with Christopher Columbus.[17]

The Franciscans evaluated the situation with him. They surely spoke of his expedition, of the need for gold for the Crusade, and so they returned to Rome, to Giovanni Battista Cybo.

Jem had left his wives and children under the protection of the sovereign in Cairo. Did pontifical diplomacy take advantage of this in order to enter into new negotiations with the sultan of Egypt? The moment had come to speak the final word regarding the war in Spain against the Moors, to reach an agreement with Boabdil, the Muslim king of the Alhambra. Without this treaty, Columbus could never have sailed.

Many historians think the meeting with the Franciscans dictated the navigator's decision to reconquer the Holy Land. In truth, the plan had always been at the heart of the slow preparation and maturation of a man who was the living replica of the giant St. Christopher, the ferryman of Christ. "The day for wresting Palestine from the yoke of the Muslims, redeeming it with the gold of the regions he would discover, was foremost in his thoughts."[18]

From Rome to Spain to America, the gold lit the new path to forge and follow, the new Easter Crusade for the Resurrection. In Constantinople, Bayezid felt surrounded. He sought to rid himself of his fears and his problems, hiring an assassin to kill both his brother and the pope by poisoning the fountain from which the water was taken for their rooms—but the plan failed. For both Giovanni Battista and John Paul II, the torch for the elimination of the head of Christianity would be passed through Turkey.

All the Holy Father's energies were now focused on finding a solution to the Eastern problem. A definite possibility existed of realizing the longed-for redemption. In early July an assembly began at Frankfurt, attended by the emperor. One by one, all the nations were won over to the cause. The pope wrote to the princes, exhorting them to join ranks against the enemy.

Circumstances were highly propitious. Such a favorable opportunity could not be wasted; all internal discord must be abandoned for the common good. Pontifical politics, set in motion on all sides, achieved surprising results: the pope "wished not only to offer all the resources of the Holy See, but also to take part in the expedition in person, should it be undertaken."[19]

In the summer of 1490, Rome welcomed the impressive assembly. All particulars were discussed. It was agreed there would be three armies: the first would be assembled by the pope and the Italian states; the second by Germany, Hungary, and Poland; and the third by France, Spain, and England. Supreme command would be given to the "king of Rome" in person, and to the emperor. Apparently, the pope's health did not cause the slightest worry. The blood of the Cybo knights was resurfacing in Giovanni Battista; the pope, described as weak, would quickly become a warrior pope in the field. The war was expected to last between three and five years.

The death of Matthias Corvinus, king of Hungary, caused fresh disputes within the Christian body, and the plan was postponed. Innocent's commitment never wavered, despite the well-timed recurrence of his sporadic and mysterious illness. Hope revived when an agreement was reached with Ferrante of Naples, overcoming an age-old obstacle to peace in Italy.

Troubled by a strange discovery, the king of Naples had gone to Rome to ask pardon of the pope. A priest in Apulia, near Taranto, had found a book bound in lead and wrapped in a cloth on which was marked a cross, the letters *CNAT,* and the words *Catalus Bani archiepiscopus Tarentinus, et non aperiatur nisi pro rege infideli suo* (Catalus Bani, archbishop of Taranto, and it is not to be opened except for his infidel king). The book, also containing Egyptian writing, gave prophecies of many things to come.[20]

✠

Mystery piled upon mystery. It was the eve of Columbus's departure.

The Crusade and the New World could not come into being without light, without the splendor of gold, the gold necessary for the Great Work. Economic objective and spiritual objective were converging. The gold would come from the farthest Indies, from the lands beyond the Indies, whose extent was unknown—the Indies still hidden from humanity, the Indies of Solomon, St. Thomas, and Alexander the Great. For now, however, the dream had been shattered.

With death already snapping at its heels, the Platonic Academy in Florence was struck down, as if by a deadly virus. Lorenzo the Magnificent died in the spring. Pico della Mirandola, Angelo Poliziano, and Marsilio Ficino attended to him at the Villa di Careggi and surely Savonarola also visited Lorenzo on his deathbed.

The drastic attempt to save Lorenzo's life apparently involved a potion made of powdered diamonds. He was only forty-three years old. The balance in Italy was beginning to swing irrevocably. The great Venetian knight Marco Barbo had already died and Innocent himself followed soon afterward. Columbus was left alone to defend the dream, yet he did not even know it.

After the fall of Granada, the Spanish court could no longer put off granting the navigator's requests. Things were gathering pace. Columbus was ready, supported by the Franciscans and the Florentine and Genoese families who were forever at his side in Iberia.[21] The Spanish monarchs could not say no to the pope of Rome, nor could they any longer run the risk of someone else venturing from a foreign port across the Atlantic to the lands that were to be discovered (or rediscovered). Two great humanists, the Geraldini brothers, two Umbrians from St. Francis's homeland and ambassadors of Rome in Spain, had championed Columbus's cause to the monarchs for some time. Antonio Geraldini was a great poet and cosmographer, an astronomer, a "father of the stars."[22]

It was certainly with Geraldini that Columbus perfected his project. No one had aided him for seven long years, "save for Friar Antonio Marchena," Columbus wrote. He often mentioned a Father Marchena as his protector. Was this Antonio Geraldini or another friar? Antonio Geraldini had welcomed Columbus upon his arrival in Spain, helped him financially, and introduced him to Isabella. Did the navigator open his heart in secret to him? Geraldini died at Marchena in 1489. In the chronicles, he was replaced by the Spaniard Antonio Marchena, long confused with Father Giovanni Perez (who would have put Columbus in contact with the Pinzón brothers). The recurring duplication of persons and names has made the five-hundred-year puzzle of Columbus all the more complicated.

The legacy of Antonio Geraldini, astronomer and "father of the stars," was handed down to his brother Alessandro, tutor of the royal couple's children. It was Alessandro who, in a moment of extreme doubt, convinced the indecisive Queen Isabella to defy the contentious King Ferdinand when it came to giving a definite yes or no to Columbus's requests. The rest, tradition has it, is a cheap adventure story: the sovereigns' refusal of the exorbitant demands, the departure of a bitter and offended Columbus, his wild goose chase, his return to the court, and the inexplicable and patronizing consent of the monarchs to the demands of the "ignoble stranger."

Church fathers such as St. Augustine and Nicholas da Lira, who wrote of the impossibility of life in the antipodes, were masters of the faith—but they knew nothing of geography, Alessandro Geraldini explained this to the skeptics in their final moment of deliberation. Columbus was right: The risk was minimal. The promised rewards were after all dependent on the success of the expedition. The one running the greatest risk, putting his life on the line in the stormy ocean, was Columbus. Alessandro's speech was convincing. The Geraldini brothers were fundamental in the preparation and execution of the first voyage, although chroniclers rarely mention them; their role and influence, their movements between Rome and Spain, have been minimized. They are recorded, moreover, as having been exclusively on the Spanish side—and thus it is necessary to return them to their correct locations in this intricate puzzle.[23]

In doing this, we discovered the Geraldini brothers were sent to the Spanish court by the pope—one played the role of *logothete,* spokesman for the pope, and the other, a geographer and a highly educated man, was the ambassador of the Vatican as well as tutor to the royal children. All their undertakings can be traced back to Innocent VIII.[24]

Thus all Columbus's problems related to financing were suddenly overcome at the most critical moment, thanks to Alessandro Geraldini. Half the sum, an incredibly underestimated amount, came from Italian sources. The necessary funds came from Genoa and Florence, from bankers and nobles related to the Holy Father. A share was deposited by Giannotto Berardi, who handled the Medici family finances in Iberia.[25]

The other half of the financing still remained—that which would ensure that "the endeavor is Spanish." The money, as has always been maintained, came from the Santa Hermandad, a secular militia. Two partners administered the Santa Hermandad,[26] and one was Luis de Santangel, *escribano de ración* (secretary of the royal treasury) to the king of Spain. The fact that Santangel was Ferdinand's man is well known.

More important, and what tends to be ignored, is that he was also the receiver of ecclesiastical revenues in Aragon—in other words, a collector for Rome. He gathered tithes and indulgences for the Vatican's coffers and went into negotiations as Pope Innocent's man. His function, moreover, was lowly compared to that of his Genoese colleague. He received money from "a certain Pinello and a certain Centurione" which he in turn lent to the king of Aragon.[27]

Queen Isabella's flaunted jewels, which she offered to give up in aid of Columbus's departure, were no longer in existence; they had already been pawned for the expenses of the war against the Moors. This sacrifice was merely a cunningly created legend, and the testaments immortalizing her gesture are pure propaganda. Strange indeed that it was a man in the service of Ferdinand, and not the queen, who offered the decisive contribution of 1,140,000 maravedis, considering the four expeditions to the Indies would be the exclusive appanage of Castile. Isabella never gave up to her consort her rule over the Indies. Santangel, finally, was from a Jewish family, a converted Jew. The characters of the plot again lead us back to Naples.[28]

A digression on the Gulf of Naples might even involve Christopher Columbus and, in part, his youth. We cannot imagine that Christopher, or at least one of his siblings—perhaps Bartolomeo—never went to Rome. A residence in Naples might at least explain the navigator's Catalan influences and knowledge of Spanish prior to his arrival on the Iberian Peninsula, as well as his use of that language throughout his life and the numerous Catalan inflections present in his writings, as pointed out by the historian Luis Ulloa. It might also explain the many geographic references in his writings to Naples and Sicily, which were part of the Catalan-Aragonese kingdom. As a final note, Llullism was particularly widespread in Naples, under the influence of Alfonso the Magnanimous and his wife Maria.

The Franciscan Ramon Llull, the martyr of Majorca, faithful to the Immaculate Conception, in his fervent reverence for the Virgin Mary (something he had in common with Innocent VIII and Columbus), predicted a Crusade brought about more by means of the Word and conversion than by the sword—bringing the good news "beyond the curve of the sea which surrounds England, France, and Spain, where, across from the continent that we now see and know, there is another continent that we do not see and do not know. It is a world that is ignorant of Jesus Christ."

The other administrator of the Santa Hermandad was the Genoese Francesco Pinelli, and much less is known about him. That he was the nephew of Innocent VIII has been ignored above all.[29] Pinelli combined the functions of ambassador, legate, and collector, which had never before happened anywhere in Europe. In some documents he is even referred to as *clericum ianuensem*.[30] Although a member of the clerical hierarchy, he was clearly able to lead a secular life—in one of those anomalies so common of the time, as might also have been the fate of Christopher Columbus. Pinelli, for his part, was related to the great families of Genoa as well as to the pope.[31]

The web of kinships, friendships, alliances, and interests was thick. From Rome, it grew to envelop Italy and Spain. Christian names and surnames were almost all Italian. Every character was a member of some rich and illustrious family, and each was a loop in a Gordian knot waiting to be untied. The threads led to Pope Innocent, to the Medici, and to Columbus. The plot, complex as it was, revealed Giovanni Battista Cybo's power, illuminating the darkness of a hidden truth, testifying to the pope's capacity for commitment and to his skill at good relations. The many elements, in the end, led to a dense network of churchmen, bankers, and merchants—but, above all, to the knights who were given special powers in view of a special moment, such as the moment at which the "mariner" pope was chosen or the moment of Columbus's departure on his voyage to reveal at last the other half of the globe.

The sum offered by the Santa Hermandad constituted a simple loan with a duration of only a few days. One essential detail has always been glossed over: the repayment of the loan, which was done immediately afterward using the funds from the bull of the Crusade coming from the knights of the Order of Santiago (St. James). It consisted of contributions to the Church of Rome, mostly from the humble and pious people of the province of Estremadura. "The most interesting item on the accounts of universal history," the famous sum of 1,140,000 maravedis, passed through the treasury of the diocese of Badajoz to Bishop Hernando de Talavera to pay the expenses of three caravels "sent to sail as a fleet to the Indies, and to pay Cristóbal Colón who goes with them."[32]

Everything possible was done, the study adds, in order that "a thin mist might shroud the ecclesiastic origin of the money, which formed the royal contribution for the financing of Christopher Columbus's first voyage and its provenance in the Church of Estremadura."[33]

In whose interest was it to conceal the truth? Who profited from the cards being shuffled? For all the effort made to obliterate all documentation, many sources have fortunately survived and can once again make things clear. Of all assassinations, that of the truth is the most difficult, for as Columbus wrote, "truth always triumphs."

Once every untruth was finally vanquished, once every obstacle was surmounted, once every particular appeared taken care of down to the last detail, once Columbus's departure was imminent, the pope's health began to decline again irremediably—and in a suspicious manner: In the late spring of 1492 he was afflicted by atrocious abdominal pains and strange fevers.[34]

Then events quickened. "The end of Innocence was worthy of him; the end of Innocence was edifying."[35]

✠

In a slow agony, a great spirit was extinguished. The pope's torment lasted a few days. He asked the cardinals' pardon for "not having the capacity to bear the weight of his office." His final gaze, in the Palazzo Venezia in Rome, probably fell on the world map painted on the walls of the *Mappamondo* (world map) room. Was his last thought of Columbus, his *dilecte fili?* Before his death, he urged the cardinals to agree among themselves, exhorting them to find a worthy successor. Fate and calculation dictated this would be Alexander VI, Rodrigo Borgia. Rome, Italy, and Europe fell back into chaos. The Medici lost Florence, the Crusade was set aside, and the origins of the discovery of America were swept under the rug.

What had been a universal project, economic and spiritual, became an immense nationalistic and material affair within a delirium of omnipotence. The atmosphere in St. Peter's was realistically described in a passage of a letter (as related by the historian Giovanni Soranzo) from Franceschetto Cybo to his father-in-law, Lorenzo the Magnificent: "In this court, namely in the College of Cardinals, as Your Magnificence knows, there is discord and partisanship between many passionate men, such that the College is divided into two or three parties, each with their own followers." Italy was the favored terrain in the battles of the transalpine sovereigns. The Spaniards, firmly installed at the heart of Christendom, pursued their own goals. The situation was such that "there was already talk of a double election and a schism."[36]

The first signs of the struggle to follow were heard at the Holy Father's deathbed. An example of what was happening can be deduced from another passage in Giovanni Soranzo's chronicle: "In the days of the mortal illness of Innocent VIII, a grave dispute arose between the Borgias and the della Roveres. The vice-chancellor, in the name of several cardinals, asked the dying pope to have it arranged immediately for Castel Sant'Angelo, whose commander at the time was Battista Pinelli, the pope's nephew and a supporter of Cardinal della Rovere, to be consigned to the Sacred College. Della Rovere, in quite a troubled spirit, said to the pope—as reported by Antonello Salerno in his dispatch of July 21, 1492, from Rome to Gonzaga, Marquis of Mantua—'that if it was remembered that the vice chancellor was a Catalan and intended to make Napoli pope [Carafa, cardinal of Naples, then out of favor with King Ferrante], it should then be arranged for the castle to be consigned to the future pope. The two cardinals then fell to harsh words, if not indeed to threats.'"

It was standard upon the death of a pope or cardinal for the body to be abandoned and for his earthly demise to be followed by sacking and looting, in a popular savage tradition. Miraculously, these excesses did not happen in Rome either at the coronation or at Innocent VIII's funeral. Innocent died in the night between July 25 and 26, 1492, which happened to coincide with the feast of St. Christopher on the Christian calendar. Seven days later the man named after the giant saint and the dove set sail from Palos. A great pope had departed. At his election, someone had predicted the coming return of the golden age of Saturn, the planet that was shining in the sky when Columbus landed on the first shore of the Indies. Saturn also lit the celebration of 1992: "The only planet above the horizon of San Salvador on that evening five hundred years ago was Saturn; on that day, just as today, the ringed planet was in the constellation of Capricorn."[37] These were mysteries in the stars by which the ships steered.

The period of the pope's illness and the time following his death were characterized by a truculent atmosphere. The ambassadors' dispatches and accounts bear witness to it: "It is true that some people were killed, and others injured, mostly while the pope was near his end. . . . I recall how Pope Innocent sickened from May onward, and then died in the month of July, and in Rome many people were murdered, injured, and robbed, and afterward the cardinals went into conclave."[38]

Reprisals began immediately. Among those affected was Giovanni Lorenzi, the great Venetian Hellenist, librarian of the Vatican and secretary to the pope who had studied at the University of Padua and joined the circle of Cardinal Marco Barbo, administrator of the Order of St. John. A long line of knights and humanists forms the constant background for my research.[39]

In these times, thanks to the contributions of Pomponio Leto and the Roman Academy, the *aurea Roma* and the golden age were reemerging everywhere in the holy city. Latin was the language of orations, feasts, and banquets. Platina had been a member of the Academy. Other members included the refined humanists Bembo and Paolo Giovio. The latter kept one of the most accurate portraits of Christopher Columbus in his gallery. "The power that the movement of the Renaissance had gained in Rome during the time of Innocent VIII and the great enthusiasm for all things ancient that had pervaded even the common people" were documented in an event of April 1485. Among the ruins of the Appian

Way, excavations brought a tomb to light. Amid the rocks and excavated graves was found the perfectly preserved body of a young girl. The veneration of the discovered body was so immediate and intense, with processions of people, that Innocent decided to arrange a new burial in secret. The worship of the past must not be confused with superstition.

Upon the death of Innocent VIII, Lorenzi's fortune immediately collapsed. Borgia replaced him with a Catalan, who died soon afterward; Lorenzi finally went to Viterbo, where he was dispatched "by poison."[40]

The same fate awaited his brother Angelo: His throat was cut and his body thrown in the Tiber, a victim of Cesare Borgia's series of assassinations. His crime: having preserved and translated into Latin the works of Giovanni Lorenzi, written in Greek, denouncing the dynasty of the Antichrist-pope.[41] This pope had now taken possession of St. Peter's. Whatever had the faithful and erudite humanist written?

The series of deaths is disturbing. What took place after the death of Sixtus IV was repeated soon after Innocent's demise. In the few days of the *sede vacante* preceding the election of Pope Alexander VI (the Borgia pope), anarchy reigned. While Columbus's ships plowed through the waves, an extremely vicious showdown occurred over the conquest of the pontifical seat and the New World. In those few days the fate of humanity and modernity was decided. Justice was degraded and truth buried. In little more than two weeks, the streets of Rome saw more than two hundred murders, twelve per day, one every two hours.[42]

The wave of bloodshed continued for years. Another of its victims, after the death of Alexander VI, was Pope Pius III (Piccolomini), the Sienese nephew of Pius II, whose pontificate was one of the shortest in the history of the Church: little more than ten days. Poisoning has been suggested among the possible causes of his unexpected death. Perhaps this pious Franciscan wished to reveal the hidden truth—but by now, Rome, where the factions fell back into ferocious fighting, spurred by motives that had become universal, no longer deemed it possible. Popes, kings, and emperors had lost face in front of all of humanity. The new pope immediately chosen, following an ironclad pact made with Cesare

Borgia, was Julius II, a warrior pope. He would have to defend and reinforce the papal states. "The agreement between Giuliano della Rovere
on the one hand and the Spanish cardinals on the other was reached on
October 29. . . . Few details escaped regarding what occurred there."[43]

Was it this pact made in secret that sanctioned the injustice and the
untruth?

✠

The deaths by poison or by hanging in this long history may seem too
numerous; but poisonings, stabbings, and other murders formed an inevitable part of the struggle for power at the end of the fifteenth century. A
great mystery such as the one we seek to solve, with all the implications it
contains or may contain, must have many victims and many executions.
According to Cesare Borgia, who outlived Alexander VI by a few years,
via Machiavelli: "I had thought of everything that would result from my
father's death, and for all of it I had found a remedy . . ."—for all except
the imponderable.

It appears that everything possible was attempted to save Innocent's
life: First a potion made of powdered diamonds, then his Jewish doctor
supposedly injected him with the blood of three young girls who died in
the atrocious experiment. History has proved this wrong, but the legend
of the vampire pope took hold; though perhaps it was simply a matter of
a pioneering attempt at blood transfusion. The Jews were forever accused
of eating babies, an accusation aimed at political opponents even today.
To defend the accused from infamy, Pope Innocent IV wrote in a bull of
1247: "The Jews are falsely accused that at Passover they make communion with the heart of a slain child, on the pretext that such practice is
said to be written in their law." Around the end of the fifteenth century
the Jews were considered the "older brothers"—but the converted Jews
who continued to practice their law in the secrecy of their homes while
seeming to be converts were an ongoing danger to Christianity.

For this reason, the term *marrano* (converted Jew) was a tremendous insult. Who was Pope Julius II (Giuliano della Rovere) referring to
when, passing into the Sistine Chapel and speaking of a predecessor, he

uttered the invective: "*Marrano,* Jewish and circumcised." Julius's relationship with Pope Innocent VIII appears to have been unstable, considering that "Innocent VIII was more determined than most to be his own master, and was even heard to speak critically of Vincula [della Rovere's title as cardinal] in public." [44] The new pope cursed while upon the frescoed walls of the hall stood unparalleled decorations and woodcarvings, apparently dating from the time of Alexander VI or even Innocent VIII before him. In a corner of the immense artistic masterpiece where the conclave still takes place today, the crowds of the damned are depicted with exotic features—surprisingly reminiscent of the faces of the Maya and Inca people. [45]

They were the heathens waiting for Christo Ferens to sail from Palos, as he repeated a voyage that had already been made earlier. This is but one of the many enigmas in this history.

The greatest enigma is the inscription in the marble tomb of Innocent VIII, carved a little more than a century after his death:

INNOCENTIO VIII CYBO PONT MAX

ITALICAE PACIS PERPETUO CUSTODI

NOVI ORBIS SUO AEVO INVENTI GLORIA

REGI HISPANIARUM CATHOLICI NOMINE IMPOSITO

CRUCIS SACRO SANCTAE REPERTO TITULO

LANCEA QUAE CHRISTI HAUSIT LATUS

A BAIAZETE TURCARUM TYRANNO (IMPER)

DONO MISSA

AETERNUM INSIGNI

MONUMENTUM E VETERE BASILICA HUC TRASLATUM

ALBERICUS CYBO MALASPINA

PRINCEPS MASSAE

FERENTILLI DUX MARCHIO CARRARIAE ET C

PRONEPOS

ORNATIUS AUGUSTIUSQ. POSUIT ANNO DOM. MDCXXI

("To Innocent VIII Cybo, supreme pontiff, perpetual custodian of

Italian peace, distinguished for the glory of the New World discovered in his time, for having imposed the name Catholic upon the king of Spain, for having received the titulus of the holy cross, for the spear that pierced the side of Christ sent as a gift by Bayezid, tyrant (emperor) of the Turks, [This] perennial monument, moved here from the old basilica, Alberico Cybo Malaspina, prince of Massa, duke of Ferentillo, marquis of Carrara etc., his great nephew, placed with great decorum and magnificence in the year of our Lord 1621.")

The tomb of Innocent VIII, signed by Pollaiolo, was moved from the old Basilica of Constantine to the new St. Peter's in homage unique in the history of the papacy—and especially strange considering this was a pope upon whom a *damnatio memoriae* had been passed. His epitaph is a summary of his life, carved in the days of Pope Paul V (Borghese), a native of Siena. It commemorates for all time to come a pope who was the eternal guardian of peace, bringing the peace of Italy and Rome to the world. Innocent, the pope who was called by the monarchs of Spain "most Catholic," received the titulus of the cross and received the lance that pierced the side of Christ, given to him by Bayezid.[46]

The monument, reconstructed in the early 1600s, was changed from its original composition. Today, it has the appearance of a truth turned upside down. What was at the bottom ended up at the top, and vice versa. On it appears the phrase, carved in marble for the remembrance of posterity: *Novi orbis suo aevo inventi gloria* (In the time of his pontificate the glory of the discovery of the New World). It is a disturbing declaration in the temple of truth, and it is not the only mystery.

Further up, above the triumphant image of the pope, not legible to the naked eye, there is a different and cryptic inscription: *Obiit an. D.ni MCDXCIII.* The date corresponds to 1493.[47]

Another year added to his life, albeit unbelievable, would change everything. Is this an error—or a clue? Remarkably, in Genoa in the Church of San Lorenzo, where the Grail and the ashes of John the Baptist are kept, there is a bull signed by Innocent VIII and dated 1493, and on his portrait, hung in the cloister along with those of the other Ligurian popes, the date of his death is also 1493.[48]

The falsity, it is said, was the product of an attempt to lay claim to the discovery of America—as if the jotting of two numbers at random were enough to correct the paternity of an epochal project before the eyes of the entire world. Were the errors made in order to attribute to him a discovery that was not his or to affirm a role or presence that had been suppressed? When exactly did Innocent VIII die? Was it really in July of 1492, or was this date of July 25 merely chosen for its esoteric and astral significance?

Looking at his casket in St. Peter's, in front of the black marble tablet, the words of Panvinio's biography resound. They are the unthinkable, incredible conclusion of the life of Innocent VIII: "Great things occurred, and among others, almost at the end of his pontificate, the greatest that has ever taken place in the memory of man, in which Christopher Columbus discovered the New World. And not without mystery it came to pass that while a Genoese man was ruling the Christian world, another Genoese man found another world in which to plant the Christian religion."

The words are few, but the meaning arising from them is unequivocal. They coincide with the inscription on the tomb. The discovery occurred during Innocent VIII's pontificate. Panvinio writes the event took place "not without mystery." Two negatives make a positive. Mystery shrouded the events. In the *other* world (the same adjective used by Columbus, although the custom of calling it *new* had already taken hold), the Christian religion had to be planted. Do these words allude to a religion renewed (to be planted) with respect to tradition?

A century later the same idea was repeated once again: "Near the end of his pontificate there occurred an event, perhaps the greatest event ever in the memory of man, in which the Genoese Christopher Columbus discovered the New World. In what truly appears to have been divine ordination, while a Genoese man was ruling the Christian world, another Genoese man found another world in which the Christian faith would be planted."[49] The endeavor, then, followed a divine ordination.

With the death of Innocent VIII, innocence perished and the dream of universal peace was extinguished. "His death brought great hurt to all the good of the times, for it appeared that the loss was not merely singular, but common and general to all of Christendom. And truly, with his death, the most beautiful, the most glorious, and the most laudable endeavor was disrupted, which had never before been thought of, much less carried out; but perhaps it pleased God Almighty, by his fair justice, which is hidden from us, to reserve it for a different time."[50]

What does this refer to? More than merely a discovery, this was "the most beautiful, the most glorious, and the most laudable endeavor," to be first planned and then carried out. In particular, it was disrupted and postponed. The passing of Innocent was a loss for the entire human race. With Christian resignation respecting the hidden justice of Providence according to the rule of obedience, the sacrifice was accepted, ascribing the event of the discovery to a different time.[51]

The tomb is still there today, in a dark area of the basilica, along the nave on the left from the entrance. We need only walk into St. Peter's to see it: an epigraph, shadowy and mysterious, like a treasure map.

✠

FIVE

The Witches and Pico della Mirandola

"IF NOT PEACE, at least money." The phrase, referring to Innocent VIII, is terse and categorical, highlighting the fortunes of the Church and the dispositions of the popes in the second half of the fifteenth century. It gives a new perspective on the recurring platitude of a pontifical state often troubled by economic difficulties.[1]

The recent news comes from a discovery by a scholar after three years of fruitless research: "The documentation . . . allows something to be proved," writes Jean Delumeau, "which time has caused to be forgotten: that a great mining endeavor of international fame and dimension was begun and successfully continued for many centuries in the areas of Tolfa and Allumiere, and that alum was a great 'character' in history." For five hundred years this history was constructed and reconstructed in the absence of the truth, numerous characters, and many forgotten elements. From the archives traces suddenly reemerged of an important and completely forgotten financial influx—which connected with the actions of the pope and Columbus. The safety of Rome and its domain and the fulfillment of the Crusade depended on economic resources in a time when the Vatican was often impecunious, especially when kings, princes, cities, and churches refused to pay taxes for war.

As if by a miracle—as indeed the emotional populace interpreted it to be—the Vatican gained a new, unexpected, limitless possibility for income. "The backbone of the war against the Turks was money . . . when suddenly, in May of 1462, a new source of wealth emerged, right within the Patrimony of St. Peter. These were the alum mines of Tolfa, discovered by Giovanni di Castro."[2]

Amid the forests and hills, among oaks, chestnut trees, hornbeams, and beeches, in the green thickets of the ancient metal-bearing regions of the Etruscans the past came in contact with the present. Among the lights and shadows of the forest, the Paduan Giovanni di Castro, a relative of Pius II (Piccolomini), discovered the providential mineral vein. He was delighted to declare to the pope: "Today I announce to you the victory over the Turks."[3]

Alum, an essential ingredient in the dyeing of fabrics, was indispensable for the wool trade. It was exported to Florence, where manufacturing was thriving.[4] The rivalry, or affinity, between Genoa and Florence also came up in the extraction of this mineral. With Innocent VIII's accession, the interests of lords and family clans who had been rivals until the time of Sixtus IV converged in order to profit from this opportunity. Alum, one of the most important products of medieval commerce, could be compared to petroleum, the black gold of our age. The alum trade had been in the hands of the Genoese since the age of the *maona,* the society founded on the island of Chios: the same Greek island where the trade was concentrated, from where the Cybo family came, and where Columbus—allegedly the son of a wool merchant—would land.[5]

Another debacle, this time financial more than anything else, involved the Italian nobility after the fall of Constantinople. Previously, alum was always imported, mostly from Turkey, in a kind of forced, centuries-old dependence. After 1453, this route seemed closed forever, constituting an ultimate weapon of extortion in the hands of the infidels.

Giovanni di Castro had also traded alum in Byzantium for many years. After the fall of Constantinople he was forced to return to Italy, where Pius II made him treasurer of the patrimony. One day, he discovered a number of white stones and some plants, among them holly with its light and dark leaves (like the squares of a chessboard), very similar to those he had seen around alum mines in the East. This awakened his intuition; he gathered the rocks, had them baked at length in a smoking furnace, and obtained an extremely refined product.

In the hands of the pope, this was a supernatural omen and at the same time an offering from nature, a divine sign. The alum was earmarked to be sold exclusively to all the courts of Europe. Well might the treasurer say to the pope: "Today, I bring you victory over the Turks . . ."[6]

The pope was initially skeptical: The usual denigrators assumed the finding to be an astrologer's fantasy. In a strangely parallel life course, the discoverer was treated "as foolish, like Columbus, until the facts proved him right."[7]

Di Castro was a lover of the natural sciences, an experimenter from Padua, that furnace of knowledge and seat of genius. His innate curiosity had been fueled by an astronomer, Domenico da Padova. The Genoese Bartolomeo di Framura was also his colleague. Locations converged in a remarkable confluence of science and knowledge. Giovanni prepared a furnace in which the mineral was cooked, dissolved with water, and left to soak for several days. It was then cooked again. After twenty-seven days, the familiar crystals had formed on the sides of the container. Thus was born the Roman cubic alum.[8]

Astrology, Pope Pius II, the Crusade against the Turks, the need for money, cubes like the checkers on the Cybo shield, the analogy to Columbus: the pawns in the great game were moving. The Crusade was the end, the East the means. Pius II gave thanks to the clemency of heaven for coming to the aid of the Christian people, and the discovery was consecrated in a bull. The proceeds from the mineral were destined to be spent on war, as was announced in the constitution of 1464 and reasserted in that fateful and long-awaited year 1484, with the accession of Innocent VIII.[9]

The pontifical state had an estimate made confirming the amount the Christian nations had paid to the Turks for imports of alum, according to Giovanni di Castro. The sum turned out to be three hundred thousand ducats paid annually to the Muslims, equivalent to 2,239.5

pounds of fine gold.[10] The new discovery was a vein of gold with the power to speed the voyage toward more gold.

Sales were immediate, payments began to roll in, and the bards sang of the event. It was indeed an exceptional occurrence, all the more so considering the quality was superior to alum imported from the East. Extraction was organized on an industrial scale, with at least a thousand workers, perhaps more, coming from all over Europe.

The complex was called the Allumiere delle Sante Crociate (Alum Works of the Holy Crusades), and near the port of Civitavecchia the Depository of the Holy Crusades was instituted. The revenues from Tolfa allowed Pius II to prepare his Crusader fleet. The principle was reasserted by Innocent VIII. During the course of Innocent's pontificate, the mining rights passed to the Cybo entourage: the Doria, Visconti, Cicala, Medici, and Gentili families. The Gentili were the administrators of the funds for the Crusade in Spain.

Production continued busily.[11] Smokestacks, furnaces, barrels, and patient manufacturing produced a nacreous substance consisting of crystals in cubic form upon which, by means of water and fire, a kind of transmutation was achieved.[12]

From the nearby hills, "an inestimable treasure" came to Rome; a torrent of "gold" passed through the hands of the alchemists. Today, all that remains of the excitement are a few trails and a little chapel in the area of Cibona (clearly derived from the surname Cybo), indicating the traces of the great dream, helping to rebuild a damaged justice. In the chapel is the image of a miraculous Madonna, a Virgin carrying a child and a pomegranate (the fruit symbolizing Christian unity), flanked by St. John and St. James, patron saints of knights and of Christopher Columbus.

Innocent, susceptible to gold and precious stones, as the chronicles relate, must also have sensed something akin to a proclamation from the heavens and the stars in that mineral, those processes, and that quarry, working toward the transmutation of the world. *Calcination, refinement,* and *dissolution* are part of the vocabulary of the alum industry, but they are also words in a language as exclusive as it is initiatory.

The many offices created for the so-called *plumbatores,* instituted by Innocent VIII, recall another indispensable component in the alchemical Great Work which so fascinated the Renaissance: a coagulation of energy concentrated on a single purpose, drawing in artists, scholars, scientists, and men of power. Of course, the monks were also included, and in 1486 Innocent issued a constitution in which he decreed that the *piombatori* would belong to the Cistercians of the abbey of Fossanova, as established in the thirteenth century by the creators of the greatest and most mysterious cathedrals. Many sales of church offices appear to have been specifically due to the inheritance of an elite knowledge. The fact that Innocent was the first pope to use a ciphered code in pontifical documents shows secrecy was an integral part of his ministry.[13]

✠

We have now reached the point at which alchemy, parallel to the Kabbalah, emerges and will continue emerging from all sides of the story. It is a discipline that now reaches us only in folklore. Most of the enthusiasts who considered it a true and genuine art, the supreme art of the individual good and the collective good alike, are now seen as sorcerer's apprentices intent on creating diabolical works in their secret caverns. Alchemy was not this—it was much more.

It was an extremely profound and endless study of the possibilities offered by nature, following a magical path in search of the philosopher's stone and the elixir of life. It was a way to the absolute, a return to primordial perfection, to the lost Eden, and in a way to the resurrection of the body by means of the spirit. The influences of the stars, herbs, plants, stones, and medicine with its recipes formed part of an exclusive and valuable tradition, a divine tradition in which Islam, Judaism, and Christianity merged. Yet in it the messages of angels and demons were not always easy to distinguish in operations that always flirted with the bounds of legitimacy.

It was a highly risky discipline and, as we have seen, there were many enthusiasts at the University of Padua—in a parallel course once again linking Innocent VIII and Columbus. It is surely no coincidence that one of the greatest English alchemists of the fifteenth century, George Ripley (1415–1490), spent about twenty years in Italy and was one of the favorites of Innocent VIII, who made him his private chaplain and master of ceremonies.[14] Legend has it that Ripley discovered the philosopher's stone, from which he produced a large amount of gold, about one hundred thousand pounds, which financed the Knights of Rhodes in their defense against the Turks. Even the name Rodi, commemorated in the Sacred Grove of Bomarzo, is connected with alchemy.[15]

The constants were money, gold, Crusades, knights, and the triumph of Christianity: "Gold means immortality." The golden lands across the ocean promised to be the source of eternal youth, the elixir of longevity. There had been a relationship between the popes and alchemical craft ever since that knowledge arrived on the shores of Europe, brought through contact with Islam. It was an age-old tradition that, before Innocent VIII, had won the hearts of Clement IV and Felix V, as well as Pius II himself.[16]

Alchemy was already linked inseparably to the Franciscans through Ramon Llull. The sacred art of making gold would open the way for illuminating the soul; thus "the alchemists were mystics without being orthodox Catholics."[17] They were believers who moved above all faiths, albeit in opposing camps. Many considered them a gift from God and even divine. Those in power were extremely fascinated with them, in view of their premise and potential.

A man such as Innocent VIII, a composite personality combining a triple theological path within himself, a man of an enlightened mentality aspiring to harmony, the son of a Jew and nephew of a Muslim, gives every indication of having a strong alchemical inclination. The peacock,[18] the iridescent-tailed bird native to the Indies, was on his seal, inherited from his father Aronne, to whom it was apparently granted by the French king René d'Anjou. The peacock's tail represents a phase in the alchemical process. Even though many of the peacocks that once lived in the Vatican have vanished, the bird of a thousand colors remains as the pointer to a labyrinth of unequivocal signs surrounding the intentions of Pope Innocent: The peacock's tail "heralds the dawn and the return to the soul."[19]

It is a slow and arduous process, changing blackness to light, from *nigredo* to *albedo* to *rubedo,* a procedure arriving at regeneration out of corruption: "The volatile principle of mercury flies through the alchemical air within the microcosm of the Philosophical Egg, 'in the belly of the wind,' receiving the celestial and purifying influence from above. It falls again, sublimated, on the New Earth, which must eventually emerge. As the outer fire is very slowly intensified, the moist yields to the dry until the coagulation and desiccation of the emerging continent is complete. While this is happening, a great number of beautiful colors appear, corresponding to a state known as the Peacock's Tail."[20]

These are enigmatic words ("New Earth," "emerging continent"), appearing to be metaphorical of things to come. Paradoxical as it may seem, despite what is written about Columbus's scant education, it can no longer be denied that the navigator, with his obsession with gold, must have been a savant and scholar of the texts of mysticism and alchemy. "He who 'adventured' upon the sea . . . was a mystic, a warrior who fought not against other men, but against the mystery of the unknown. Columbus desired to return to the gold of the Indies, to the source of light, the sun, the dawn, crossing and rounding the West, the land of the sunset, because he took for granted the spherical shape of the earth. In all places at all times, gold evokes the birth of the sun and the light, and its possession has a value not originally monetary, but symbolic."[21]

The circle closes tighter, surrounding the explosion of colors, the rainbow of the peacock's feathers, the bells chiming the coming event: "[W]hile the one's corruption is the other's creation, thus many things arise from this twofold carrion: first there emerges a raven, which, while it rots again, vanishes, from which a peacock emerges . . . [W]hen this perishes, there emerges a dove, which, because the raven could find no dry place, finds one such, but a new one because the previous Earth was corrupted by the Flood, but this is the virgin chalk of the philosophers."[22]

Peacocks, doves, and new worlds—the language is abstruse, but as in the prophecy, it seems to indicate the coming of a new Noah-dove *(colombo),* as had happened once and would happen again.

The symbol is more apparent than ever on Innocent VIII's escutcheon, with its band of black and white checkers, squares of argent (white) and azure or turquoise (black), recalling the *baussant* of the Templars. The same squares are on the arms of the Adorno and Doria families of Genoa. Interesting analogies appear at this point between the Cybo arms and a section at the bottom of Columbus's first shield, which later disappeared and was replaced by five anchors. In this part of the old shield, in the record of the original coat of arms, there are heraldic elements having the same colors as the Cybo family's shield.[23]

✠

The squares of the chessboard also came from the East, the origin of the game that was such a great success in medieval Europe, its sources lost in Persian or Chinese antiquity. The squares might have had their forerunners in astrological signs, in the voice of the firmament: White and black symbolized the eternal opposition between light and darkness, good and bad, yin and yang. They came to form a virtual war game, which unlike a roll of the dice, involved the player's choices, the participation of free will and intelligence.

Chess also had an ongoing relationship with the Church. In the *Liber de moribus hominum et officiis nobilium sive super ludo scacchorum,* the Dominican Jacopo da Cessole, through an interpretation with chess pieces, gave one of the most fascinating descriptions of the society and mentality of the Middle Ages. The priest who spent a long time in Genoa knew a great number of people from all social classes through his work. Almost his contemporary, a Genoese physician "had suggested deriving 'the harmony of justice' from chess, symbolically illustrating the work of the subjects and the duties of the rulers," and was "a most devoted friend of the order and the convent of the lesser brothers of Genoa."[24]

Curiously, even Odysseus is involved in the origin of chess, and there is no lack of similarities between Columbus and Odysseus. Chess was also not without its detractors, who feared the game might draw the priests away from their duties. But Leo X (Medici) was a passionate player, as was Pius V, the pope from Lepanto. In his youth, John Paul II wrote a column on chess for the university magazine at Krakow.

For the purists chess is not simply a pastime, but a way of life: "We do not say Game, but miracle, a paragon of Games." Requiring patience, it is a means for improving oneself, a celebration of morality that leaves nothing unforeseen or up to fate, right from the first move of the white side that begins the game. "The chess player has his own value system involving loyalty and reciprocity, and his greatest satisfaction is winning a good game, because a good game makes everyone happier, the winner and the loser, because it is in the contact between the two players that the common experience is realized."[25]

These are the rules of the code of chivalry converted into an intellectual exercise, the art of war sublimated into a duel through a progression of moves, following precise rules according to an ancestral philosophy. It is surely no coincidence that, in a miniature in a codex preserved in the Escorial Library near Madrid, the contest for the Holy Land is shown with a Crusader knight and a Muslim knight peacefully facing each other "in fellow feeling" across a chessboard. "The world is a chessboard of existence," as we can read on the mosaic floor of the cathedral of Otranto in Apulia and in the frescoes of *The Allegory of Good Government* in Siena.

Chess was introduced into Europe via Muslim Spain. Arabs playing chess are depicted on the ceiling of the Palatine Chapel in Palermo. Dante knew the game; Boccaccio and Petrarch were experts at it. It spread to Italy in the 1400s. "[T]he rich fantasy of Francesco Colonna conceived the first recorded chess pantomime."[26]

Colonna was another preaching friar, raised in the circles of Venetian nobility. He was an expert in theology and is credited with authorship of one of the most enigmatic books of all time, the *Hypnerotomachia poliphili* (The Strife of Love in a Dream), a sacred text of magic with lofty moral content. The Venetian branch of a Colonna family, the collaboration with Mantegna for the illustrations, the study of chess, and the professorship at the University of Padua—all are elements pointing toward the life of Innocent VIII, and possibly to a maternal Colombo-Colonna line, with that ciphered surname of so many interpretations.

The chessboard, with its kings, queens, bishops, knights, and pawns (representing the common people), provides a path to a series of ethical teachings and spiritual training.

Thus, looking at the chessboard on the Cybo arms, we find ourselves facing symbols that vanish in the mists of time and mask the indelible characteristics of a dynasty and a knowledge forever on the fringes of orthodoxy, faithful to unbreakable principles. This holds true whether we look back over the centuries or forward to the descendents of Innocent VIII—especially Alberico, who, having landed in Massa, always fought for the reassessment of his lineage and obtained permission to place the inscription on the pope's tomb containing the reference to the discovery of America.

Of course, Alberico is also a controversial character precisely because of this desire to dignify his ancestry, which is often viewed as the whim of a vain man. Remarkably, though he was able to claim a tie to the Malaspina family, Alberico completely ignored his maternal genealogy, as if his will were directed solely toward the righting of an enormous wrong endured by his most illustrious ancestor, Innocent VIII, the pope condemned and obfuscated by history.

Alberico's figure follows the path of the great dream of the Renaissance, in line with his provenance in a branch originating from the marriage between Franceschetto Cybo and Maddalena de' Medici. Alberico had considerable means at his disposal, thanks to his two marriages: to Elisabetta della Rovere (illustrating another traditional family tie) and then to Isabella di Capua, from the city where Aronne Cybo was buried.

He opened the doors of his fiefdom to the Jews. The tradition had evidently been passed from father to son. It was a period during which many doors were closed to them, and contact between Jews and Christians was frowned upon by the clergy. Alberico founded a pawnshop, granting privileges to the Jews.[27]

Alberico was a man of great ingenuity. Like some of his predecessors, he had an acute head for business and negotiations and a particular eye for gold. He had the power to make counts and knights of men and to strike coins. He received the cross of the Order of Christ in Portugal.[28]

Franceschetto Cybo had received a similar honor at the hands of Frederick III. The much-talked-about count of Anguillara, by the power vested in him, permitted Franceschetto to wear a gold cross on his chest. A yellow cross on a sky-blue background, surrounded by gold stars, appears in a sixteenth-century fresco in the Palazzo Pitti in Florence. It also shows Columbus studying with an armillary sphere and compass among a collection of alchemical and Masonic symbols.

In the *Book of Memories* he began writing once he had returned to Florence after his father's death, the pope's son preceded the text with this auspicious quote from the Gospel of St. John: *Iesus autem transiens per medium illorum ibat* (But Jesus, going through the midst of them, passed by). It was a passage condemned by the Church as "vain superstition."[29]

The mint of the marquis of Massa faced a large piazza dedicated to Mercury, the god of the mysteries. At the center of the square stood a large statue of Hermes. Alberico had a series of coins struck in precious metals, sought after "as much for their weight as for their denomination" and extremely interesting from the Hermetic point of view. Production was very intense until Emperor Maximilian II obtained the title of Holy Roman Emperor, at which point Alberico was also able to decorate himself with the double-headed eagle and the motto *Libertas*. The motto *Anno Pacis* was on the first significant issue of coins from 1559; they were struck in the name of peace, the calling of the Cybos.

There are other precise references here besides coins and drawings, mixing real events with allegory: pawns, barrels, crucibles, obelisks, anvils, temples, and pyramids in a crescendo of architectonic and philosophical concepts relating to esoteric symbolism. "Between the early days of the first gold *doppia* and the final minting, the coin showing three stags [crossing the waves, like three caravels] challenging adversity, [there was] another half-century in the history of the territory whose prince had continually sought enthusiastically to bring together his success and the gold of his coins in the creation of an ideal principality."[30]

As a key to the interpretation of existence, the occult sciences were a discipline cultivated by the Medici and Cybo families, always in pursuit of the ideal state, always seeking to interpret the messages in the stars: "In that same year 1569, a physician philosopher from Piedmont . . . who said he was a nephew of Nostradamus . . . drew up the nativity of Signor Ferrante Cybo . . . who himself was an astrologer."[31]

Despite everything, Alberico persisted in concentrating experts on alchemy within his small state—including Cipriano da Piccolpasso, a native of Castel Durante, whose name was clearly a cipher. Cipriano recalls Cyprus, the Greek island that was the seat of the Templars and the Knights of St. John[32] and where the Franciscans went who were exiled from the Holy Land.[33]

Cipriano was the author of *Le tri libri de l'arte del vasaio* (The Three Books of the Potter's Art), at a time when the art of ceramics—which Innocent VIII employed for some of his magnificent shields and for the inscriptions in Santa Croce in Gerusalemme—was admired "for its principal basis of two derivations, the one coming from the art of design, the other coming from various secrets and alchemical mixtures."

In the Renaissance, ceramics, which until then had been considered subordinate to the other arts, gained enormous prestige. The book concludes with some moralizing reflections. The ornate letters hark back to mythological images. The technique of majolica (the name derives from the island of Majorca in the Balearics, Ramon Llull's homeland), known as *lustro ad impasto,* using metallic salts, was of Arabic origin, part of the Moorish ceramics to spread throughout Muslim Spain, where *obra dorada* imitated gold by gilding clay—the primal substance of humanity, going back to the creation of Adam.

The potter's wheel thus became the Demiurge ruling the four elements: earth, water, air, and fire, achieving circular perfection. Once again, ceramic technique was a process developed through learning the sacred art of antiquity. This art often used the dove as a symbol, and "in the Hermetic Kabbalah, played on the similarity between the words *cavalla* (mare), *cavallerizzo* (rider), and *cavaliere* (knight)."[34]

Chivalry, therefore, was the eternal, inextinguishable "crimson thread" of a knowledge jealously guarded over the centuries. In a certain sense, Cipriano was an heir to della Robbia, who had worked for

Innocent VIII and studied at the workshop of Mastro Giorgio, the potter from Gubbio who left behind works of incomparable brilliance and whose signature is astonishingly similar, albeit with a different arrangement, to the esoteric cryptogram used by Columbus.

✠

A Massanian enthusiast[35] has pointedly corrected the birth date of the new Cybean city wished for by Alberico using, for the first time ever, the Gregorian calendar: It came to light in concomitance with the spring equinox and the summer solstice. The true founding dates make Massa the city of the sun, couched in a language dedicated to an endeavor in which figure the cube, the stork, the sun, and the springtime zodiacal signs. This allegorical framework lends itself to many different interpretations, one of which corresponds to a perfect alchemical transformation from coarse rock to the philosopher's stone.

Walking the streets of Massa, we can sense the remnants of a time when the hospitals were dedicated to St. James, St. Christopher, and the Virgin Mary in an ensemble of suggestive and puzzling references. Even today, we can discover and read them hidden in the frontispiece of the Statutes of Carrara from 1574 as designed by Alberico Cybo. The symbolism, derived from Masonry and beginning with the chessboard, seems to multiply into a tangle of signs as abstruse as it is clear in light of what has been written about these signs and what remains to be written: obelisks, radiant suns, the peacock's tail, the barrel, the anvil, wreaths. . . . Together they form a kind of esoteric encyclopedia condensed into a series of pictures in which every image has its own precise and hidden meaning. Many of these symbols appear on the American dollar bill, as if there were a continued and unacknowledged connection between those responsible for the discovery and those who subsequently gained control of the far side of the Atlantic, becoming the Founding Fathers of the United States of America.

In this context, something written by the Mason Abraham Lincoln, in which he assumes that tone of prophecy recurring so often in this history, takes on exceptional significance. Here, he expresses singular ideas regarding the need to return to the fold of Rome in order for future society to be content. Lincoln wrote the following in 1853 to his friend Macedonio Melloni of Parma, one of the more noted physicists of the nineteenth century:

> I am convinced that the barbarians coming from the far-off tundra, whose abominable hordes invaded, plundered, defiled, robbed, and annihilated, brought about the reversal of the centuries-long triumphal march of human victory over the universal conscience of the united people. They had begun, imperceptibly, to become a single family, yet suddenly the thick darkness of barbarian destruction descended upon the civilized world of the times, upon the noon-day light of Rome, immortal and eternal. On that glorious Rome, my friend, which has brought civilization to the whole terraqueous globe, which has discovered us, created us, saved, educated, morally nourished us . . .[36]

Lincoln wrote of a Rome "which has discovered us." He believed in a just God and he did his utmost for the abolition of slavery, considering it an abuse of power "founded upon injustice and political evil." Lincoln hoped for a political reorganization of Europe that would reinstate Rome in its eternal central role as the prophesied caput mundi. Like many others who sought to improve human society, and like many of the main characters in our story, Lincoln was assassinated.

As we can see by now, medicine, astrology, and a reverence for plants and herbs, the vehicles of natural forces, formed part of the Cybo family's intellectual background. The first gardens in the Vatican were created by Innocent VIII in front of the Belvedere. Alberico created gardens full of statues. Gherardo, a nephew of Innocent VIII born in Genoa, established a remarkable herbarium. The greatest curiosity in his first collection was an ear of maize, a plant clearly unknown at the time.[37] Gherardo Cybo personally made note of it when consulting a book in which the plants were illustrated according to the alchemical cycle.[38]

✠

The mystery remains as to how all this might relate to two of the major accusations leveled against Innocent VIII: that he was the pope who railed against witches, causing their persecution; and he censured the Phoenix, Pico della Mirandola, during his pontificate, condemning free thought and tolerance. Once again, our careful exploration will find that events unfolded in a different way from how they have been recorded. The truth has been continually distorted and justice repeatedly violated.

In those days, confronted with increasingly adventurous scholarship and research, popular superstition grew exponentially, requiring a precise and necessary division to be put in place between acceptable and unacceptable magic, with all its perverse and diabolical implications. This was also necessary to defend against charlatans, who were having a field day with the naive populace.[39]

The bull *Summis desiderantes affectibus,* issued December 5, 1484, was part of a broader action against those considered the true heretics. This followed preceding interventions and admonitions on Rome's part. Innocent's initiative was not in itself a particularly severe action, if we see it in context of the times and events and consider widespread gullibility and the resulting risks posed to the most credulous people. The dark legend surrounding the bull comes from its connection, through one-sided interpretation, to the introduction of the notorious *Malleus maleficarum* (*The Hammer of Witches,* issued a few years later) by Heinrich Kramer and Jakob Sprenger, two German Dominicans and inquisitorial zealots.

The book, which became "one of the most deadly pieces of literature in the world," was used mostly in later times in actual witch hunts. It opened the way for a continuous series of burnings at the stake in Germany and especially in the dioceses of Mainz, Bremen, Cologne, Trier, and Salzburg. This area adopted the fiery words of Martin Luther, spoken against "the women of Satan": "[M]ore than any other, they are subject to the superstitions of the demon." This was followed by even more slanderous anathema: "Witches are the devil's whores."

The *Malleus maleficarum* proceeds by distinguishing between the various forms of magic. The work is merely a late-scholastic collection of writings relating to witchcraft, compiled by numerous *auctoritates* (authorities deemed unimpeachable). It is a systematization of representations of magic and of the figure of the magician furnished by literary documents, "a popular summary of the magical theory of the times, fixed in writing, which would have been innocuous had it remained only that."[40]

The text, which is almost always quoted out of context, is chiefly limited to discussing "the true arts of witchcraft" in precise differentiation from other forms of magic, which are not covered in the treatise: "In effect, such persons would be better defined as soothsayers or magicians than as witches."[41]

In truth, broadly speaking, the treatise contains nothing original,[42] but the widespread diffusion it enjoyed in the course of numerous publications (thanks to the invention of printing) produced deadly consequences. The *Malleus,* indisputably pervaded by the pathological misogyny that was so prevalent among monks, was often a tool used by individual inquisitors. Over time it became a weapon that helped to send some twenty-eight thousand witches to their death.

Except for a few lulls, this slaughter increased from the end of the fifteenth century to the end of the seventeenth. The massacre was mainly Protestant in origin; most of the pyres were ignited far from Rome, in places where secular powers were forced to create diversions to distract the people from injustice and famine. After the Counter Reformation,[43] this recrudescence also reached Italy with the condemnations of the philosophers Campanella and Bruno and the scientist Galileo.

The bull gives no indication of taking a dogmatic position with regard to witchcraft. The fundamental idea is the hypothesis, long and firmly sustained by the Church, of the possibility of a demonic influence upon humanity.[44]

This influence involved practices which, along with "incubi and spells," sometimes included "cruelties, crimes, and murders." "The pope was not concerned solely with the souls of Christians, but with the organic world, with 'men, women, and beasts of burden.' In his original intent, the fight against witchcraft served to protect the natural world, to defend life from death, fertility from sterility."[45]

Ultimately, it was intended to assert the supremacy of the judiciary power delegated by Rome over the lay and imperial power that sought to hand over confessed criminals to the secular arm. In fact, in a letter to the archduke of Austria, Innocent pointed out the law prohibiting the use of hot iron in trials and that proceedings must follow the holy canons and imperial laws.[46]

It is absurd, incidentally, "to claim that this bull sparked the persecution of witches already condemned to the stake by civil law, just as it is absurd to talk of the Church's credulity."[47]

✠

The Renaissance proclaimed the *renovatio saeculi* (renewal of the ages), but it dragged behind it centuries of superstition and necromantic brutality, in a dichotomy that is difficult to distinguish as scholars were pursuing new things, rediscovering the hidden language of natural laws. Baggage from a pre-Christian or paleo-Christian culture might easily mutate into non-Christian or even anti-Christian practices—against which the Church's vigilance was most attentive.

For a long time, for example, a popular practice had been the opening of the gospels to a random page where the first verses to present themselves inspired the decisions even of the clergy. In the *Life of St. Francis,* Thomas of Celano writes that Francis made use of this practice, which was considered tantamount to a magical rite and thus also an act subject to condemnation. In the *Legend of Three Companions,* it is hastily explained that the opening of the book three times by St. Francis was justified because he "was a true adorer of the Trinity."[48]

It was in the name of the Trinity that Christopher Columbus sailed; and during his return from the first voyage, fearful of perishing in a shipwreck, he placed himself in the hands of fate in a triple drawing with the members of his crew, using *sortes,* which may have been counters or straws. On board, Columbus also used chickpeas marked with a cross, and in two drawings, apparently he was the person chosen. It was a practice going back to Roman augury, a method for interpreting events in terms of good luck or misfortune.[49]

This was in keeping with the existence of harmony between all things in creation, involving the heavens, the planets, nature, plants, animals, metals, stones, and finally, man himself—who, in his essence, reflected everything in a reciprocal, floating reflection.

In the Celtic north, another saint, St. Colomba, was one of the most highly respected priests of white magic. Around 1300 the physician and astrologer Pietro d'Abano, who operated in Padua, successfully avoided capital punishment, although not prison, for his bold theories of Arabic and Hebrew origin. The legacy that accumulated in the Iberian lands during the time of the Reconquest was epitomized by the reign of Alfonso X, known as the Wise, but also as the Magician, the king of Castile and Leon whose court was a true cultural crossroads.

A great deal of attention was paid to the stars and to an implacable division between witchcraft and magic by Giovanni Pico, lord of Mirandola and count of Concordia. These are names that, as often before, appear to hold the seeds of human destiny. In his *Apologia* inspired by Ramon Llull among others the precocious philosopher wrote of the permutation of names. Was the name Christopher Columbus a permutation?

Pico's family boasted ancestors on the maternal side from the emperor of the East. This was revealed to be false, but in any case, they were knights. They showed interest in the new religious orders and their Church of St. Francis was one of the first dedicated to the new saint.[50]

Count Pico della Mirandola studied for two years at Padua, where memory was preserved of Marsilius of Padua (1275–1342), author of the *Defensor pacis,* considered the greatest study of political science of the Middle Ages. Pope John XXII condemned five of Marsilius's positions as heretical. At age twenty, Pico attended this university. He had grown up between Ferrara and Mantua, in an area where humanism was being asserted in the splendor of the courts. His *Oration on the Dignity of Man* was considered the theoretical, programmatic, and spiritual manifesto of the Renaissance. Among his teachers were Elia del Medigo, a Jew from Crete, one of the greatest Averroists, and destined, like Pico, to die young; and Raymond Moncada, a converted Jew. He also studied with another Jewish professor of French origin, Jochanan Alemanno, according to whom there were seven stages (the perfect number that so often appeared in Pico's books and that would become one of Columbus's obsessions) on the human soul's ascent to God, and according to whom Moses, the prophet to whom Columbus compared himself, represented the model magician who possessed perfect knowledge of the spiritual world.

The young Pico was protected by Lorenzo the Magnificent and became a member of the Florentine cultural circle that had made ancient books and knowledge the foundation of a new era. He was increasingly influenced by the preachings of Girolamo Savonarola, a friend of Ermolao Barbaro, the Venetian patrician who had studied at Padua.[51] For a long time Pico was a comrade of Marsilio Ficino[52] and his academy; he dreamed of "reconciling Aristotle and Plato."

Savonarola was one of his admirers. According to the austere friar, if Pico had lived longer, "he would have eclipsed all the men who had lived before him for several centuries, by virtue of the number and the value of the monuments to his genius that he would have left behind . . . this man must be considered as one of the miracles of God and of nature for the greatness of his spirit and his doctrine; he was not inferior to the first Fathers who were the most celebrated of the world . . . You are the sun of our epoch who knows perfectly the philosophy of all the ancients, as well as the precepts and laws of the Christian religion."[53]

✠

The reactionary monk was thus infatuated with Pico's knowledge, as was Lorenzo the Magnificent. Pico's view of the world and of existence, admired even by detractors of the faith, remains fundamentally mystical. He sought links between the Hebrew scriptures and Christian scriptures, which were painted by the greatest artists of the period in the magnificent fresco cycles to embellish churches and palaces. According to him, in the *Conclusio cabalistica,* the three names of the divine tetragrammaton, Eheyeh, Jehovah, and Adonai, were the names of the Father, the Son, and the Holy Ghost—the last, for some kabbalists, was not only the voice of God, but also the "breath" that engulfed Moses on Mount Sinai. He was particularly influenced by the words of Jesus as reported by St. John: "Peace I leave with you, my peace I give unto you."[54] It was the same peace Innocent VIII pursued with all his means, the peace Columbus's voyages were meant to have realized.

A fourth golden age would begin, according to Pico, by means of the unifying golden thread running through time, in a kind of alchemy of thought—the only weapon capable of waging a holy war to reconcile the people of the world. "All religious systems, remaining as they are, will lead to the same end, by different ways; each is one of the exoteric forms, adapted to the imagination of the common man, of the superior esoteric truth, the privilege alone of the philosophers secretly guided by the universal mind."[55]

The gold of the spirit would be joined with the gold of the Indies, soon to be obtained. Columbus revealed it, reading the verses of St. John, confident that the breath of the Holy Ghost would blow in his sails. The soul (the breath, the wind, the spirit) was, Pico declared, the instrument to progressively change man in a succession of levels of knowledge, in the unveiling of truths ever more occult and secret in order to gain theological wisdom. The intellective soul, like the truth, was one and the same for all the human species. The use of magic was necessary for investigating the mysteries of nature. To understand the divine mysteries, the Kabbalah was required with the revelation of the symbols of the Holy Scriptures.[56]

His theses were "dialectic, moral, physical, mathematical, metaphysical, theological, magical, and kabbalistic, partly personal and partly drawing on the 'monuments of Chaldean, Arabic, Hebrew, Greek, Egyptian, and Roman wisdom,'"[57] covering the entire range of human knowledge. If ideas of this kind could have been established, harmony and philosophical concordance among peoples would have proved less difficult and peace less unattainable—and Innocent VIII's pontificate, as well as Columbus's voyage, could have had a different meaning.

A fascinating young man with delicate features, an ardent lover involved in the abduction of a noblewoman, Pico possessed incredible knowledge considering his youth and was gifted with a memory that became legendary. He loved the languages of the East and the Hebrew Kabbalah and attempted in his studies to achieve the definitive mediation between past and present, between East and West.

Nothing in the knowledge of the giants who preceded him was unknown to him. In his universalistic and encyclopedic mind, everything could be traced to the one doctrine of a human race on its way to the Kingdom of God. Thus the doctrines preceding Christianity and the teachings of the Church presented no contradictions to Christian law, but instead were its heralds and its confirmation in the common destiny of an Edenic age of restoration. Through Hermes Trismegistus and Orpheus, one inevitably arrived at Christ.

This *summa* was collected in no fewer than nine hundred theses. He stopped at the threshold of a number he considered to be magical, saying he had limited himself, given that he wanted to write at least a thousand. His language was not always clear—indeed it was decidedly abstruse at times, lending itself to all manner of interpretations. His writings on the Kabbalah, according to some—including those envious of his knowledge—formed a Trojan horse to be introduced into the stronghold of Christianity. Even today's readings of Pico—mostly referring only to a few extracts—are inconsistent if not contradictory. Each scholar tries to extract from Pico his own definitive and convenient truth. Yet the principle upon which Pico based his ideas was that of not swearing on the words of any master.

Despite this endless supply of revolutionary ideas, Pico was called to Rome in 1487—when he was only twenty-three years old—to dispute his theories in the oratory contests so popular at the time. This was at the height of the pontificate of Innocent VIII. He had himself accepted the dedication of such a text as the *Corona regia* by Pablo de Heredia; one of the great Spanish kabbalists and a Jew converted to Christianity.

The pope's consent showed, in itself, a noteworthy openness to Pico's ideas. If Innocentian Rome was really as it has been portrayed, the brilliant philosopher should not have escaped execution in the public piazza, as would be the fate of Giordano Bruno, another heir to the legacy of Hermeticism. When he reached the capital, Pico's reputation had preceded him: "Upon his arrival in Rome, the pontifical court 'welcomed him with great honors'; he was received in an audience with the pope; the doors of the Apostolic Library were opened to him, from whence he was also permitted to borrow books."[58]

The history of humankind and of philosophy, as Pico maintained, supported by the most original and heterogeneous authorities, was nothing other than the obvious confirmation of a substantial, fundamental concordance that had traversed the centuries, spanning temporal and geographical space by means of a secret transmission contained in the laws. This began with Moses himself, "master of human wisdom in all the domains of the sciences and letters, and learned in all the doctrines of the Egyptians."[59] The ancients, therefore, were merely the anticipators of the present.

In its flood of propositions, Pico's *Conclusiones,* submitted to the judgment of the pope, were at first suspended; the public posting had actually been minimal. The famous condemnation attacked about 1 percent of his theories—in short, a mere trifle. The pontifical document began thus: "Recently, the noble and magnificent Signor Giovanni Pico, count of Concordia, has publicly posted in several places in Rome numerous and diverse theses on various disciplines." These words do not smack of interdiction. Some have gone so far as to claim that Innocent VIII's words were written "with courtesy, and almost in the tone of an apology . . . 'We have received news that our beloved son'" (the tone is familiar; Alexander VI used the same words, *dilecte fili,* in reference to Columbus, upon the admiral's return from the first voyage) "'Giovanni Pico, count of Concordia, has exposed many and diverse theses on various matters for public discussion. Some of these, as far as can be understood from the tenor of their words, appear to deviate from the correct path of orthodox faith; some of them, also, are of dubious and ambiguous meaning, because they are composed with new and unfamiliar vocabulary, and are involved and obscure enough to require explanation.'"[60]

This is not an absolute condemnation. Pico's writing often lacked clarity—something unacceptable in matters of faith.

Moreover, upon careful examination of the response, it becomes apparent the inquest was extremely lenient. The theses considered heretical were required to be reexamined in Pico's presence; those remaining obscure were required to be elucidated in simpler terms. The pope acted through Giovanni, bishop of Tournai. It is easy to guess that a great portion of the Curia, which had to be taken into account, was agitated. Among the theses rejected was one stating that neither the cross of Christ nor any other image should be worshipped.[61] It is continually claimed that the Templars renounced the cross. Another thesis asserts that no other proof of the divinity of Christ is more convincing than magic and the Kabbalah (a total of forty-seven theses were inspired by the Kabbalah). As we have seen, these were arguments of no small impact; they presented the danger of undermining the very foundations of the faith, of completely overturning theology. The debate must have been bitter, with nothing taken for granted. Among the fifteen commissioners there was a close division: eight against seven.[62]

Innocent VIII had to be prudent. As a scholar who had studied the history of all the heresies, he was a man of consummate prudence. Perhaps, as would happen again later, he was not prudent enough.

The verdict was not definitive. Pico della Mirandola did not present himself at a subsequent invitation; negotiations proceeded. Fundamentally, only three of his theses were judged decidedly heretical. One was considered scandalous, the others unclear and false. The Church could not back down on all points; the repercussions upon the flock of simple souls might have been harmful in a time when Rome had countless problems and was at risk of a schism, and all things considered, the Church could not risk going back on its word.

Perhaps the young Pico was guilty of the sin of pride. Perhaps he was ill advised, and it was not sufficient to sign a document of submission to the Holy Father. Also, an *Apologia* followed (apparently printed in Naples) in which Pico upheld his ideas and defended the thirteen propositions of his *Conclusiones,* which he deemed "worthy of the city of Rome" and to the liking of the "Prince of Christians." The work had thus been conceived as homage to Innocent VIII. Did this initiative now constitute an affront to the pope, going back on his given word? However this may be, Innocent showed clemency once again, writing on August 4: "I declare that the aforesaid count has not incurred any blame denting his reputation, because he has merely proposed and published his theses in view of a scholastic discussion and under the control of the Apostolic See."[63]

From this moment on, the exact dates and chronology of events become jumbled. The two sides entered into a definite struggle. The most defamatory accusations aimed at Pico were similar to those to which Columbus would be subjected: being a heresiarch, a Muslim, and a Jew. Catholic fundamentalism and the tireless opponents of change had uttered their anathema. Innocent VIII could not ignore them. Who were the promoters of the false accusations? Who were the true enemies? In this same period, the Spanish current had entered the stream in the form of Cardinal Pedro Garzias, who became librarian under Alexander VI; the refutation of the *Apologia* appears to have been written under his cardinalate.[64]

Spain was fighting against the Moors, had attempted the forced conversion of the Jews, and was scheming to place her candidate upon the throne of St. Peter. Garzias solicited Isabella and Ferdinand, who sent Torquemada, the dreaded head of the Inquisition, to intervene and present to Innocent VIII the danger posed by Pico's writings.[65]

In Spain Columbus had been waiting for years. His voyage could not be compromised. Thus, the thirteen most dangerous theses tarnished Pico's entire work ("a little mold can spoil the whole loaf," declared another Spaniard, Antonio Flores, one of his most vicious detractors), and so its condemnation was issued under pressure from the cardinals.

Pico prudently took refuge in France—albeit with a great deal of calm for a heretic who might have been under pursuit. In this time of disgrace, there might also have been danger from someone wishing to exact revenge upon him for the rash love affair of his youth. Also during this time a young graduate, Jean Laillier, wrote to Innocent VIII from Paris, proposing a series of audacious debates, including one on the marriage of priests. Pico was finally arrested outside Italy under circumstances that may have resulted from some secret political activity.

It is certain that Innocent VIII, whom history has presented as the guiltiest party in Pico's exile, turned a blind eye to the cardinals and, at the request of Lorenzo the Magnificent, agreed to Pico's release. Among other things, the two family trees, those of Pico della Mirandola and Cybo Malaspina, would quite soon intersect on at least two occasions.[66] This would certainly not have happened if Innocent had really been the philosopher's assassin. The Pico family even had the same chess squares as the Cybo family on the middle of their shield.

On his way back to Florence, Pico had the idea of traveling to Germany to consult the library of the late Cardinal Nicholas of Cusa, who had introduced the subject of peace after the fall of Constantinople, dreaming of a heavenly harmony among all people—while the sages "would gather in Jerusalem as their common center to receive the same faith and build upon it a perpetual peace, so that the Creator of all things might be praised and blessed through the ages."[67] Christopher Columbus's voyage round the world was to culminate in Jerusalem.

In another exquisitely political action, Pico was subsequently pardoned by Alexander VI, the pope of Machiavellian duplicity, the poisonous pope. The young count of Mirandola, after having given increasing demonstration of his true Christian faith, died during the Spaniard's pontificate on November 17, 1494. He was poisoned by his secretary. Savonarola was executed a few years later. The Borgia pontificate constituted a massacre of great spirits.

In the conflict between Pico and Innocent, many accuse the pope of doctrinal blindness, of theological rigor, and of not being in a position to comprehend the cultural breadth and tolerance of a man of such boundless knowledge. In Alexander's pardon, others erroneously see the consonance of a pope more open to magic and new ideas. A few days before his death, Giovanni Battista Cybo requested a consultation, through Ludovico Sforza il Moro, duke of Milan, with the famous Ambrogio Varese da Rostate. On July 20, just five days before the pope's death, Ambrogio consulted his charts and read a fatal horoscope, predicting "this pontiff must die."[68]

Like Pico and Columbus, the pope evidently believed right to the end in the mathematical harmony of the stars that reigned over his ministry—stars that perhaps prognosticated another passing ("this pontiff must die") for five hundred years beneath the veils of history.

SIX

✠

Santa Croce and the Lance of Longinus

CENTURIES LATER, VISITING Rome, we can see the churches still conceal messages waiting to be decoded, raising a multiplicity of questions, but also providing the keys for solving the great puzzle of the vanishing pope and the discovery of America. It is a more truthful and just version of history, beginning long ago and locked and guarded in a sacred and evocative place, continuing to form part of the Jubilee route, the devout pilgrimage that passes through the *seven* gates of the *"seven* churches." Among these, ideally connected to the nearby Basilica of St. John Lateran, is Santa Croce in Gerusalemme—one of the oldest basilicas in the city along with those of the Vatican, Lateran, Ostiense, and Verano.

The great edifice, now with a pompous baroque facade, is whitish and rounded at the front. Scholars liken the interior to the Basilica of Maxentius, the *Templum Pacis,* the quintessential temple of peace: the peace pursued by Pico through intersecting interpretations of the scriptures, the peace desired by Innocent VIII in his ministry, the peace Columbus was meant to bring about with his gold. The events began with St. Helena, mother of Constantine, the Roman emperor who defeated Maxentius in the famous Battle of the Milvian Bridge in AD 312—when, following a dream, the typical vehicle of prophecy, he decided to place the monogram of Christ on his army's insignia.

This was the first act of official recognition and establishment of the Christian faith.

"In this sign you shall conquer" *(In hoc signo vinces),* the Lamb of God announced, and Constantine saw a brilliant cross, brighter than the sun. The prophecy came true on the battlefield, and the emperor triumphed. It was after this dream and the famous donation[1] that Christianity acquired freedom of worship and its own state. So, its expansion began.

Constantine renounced paganism and converted. He summoned the first ecumenical council at Nicaea. He united the empire and rebuilt Constantinople, the capital and new seat of the Roman Empire of the East. The "second Rome" remained forever indissolubly linked to the city of the popes, albeit through inevitable mishaps and conflicts—until its dramatic fall in 1453 at the hands of Mehmed II.

The emperor, who was considered like Christ, the so-called thirteenth apostle, signaled the passing from the cult of the sun to the cult of Jesus. Little more than a thousand years later the Renaissance saw the light of the Creator in the stars, seeking to reconcile Christ with the expressions of various beliefs that had gone before him in the execution of a single divine plan. The path, winding through the labyrinth of time, recovered its direction and its lost meaning in the fifteenth century. It joined with the new paths offered by a new and more correct reading of the past and its writings.

If Constantine's inspiration was the fruit of a political need, we must not forget his mother was fervently religious; she traveled to the birthplace of Christianity and was later made a saint. At the venerable age of seventy-seven (no reference to the Holy Land is complete without the numeral 7), she made a pilgrimage to the places of Christ's martyrdom in search of surviving remnants of the Redeemer's earthly presence, particularly the Holy Cross.

As always, truth and myth overlap. In Bethlehem, Helena is said to have built a sanctuary near the Grotto of the Nativity and another on the Mount of Ascension. From there and from the Holy Sepulchre and Mount Calvary she brought rocks, earth, and the remains of the cross, as well as the Titulus of the crucifixion. In the Chapel of the Saints in

Santa Croce there is still a Latin inscription attesting to the soil soaked with the blood of Jesus. Only the popes may officiate in ceremonies there: "Here the holy soil of Mount Calvary in Jerusalem was strewn and preserved by the blessed Helena in the hollow beneath, upon whose vault she built this chapel which bears the name of Jerusalem." The soil of the holy blood, the holy Grail, the blood of the Redeemer also brought promise of redemption to Rome.

The queen mother placed her findings in her palace, the Sessorium. Santa Croce is thus doubly bound to the roots of Christianity, by the cross of Jesus and by the cross that enlightened Constantine. It was considered the second Jerusalem, a concentration of events and spirituality for the men of the Church and the faithful of the times, superior even to the Basilica of St. Peter. The legacy went back to the poor community of the original Christianity, Eastern and apostolic, which the mysticism of the High Middle Ages strove to restore to a Church that risked losing its way.[2]

The layout of the church follows the arrangement of the Constantinian Basilica of the Holy Sepulchre, and that of the Church of the Nativity. In Rome the mystery of Jerusalem is repeated and renewed. The two cities are joined together indissolubly in a perfect topographical transfusion. The surrounding area contains the *Horti Variani* and is bordered by the Aurelian walls, which meet with the remains of the aqueduct of Claudius, the baths, and an amphitheater. It is also near Caelian Hill and the Colosseum. At the midst of this concentration of pagan elements there stands a small temple dedicated to Constantine and originating in close connection to the holy places of Palestine. Its structure, with doors on all sides, is remarkably similar to that of Syrian and Armenian churches. Paganism had yielded, blurred at the edges, and flowed into Christianity. The East was married to the West; the sun was reflected in the Christian light. It was once again necessary to follow the path of the sun, the path of the chosen; Columbus did so.

In Rome, then, an image of the original Jerusalem was replicated and in a way reconstituted in an affinity "confirmed by the fact that the entire area around the Caelian and Esquiline Hills was dedicated, at least until the end of the Middle Ages, to the figure of Christ. The Basilica of Santa Maria Maggiore, consecrated to the Virgin, commemorates the birth of the Redeemer and Bethlehem; Santa Croce, known simply as 'Jerusalem' at least until the end of the sixteenth century, commemorates the death of Christ, and the ceremonies of Good Friday take place there, a short distance from the Lateran Basilica, originally dedicated to the Savior and therefore to his work of redemption."[3]

Such concordances, evocations, and natural and magical virtues at the heart of the Renaissance could not escape a pope such as Giovanni Battista Cybo, with his Eastern ancestry and love of esotericism. History repeats itself in the course of humanity, like the courses of the stars. Another Innocent—Innocent III—had gone barefoot to the same Lateran Basilica to pray to God for victory over the Saracens.[4]

This was the same prayer that stirred the efforts of Pope Innocent VIII once he was elected, with the holy places of Jerusalem, as well as the city of Constantinople founded by Constantine, once again in the hands of the infidels.

The elements that might reinforce the supernatural significance of Santa Croce deepened and intensified; it was a *unicum,* a highly important place, secluded and abandoned for a long time, according to the directive of that sacred geography which prevails through the ages, absorbing and integrating many and varied sources in a process we could call stratification of spiritual energies. Ever since the sixth century the pope had celebrated the rites of Good Friday there—also a fateful and sacred day for Christopher Columbus.[5]

The work of transforming the Church is dated to the pontificate of Lucius II (1144–1145) at the hands of a monastic order whose calling was to regenerate religious life by bringing it back to ancient Christianity—a project reflected by new architectural styles—in loyalty to a never-forgotten origin, strengthened by the presence of a precious and miraculous relic. "The value of the new foundations laid by this work is confirmed by the presence of the titulus of the cross in a lead casket, built into the top of the triumphal arch. . . . The consecration of the new church thus takes place through the placement of the relic in the very body of the church. Significantly, a similar intent guided Paschal II in the consecration of the apse of San Clemente (1112), where a fragment of the True Cross was built into the wall behind the crucifix of the apsidal mosaic."[6]

Twelve (like the apostles) Carthusians plus a prior (a number already suggesting the reconstitution of a new Church) settled there around the end of the fourteenth century. Legend has it that they were called to bestow a soul upon the desert of the uninhabited area. It was the start of the construction of a great Carthusian monastery, which was to last through the ages. Sadly, it was mostly destroyed. Santa Croce was thus progressively reinstated in the New Rome, which was growing and would grow even more after 1450.

In the second half of the fifteenth century, the history of Santa Croce came together with the characters in our story with the new works initiated by Cardinal Angelo Capranica.[7] From around this time, in the apsidal cupola of the high altar, there is a fresco, apparently not inspired by the Genoese Cardinal Jacobus de Voragine's *Legenda aurea* but by an eleventh-century manuscript preserved in the Fondo Sessoriano,[8] a beautiful cycle depicting the finding and exaltation of the cross. This further embellished the reliquary church.

Contemporary with this, there occurred a spectacular and shocking *coup de théâtre* for Christianity: the finding of the titulus of the cross. It was an accidental discovery, a perfectly arranged miracle. Right at the center of the church stood an arch with two small columns, an apparently insignificant aedicule. The workers, intent on their labors, were suddenly alerted to the presence of a cavity within the brickwork.

Work reached fever pitch and emotions ran high as fragments of the wall fell away. The wall opened to reveal a small recess in which lay a lead casket with two palms engraved on it. It was hermetically sealed, with a cubic stone upon it on which was engraved *Hic Titulus Verae Crucis* (Here is the Titulus of the True Cross). This was a discovery that, in some ways, recalled the prophecy in the dream of the "thirteenth apostle": *In hoc signo vinces.*

Finding the titulus sounded a reveille for wounded Christianity.

The tablet had been thought to be lost forever; now it reappeared, or rather had been made to reappear, at the very moment it was needed. The cubic stone was removed, and beneath it in the reliquary was a tablet of walnut with the inscription *"Iesus Nazarenus Rex Iudaeorum"* (Jesus of Nazareth, King of the Jews, abbreviated INRI), in Hebrew (or Aramaic), and also in Greek and Latin written in reverse, running from right to left like Hebrew writing. The treasure was completed by some fragments of the cross—a five-inch-long nail and two thorns from the crown Helena had supposedly retrieved. This was a fairly substantial collection of tangible signs of the Passion of Christ and offered for the salvation of humanity. The miracle was fulfilled. Only later did research reveal the wooden tablet had been recorded earlier, in a description of Rome from 1452.[9]

The titulus had reemerged, and now Paradise could reemerge: America, a land of new crosses, inspired by the first cross.

The Christian world stood amazed and astounded and bowed before the sight of a past resurfacing in the most ancient and most venerable symbols of the faith, the direct evidence of the Passion. The discovery in Santa Croce, charged with profound and recondite significance, posed many questions and demanded many answers. It was the announcement, the prologue, and the promise of further victories, further discoveries, in a time when the revelation of the secrets of nature was believed to be reserved for great minds alone.

Toward the end of the fifteenth century, as had happened in previous centuries, relics represented a downright obsession, spreading rampant throughout Europe, drawing in common people and nobles alike. It was even believed that if a more or less precise copy of a relic came in contact with the original, the replica would absorb all the power of the original, which would then be transferred by supernatural means to whoever possessed it. In medieval culture, these sacred findings had incredible thaumaturgical virtue; they were vessels of power and divine grace. This belief was also useful from a political point of view.

Relics thus became tokens of grandeur and immortality in a business that reproduced them without control, making an endless series of copies.

All people in power, Christian or not, sought relics as the affirmation and enhancement of their own offices. It is impossible for us today to imagine what a pope such as Innocent VIII could have represented for the multitudes of Europe, having direct access to these symbols brought straight from the site of Calvary and appearing to legitimize Rome as the dawning place of Christianity, the fruit of the legacy from the saintly mother of the first Christian emperor, the founder of that other city that had fallen into the profane hands of the Turks. The miracle occurred at just the right time, infusing St. Peter's throne with a rejuvenated univer-salistic spirit, summoning Christendom to renewal. Innocent knew this well and planned his moves, playing adeptly in this chess game of sincere faith and wild fanaticism. His last move would have been Columbus's departure; but the gathering of symbols was still not complete.

The staging could not have been more perfect. The appearance of the tablet coincided with the arrival in Rome of news that the Muslims of Granada had surrendered to Spain. Vatican politics were achieving all the successes that had been hoped for. As one objective after another was reached, events followed in an ever more insistent rhythm. Now that testimony to Christ's sacrifice had reemerged, all that remained was to bring about the Resurrection. "The event became charged with inevitable religious and political implications and had great resonance, especially following a visit by Innocent VIII."[10]

Innocent went to see the titulus on March 12, 1492.[11] The pope went into meditation; everyone prayed on their knees, and the emotion was extreme. The celebration of the victory over Granada, still quite alive, was surpassed only by the jubilation at this new finding. God had reinforced Rome's supremacy. Thus the pope went in person to welcome the authentication of the object that had come directly from the Lord and to give his imprimatur to the discovery. It was as if the hand of God had placed his benediction upon Innocent's politics.

Rome was confirmed as the New Jerusalem. Santa Croce, the second Jerusalem, had retrieved its Holy Sepulchre and taken up the role of the earthly Jerusalem in miniature. St. Peter's throne was united forever with the city of Jesus, which was still writhing in the grip of the beast—from whence it must be wrested without delay. Christ in person had chosen his vicar to pave the way for an operation which, using the gold of the Indies and an agreement to be reached with the heirs of the Great Khan and through the voyage of the messenger Columbus, would give the signal for an inevitable crusade—by love or by the sword.

Meanwhile, the whole area around Santa Croce assumed a divine and deified quality, forming a mystic triangle whose most important side, from an esoteric point of view, was formed by the line running from the Basilica of St. John Lateran to Santa Croce. The area was made all the more sacred by the presence of the nearby Holy Staircase, right by the Lateran, which is also the official residence of the bishop of Rome and which bears the names of the Holy Savior and the two Dioscuri of Christianity: St. John the Baptist and St. John the Evangelist. In the chapel dedicated to St. Lawrence, we can admire another relic, a miraculous image of the Savior, not made by human hands.

The Holy Staircase, with its twenty-eight steps believed to have been walked by Jesus on his way to Pilate's tribunal, was one of the required destinations for pilgrims. Before the schism of 1510 even Luther climbed it, chanting on his knees. It is a symbolic ascension between Earth and heaven. This unique pantheon of Christianity is completed by the Sancta Sanctorum, the pope's chapel, the Sistine Chapel of the Lateran. The name comes from the innermost chamber of the Temple of Jerusalem where, in a wooden box surmounted by two gold cherubim with wings spread, the Ark of the Covenant was kept, containing the tablets of the Ten Commandments. Here, once a year, only the high priest could officiate with blood, in a sacrifice and an expiatory ritual.[12]

✠

Thus Santa Croce was integrated into a supernatural space, containing the majority of the emblems most representative of Christian and other religions. In the adjacent piazza stands an Egyptian obelisk that was brought from Thebes following a mystical and esoteric journey out of time.

Entering the interior of the basilica, beneath the three great naves and the later additions made to enrich this place of worship, the church presents messages hidden by time and by interventions that sought to cloak the manifest truth. The chapel of St. Helena lies beneath it, modest, austere, and evocative. Before reaching it, however, if we raise our eyes upward in the antechapel, we see a polychrome mosaic on the walls and the great vault. The identity of the artist is not precisely known.

There are many candidates, from Pinturicchio to Perugino (who, as we know, worked for Innocent VIII in Rome), from Antoniazzo Romano to Melozzo da Forli, who executed it in 1484. Scholars have not managed to reach an agreement, especially because included within the mosaic, among the many chalices of the Grail, there is an Amazonian parrot, some long garlands of flowers, and fruits and other produce that could not have come from Rome. Among these, noticeably, are numerous pineapples and varicolored corncobs.[13]

Melozzo's Neoplatonism leads us back to the Tuscan circle of Marsilio Ficino and Leon Battista Alberti, the builder of Santa Maria del Fiore, with "a worldly aesthetic of the beautiful and the good, in a lovely form open to the future . . ."[14] Fauna and flora in a riot of color and detail are not the only resounding clues present in this work. At the center, where the four walls converge, are two beautiful peacocks, their tails overlapping.

The peacock, as we have seen, is one of the favorite figures of alchemical symbolism. It constantly appeared in the Cybo family's heraldry, especially in that of Giovanni Battista, Innocent VIII, the pope who came from the sea and carried within himself this allegorical ensemble: Christ on Earth, the precursor, the baptizer, the new peacemaker Constantine, the redeemer, the new Christ for a New World where he would send his messenger, his Moses—to whom Columbus equated himself. The thread leads from the first Christian emperor to the *dominus orbis* of a world that no longer had boundaries, within sight of the great Jubilee prepared for the year 1500.

Melozzo also fits into the Franciscan context as a follower of the restless friar Luca Pacioli, an exceptional scientist and friend of painters, "most mobile ambassador and propagandist of mathematical culture, even as applied to the arts."[15] The story is continually allusive, enriched as it proceeds through solar quadrants, armillary spheres, astrolabes, and philosopher's stones, leading to a superior cosmic order through a harmony to be restored.

In particular, the solids—one of which was naturally the cube— lost their connotation of abstract geometric constructions for Luca Pacioli but gained life as stereometric sculptures, sometimes in wood, sometimes in crystal or marble. These mystical projections became the subject of lectures given by the friar in all the courts of Italy after he delivered them in the palace of Giuliano della Rovere in the presence of the pope.[16] Science, from mathematics to geometry, formed the basis of astrology, astronomy, and geography. These disciplines lead us back to Christopher Columbus, the exemplary personification of Leonardo's *Vitruvian Man*.

The great apse of Santa Croce in Gerusalemme is a Renaissance masterpiece, the fruit of a collective endeavor. Melozzo was surely among those who worked there, and his sojourns in Rome coincided with the pontificate of Innocent VIII. A friar, Sabba da Castiglione, wrote of him: "The works of Melozzo da Forlì, through their perspectives and secrets of the art, are even more pleasing to the intelligent than they are beautiful to those of lesser understanding." Secrets hidden from the eyes of the many, truths concealed beneath the artistic canvas, secrets saved from the lasting misfortune that sealed the fate of his many lost works— for all this he was called a *pictor papalis* (papal painter).

To gain access from the church to the chapel of St. Helena beneath it, we must walk along a funnel-shaped, descending corridor, which remains dark and silent. On the side wall the visitor is accompanied by two long inscriptions in capital letters executed with majolica tiles in Pacioli's own mysterious Roman lapidary style. Of these inscriptions, "only a part remains, this being the result of a natural degradation of the inscription over time, but also, it appears, because it was removed during the restorations carried out in the eighteenth century by order of the ecclesiastical supervisors, who saw, in the content of the inscription, a historical truth that did not correspond to their own. In fact, they enacted a scrupulous inquisitorial revision."[17]

The inscription was damaged because of its intrinsic truth, in the centuries-long iconoclastic fury following the death of Innocent VIII, of whom all traces had to be buried in the interment of truth and justice. The tiles must have been made in Rome, where renowned ceramicists worked at the time.[18] The capital letters in ceramic are all perfectly square, measuring twenty-two square inches: "The final effect is one of white bands bearing the writing, alternating with dark bands illuminated by gold lace."

Squares, white, black, and gold: This looks like a familiar signature, that of Innocent VIII. In the inscription set in the left wall of the descending corridor there are many gaps—just as in the history of the Church and the relics—where tiles have vanished, and two large, white patches remain. The censorship, surely the work of Spanish hands, was performed subtly: The original was not suppressed, but instead was counterfeited in order to hide Innocent VIII's role and exalt that of the king of Spain and Alexander VI.

The missing letters are those relating to the disappeared pope; nothing of them remains but a numeral (V) and a date (1492). The crucial phrase, fortunately, can be reconstructed thanks to a transcription made prior to the censorship and appearing in a work from 1592: . . . *titulus staret quae iam litterae prae vetustate vix legi (poterant, sedente Innocentio) V(III p)ientiss(imo Pontifice anno Domini) MCCCCXCII. Pontificatus sui an(no VIII cum bonae memoriae)* (Though it can scarcely be read on account of its age, it can be translated as: [during the pontificate of Innocent] V[III] most holy [Pontiff in the year of our Lord] 1492, his pontificate's [eighth year of blessed memory]).[19]

Once again, the devil had done his best, but it was not good enough. The truth intervened, despite inquisitorial revisions, and Innocent VIII was once again unmistakably resuscitated.[20] Here is further proof that an authentic source can be falsified, succeeding even today in deceiving researchers.

The revision of the text in the remaining inscription allows only the harmless record of Innocent VIII's visit accompanied by the senate of Rome: *Innocentius ipsa et hanc basilicam cum Senatu devotissime visitavit et quotannis eam ipsa die visitantibus plene indulsit primum Alleluia referens / contra bestiam babylonemque Mahumetem in ecclesia sanctorum iuxta Apocalipsim ea die fuisse decantatum.* (Innocent himself, together with the senate, most devoutly visited this basilica and declared a plenary indulgence to those visiting on this day each year, noting that an Alleluia should be sung on the same day against Muhammad, the Beast of Babylon in the church of the saints as in the Apocalypse.) This is enough to confirm, if nothing else, Innocent's strong will in wishing to fight Mehmed's Babylon.

Santa Croce's collection of relics is further enhanced by the index finger of St. Thomas. This apostle who wanted to touch Christ's side with his finger supposedly died in western India, the first missionary of the evangelization of the Indies, the Indies Columbus was preparing to discover. St. Thomas was called the apostle of Asia. Whither did he travel? In the thirteenth century his remains were brought to Chios and thence to Ortona.[21]

Once again, Chios: the island of Homer, creator of Odysseus; the island of the Cybo family and the island of Columbus; the last Eastern outpost remaining in Christian and Genoese hands after the fall of Constantinople and where the young navigator landed on one of his many voyages. Innocent VIII and Columbus might have prayed at the tomb of St. Thomas on this island; perhaps they even prayed there together. The admiral dedicated to St. Thomas the first fort built at Santo Domingo.[22]

If we are to pursue further our study of Santa Croce in Gerusalemme, we must mention that the most frequently recurring presences in connection with the assignment of the basilica after the pontificate of Giovanni Battista Cybo are Iberian. Out of sixteen cardinals in succession from the end of the fifteenth century to the beginning of the eighteenth, no less than nine were Spanish.[23]

Was this a sequence that would guarantee censorship and the necessary silence through the centuries, resulting in the elimination of Innocent's record and covering up the presumed historical and pictorial incongruences? It was, at the least, intended to impede the correct understanding of the inscription set in tile, as well as that of the Grails, peacocks, parrots, sweetcorn, and pineapples . . .[24]

Today, the church (coincidentally?) is in the hands of the Cistercians, the order of St. Bernard of Clairvaux, the spiritual father of medieval knights and of the Templars.

The relics of the cross, still much revered today, are scattered throughout Rome. One part is in the top of the obelisk that stands at the center of the piazza at St. Peter's, directly opposite the basilica, next to one of the two fountains whose origin is attributed to Innocent VIII. It repeats the synthesis of a spiritual path leading from ancient Egypt, from Heliopolis, the city of the sun, to Rome. The remains of the sacred wood are also hidden in the apse of the Church of San Clemente, within another framework of symbols. In the depths of the church is a sanctuary to the god Mithras, with a carving that seems almost to leap out of the stone, armed with a dagger "with which he will slay the bull in order to rise to the heavens and rejoin the sun."[25]

San Clemente was built on the site of a series of previous religious monuments, which lead back through the ages to a mystery cult of the Roman Empire. Descending into the grotto, we can still hear the waters of the sacred river, the Tiber, flowing along one of its four natural channels located at the site of the Mithraeum. Mithras was an ancient sun god, bearer of grace and peace battling taurine forces, the symbol of the alchemical *prima materia*. The analogies to Christ are striking. His name means "pact," implying an alliance with God, which was repeated with Noah and Moses—and thus also with Columbus in a symbolic web.[26]

✠

Despite all efforts made, despite all attempts to avoid it, despite all movements in time, space, myth, and legend, enigmas and esotericism emerge at every point, reinforcing the conviction that humankind's religious knowledge and sentiments have always been similar and only their apparent form has been changed over the centuries, adjusting to the path of humanity, to the times, to politics, and to faith. The intrigue is infinite, and sometimes apparently unsolvable.

✠

San Clemente is also near the Colosseum, not far from Santa Maria Maggiore, the Basilica of St. John Lateran, and Santa Croce in Gerusalemme. San Clemente is named for St. Peter's third successor, who died around the year AD 100. Little is known of this saint's life, but according to recent study, "his work reveals a Hebrew origin."[27] St. Clement was also the author of the *Letter to the Corinthians,* a "singular testimony to the self-awareness of the original Church," hoping for a return to peace.[28]

Judaism, the evangelical church, discord to be overcome, peace to be regained, the capacity for self-renewal, the reemergence of the paganism that preceded the birth of Christ: All these themes were vibrantly alive during the fifteenth century.

It is no simple task to reconstruct the vicissitudes of the holy place. It is certain only that in 1403 Pope Boniface IX, known as Tomacelli Cybo, entrusted it to the Augustinian congregation of Sant'Ambrogio in Milan.[29]

San Clemente is a fascinating church. The vault of the central mosaic above the altar is dominated by Christ with a seraphic expression; his cross sprouts from a luxuriant Tree of Life. Jesus is accompanied by the apostles, represented by twelve white doves. "If the cross in the mosaic at San Clemente is the Tree of Life, then this is at the same time the vine 'from which the sweet wine flows amply—red as blood' (Venanzio Fortunato, 535–600). 'We liken the Church of Christ to this vine,' reads the inscription beneath the mosaic. In the various pastoral scenes depicted amid the foliage, we see its branches spreading and giving life and sustenance to men and women of every human condition and, in truth, to all creation . . . On the triumphal arch . . . the whole scene was inspired by the Apocalypse."[30]

Here we see the cross–Tree of Life, a fragment of which is kept in San Clemente, the True Cross to be planted in America, in Vinland, the Vikings' land of vines, the land of God's age baptized in the enterprise of the messenger Christopher Columbus, Christ bearer and cross bearer. The unambiguous inspiration and aspiration flowed together in an eschatological vision, promising a reformed and new world, as in the Apocalypse.

Lurking everywhere around the church are anchors, like the one on Columbus's shield. These are in remembrance of St. Clement's martyrdom. One painting primarily caught our attention at first sight: a large St. Christopher carrying the infant Jesus on his shoulders. The latter, for his part, holds the orb of the world in his hands. The light was no help and the height of the detail made it hard to see, but in this depiction on the southern hemisphere of the globe there is a surprising expanse of land. The date of its execution is not known; critics waver between attributing it to Masaccio and to Masolino, taking the position that the latter limited himself to completing the work of the former.[31]

Did this spherical world, shocking to some people, anticipate the "heresy" of life in the antipodes, perhaps in Africa? Was it the revelation that Rome held in store for the apocalypse soon to come?

Piece by piece, the sacred evidence was flowing toward Rome in a spiritual current that pervaded St. Peter's city. The collection was almost complete, because Genoa held the chalice, the green cup of the Grail that had caught the blood of Christ, and the sacred Mandylion. The last pieces of the unknown mosaic were being assembled: the collage of relics and works of art, the final steps in this ideal pilgrimage, leading up to the late spring of 1492.

Columbus was on the brink of departure. Rome held the sultan of Constantinople in its teeth, politically speaking, taking advantage of Jem's presence in the Vatican court. Peace with King Ferrante of Naples had just been achieved. The question of the Crusade, forever open, had found a new ally. Taking this into account, Bayezid was seeking to ingratiate himself with the pope, showering him with gifts and also remunerating him lavishly in coin.

In May, "the envoy to Rome brought, at the sultan's command, a valuable emerald and a precious relic, the lance with which Longinus pierced the Savior's side at the Crucifixion. By order of the pontiff, the sacred relic was received at Ancona, from whence the Crusade of Pius II

Piccolomini had been intended to sail, by Niccolò Cibo, archbishop of Arles, and by Luca Borsiano, bishop of Foligno, and was thence brought to Narni inside a crystal vase embellished with gold."[32]

Giuliano della Rovere, the future Pope Julius II, also went to accompany the gifts on their entrance into Rome. Innocent VIII was unwell but went to meet the procession at the Porta del Popolo, where he gave a sermon on the Passion. He then went with the solemn procession to St. Peter's—but he wanted the relic placed in his private rooms. The lance would be among his final thoughts on his deathbed.

With the arrival of the lance, the Vicar of Christ had at last come in contact with the final moment of Jesus' life, with the iron that had marked his passage from life to death (as would soon also happen for Innocent), almost in a form of transmutation, in a springtime, close to Easter, that oscillated between Passion and Resurrection. Finally, from the choirs of its two basilicas built upon the heart of paganism, Rome had returned to being and hymning the New Jerusalem—from whence would blossom forth the celestial Jerusalem to which Columbus's voyage was aimed. The lance pointed along a path from which no deviation could be made.

The gem, with the image of Christ, the precious emerald, also had a formidable power in a time particularly sensitive to the true portrait of Jesus. This stone also came into the hands of Innocent VIII. In the Renaissance it was understood that the longstanding image of Jesus imposed by canonical learning and power had tampered with the truth. Traces of this truth were passionately sought. The profile of the Son of God, for example, represented something completely new. The first one appeared in the mid-fifteenth century on a medallion, and in that fatal year of 1492, history locates the reemergence of the incredible talisman upon which the features of the Nazarene materialized: "A medallion which, in many respects, remains an enigma. It presents a different type of representation of Christ, often called Nordic, characterized by facial features that are not classical and varyingly accentuated depending on the version: a receding forehead terminating in a fairly fleshy nose with a prominent bridge. The lips are full and slightly protruding, the chin a little receding and covered by a short, rather sparse beard. . . . In one of the variants, the reverse of the medal bears a text that enriches the image through a legend regarding its provenance. According to this legend, in return for Jem (with whom he was involved in a struggle for the throne) being kept on a forced sojourn in Rome, Sultan Bayezid had given Pope Innocent VIII an ancient emerald upon which were depicted Christ and the Apostle Paul. . . . [T]he emerald (in its natural form) had great value as a precious stone, and in Christian allegory it was connected to Christ, because allegorically, the emerald is analogous to the mirror. This stone would have been the ideal medium for an image of Jesus. It is not clear what was really depicted on this stone, however, because no examples of the combination of a portrait of Christ and Paul are found in late ancient and medieval iconography.[33]

✠

Miraculous emeralds, an unheard of and not exactly orthodox image of Christ: These were novelties, mysteries, and items without precedent, origins of the faith worthy of reconsideration. Whenever reference is made to Innocent VIII, it seems such words and such reflections cannot be disregarded, confirming the underground course of a pontificate that was seemingly tireless in pursuing the authenticity of a theology that had become Catholic and Roman but was in part distorted. The path to be retraced could begin only from the places and objects of the Passion, places and objects to be relocated to Rome and ideally brought across the ocean by means of a Christ bearer—to a land viewed as the lost Paradise, which would be baptized by grace, by the holy cross, and where the city of the True Cross was to be built.

The new destination was indicated by the point of the lance of Longinus, representing in metaphorical language the axis of the world along which the spiritual influences descend by way of the drops of blood which, flowing along the iron, were caught in the Grail and which, falling upon the earth, made it fertile: drops of an elixir for an eternal life to be regained. This was the transmission of a supernatural power granting rule over the world and over all of humanity to him who possessed the weapon, for good or for evil. This was the hidden significance of the lance, which can still be seen today in the hands of Innocent VIII on his funereal mausoleum at St. Peter's. And this, broadly speaking, forms the background for the events and for the idea behind the words in that carving, which never ceases to amaze and surprise: *Crucis sacro sancte reperto titulo / Lancea quae Christi hausit latus / A Baiazete Turcarum tyranno dono missa.*

Thanks to copying, and the medieval craving for relics, there is also more than one lance. Which is the true one? "The true sacred lance—at least as far as we can guess—was part of the treasure of the Byzantine emperors, along with many other relics. After the Ottoman conquest of Constantinople, the point of the lance was sent to Pope Innocent VIII as a gift from the sultan, and since then it has been kept in the Basilica of St. Peter. The shaft, however, had already been sold by the Byzantine emperors to the king of France in the thirteenth century, and it can be seen today in [his] private chapel, the Sainte-Chappelle."[34]

The extent to which the power of Longinus's spear influenced the path of humanity, even up to the twentieth century, is demonstrated by the fact that the iron bathed in the blood of the Savior was sought by Charlemagne, Napoleon, and even Adolf Hitler. "Hitler became utterly fascinated with the passage of the Spear through the era in which all his childhood heroes had lived. He found to his astonishment and delight that the great German figures that had filled his youthful dreams had held the Spear as the holy aspirations of their ambitions, their talisman of power. Altogether forty-five emperors had claimed the Spear of Destiny as their possession between the coronation in Rome of Charlemagne and the fall of the old German Empire exactly a thousand years later. And what a pageantry of power and gallantry it was! The Spear had passed like the very finger of destiny through the millennium forever creating new patterns of fate which had again and again changed the entire history of Europe."[35]

In his folly, the German dictator hoped, by means of the powerful sacred object, to start a new golden age, in a magical symbiosis with the natural laws of the universe. Frederick II Hohenstauffen (1212–1250), half saint and half demon, the valiant knight and poet (whose funereal monument Hitler had brought to Germany), who had his people sing of the Holy Grail, who believed in astrology and practiced alchemy, "prizing the possession of the Spear beyond all things, made it the focal point of his whole life—especially calling on its powers during his crusades (in which Francis of Assisi once carried the Spear on an errand of mercy) and throughout his running battles with the Italian States and Papal Armies."[36]

It was a supernatural assegai, like a finger pointed in an unknown direction, like the bloody javelin of the wounded Fisher King in the Grail legend: an extraordinary and most powerful discovery to which was added the finger of St. Thomas, pointing to the route of the Indies.

Could the leader of the faith, at the height of the Renaissance, ignore the signs of his election, his investiture as the guide of Christendom along a path leading to the Christianizing of a whole world? 1492 represented a year of miracles in all senses, a concatenation of events charged with ideas, accompanied by coups de théâtre, prefacing events in Spain before Christopher Columbus's departure.

Rome was filled with the evidence of the life and death of Christ. After the fall of Granada, Spain was further pressed into the role of the most Catholic nation. People lined up for baptism in front of the frescoed walls of the churches of Rome. Fulfilling his mission, a dove *(colombo),* like St. John the Baptist, would bring the waters of salvation: A new prophet, like Noah and Moses, would cross the sea.

SEVEN

✠

VATICAN, CAMPIDOGLIO, AND QUIRINAL

A MAJESTIC CUBE, like the geometric figure and the magic contained in the etymology of the name Cybo, was once erected at the Vatican, visible from all of Rome in the late fifteenth-century, solitary, detached from the other buildings of the holy city. In old prints, especially in a view printed in a book *(Liber chronicarum)* published at Nuremberg in 1493, it appears more imposing than the structure of St. Peter's Basilica itself. It was a powerful solid with square sides, rising upward with a series of arches one upon the other, at ground level numbering *seven,* the perfect number.

Even today, despite all changes, Innocent VIII's mark is still visible upon God's hill, on the heights of Monte Sant'Egidio, where the oldest botanical garden in Italy dates to the same era, a vision of colors, a symphony of perfumes, a passion remaining in the blood of the descendents. The plants had mysterious properties, a meaning, and a voice—the voice of nature. They were the ingredients for magical recipes used by the Cybo family and by Columbus.

The imposing cube was the first great building outside the walls of the patrimony of St. Peter in a spatial expansion typical of Innocent's pontificate, looking beyond all confines, overturning all rules. Of Innocent only a distorted reflection remains, implicating the humanistic side of this great patron of the arts. It was a unique time, during which Europe gazed in admiration at the unparalleled explosion of the Renaissance, during which the artists and thinkers of the Italian peninsula were a guiding light for all the Christian courts.

"Never before," wrote the Florentine historian and diplomat, Francesco Guicciardini in his *Storia d'Italia* (he was in the service of two popes from the Medici family, Leo X and Clement VII), "has Italy shown such prosperity nor found herself in such a desirable situation as in the year of grace one thousand four hundred and ninety and the years directly before and after. Italy enjoyed miraculous peace and tranquility: she was not subject to any emperor but only to herself, and was home to many inhabitants and a great abundance of goods and riches. She was further adorned by the magnificence of numerous princes, by the splendor of many and noble cities, by the seat and the majesty of religion; she abounded with excellent administrators of public works and with spirits excelling in valor in all disciplines; and she was dedicated to all the arts and renowned for them . . ."[1]

The "majesty of religion" reached its acme in 1490: prosperity, riches, splendor, magnificence, the triumph of the arts and all the disciplines, and "spirits excelling in valor" all pervaded this fateful decade. Men are always faithful expressions of their own time, for both good and evil. Of the evil of Innocent VIII everything possible has been said, extending into every branch of his activities. Of the good nothing more is spoken. On the magnificent fresco of the Renaissance, Giovanni Battista Cybo's figure appears in many pseudohistorical reconstructions as a great absence, a total nothingness. His great rival, the sinister Alexander VI (Borgia), has, however, been reevaluated in light of the artistic magnificence of his pontificate, which was simply a continuation of the trend that had preceded him.

And yet Innocent's contemporaries were unanimous in celebrating the importance of the works of architecture that he caused to be executed, which satisfied an impulse that had originated in the pontificates preceding Innocent—an impulse to beautify Rome. If we retrace the steps of this beautifully artistic and cultural path, we cannot help but see Innocent VIII does not correspond in the slightest to the superficial image of the ignorant simpleton, the man foreign to the mentality of the munificent lords and at odds with his epoch. On the contrary, he represented in his time a more perfect synthesis of the absolute than any of its other pursuers in a trajectory that has left behind indelible traces—complete adulteration notwithstanding.

Today, walking along the bastions of Michelangelo in Rome, it is possible to catch sight of the Belvedere, the villa consisting of six rooms and a chapel. It has an imposing facade and at the top is a twenty-inch-high inscription celebrating the pope Genuensis, crowned by a number of characteristically Renaissance festoons and the Cybo family arms. The crenellations should have been Guelph style, this being the very heart of Christendom—but no, they are in the style of the revolutionary Ghibellines in one of those many clues pointing to a desire to reconcile opposites.

The charge of building the edifice, according to Vasari—who was simultaneously a painter and the first great art critic—was entrusted to another great artist, Antonio Pollaiolo.[2] Antonio and his brother Piero Pollaiolo were both painters and sculptors. They had been trained in a goldsmith's workshop in Florence and were familiar with the working and polishing of precious metals. Perhaps they also believed gold could change the course of human events—the final goal, material and spiritual, of every alchemical process.[3] It was the same gold Innocent VIII wished to use, once Columbus's voyage was completed, to change the face of Rome and the world, in his action of renewal.[4]

The crenellated castle faces east toward the rising sun, identified at the time with the Christ, the sun that guided Christopher Columbus, the crusader, monk, and cavalier. The fortress towers above nature, above the countryside, above the secret garden, the completed Eden. It is a beautiful place with a beautiful view (Belvedere or Bel Videre means "beautiful view"), a mysterious and massive retreat rising above the hill in yet another failed operation of Pope Cybo. The Belvedere signals an all-embracing reform, a summit to be looked upon from an ever-increasing distance.

The Belvedere quickly became an actual residence, intended for long stays and as guest quarters. The villa had a rectangular courtyard and a "famous octagonal courtyard," 8 being a numeral particularly dear to knights. "This expansion of the original project was such that the Belvedere can be said to be the first villa built in Rome since antiquity."[5]

It is no stretch of the imagination "to believe that the thirteen masks which, according to tradition came from the Pantheon, might have once decorated the villa."[6] In new buildings, gardens, and statues, antiquity was the model of perfection to imitate, the fulcrum of knowledge to revise and pursue. Innocent VIII accumulated and superimposed them in a multiplication of energies.

Inside in the first chamber, with its arches containing lunette windows, the visitor is drawn in by a sequence of bundles of golden rays upon which stands the pope's shield; and among a number of Chinese arabesques, constant reminders of the East always on a gold background, is Innocent VIII's favorite symbol, a peacock, with its plumage displayed and forming a great wheel, with the inscription in the original French (the language of the first monks of the Temple): Loyalty above all. It was one of the family's mottos.

Loyalty was a characteristic of the lives and customs of the knights of the Temple and the Holy Sepulchre, as well as the Knights of St. John, as confirmed in the depiction of St. John the Baptist and St. John the Evangelist. They are portrayed among children playing musical instruments amid floral decorations and more peacocks. They are the omnipresent Johns, the dioscuri of a Church to be rebuilt in a harmonic conjunction of exquisite beauty, so that "this ornamentation truly served as a prototype for that of the Borgia apartment."[7] Some of the most admired masterpieces of the Renaissance thus had their forerunners in the works accomplished by Pope Innocent VIII.[8]

Bunches of fruit and flowers were everywhere; "Of these only one remains," while there are "four of the pope's shields in colored stucco relief amid golden rays. An analogous decoration is in the pope's two rooms (today no longer separate from the rest of the loggia), but in place of the musician angels, in the lunettes of the first room, we can see pairs of philosophers flourishing scrolls, while in the two unbroken lunettes of the second room there is only one personage in each, with his own scroll but without any writing. The sphere held by one of them identifies him as a geographer."[9]

A geographer with a round globe: the sign of a vocation—and there are also Greek crosses and radiant suns, rare techniques, vanished or altered originals and complete suppressions, despite the excellence of the artists in the pope's service. "The majority of works from the time of Innocent VIII have been destroyed or in part rendered entirely unrecognizable."[10]

It seems as if a curse, where it did not obliterate everything, resorted to cunning concealment. Why such tenacity? Innocent's story is also the story of those lost works of art. The building on the hill remains, but looking down from it upon the fated city and the gardens, the view has been lost. From those heights, Rome once appeared as a jewel, resplendent as in the age of the Caesars, but the dream has crumbled, like the frescoes.

Critiques are full of admiration for the innovative and marvelous work within the frescoes. The family's shield, supported by two angels, is distinguished "by a rich festoon of various leaves and fruits in terra cotta color, skillfully glazed. This technique of glazing terra cotta allows such sculptures to resist the ravages of time without alteration of their true colors."[11]

The building as a whole constitutes an astounding achievement. The equally exquisite and colorful floor bears the signature of Luca della Robbia, another artist, a Florentine genius of the goldsmith's alchemical art. He devised *invetriatura*, glazed terra-cotta, the alchemists' miracle, a style of ceramics unknown anywhere else in the world.

The Belvedere was a brilliant construction, a melting pot of the greatest artists, mostly coming from Florence, the new Athens, thanks to the patronage of Lorenzo the Magnificent. A considerable number of artists hailed from Umbria, home to the brothers of St. Francis. Among the most famous of these was Pinturicchio, apprenticed to Perugino, who frescoed the Italian cities and the greatest maritime republics, homes proudly claimed by the Cybo family.[12]

These artists formed a kind of Italian league, drawn together to make peace in the peninsula, watched over by the Madonna. Along with Pinturicchio and Perugino, the Mantuan Mantegna—already in the service of Gonzaga—was particularly admired. He was of humble origins but "obtained the honor of a knight" and proudly signed his works *Andreas Mantineas Comes Palatinus eques auratae militiae* (Andreas the Mantuan, Count Palatine, knight of the golden militia).[13] A talented man of noble character, he was called to Rome after being taken in by the Paduan painter Jacopo Squarcione, who served "the Carrara, the Lords of Padua."[14]

In Padua, where Innocent VIII had studied, Mantegna the knight frescoed the stories of St. Christopher and St. James, preludes to the enterprise of the brothers Christopher and Diego (James) Columbus. Mantegna was called upon to decorate the pope's private chapel, where he "worked on every detail with such love and precision that the vault and walls seem more like illuminations in manuscripts than paintings, and the largest figures in the work are over the altar, which he did like the other parts in fresco; while St. John the Baptist is baptizing Christ, people standing around him are removing their clothes and making signs that they wish to be baptized."[15]

Pastor's description of this beautiful work also mentions a series of paintings, among them an Annunciation, a decapitation of the Baptist, St. Peter with the pope, and the four Evangelists on the spandrels of the dome. On the same vault there is a loggia with children holding garlands, as in the famous Sala degli Sposi in Mantua, where a peacock is among the figures on the ceiling. The famous composition, considered one of the greatest artistic masterpieces, therefore has a counterpart inside the walls of the Vatican.

The iconography described by Vasari, in addition to the Madonna and the pope as a new Peter, includes St. John the Baptist washing away the sins of the world and the savages who, as Jesus arrives, undress and offer themselves naked to the Word of the gospels and the purifying water of baptism. Who are these people in an all-too-open allegory? Whom might John the Baptist have represented? Who was the Christ bearer, the Christo Ferens, as Christopher Columbus signed his name? These visions shimmer in the chronicles and paintings of a vanished past.

Vasari also records an episode offering a significant insight into the relationship between the artist and his patron, providing a useful indication of the pope's character, his bonhomie and generosity contrasting with current anecdotes, which portray him as avaricious: "It is said that because of the many commitments he had, this pope did not give Mantegna the money he needed often enough. Because of this, when he painted some Virtues in monochrome, Andrea included among them the figure of Prudence. When the pope came to see the work one day, he asked what that figure represented, and Andrea replied: 'That is Prudence.' Then the pontiff added: 'If you wish her to have a proper companion, paint Patience beside her.' The painter understood what the Holy Father wished to say, and never again uttered another word. When the project was completed, the pope sent him back to the duke with his favor and very honorable rewards."[16]

There were minor skirmishes among knights, among minds that could look behind the scenes of everyday events. The pope's political responsibilities were hectic and his office kept him away from works in progress. The artist could understand that, but in the end the promise was abundantly honored.

Even the front of St. Peter's, along with the piazza, underwent a transformation during Giovanni Battista's pontificate, but of these no trace remains. The pope's hand was everywhere, giving meaning to a profound change pervading all of the Vatican and the papal states. "Although Cybo was a great builder in Rome and in the Vatican (it suffices to recall the facade of the destroyed Curia Innocenziana in the square of St. Peter's), only a single building in the new pontifical residence bears his arms: the sacristy, which he had joined to the Sistine Chapel, inexplicably 'forgotten'! It adjoins the west side of the chapel. . . . Subsequent additions and modifications . . . have altered the internal and external appearance of the Innocentian sacristy to a considerable degree."[17]

Every trace of verification is blocked by the usual obstacles; nothing is left behind. Of Innocent, as of Columbus, only the memory remains.

In the meantime, work had begun on the Sistine Chapel and continued in the following years. Innocent surrounded himself with a court attended by the most illustrious artists of the epoch, radically changing the face of his pontificate. And yet in the Sistine Chapel—the huge and astounding space whose measurements correspond to those of the Temple of Solomon in the Bible, forming an indissoluble link between the Hebrew and Christian scriptures—there is no record of this pope, the son of Aronne. Historians of every discipline have passed directly from Sixtus IV to Alexander VI and Julius II.

We know an entire wall was leveled to make room for Michelangelo's grandiose *Last Judgment,* and many of the artists who painted the Sistine Chapel had also worked for Innocent VIII. The lost frescoes appear to have been signed by Perugino. The Sistine Chapel was inaugurated in 1483, and it is impossible to think that Giovanni Battista Cybo could have completely neglected it between 1484 and 1492. Yet that which no longer exists, that which has disappeared, ends up never having existed at all.

✠

The Belvedere was immersed in green. It was a place for meditation, a place for repose and prayer far from the pressing duties of the pontificate, far from the mobs of the corrupt and disloyal city, which was torn by patrician rivalries. It was a place for reflecting upon the harmony of a world to be rebuilt while listening to the music of a fountain. There had to be water. This was also an Eastern custom—especially for a pope who identified water with purification, the sacrament of baptism, membership in the body of Christ. In the magnificent flow of words in St. Francis's *The Canticle of the Creatures,* "Sister Water" is praised among them.

In front of the Belvedere, still standing today, is one of the lesser known fountains of the Vatican, even though it is the most beautiful in the whole area of St. Peter's, the Galleon Fountain. A green, transparent bowl enclosed in a square basin, its base was originally a playful mass of hollowed rocks with rustication resembling the scales of a pinecone (which we shall discuss later) or a fish and with an inflorescence of mosses converging upon a statue of Neptune, lord of the waters, reclining amid the endless bubbles of the foaming cascades. Hercules, with his club, stood guard.

In the middle of the water there was a ship, a handsome galley, perfectly executed down to the smallest detail. It is a warship with a row of cannons jutting from it, water pouring from the mouths of the cannons' barrels. On a marble plaque attributed to Maffeo Barberini, who had not yet become Pope Urban VIII, are the words: *Bellica pontificem non fundit machina flammas / sed dulcem belli qua perit ignis aquam* (The papal cannon does not shoot flames / but instead the sweet water that quenches the fire of war).

A singular coincidence right next to the most spectacular edifice built by Innocent VIII, this small ocean of serenity existed with a ship (what vessel might it represent?) at its center, speeding with spring water to the conquest of peoples, to a battle to be won by means of a purifying bath, in the peaceful spirit of baptism. Today, the fountain is noticeably different. Under a vault painted with a great Tree of Life, Neptune is still present, and Hercules also remains, the hero of the Hesperides sailing, like Columbus, to conquer the golden apples.

The date claimed for the fountain's construction does not correspond exactly to Innocent's pontificate, but research is always full of surprises; we have already seen a fountain mentioned, near the Belvedere, during the time of Innocent VIII. What might have been a mere suspicion receives incontrovertible confirmation in an assassination attempt that occurred in 1489, while the pope was intent on preparing the Crusade against the Turks thanks to negotiations with the sultan of Egypt, among other factors. Bayezid, the ruler of Constantinople, his worries increasing with the presence of his brother

Jem in the Vatican, took extreme action "by one of those means unfortunately often employed in those times, even by Western powers. At the hands of a degenerate nobleman from the march of Ancona, a certain Cristofano di Castrano known as Magrino, the fountain next to the Belvedere was poisoned, whose water was served at the table of Prince Jem and Innocent VIII. . . . By all appearances, even some people in Rome were aware of this plot."[18]

Therefore, the fountain, which may have been the Galleon Fountain, was already in existence along with all its evident symbolism, while the widespread attempts at the physical elimination of Innocent VIII were beginning. Who, besides the Turk, would have benefited from his death? Who might have known about it? Who might have aided the attempted poisoning if not the future Alexander VI, anxious to hasten the moment of his inauguration, the pope-Antichrist who would never carry out the Crusade against Bayezid?

The water was the humus from which Innocent VIII, the sailor pope, sprang forth. Was his fountain the first one built in front of St. Peter's, the one that can still be seen today in the grand piazza, looking to the right of the basilica? Its base is said to be original, conceived by commission of Innocent VIII and quickly transformed by Rodrigo Borgia. Was this fountain the first one, or was it another? "The fountain was decorated with ornaments in wrought or chiseled metal by the goldsmith Alonso."[19]

The golden path from the Cybos to Columbus keeps reemerging like a great highway. "The goldsmith's art, which grew to dominate the forms of the Renaissance, took a great leap forward under Innocent VIII."[20]

Rome, with its goldsmith pope, with its messenger Columbus sent toward the golden Eden, was regaining the splendor of golden Rome. Its past was being rediscovered, day after day, emerging in excavations in all quarters to the amazement of common people and great lords alike as they quarreled over all these beautiful discoveries. Under Innocent VIII the Vatican, after having long remained immobile, was transforming into an experimental alembic.

The Vatican's first fountain materialized almost magically in the catalog of the exhibition in Rome dedicated to the Borgias, in a sort of subliminal compensation. The lost fountain of Innocent VIII has never been found. It is shown in an old print depicting the Constantinian basilica before the start of the demolitions that began in 1506 under Pope Julius II. This is how St. Peter's must have appeared in the time of Innocent VIII. In front of the façade, at the center of the square, a marble baldachin stands over an enormous bronze pinecone from the Roman era, dating back to the time of Constantine—another connection to ancient Rome, to the first Christian Roman emperor, and thence to the East and to Giovanni Battista Cybo. His surname's etymology is in the cube, the founding stone, the ciborium, the *cibo* ("food" in Italian) and water for the souls—and also in Cuba, the island first christened Juana (Giovanna, the feminine version of John), and finally *ceiba,* the plant sacred to the Native Americans, the Tree of Life for another world.

In another print we can read, inscribed on the architrave of the temple: *Symmachi fons.* The name of Symmachus on the fountain at St. Peter's is written with the Greek *y.* It may have a double meaning, harking back to a primordial church and a Jesus uniting East and West.[21]

Why should this specific fountain be that of Innocent VIII? Because at the top of the baldachin is an unequivocal signature: two splendid peacocks of Roman origin. In the old print the two birds are nearly invisible, just like everything relating to Innocent VIII. Yet the pinecone and peacocks are still there today. They can be seen in the Vatican, in the spectacular Cortile della Pigna, rivaling the sculpture by a modern Italian artist, Pomodoro (a name containing a subliminal cipher, literally meaning "golden apple"), famous for his decayed and broken worlds rendered in golden spheres. In this courtyard, the gaze of one peacock is now directed toward the globe! In the passing of the centuries the power of symbols is eternal in the Vatican, whether conscious or unconscious. The Cortile della Pigna just happens to be directly above the underground bunker that forms the most futuristic room of the Vatican secret archives. The pinecone must have been a symbol, but its most magical and profound significance is lost.[22]

If we now move beyond the walls and out of the center of Rome, entering what used to be the wild Roman countryside, we will find another interesting exhibit, completely abandoned in the early decades of the twentieth century. During the two decades of fascist rule it was earmarked for restoration, amid plans for renewing and reclaiming the Agro Romano, the area at the edge of the Pontine Marshes; but it was not until the 1950s that work on the monument went forward. The task just happened to fall to the Sovereign Military Order of Malta (SMOM), the modern-day heirs to the Templars and the Order of the Holy Sepulchre, the knights of St. John who were involved in the operations of Pope Innocent VIII and Columbus.

This edifice is the Castello della Magliana, by the Tiber in the Portuense suburb on the edges of the *urbs nova* Rome, whose rebirth into a universal destiny had already resounded in the testament of the Ligurian Pope Nicholas V: "And Rome shall be monumental, and shall impress those who come there from all over the world, in order to convince all, imposingly, of the superiority of the Church of Rome and the Catholic faith." The Renaissance was also born out of this intent.

Magliana was on the route to the seas of Ostia and the Lazio. There, in open countryside amid gentle hills and luxuriant vegetation rich in fauna and flora, the remnants of ancient Rome and the pagan cults jut out from the landscape. It is a kind of *lucus,* a sacred place where devotion to St. John the Baptist was particularly intense in the mid-fifteenth century. In 1510 Michelangelo was summoned to paint a fresco in the chapel, depicting "a St. John baptizing our Lord Jesus Christ painted in fresco, and of not very great size."

It was Pope Gregory VII who, in 1074, gave the monastery of San Paolo fuori le Mura a small church dedicated to St. John "in Manliana," from which a chapel remains—a reference to St. John that cannot have escaped Giovanni Battista Cybo. But his power was diverted toward more mundane activities.[23]

In the castle beneath the cross vault, Innocent's shield stands at the center of a multitude of flowers and seashells in another of those constant references to sea life. The road that led to Ostia was the high road to more distant shores, but the road was also open to enemy incursions: "It is known that one of the actions taken during the time of Pope Innocent VIII was that of providing Rome with a certain defensive security. To protect the city from dangers coming mainly from the sea, a number of guard towers were built all along the littoral zone, which in case of an unexpected attack would allow not only Rome, but also all the coastal lands, to organize rapidly their own defense."[24]

The thought of imminent danger from the Turks drove Innocent VIII to provide more secure defenses should peace prove impossible to achieve. These were the precautions and the global strategy of a Holy Father who, in spite of everything, is always described as lacking in courage. The castle of Magliana, upon Innocent's death, was neglected by Alexander VI but was frequently inhabited and improved by Julius II. It became truly splendid, finding its worthy heir under a Medici pope: Leo X, son of Lorenzo the Magnificent, who was made a cardinal in his youth by Innocent VIII—in a precedent recalling Columbus's request, in an astounding letter only recently discovered, of a cardinal's hat for his son Diego, who was still a minor.

The veneration of St. John the Baptist and the presence of a pope who dedicated his pontificate to the beheaded saint: Is it any wonder that today this property is in the hands of the Knights of Malta, whose shield is identical—albeit with reversed colors, as is wont to happen—to the emblem Columbus bore on his sails? Is it any wonder that in this same place, at the old farmstead, a modern hospital has sprung up at the hands of the Hospitalers? Such is the tradition of an order that had always cared for the sick and for pilgrims, just as Columbus cared for those of his men who were injured or taken ill in the Indies. The ancient link seems to live on secretly, still operating in a reciprocal exchange of favors and concessions—but also, most likely, of disputes and blackmail.

The activity of building and restoration during Innocent VIII's pontificate has left its marks in varying significance and visibility, but in all cases these are ignored along the many streets and in the churches of the city and of course at Santa Croce in Gerusalemme.[25]

There was also Sant'Agostino, where an image of the Blessed Virgin was kept in secret, taken from the enemy Turks after the fall of Constantinople thanks to some nobles of Greek origin. According to tradition, it was painted by the hand of St. Luke the Evangelist. In August 1485, during the plague, it was displayed for the first time in St. Peter's by order of Innocent VIII after being brought through the city in a solemn procession, amid general commotion and devotion. This Stella Maris, like that of Molfetta, was part of Innocent's Marian project, which was to unfold the wings of the *Santa Maria*.

✠

Finally, the works undertaken by order of the pope inside St. Peter's itself were quite varied and significant. They began with the ciborium of the holy lance. The sacred iron spear that had pierced Christ's side— sent to the pope by Bayezid, as we know—had to be protected and displayed for public veneration. It was a unique and supernatural artifact capable of guaranteeing all manner of abilities to its possessor. There is a surviving design for the ciborium, apparently by Bramante, who proposed two aedicules, one atop the other: In the lower was the image of a Madonna by Pinturicchio, with the pope depicted kneeling. In the upper one were two angels adoring the lance wielded by the Roman centurion Longinus.

This work of art has not survived except for a few fragments kept in the crypts of the Vatican. But the lance of destiny, the relic symbolizing power and immortality, the relic pursued for so long and finally obtained, is still held in the hands of Innocent VIII in one of the two statues of him in the funereal mausoleum by Pollaiolo. His stance, the tomb, the carvings, the inscriptions, and the dates are all at odds. They appear to form an ensemble of factual errors, the fruit of ignorance. In light of what we have learned, they may reveal what could not be explicitly said.

It was Vasari, again, who gave firsthand information on the activity of the Florentine Pollaiolo brothers and in particular Antonio, master of the art of fusion who, in order better to study the human body, didn't hesitate to perform experiments and anatomical investigations, which might have had him condemned for witchcraft: "He skinned many men to see their anatomy beneath. . . . For this reason, having become famous after the death of Sixtus IV, he was brought to Rome by his successor Innocent, where he made a metal tomb . . . in St. Peter's next to the chapel containing the lance of Christ."[26]

The lance thus formed the central axis of the link between the chapel of Longinus and Giovanni Battista Cybo's mausoleum. It was a connection charged with significance.

Both figures of Innocent VIII immortalize him in bronze in a sempiternal dualism uniting life and death, light and darkness. It is an innovative and unusual design. On the lower level the pope, clad in sumptuous pontifical vestments, is in the act of benediction; the lance is in his other hand. His shoulders point exactly north—a positioning contradictory to his great hopes and endeavors. Up above, the pope reclines on his deathbed. It is a proud portrait that speaks with an introspection that was rare for Antonio Pollaiolo, who was "little interested in the psychological individuality of his figures." All the virtues, theological and cardinal, submit to the pope: faith, hope, charity, justice, fortitude, temperance, and prudence. It is a complete iconography, one that could be reconstructed in a purely alchemical interpretation.[27]

In the early 1600s the monument was moved and reassembled. Finally, in 1621 it was inverted in an entirely arbitrary manner, like a truth reversed. Thus it lost, in part, its complex harmony and hidden meaning. The remains of the popes that had been in the old basilica were distributed throughout the churches of Rome. Sixtus IV was put in the Vatican grotto and Alexander VI was actually buried beyond the Tiber, in the Church of Santa Maria in Monserrato—in a plain wooden casket. Among the many popes prior to 1500, with the exception of St. Peter, only the "damned" Innocent VIII is still in St. Peter's. It is a strange honor.

The new location is the tomb on the left as one enters the basilica. When the casket was opened, the pope's body was still intact, with the odor of sanctity. Some wrote of a strong smell of violets. "And in the pontificate of Paul V, the grace and honor was done of placing him where he is now, in that beautiful and honorable place; but first, in the presence of Sig. Car. le Bandini and other prelates, with my agent [that of Alberico Cybo Malaspina], the bronze casket was opened and the body was found complete with the brocaded cope, slippers, little worn, silken gloves, and many medallions . . . The remains turned to dust, whereupon we placed the bones in a lead casket, as was done with those of Count Francesco, my uncle, and his wife, Signora Maddalena di Medici, whom we placed in the chapel."[28]

The body was wrapped in a red satin cloth, like the robes of the Roman priests, with gold and pearl decorations. On the coffin there were gold coins and the images of three women with the inscription "Justice, peace, abundance."[29]

A perfect spiritual statement: The plan that had inspired Innocent VIII from the beginning of his pontificate was made eternal. Gold and pearls (the riches that would come from America) together with justice, peace, and abundance had been the guides for a pontificate much more innocent than accepted history has taught us.

Bones and dust, if they still exist, could be examined today to test whether a blood relationship between the Cybo and Columbus families is truly possible. A similar test was attempted in Spain with the navigator's ashes, in order to ascertain whether the remains contained in the tomb in Seville are actually his—in pursuit of that truth which the pope's tomb seems to make every attempt to hide in a mishmash of numbers, or in order to attract an attention too long distracted.

It is an unsolvable puzzle, thwarting the pious invocation *In innocentia mea ingressus sum redime me Domine et miserere mei* (For I have walked in my innocence; redeem me, Lord, and have mercy upon me—Psalms 26:11), inscribed on an urn upon which the pope's

statue reclines. How far does the phrase go back? Was it on the original monument or was it added later? Perhaps it means innocence will
be honored and redemption *(redime me)* finally achieved only when
the inscription can be interpreted definitively, without a shadow of
doubt, anachronism, or ambiguity. In the meantime, only commisera-
tion remains *(miserere mei)*.

Alexander VI and Spain gained further allies when the Church
renounced and put an end to the Renaissance with the Counter
Reformation. It was Pius V (1566–1572) "who had everything removed
from the pontifical palaces, including those things he defined as 'ancient
idols,' which he deemed unworthy of the true spirit of the post-Tridentine
Catholic reform. During those years, the considerable collection of
antiques decorating the internal corridor and rooms of the Belvedere
was also put at serious risk."[30]

✠

Faced with the dangers humanism and the Renaissance presented to
orthodoxy, even within the very walls of the Vatican, the least risky path
was chosen.

If it is easy to bury a man, even a pope, it is harder to bury the ideas,
the memory, the truth and justice. It remains only to follow intuitions
and hypotheses, pursuing every possible clue. The reconstruction proceeds from marble to marble, from carving to carving, from stone
to stone, groping for one handhold after another as if on an arduous
climb.

For this it is best to leave Rome and the Vatican and move up into
the surrounding hills. The place is, even today, the favorite vacation
area for the church fathers. Atop Monte Porzio Catone we open the
last chapter of a riddle full of mysteries. The place was given the title
of principality at the Vigil of Christmas 1614 by papal bull: "Paul
V went to Monte Porzio from his country seat at Mondragone on
June 2, 1614. He was received in the house then belonging to Lorenzo
Colombo. . . . To preserve the memory of the pontifical visit, the following inscription, now no longer in existence, once stood upon the

exterior walls of the house: *Paolo V Burghesio. P.M., Qui IV nonas Iunii MDCXIV, Hanc ingressus domum, Ex supreme fastigio, Descendit ad infimos, Fines omnes benignitatis egressus, Laurentius Columbus hospes, Grati animi testificationem posuit* (Paul V Borghese, Pontifex Maximus, on the fourth nones of June, 1614, entered this house. He descended from the highest place to the lowliest, exceeding all bounds of generosity. Laurentius Columbus, his host, placed this memorial of his gratitude)."

The inscription is followed by some verses.[31] The carving is still there today in part, but has been altered from the original and then confined beneath the stairs of a house in the same town.[32]

One pope was never in a private house in Monte Porzio. Would Paul V (Borghese), the pope with delusions of grandeur, whose love for the splendor and magniloquence of his own person is still visible today in the great inscriptions carved along the façade of St. Peters, the pope who changed the face of the basilica and also reorganized the secret archives, have chosen to enter this "lowliest" house, as the guest of an unknown Lorenzo Columbus? Who was this Lorenzo? Was he a descendent of a branch of the Cybo-Colombo family originating from the relationship with Lorenzo the Magnificent? What might the two men, so different in social status, have said to each other in a time when such a visit appears impossible? These were the years in which it was being decided how and where to position the sepulchre of a pope who was to be forgotten.

The house in Monte Porzio belonged to the Statuti family for a certain period. Nicola Statuti was a knight. "In the courtyard of his residence, Nicola Statuti, in 1882, had a stone inscription put up so that posterity might remember not only the visit of Paul V to Monte Porzio on the second of June, 1614, but also the first inscription, by then destroyed, which Lorenzo Colombo had set in the wall of his house during his time."[33]

✠

Stone and marble only deepen the great enigma of Innocent VIII and Christopher Columbus. It is a search that never ends but only reveals new paths to follow in every direction—and the coincidences, if we still choose to call them that, keep intersecting more and more in a manner at times almost prophetic.

For example, those Latin words inscribed in the marble at the base of the tomb in St. Peter's represent a mine of information to be excavated. The first phrase referring to Innocent states: *Italicae pacis perpetuo custodi* (A perpetual defender of Italian peace). Yet at this time Italy itself did not yet exist. Was he a tireless paladin of harmony, presumed indispensable for the harmony that was to spread throughout the entire world? This does not tell us much more than we already know. But why *perpetuo,* as if something had to be asserted that only the future could confirm? And yet on careful investigation even this chance phrase, carved in stone, just like a prophecy, gains an almost subliminal meaning.

The Cybo family, after the pope's death, intermarried with the branches of the Malaspina and Este families. The Malaspinas would settle between the sea and the mountains, near the white marble quarries, becoming princes and dukes of Massa. It is there we shall now direct our attention, with a necessary assumption by now taken for granted: "The study of things in Massa, if we wish to attain even a mental inventory of the works of art, furnishing, and valuable objects collected and left behind by two centuries of this dynasty, yields the most disagreeable sensation of finding oneself before an absolute void."[34]

Yet patience reveals the void is in fact not so absolute if we are willing to dig into what remains.[35] This is a matter of a series of structures ravaged by time, piles of stones not always in a happy state of preservation, requiring "rereading" word for word. The clues, as usual, are not lacking—especially regarding the Villa di Sopra la Rocca. Today it bears a singular name: dei Massoni (of the Masons). The terminology seems as casual as it is obvious. The building has a large garden full of sculptures whose ensemble must have some meaning. Sculpture gardens often illustrating the arts and trades are perhaps the most obvious and significant common characteristic of the Cybo villas and palazzos. Their legacy is scattered, divided through hereditary disputes and largely vanished amid alienations to various Genoese knights and to kings, even abroad. Among their various peregrinations, many of these statues were brought to Rome, at Ripa Grande, at the foot of the Aventine—below the house that was first of the Templars and then of the Knights of Malta. They finally ended up at Castel Gandolfo and there form part of the current holdings of the state of the Church—in that same region where, in ancient Alba Longa, the first Latin people ventured across the plain to found Rome.[36]

It was a destiny the Cybo family felt themselves called upon to fulfill: founding the new caput mundi. Correspondences and occurrences and reoccurrences form a plot line without end made up of astounding concordances—such as that pinnacle or pyramid-obelisk, with all the symbolism that emerges from it, surmounted by a rising sun and the motto *sine fine* (without end), the emblem of Lorenzo Cybo. The metaphor is reproduced almost exactly on the U.S. dollar bill on which the spirit that discovered the New World becomes the *novus ordo seclorum* (disquietingly adding the word *ordo,* making the motto "New World Order") in the unifying language of Latin. However, here the course has changed, and the gold of the Indies has been transmuted into multinational finance.

Atop the hills of Rome—in a setting similar to that of the castle of Massa, similar to that of the Belvedere—the Cybo family, within their villas and gardens, reproduced to scale that paradise of lost harmony to be regained, the new order to be given to the world.[37]

From Castel Gandolfo, our view wanders toward the Quirinal Palace. On one of the *seven* fateful hills of Rome stands another palace fundamental to Italian history. It was once a papal palace and today is the palace of the president of the Republic. There, many of the works of art from the legacy of the Cybo family are scattered in the open air of the beautiful gardens. There are a number of statues: mannequins, testimonies carved into stone. There are laundresses, cobblers, knife sharpeners, milliners, mendicants, jesters, commoners, Pierrot and Pulcinella, the memories of a Naples never forgotten, a true gallery of the arts and crafts that were so dear to the Masons. There is also a stupendous sundial; a company with the mythical Hercules fighting the dragon; clowns; satyrs; Bacchus; the great forge of Vulcan with the metal-forging Cyclopes; a Fortuna with a great wheel; Menelaus and Patroclus; Andromeda and Perseus; a young nude who might be Apollo, Adonis, or Orpheus—and an exquisite pavement of black and white checkers, like those appearing in Masonic symbolism.

Snapshots of daily life, protagonists of legend, geometric figures and motifs, masters of the occult: The exact meaning of this succession is difficult to reconstruct, all the more so because (as usual) the archives and documents have gone missing, fueling the mystery without end. The reasons behind certain gifts are not understood. It was Alberico Cybo Malaspina who made greater efforts than anyone else in the name of the family beyond the restoration of the monument to Pope Innocent VIII in St. Peter's Basilica: "He worked with patience, but his efforts toward Popes Pius IV, Gregory XIV, and Clement VIII did not produce the desired effect, and Alberico died in 1623, having achieved progress only in the basic necessities. . . . [N]othing was easier than to obtain the cylindrical base [of the sundial] as a gift from the prince of Massa to one of the popes whom he so actively entreated for elevating the Church of Massa to diocesan or at least collegiate status. The sculpture with the peacock may have been meant to remind the pope of the Cybo file; but this remains within the realm of hypothesis."[38]

Vain efforts, hypotheses, and "files" increase the scope of a Cybo mystery, demanding a further examination of truly vast proportions. The base at the Quirinal, with its great carved peacock, served to support the sundial of Francesco Castelli, son of Battista. It was made by Borromini, yet another esoteric scholar. Several statues were later placed in a beautiful fountain known as the Fountain of the Organ on whose vault we "can see the most beautiful stuccoes, capped by a frieze of rustic mosaics depicting the seven days of creation, the story of Moses and the Hebrew people, and figures from the mythology of the waters."[39]

It is an infinite sequence of personages linked to history, but even more to mythology and to the recondite meaning that transcends immediate meaning, whose explanation eludes common sense—amid events and actions that conglomerate and make even the Cybo sculptures an unsolvable brainteaser. Among the many questions left unanswered is the reconstruction of the complicated movements of these statues.

The same thing always happens in every aspect of a family that has left many strange messages over the centuries in the panorama of public religious and civil life and on the most select offices of the state. "Perpetual defender of Italian peace," reads the epigraph on Innocent's tomb, marking a death that occurred on July 25, 1492, at the Palazzo Venezia—where, as we shall see in more detail later, there is a Mappamondo room. The room, the palace, and the date connect to another central episode in the history of modern Italy: the fall of fascism and Benito Mussolini. In addition, often enough, in the events we are patiently seeking to reconstruct, we encounter the names of various ancestors of the Savoia family, especially in connection with the area of Monferrato (another of Columbus's possible homelands), rich in Crusader knights and lovers of mystery.

We seem to be on a bizarre wild goose chase, bouncing around in time, as in the case of this latest heraldic shield found on a wall of the Palace on the Campidoglio, facing Trajan's Forum—watching over the remains of an ancient grandeur, overlooking St. Peter's prison in memory of the martyrdom of the first pope of Rome.

It is an Ariadne's thread made of stone, running endlessly through past and present among the highest powers of the land: from the president of the Republic to the royal families, the pope, Mussolini, and the first citizens of Rome. All are inseparably linked and alternately placed at the helm of the fate of the eternal city, the caput mundi that was once golden—and would become golden again, thanks to a man who brought together all the powers, religious and civil, in a single person. This man, in an age of destruction and blood, aspired to become a great builder, a grand architect of the universe in addition to being the Vicar of Christ. We owe thanks, too, to a *dilecte fili* (beloved son), programmed and now ready to find and found another world.

EIGHT

Monks,
Knights, and Vikings

AMERICA WAS NOT discovered by chance. Kings, princes, monks, and
knights searched for it. Cartographers attempted to depict and reconstruct it. Christopher Columbus, on his voyage, did not sail into the
absolute unknown. A new world desired to be baptized with water and
gold. Christendom hoped for it, and the pope of Rome wished for it.
America was not just in the air, not merely in the intuitions or fantasies of many lost islands and shores. America was there, albeit not in its
current form, not whole. It was an indistinct land, as concrete as it was
imaginary, made up of a series of individual landfalls independent from
each other and yet at the same time connected. It was the sum of what
had been found on ancient maps and documents, supplemented by the
findings of the most recent explorations and voyages, starting around
the year 1000.

At the time, America presented itself as a fractured series of islands,
an endless archipelago sometimes consolidated into a single great island,
sometimes in the East and sometimes in the West. Sometimes it consisted of scattered and discontinuous pieces of land that awaited further
exploration before obtaining entirety. Indeed, the case was the same for
lands much closer to home, whose depictions often only vaguely corresponded to reality. Further, the term *island* generates the utmost confu-

sion, especially in minds constrained by the modern concept of language, which has lost the meaning of the word.

America was in the maps, books, and minds of ancients, scholars, and geographers, almost all connected to the body of the medieval Church. It was in many minds, in those of the lords and nobles of the world. It was in the sights of those who believed they had the right and the authority to set humanity on a new course. One figure rose above all the rest: the Roman pope. For the others it was a matter of expanding the boundaries of their own dominions. For the pope it was a matter of repudiating what the Church had preached over the centuries—of performing the transition into heterodoxy in the least painful way possible. Could it be admitted that the holy scriptures and fathers of doctrine were bearers of lies? Had Rome been one of the contributors to an age-long darkness?

The error, it was argued in secret, had been only human. The sacred texts were not scientific treatises but had to be read with a symbolic key. Also, the prophecies had continually predicted the New World, the apocalyptic revelation. How could it be interpreted, how could it be realized among men? In the eternal course of history, in the endless battle between hawks and doves, a dove *(colombo)* had been chosen: "Who are these that fly as a cloud / and as the doves to their windows? / Surely the isles shall wait for me, and the ships of Tarshish first, / to bring thy sons from far, their silver and their gold with them, / unto the name of the Lord thy God, and to the Holy One of Israel, because he hath glorified thee . . . Thy sun shall no more go down . . . I create new heavens and a new earth . . . I will gather all nations and tongues . . . the Gentiles shall come unto thee from the ends of the earth."[1] *Isaiah & Jeremiah*

✠

Christopher Columbus made notes in his own hand. Had he not, things might have gone differently and the hawks might have won. Little or nothing remains of the utopia reached five hundred years ago and the transmigration from the dreams of the old world into the new. Yet even today in America there persists the idea and ideal of living in the best of all possible worlds. It is a legacy never completely lost, passing from the age-old dream into the American dream.

Who, then, discovered America before Columbus? Mythical forerunners sinking back into legend: Jason, Hercules, Odysseus . . . and others, more recently recorded in history. What, beyond the sacred waters of the Nile, could have been the distant land of the Egyptians who were so aware of gold and of the sun's path? This question has become all the more pressing because traces of drugs and tobacco, of plants existing only in the other world, have been found bundled with the mummies of the pharaohs—seeds planted in time, sprouting questions as yet unanswered.

There were also sea voyagers of Jewish and pagan blood, voyagers from the long-ago days of Tartessus (the biblical Tarshish?) and the thalassocracy, the Empire of the Sea, and then the Phoenicians, Greeks, Romans, saints, and Vikings—that is, if we keep to the West and especially the Christian world, ignoring the other worlds whose civilizations were not mere spectators. The question is no longer who discovered America, but who succeeded in bringing it definitively into the consciousness of humanity as a piece of information acquired at that moment and retained for all time.

All over the Americas new discoveries slant the statistics in favor of possible "accidental" expeditions, though science persists in ignoring them. The discovery of ever more complex buildings and knowledge renders less and less plausible the myth of the "noble savage" with which the indigenous peoples of the West Indies were identified. Caution is necessary. How much longer can the defenses stand against written and oral tradition, against clues hidden in the etymology of names, against documents, stones that speak, inscriptions that reveal, and objects that do more than simply stir doubts?

The findings keep multiplying; individually they can be refuted, but together they form an unstoppable avalanche. How long will the excuses, silence, and lies remain entrenched, keeping the truth at bay? Lies can be retracted, but when silence reigns—especially where no fault can be proved—silence sounds like assent, despite the courage and brilliance of scientists and scholars working against the current, operating not only amid books but also in the field. Recent solo Atlantic crossings (including those by women), some successfully completed in rowboats, demonstrate that tales often ring truer than science; science—just like the Church, in its day—has told too many tales.

The voyage of the pharaohs' sun, the *sol invictus,* the sun upon which all things depend, has forever fascinated people. Nothing could be more natural in an age when the sun was the supreme expression of the divine for all people—priests, warriors, and laypeople alike—ready to face any danger to solve the mystery of the horizon where each evening the star of day, beneath which all things moved, went to its rest in the bosom of the ocean, in that *ultra,* ripe for exploration, into which the sun ran the risk of vanishing forever. To these people every dawn was a miracle, driving away the fear of the sun's death, but the danger remained, rendered more real by the regularly renewed terror of an eclipse.

Not to mention the primeval instinct for the unknown in men such as Odysseus, the persecuted man condemned to exile upon other shores, the businessman in continual search of riches, never fearing the dangers of injury and shipwreck. With all this, we cannot help but consider the question of an America that was prediscovered and then covered up again by time.

Seneca wrote of this very subject in the tragedy of *Medea,* as Columbus punctiliously noted: *Venient annis saecula seris, quibus Oceanus vincula rerum laxet et ingens pateat tellus Tethysque novos detegat orbes nec sit terris ultima Thule* (In the late years of the world, Ocean shall slacken earth's bonds, and a great land will appear. Tethys will uncover new globes, and Thule shall no longer be the last of the lands). The philosopher had sojourned in Egypt—in Alexandria, that center of knowledge with so many mysteries hidden in its unparalleled library.

Jason, Tethys, and Thule, an unknown *finisterrae* waiting on the other side of the Atlantic.[2] In what direction did it lie? To the north of Hyperborea, as was commonly believed, or in the Hades of the Cimmerians? Hades meant "darkness," "obscurity," and also "the land of the sunset."

On the Mexican coast, far from Europe, in the littoral zone—the area of flat land reaching out toward the turquoise sea—is a Maya settlement still called Tulum, like Thule. It was one of the many sites where the people waited for the return of the white god with the golden beard and handed down his legend: He would arrive riding the waves, a divine knight heralding a new era. The signs were converging on both sides of the world, and the last of lands could only announce the last of times. Matthew confirmed it, as transcribed by Columbus: "And I say to you that many shall come from the East and the West and shall sit down with Abraham and Isaac and Jacob in the Kingdom of Heaven."[3]

"Of two flocks," adds St. Gregory in his homilies, "he makes one, uniting Jews and Gentiles in one faith."[4]

✠

On his journeys the mariner Columbus traveled in all directions before that fateful year 1492. To verify his readings and studies, he went to the north, to Ireland, Iceland, and almost certainly Greenland.

In the month of February in 1477 I sailed a hundred leagues beyond the island of Thyle, the southern part of which is distant from the equinoctial 73 degrees, and not 63 as some wish it to be; nor does it lie upon the line where Ptolemy's west begins, but much more toward the West. And to this island, which is as large as England, the English come for traffic, and especially those of Bristol. And at the time I was there the sea was not frozen, but there were great tides, so that in some places the sea rose 25 *braccia* twice each day, and fell the same.[5]

On this voyage, Columbus relates, Ptolemy's incomplete globe was modified, adding the world of the great beyond, located "much more toward the West." These were coasts to which the English regularly traveled. The vainglorious Columbus could have hidden this fact in order to claim primacy, but the navigator did not cheat; he chose the path of truth, progressively gathering all the elements of those who ventured before him on this unknown path, leaving no point of the compass unattended.

He went to the west as far as the Canary Islands, the Spanish trampoline from which to make the leap farther forward into the Atlantic. He rounded the coast of Africa to the south, as far as Guinea, with its Portuguese gold mines. He went to the East, to the island of Chios, the island of the Cybo, the last Christian outpost in the body of Islam. His thorough and painstaking search reached to the limits of a knowledge he increased first-hand, through direct experience, as far as possible given the geopolitical conditions of those years.

Columbus studied the winds, the currents, the movements of the seas, and the hourly changes, gathering written documentation and oral tradition. He observed, compared, summarized, and catalogued. He examined the evidence washed up on shore: unknown fruits and plants, strange woodcarvings, and the bodies of shipwrecked alien creatures the ocean deposited on its beaches. The land to be reached was speaking, sending messages, and calling out. Columbus's modernity lay in not being content with hearsay or with the writings and accounts of those who had preceded him in his incessant quest like a paladin of the Grail.

Greek texts, Roman texts, documents, and ever more remote maps told of long-ago voyages that alone were enough to belie another dogma— that the ancient navigators had never sailed far from the coast. Such caution may suit the bulletins read by today's Sunday sailors, but not men who burned with the desire to conquer and overcome whatever seemed forbidden to them. For a man with a thirst for knowledge, no challenge is more urgent than stealing the forbidden fruit—especially in a historical epoch in which risking one's life counted in certain cases as a holy sacrifice and death as an auspicious event in the cycle of existence, a mystery not to be confused with terror but rather to be transmuted into a prize.

If we were to make a list of Columbus's forerunners, a single volume would not suffice. Thus we will limit ourselves to a few examples, not neglecting the most recent research revealing a Greek presence on the

Atlantic coast of Iberia, in many cases leading to the area in Spain from which Columbus sailed.[6]

The Greeks and Phoenicians were maritime peoples united in the curiosity that defied the Pillars of Hercules. They were present in settlements that formed the historic counterpoint to the neuralgic zone: Huelva, Palos, and Cadiz, the "wings" of Christopher Columbus. Was this a predestined geographic area, a matter of chance, or a willed outcome? This might be elucidated in the prophecy Columbus mentioned in his writings: "The Calabrese abbot Joachim said that he who is to rebuild Mount Zion must come from Spain."[7]

This might explain Columbus's move from Portugal to Spain, contemporary with the accession of the Greek-Genoese Innocent VIII to the throne of St. Peter. Near Huelva is a Franciscan cloister where, according to tradition, a penniless, ragged, and weary Columbus, accompanied by his son Diego, came seeking aid. On old maps we find a "point of Umbria" and a "tower of Umbria," because the area was *ombrosa* (meaning "shady" or "shadowy"). This seems, moreover, to indicate a green, shady Italian enclave on Spanish soil. Umbria, the region of St. Francis and his order, left an indelible and lifelong imprint on the navigator's destiny.

✠

Columbus's move to Spain and Innocent's accession coincided—and not in the sense of a coincidence. Modern times connected perfectly with ancient times in the *forma mentis* of the Renaissance. Spain's sails were set for the world of the hereafter where today Mexicans celebrate the *calavera* (meaning "skull") or perhaps *vera cara,* "dear truth" in Italian, the true face of the netherworld). The skulls now appear as candy and in wild dances. Columbus's caravels sailed toward the *calavera* in a suggestive play on words veiling and unveiling the unrevealable.

This was a time in which every name, like every number, concealed profound meanings, as in the ingenious art of the Kabbalah. Columbus's departure from the Canary Islands appeared as a farewell to the farthest point of the known West, but it would forge a path toward the revelation of the farthest, still unknown West, the West that, in its turn when the world was circled, would become the East, the birthplace of a new day. Thus the alpha is identified biblically with the omega, as in St. John's Apocalypse, as in Columbus's words: "Like the Ouroboros, the mythical serpent wrapped around the globe, devouring its own tail, thus opposites meet and are reconciled, in a perfect Great Work."

The enigma of the flat earth remains to be solved, as does that of Ptolemy's earth terminating to the south. How could such a thing be possible, considering the ancient Egyptians had believed Africa to be surrounded by sea, and the Greeks had believed the ocean embraced the whole earth like a great river? Had not Homer and Herodotus[8] written of a circumnavigation to the south, from east to west? And had not the Phoenicians' voyages proved it?

For many ages, the maps had spoken a language different from the chorus, and no one seemed willing to listen. It is continually asserted that the ancients did not confront the open seas. It is repeated *ad nauseam* that medieval people believed the earth was flat. "It is only in recent times (within the last two centuries) that this strange belief has been attributed to medieval people. . . . Secular thought in the nineteenth century, irritated by the fact that the Church had not accepted the heliocentric hypothesis, attributed to all Christian thought (patristic and scholastic) the idea that the earth was flat. This idea was reinforced in the course of the prolonged struggle of the defenders of the Darwinian hypothesis against all forms of fundamentalism."[9]

At a distance of centuries, even with enlightenment and reason triumphant, the earth continued to be deformed by intellectual battles, by the scientific Taliban. Obscurantism was not a one-way street limited to those so-called Dark Ages. Thus even the Church might be partially acquitted in the great argument over the shape of the world.[10]

"How," Umberto Eco inquires, "could the sphericity of the earth be unknown in an age when armillary spheres were studied?" This is a prosaic and elementary question that has been posed time after time. Similar questions can be asked when we look at Roman coins[11] or think of the shadows cast by eclipses—but above all, when we consider iconography over the centuries. God Almighty, Christ, the Infant Jesus, Madonna, saints, emperors, rulers, and lords—all are commonly depicted holding a sphere in their hands or beneath their feet. The depiction of their fingers and hands shows the palm always in a concave position, holding a sphere and not a flat disc. No one disputes this when looking at sculptures.

To this we might add the singular discrepancy between nautical maps and world maps.[12] Nautical maps are almost perfect, and they appeared quite suddenly. What maps inspired them? Did the world maps complicate them to the point of deforming reality, perhaps in order to preserve the unknown or to hide secrets?[13]

Due to widespread illiteracy and lack of education, the possibility of a voyage to the south, where the lands would presumably be upside down, was thought to entail some difficulties. The fear was the product of naïveté and ignorance, and those who held the power of knowledge, albeit only approximate knowledge could not have had this fear.

How was the deception devised? Perhaps it was successful because the earth was represented and illustrated as though on a plane or through symbols and metaphors, which was the most widespread language. Was it a consequence of the principles of projection and various calculations, lost to us today, regarding the shape of the world? Doubt as to the roundness of the world no longer seems to persist. The so-called T maps are inscribed in a circle: The *orbis terrarum* formed a Tau; a perfect trinity; the union of Europe, Africa, and Asia. At the same time, it was the cross and the Tree of Life, the projection of the Tau of the earthly Jerusalem and the Franciscans.

Then, after some five hundred years of silence, in two world maps the three familiar continents were joined to a fourth at the extreme West. Its resulting shape is one of a small half-moon.[14]

The map from 1086, preserved at the cathedral in El Burgo de Osma, shows, in somewhat rough illustration, a condensation of many of the elements forming the background for the discovery of the Americas: Paradise, the evangelization of all the lands preceding the Last Judgment, St. James Matamoros—the enemy of Islam, and those monsters with a large single foot guarding the unknown which had to be faced. The fourth continent posed a problem to the faith. Columbus was convinced and could not be persuaded otherwise that North America was part of the Indies, a continuation of the land route but separate and far beyond known Asia and having nothing to do with China. This, in the Western view, made it part of the Indies. There remained the theological obstacle presented by South America, which the navigator held to be separated from North America by a strait, on the basis of the ancient maps in his possession. The fourth world, he thought, would appear only after crossing this theoretical span of sea, upon reaching the true antipodes.

Because the southern regions of Africa and America are more or less on the same parallels, it was obviously believed the heat of the sun would be equal in those hypothetical regions, and the monsters inhabiting these scorching lands would be similar. This explains the presence on the "heretical" Osma map of an antipode and a monopod (a human with a single, great foot) standing guard over the fourth world, which was inhabited by a race that was animal in that its members were not Christian—beings who, by reason of their separation from the rest of the world, could not be descendents of Adam, sons of God. A great deal of salt water and Native American blood would pass under the bridge before it was admitted that these people also had souls and were human. The question was debated throughout the sixteenth century. Moreover, Columbus's presumed erroneous geographic ideas were upheld for many decades after his discovery. Not even the glorified Amerigo Vespucci—he who became the tool for giving a convenient name to the new continent, and would hide Columbus's role—would be immune to them.

The problem of the acceptance of a terrestrial globe that was no longer the geographic expression of the Trinity was so divisive that the novelty was long refuted, even in the face of what had, by this time, become full-blown evidence.[15] Thus people took refuge in the myth of Atlantis, the lost continent, and of lands that had always been known.[16]

Difficulties and obstacles clearly emerged to impede the modernization of geography. A series of more or less unconscious mechanisms sprang up, sometimes in good faith, defending the more reassuring old world and confronting the new to the point of refuting it. Such was the aftershock of the devastating impact caused by Columbus's theories and voyages.

Columbus knew and understood that the ancient maps he possessed, like those of Innocent VIII, were the most accurate. He acted as a Christian in the best possible ways in order not to bring damage to the image and traditions of the Church. It was the other people who did not understand or who refused to understand, the others who persisted in not understanding or allowing anything to be understood, mixing up the maps and hiding the truth.

Geography was unstable, elastic, and counterfeited, interpreted and rendered according to biased interests, governed by the words of the Church. Nascent science, almost exclusively in ecclesiastical hands, sought to defend tradition and remain faithful to the providential design foretold in the prophecies—but the appetites of the potential masters of the world were growing dangerously in proportion to the novelties they saw before them. Islands and nations appeared and disappeared and shifted and multiplied and would continue to do so—Atlantis, Antilya, Cipango, El Dorado . . .[17]

Geography was as errant as the waves of the ocean in a maritime labyrinth in search of a new Neptune who would reimpose the lost order. A Columbus-Neptune, in the geographic corridors of the Vatican, would ride the waves of the water replete with new lands.

If the ancients, the pagans, were among the first forerunners of Columbus, then what Christians had preceded him? Let us begin with the legend of St. Brendan, the Irish monk who just happened to decorate his sails with a red cross on a white background—the same cross that was on Columbus's sails—and whose destination just happened to be the Promised Land. The route, this time, passed through the Great North. The expedition sought a route not through the "boiling" world, but through the frozen world, and left from one island in search of another.[18]

It took the monk seven (the apocalyptic number *par excellence*) years to reach the "western land." He confronted vicissitudes and dangers of every type, brushing past mountains and menacing crystal towers (icebergs) along a route that must have gone via Iceland and Greenland, finally landing on the North American coast in the northern regions of Newfoundland (Terranova, the "new land"). In those times the climate conditions were apparently favorable and tempests were less frequent. The legendary chronicle of this learned monk and navigator saint is peppered with recurring numbers. "The medieval author was often tempted to use his numbers symbolically—perhaps three to reflect the Trinity, twelve the apostles, and of course that vague favorite of 'forty days' to represent 'a long time' which is used regularly in the *Navigatio.*"[19]

The proof is lacking, but on the Faeroe Islands record was preserved of the *papars,* as the Irish monks were called. The Irish landscape, a contrast of rugged and smooth, always facing the sea, leads to meditation and inspiration to breach the limits of an aquatic horizon that is simultaneously a space of endless freedom and a prison—a maze in which to venture, a playground of light and dark, like pawns on a chessboard, beyond which the mythical opposite shore might hide those same delights. The landscape is a destination as green as the Garden of Eden, a land of holy and pious men, a land of redemption.

After St. Brendan had completed his long voyage, he encountered a man who told him, "Return, then, to your native land, carrying with you the fruits of this land and as many jewels as your little boat can hold. . . . After many ages have passed, this land will be made known to your successors at a time when Christians are undergoing persecution. This river that you see divides this island. Just as it appears to you laden with fruit, so the land will remain forever without the shadow of night, for its light is Christ."[20]

It was a land to be revealed, an Edenic and earthly reserve. It is hard to establish whether these words were prophesy, legend, or truth. Although St. Brendan left a lasting record of his voyage, little or nothing is known of those who went before him: St. Barrind, another Irish monk, who was accompanied by an abbot named Mernoc from western Ireland, traveled regularly to and from those far-off lands, as St. Brendan's *Navigatio* records. Such voyages became increasingly frequent, bearing the stamp of pastoral missions stirred by a single religious inspiration as men took to the seas in the service of God, trusting Him to be merciful and to guarantee their salvation in all senses. The destination, first for the Irish and later for the Vikings, was a Nirvana far removed from the evils of the world: "Europe from the tenth century onward was already perceiving the New World in the manner of the time."[21]

The epic of St. Brendan spans a period from between 489 to 583. It was a time of favorable climatic conditions. Such conditions returned between 900 and 1200 and also during Columbus's time.

The Norwegian expeditions took place around the fateful year 1000, about the same year Christianity was introduced into Ireland, a time consequently peaceful yet suffused with apocalyptic implications—though not as pressing as at the end of the fifteenth century. First, the Vikings reached Iceland, and then Greenland. Christians, who could no longer coexist with pagan peoples, had already reached Iceland. Some of the first people to settle there came from Ireland, almost certainly followers of St. Brendan. In the north, as in the south, every move forward was made in the name of the advance of Christianity. The transition from monks to Nordic pioneers was swift.

The millennium brought the arrival of Erik the Red, the great conqueror chief of Greenland. The saga of Erik and his companions, just like that of St. Brendan, involves a long, inhospitable journey along the edge of the endless ice in the arctic regions. Based around the North Sea and the Baltic, the Vikings were the epitome of a proud and courageous people. Around 886 they had even reached Constantinople, the source of many maps. They took to the sea in swift, light boats, and their oral tradition included the voyages of their own version of Odysseus. This legend was passed from one generation to the next, but was not written down until the fourteenth century; a written version is preserved in the Copenhagen library.

Long-ago Icelandic chronicles tell of Greenland, Helluland (Labrador or Newfoundland), Markland (Nova Scotia), and Vinland, retracing familiar routes. Three texts survive, parchments and manuscripts telling of people who lived in the mist and fog and now live on in the mist and fog of history: Erik the founder; Bjarni, who followed in his footsteps; Leif the Fortunate, who bought his ship and set sail upon the waves exactly at the millennium.[22]

It was an apocalyptic year, a year of revelation. Leif christened the shores on which he landed during his voyage. Finally, after leaving the great ice, he reached a land with a milder climate and green foliage, where the day and night were nearly equal in length. The natives lived in grottos and caverns. They told of a great, vast land where the men wore garments and had white skin. The place would be called Great Ireland.

Grape vines and wild grains grew in abundance; they called it Vinland, the green land, the land of vines. It is strange that in view of all the gifts from God this land placed before their incredulous eyes they limited themselves to speaking of the plants already known—and wild plants at that. Yet the green land, with grains and grapes, assumed significance and profound meaning in symbolic terms. The green land is Paradise—green is the color of hope—and the grain is the symbol of rebirth and resurrection—the wheat grains, like the seeds of the pomegranate, represent the people united by faith. The wine made from grapes is the blood of Christ. Christ is the vine, its trellises the apostles. The vine is the Tree of the Cross and the Resurrection (death and life), and the grape harvest announces the Last Judgment and the end of time. Such was the harvest Leif gathered in the year 1000.

Leif's brother Thorvald followed in his wake. The saga continues: There was a first battle with the natives of this land, who fought from their three canoes. Struck by an arrow, Thorvald asked his men to bury him in the new land, where he had wished to dwell: "There shall ye bury me, and set crosses at my feet and head, and call the place Krossaness [Cape of the Cross], forever, in all time to come." Perhaps it was the first cross planted in American soil in the land that, even in Columbus's time, was called the Land of the Holy Cross.

Leif's other brother, Thorstein, sailed in search of the slain Thorvald, taking his wife Gudrid with him. He also died, and Gudrid returned to Greenland. She did not remain a widow for long. A rich and powerful man appeared, a descendant from a noble family, a revered and prestigious man with blood ties to kings and nobles. His name was Thorfinn and he was known as Karlsefni, an appellation implying predestination. The anointed and cross-signed man could not remain deaf to the call of Icelandic legends told by the fireside, and Gudrid did not hesitate in enticing him to new adventures.

This time it was an expedition in full regalia, involving the large family of Erik the Red. Three ships, one hundred and sixty men, and the objective was to colonize and Christianize the New World. As the expedition proceeded into the unknown, the climate became more temperate, the landscape more luxuriant and wooded. They were catching glimpses of Paradise—until they landed and encountered the natives with their canoes.

The first encounter was amicable. The Vikings and the indigenous people fraternized and did some trading. The natives had a liking for red fabrics, glass beads, knives, and spears, the kind of junk Columbus is reproached for having brought in order to cheat the natives. The explorers brought their livestock on shore. Gudrid gave birth to a son: a new child was born, as if in a manger. Soon enough, as winter approached, the situation grew complicated. Relations with the natives had changed; harmony was broken, and there was war.

Karlsefni, who had earlier borne a white shield as a sign of peace, now raised the red shield. It signaled a long journey. Forced to return to the seas, the Vikings later believed they had sighted the land of the monopods, people with a single great foot. The saga continues, but the most important elements in terms of our research have already been enumerated. Myth and legend, fantasy and reality, geography and history are once again joined and mingled, making it difficult to pick out the thread leading to the truth. Yet a number of conclusive facts and precise references do remain.

Conversion to Christianity made the transcription of the sagas of the Nordic cultural heritage possible in a pagan-Christian syncretism. Among the authors of the texts were two churchmen of the Benedictine abbey of Thingeyrar, where the first sagas of the missionary kings were also written down. The originals were manipulated.[23]

✠

From St. Brendan to the Vikings, there appears to be comprehensive proof that others preceded Columbus's adventure—and in the name of the faith. The dates 500 to 1500 were marked by predictions of the end of the world. Many things resonated in time periods marking five and ten centuries—as if the story of the *Navigatio* were being replicated with only the route being different. The means and end remained identical.

Edenic lands and boundless forests brimming over with all the gifts of God; pre-Adamites with one foot; men in canoes; white-skinned and white-clothed natives (also encountered by Columbus's sailors); predestined Christian navigators, propagators of the faith; crusading expeditions; lands of the cross; red fabrics; glass beads and blades—in a sequence of events returning to the number three of the Trinity: three days, three ships, three children, three lands visited, and so on. The monk St. Brendan merges with the Viking sagas, and the Viking sagas lead to Columbus. Did Columbus read about St. Brendan's voyage and the sagas? In any case, Columbus had been to Ireland and may have traveled farther to Iceland and Greenland and even to North America. With whom did he go?

The history of the north and explorations from there into the great beyond as the millennium drew near grows increasingly closer to the history of Christianity.[24]

Rome was well aware of events, especially since Gudrid, the intrepid woman who had traveled to Vinland, went to the holy city as a pilgrim. She was received by Pope Benedict VIII. She told him of the "green land" and the world still unknown. Once she returned to her homeland, she spent the last years of her life in a nunnery.[25]

Greenland, which was believed to be joined to the continent of Europe, had its own bishop elected under Pope Paschal II, around 1100, for the *regionumque finitarum*. His name was Erik Gnupson. Pilgrims from Greenland and Iceland traveled all the way to Rome.[26]

In 1448 Nicholas V chose a bishop of Greenland. By then, Columbus's time was approaching: "In the late 1400s, the Christians of Greenland sent an urgent petition to Innocent VIII for their salvation, endangered as they were by the scarcity of means of sustenance, which threatened to put an end to this farthest western outpost of Christian civilization."[27]

Plot lines were intertwining. We also learn that "although Pope Innocent VIII had appointed one Matthias bishop of Greenland, he had heard nothing from him, not even whether he went there. . . . The rest is silence. What can have happened?"[28]

The usual deafening silence occurs—everything regarding Innocent VIII is uncertain and full of gaps. His universalistic interests, however, obvious by now, did not neglect the far-off north, where Christians were suffering, as in Egypt, as in the East—awaiting redemption.

The strange silence appears to have been broken when, "in a brief of August 10, 1492 [note the date], Pope Alexander VI lamented the decline of the faith in Greenland . . ."[29]

Here we see a singular mistake. Namely, in the letter the name of America appears prior to that land's christening. Moreover, reference is made to another pre-Columbian voyage on the part of those who had deviated from "just faith and from Christianity"—heading for a continent, America, where the arrival of the Spanish grew ever closer. The most important aspect of the document is not the news of this umpteenth expedition, but its date, which represents a real puzzle.

The day of Alexander VI's investiture was August 26. On August 10, he had not yet fully taken office. Could this brief have been copied from an earlier one referring to a different pope, altered retroactively and with the date changed, as happened in other documents? Perhaps this was one of the many errors committed by the falsifiers of the discovery of America in their imperfect crime, their capsizing of truth and justice. Columbus had set sail only a few days earlier; apparently the operation seeking to change and subvert the aims of the voyage to the Americas was set in motion simultaneously with a series of counterfeit proofs.

In the end, Columbus and his pope, also moved with perfect coordination on the northern front, with Columbus visiting the possible launching places for the voyage to the New World in person and the pope weaving the web of connections and possible support. The long arm of the greedy Alexander VI also reached toward the northern front.

With the Vikings, the sciapods or monopods also reappear, those creatures drawn upon the heretical maps showing a fourth world, probably referring only to South America—or else to a Vinland understood generally as the unknown or pagan world. "It happened that one morning Karlsefni and his people caught sight of a red light approaching them, and they raised shouts of amazement. This shape moved and was a being with one foot which hopped toward the shore where they stood."[30]

Icelandic crews included sailors who came from other regions, perhaps Italians, Scotsmen, and Englishmen. From these lands sailed forth an extremely long list of other presumed pioneers coming from all over Europe. They were not fishing for people to convert; they were genuine fishermen, such as the Basques, people of Celtic-Iberian descent, yet more prediscoverers.

What led them toward America, in this case, was the codfish. It was a staple of their diet; almost half their calendar was given over to fast days, days of salted cod. The Basques were the suppliers, growing increasingly rich and fishing along a route they kept secret. The cod came from a land across the sea. "Cod became almost a religious icon—a mythological crusader for Christian observance.... But where was all this cod coming from? The Basques, who had never even said where they came from, kept their secret. By the fifteenth century, this was no longer easy to do . . . The Bretons, who tried to follow the Basques, began talking of a land across the sea."[31]

From all places people were pressing forward into the unknown toward the same goal. It is impossible to think none among them were ever able to reach it.

In Bristol in 1480 a wealthy customs official, Thomas Croft, partnered with John Jay and together they took their first voyage in search of an island named Hy-Brasil. Nothing has remained from their two expeditions; the two men were "discreet like the Basques," but the voyages resulted in incrimination because it was illegal for an English customs official to be involved in commerce with a foreigner. It was believed the cod had been purchased somewhere. Croft was acquitted; he swore he had not bought it, but that it came from the far-off regions of the Atlantic. The region *par excellence* of the valuable fish was later revealed as Newfoundland.

As if this were not enough, "[to] the glee of the British press, a letter has recently been discovered. The letter had been sent to Christopher Columbus a decade after the Croft affair in Bristol, while Columbus was taking bows for his discovery of America. The letter, from Bristol merchants, alleged that he knew perfectly well that they had been to America already."[32]

Columbus knew this well enough to write it, as we have seen, as if it were an obvious truth. He related that John Cabot had sailed from Bristol, reaching Newfoundland and Labrador. Unfortunately, the letter discovered "[to] the glee of the British press" appears to confirm the familiar claims to a nonexistent primacy, the familiar complacent advancement of the suspicion that Columbus's glory was not real. His glory remains from whatever we might think of the endless competition. Who discovered America first? It doesn't matter. Columbus wasn't the first? Of course not—he was the last, the definitive one. It was he who, with his imprimatur, made the final move in the age-old game, in the hall of mirrors reflecting the mirages of the sea. He turned a combination of known and unknown into a distinct shoreline upon which the story of the entire human race could begin anew. He projected phantom lands onto the future of humanity. What use was it being first when being first had no consequence for humanity? The consequences ensued only after Columbus made his voyage, pulling back the veil from what had been covered in an act equivalent to discovering: revealing. No one can take away Columbus's role as the revealer of the Americas.

In concluding this Nordic chapter, we must not forget the base of

La Rochelle, the port of the Templars, those eternal suspects whom enthusiastic devotees of this order hold were the exclusive discoverers of America, amid the countless other precursors of Columbus. La Rochelle, over the years, became the natural base from which to sail for the cod shoals of North America: "Of the one hundred twenty-eight fishing expeditions to Newfoundland between Cabot's first voyage and 1550, more than half were from La Rochelle."[33]

The port's location is ideal for expeditions toward a single goal: America via two possible routes, one to the north and one to the south. La Rochelle faces the Atlantic, near the island of Aix, where "St. Malo took refuge. . . . And it is hypothesized that this bishop and monk, famous in his time, may have accompanied St. Brendan on his *Navigatio*."[34]

The stories continue to intertwine. The Templars had gold and especially silver in a time when precious metals were becoming scarce in Europe. Where did they get them? At the very moment when King Philip the Fair unleashed persecution upon the Templars in France, their fleet put to sea and was never seen again. One of the order's seals bears the words *Secretum templi* and the image of a man who looks like a Native American: "Dressed in a simple loincloth, he wears a feather headdress such as is worn by the indigenous peoples of North America, Mexico, and Brazil, or at least some of them, and he holds a bow in his right hand. . . . [To] the left, above the bow [there is] a swastika with curved arms, in exactly the same form that was prevalent in Scandinavia at the time of the Vikings, and on the right, at the same height, an *odal* or rune of Odin."[35]

This voyage is necessarily vague. It concludes with Prince Henry Sinclair, Count of Saint Clair of the Orkneys, sending to the New World a fleet of twelve ships funded by the Templars' money. The expedition, guided by the Venetian Zeno brothers—yet more discoverers of America, coming from Marco Polo's hometown and originally from Padua—landed in Nova Scotia. Before 1400 they explored the East Coast of what is now the United States.[36]

A map of these lands supposedly reached Venice. A number of

cartographers in recent years have "finally proved that the Zeno map was correct after making a startling discovery. There was once a group of islands between Greenland and Iceland that no longer exists today."[37]

Also, in 1394, the bishop sent to the Orkneys by Pope Boniface IX (Tomacelli Cybo) made his voyage in a Sinclair vessel.[38] The Sinclairs, for their part, had strong ties to the Vikings. Their clan was allied to a secret society outlawed in Europe. The founder of the Knights Templar, Hugh de Payens, appears to have been related by marriage to the Norman Saint Clair family.[39] The pieces of the puzzle continue to fit together.

It was subsequently a descendent of William Sinclair, a knight decorated with the Golden Fleece,[40] who had a singular edifice built a few miles outside of Edinburgh and completed in the mid 1480s. A church sprang up that was more than a church—a sanctuary whose "symbolism is Egyptian, Celtic, Jewish, Templar, and Masonic in profusion."[41]

Resembling a miniature Chartres transplanted onto a green hill in Scotland, it was part of an even more ambitious project, halted halfway from completion. Among the many carvings, ears of American maize appear before their time. The Sinclair family always had members connected with Catholicism, paganism, heresy, esotericism, Masonry, and Rosicrucianism. They were expert builders and lovers of divination. Their knowledge went back to the builders of the Temple and to sacred geometry.

✠

Once again the paths converge, leading from St. Brendan to the sagas, halfway between dreams and reality, spanning five generations from 870 to 1030. From brave Vikings to mysterious Templars, many details lead to the same lands; many plot lines lead to the same persons. Meanwhile, amid visions and reveries, one certainty is reinforced: the terminal of all knowledge is always Rome.

The men who traveled were carrying the cross. Upon their return, all information they gathered would reach the Church of Rome, which at the time remained the single depository of those ideas, those messages, those secrets—so much so that our protagonists, in light of what happened subsequently, appear to have formed the legitimate vanguard of a great project. What was the order given to Leif by King Olaf Tryggvason regarding his exploration? "I believe that this [the voyage] must be carried out, and that you must bring Christianity there, at my order," until the time when the definitive Christo Ferens appeared. The ways and means would be established by Rome and the pontificate—even if they then washed their hands of the consequences.

The same long shadow has fallen upon more recent investigations by Thor Heyerdahl, the Norwegian anthropologist who died in 2002, and Per Lilliestrom, a Swedish expert in cartography. According to them, all the exploration of North America, reaching as far as the area of present-day New York, was performed with the approval and under the auspices of the Catholic Church of Rome. Heyerdahl pointed out the mistake, mentioned earlier, on the part of the Icelandic bishop Gisli Oddson, who used the puzzling word "America" when transcribing fourteenth-century records. Lilliestrom adds that this *ante litteram* America was already receiving visitors: The European "population peaked around the year 1100. It appears that about ten thousand Norwegian Crusaders sailed through the Straits of Gibraltar that year on their return from the Middle East, but they do not seem to have returned to their homeland of Norway."[42]

In confirmation of this thesis, the controversial Map of Vinland preserved at Yale University in the United States—yet another forgery, according to orthodoxy deaf to reason—is completely vindicated. This map tells us that in 1117, Vinland-America was visited by an apostolic legate, a certain Henricus, who was bishop of Greenland and the surrounding areas.[43] "Evidently there was a congregation existing at the time in Vinland, in America, otherwise the pope would not have sent a man of such high position within the ecclesiastical hierarchy."[44]

Thus America was discovered and rediscovered countless times, in a tangled web of interests, sometimes economic and sometimes sacred, and by an endless sequence of discoverers lured there from all directions by the dream of wealth and gold, but above all by the evangelical advance, in the sense of a return to the true spirit of the gospels. Many among the long list of voyagers, known and unknown, might have had claims and rights to assert, but the strong pacts between Spain and the Vatican would deal the final cards and draw the final maps, and so America appeared, or rather, reappeared.

NINE

Marco Polo and America–Cipango

THERE WERE NOT only geographical maps behind Columbus's project, but also a book—in fact, more than just a book. It was an old book, an ancient book, a mysterious document, and another path to the truth. It would be made known in the *Pleitos colombinos,* the lengthy suit brought by Columbus's descendents against the Spanish crown. The Turkish admiral Piri Reis repeatedly confirmed it. From what era did this text originate? Had it come from the Library of Alexandria or had it been written later? The maps have been lost in the mists of history—but Columbus read them, learned, and made notes. His notes number at least twenty-five hundred. He annotated the pages of his books with monastic and obsessive patience.

Of his library, of the sources of his dreams, very little remains. There is enough for us to understand who this singular mariner effectively was—especially if we consider that in his time books were extremely expensive and their distribution was highly privileged. They would not have been within the means or inclinations of a modest seaman. Knowledge was guarded by the men of the Church and Gutenberg's invention did not open it up to the masses, but only to the rich.

The navigator, despite the ignorance attributed to him, wrote in 1501: "Our Lord gave me what was needed of astrology [what we now

181

call astronomy], and likewise of geometry and arithmetic, as well as an intelligent soul and the ability to draw maps, and on these the cities, rivers, and mountains all put in their proper place. In this time I took care to study the books of cosmography, history, chronicles, and philosophy, and of other sciences." He was a man of universal interests. If we add, as he himself relates, that his knowledge was derived from texts in Greek, Latin, Hebrew, and other languages, then it becomes evident we are speaking of a profound scholar—all the more so considering the evaluation of Columbus is based on only his surviving books. Most of them have disappeared or were made to disappear.[1]

The fact is ignored that Columbus's youth, maturation, and formative years are a black hole. During this time, his association with the Franciscans would have allowed him access to their libraries, which were among the richest and most current with respect to the lands of the East. No heed is paid to the language barriers Columbus faced: His syntax and orthography, which leave something to be desired, are natural for someone with no fatherland and no mother tongue. The navigator switched from his original language to the cosmopolitan jargon of the seas, to Portuguese, and then to Castilian Spanish. Many of the Italian expressions appearing in his writings are in fact Maltese expressions[2] from the language of the Greek islands, which in those days was spoken by the Knights of Rhodes, now those of Malta. It was the language of a family coming from Greece, such as the Cybos. Moreover, the knowledge of Latin, the sacred language, was the prerogative of men of the Church. Finally, Columbus's handwriting, like his brother's, was the script typical of clerics—in a world where illiteracy prevailed. Thus, from the ink the phantom of a monastic knight emerges.

In the crucible of a time in which the world's wisdom was mixed and muddled, Plato was a reemerging prophet. His Atlantis was confused with Antilla, the landfall lost beneath the ocean of ages toward which the Florentine Paolo dal Pozzo Toscanelli urged Columbus to sail beyond the Pillars of Hercules, conquering the darkness of those vast waters. Plato had written of Atlantis; over the millennia, its name had entered the imaginations of sages seeking a primordial paradise created by man on earth, a mythical Shangri-La, Avalon, Valhalla, Eden . . . lost, and waiting to be reconquered. For Plato, *soul* meant the vital force, wind, and spirit "without which living beings would not exist." For Plato, *faith* "meant being so smitten by something that one put faith in that thing's existence."[3]

Like faith in the search for the East by way of the West, the faith in the soul-spirit moved in the living beings of all faiths. These were ideas and ideals forming part of Columbus's intellectual background—like the myth of Atlantis.[4]

Two of Plato's *Dialogues* to resurface in the Renaissance mention Atlantis: the *Timaeus* and the *Critias*. The former tells of a golden age nine thousand years earlier, during the origins of Athens; a sudden military defeat at the hands of a people from far away; and a lost memory following a series of terrifying natural disasters that wiped out a primordial civilization. This was the time of the Deluge. They are words humanity has pondered for centuries:

> For these histories tell of a mighty power which unprovoked made an expedition against the whole of Europe and Asia, and to which your city put an end. This power came forth out of the Atlantic Ocean, for in those days the Atlantic was navigable; and there was an island situated in front of the straits which are by you called the Pillars of Heracles; the island was larger than Libya and Asia put together, and was the way to other islands, and from these you might pass to the whole of the opposite continent which surrounded the true ocean. . . . [T]hat other is a real sea, and the surrounding land may be most truly called a boundless continent. Now in this island of Atlantis . . . there occurred violent earthquakes and floods; and in a single day and night of misfortune all your warlike men in a body sank into the earth, and the island of Atlantis in like manner disappeared in the depths of the sea. For which reason the sea in those parts is impassable and impenetrable, because there is a shoal of mud in the way; and this was caused by the subsidence of the island.[5]

A few words, a millennia-long puzzle, an Atlantic Ocean navigable "in those days": The theme is repeated in the *Critias*. The interlocutors are the same on the same day, between 410 and 407 BC. The dialogue is incomplete, but its argument is the origin of the ideal state and the hypothesis of a political utopia: the visions of the Renaissance, the visions of Innocent VIII and Columbus.

The visions went back nine thousand years, to the war between the peoples on the two sides of the Pillars of Hercules: "Of the combatants on the one side, the city of Athens was reported to have been the leader and to have fought out the war; the combatants on the other side were commanded by the kings of Atlantis, which . . . was an island greater in extent than Libya and Asia, and when afterwards sunk by an earthquake, became an impassable barrier of mud to voyagers sailing from hence to any part of the ocean."[6]

A golden age, a utopian state, and a lost society to be refounded: the past was emerging from study as well as from excavation. Each discovery was another indicator of a cycle that had ended. Another cycle must begin, new and old simultaneously.

The Renaissance was the most concrete and confident effort made by the human spirit for a full convergence upon the ideal, a universal plenitude. The ideal was the state, the ideal city, as in the surreal and metaphysical painting by Luciano Laurana.[7]

Idealized meetings between people, such as the Queen of Sheba's visit to King Solomon, were repeatedly depicted in artistic masterpieces. Had this queen sailed across the Mediterranean and into the Atlantic Ocean, as a Hebrew document in the papal archive relates? Was it she who, "ninety-five degrees to the west, via an easy passage," reached a land known as Sypanso (Cipango), which Pinzón, the Spanish sailor who steered the caravels with Columbus, had confused with Japan—a land "fertile and luxuriant, whose vastness exceeded that of Africa and of Europe"?[8]

Man was meant to be ideal: the new Adam, like Leonardo's *Vitruvian Man,* a golden fusion as in alchemical dreams. The ultimate synthesis of opposites was pursued by minds seeking resurrection on earth in order to coincide with resurrection in heaven—but everything might also be inexorably separated, divided forever or at least until our day, as has unfailingly happened. Plato wrote of gold and of geometric figures, particularly the triangle and the cube. His writings were surely among the philosophical reading that Columbus pursued. Plato said the gravest illness was ignorance; a disease with which Columbus, unlike his detractors in life and his many academic critics after death, was not afflicted.[9]

The navigator read and reread. In his mind he tried to give the best possible form of the truth to a world distorted like a warped mirror—a world that had become, for many people, a flat disc. His endeavor intended to overcome every biased view, every geographical—and consequently political, ideological, and theological—interpretation. On the maps everyone pointed to their own places, their own possessions. Jerusalem, in the Christian view, had become the navel of the world, the center of the terrestrial circle from where the light radiated. East was often placed to our north, while the Arabs placed south at the top, completely reversing our modern view. Errors and ignorance combined to form complete misconceptions, either by approximation or by convenience. Columbus's geography nullified every preceding vision. Maps, books, and documents, rather than the actual people mentioned in legend and later multiplied for pre-Columbian and anti-Columbian purposes, are the true unknown pilots, who dictated the course of the man called to reveal the New World.

Let us begin with a text that, as usual, sinks into mystery and into the past. One of the guides for Columbus's ideas was Admiral Piri Reis, the infidel Turk,[10] in his chief work, the *Kitab-i Bahriye* (Book of Sea Lore). The Muslim admiral wrote:

They call the country Antilya [Antilla]. Listen and I will tell you of it. Let me explain how that land came to be discovered. There was an astronomer in Genoa whose name was Kolon. A rare book, no doubt from the time of Alexander, came into his hands. Everything known about navigation was gathered and written in that book. . . . Kolon found it and read it; then he took it to the king of Spain. When he told the king of its meaning, the king gave him ships. My friend, by using that book, Kolon sailed to Antilya. He continued to explore those lands; so the way there became well known."[11]

✠

Besides the maps, there is a document originating from the time of Alexander the Great! The existence of the Antilles had also been confirmed by Isidore, bishop of Seville (AD 560–636). The bishop was a doctor of the Church whose works are on the watershed between the classical world and the medieval world. Isidore encouraged the reemergence of education and literature and alluded to the antipodes, rejecting the idea of a T-shaped, cruciform world in which the three continents corresponded to the three sons of Noah: Shem to Asia, Ham to Africa, and Japheth to Europe. The idea of a civilization without fathers, independent from Abraham, Noah, and Moses, was inconceivable, much less admissible. Isidore's *Etymologiae* reads: ". . . there is said to be another continent besides the three known today, across the ocean, from north to south and where the sun is hot as in no other land of ours."[12]

Was this the paradise of his contemporary Cosmas Indicopleustes? Was it the land inhabited before the Flood or the partially vanished Atlantis? Columbus's "contraband" book is mentioned again in the lengthy caption that accompanies Piri Reis's map:

> It is reported that a Genoese called Colombo was the first to discover these territories. It is said that a book came into his hands, which stated that at the end of the Western Sea, on its western side, were coasts and islands and different kinds of metals and precious gems. This man studied the book thoroughly . . .[13]

These details reveal a precise knowledge of the hidden continent which can be traced back to the experience of earlier explorers. It reinforces the idea this land was not part of the highly civilized India already known, but of an India still savage and absent from the maps in circulation. Piri Reis even adds the inhabitants of these lands were so pleased by glass beads (the marbles that Columbus brought for barter) that in exchange they traded their pearls, which they found along the coast at scarcely two fathoms' depth.

Pearls, in the medieval imagination, were dew from heaven, and also the symbol of *gnosis,* "knowledge." The gates of the heavenly Jerusalem, which Columbus was to establish on earth, were made of pearl.[14]

✠

Lands of pearls, gold, mines, precious stones: the ancient book Columbus owned, but which no longer exists, told of these. Marco Polo wrote of them in his *Travels.* The identity of those far-off, vast, rich lands of the Indies corresponds perfectly to Columbus's expectations, incorporating the same descriptions and details. And yet this same account by Marco Polo, which Columbus read and annotated attentively, supposedly confused the navigator and made him believe he had reached Asia. Is this possible?

In this case, the book annotated by Columbus still survives, albeit damaged. The Venetian traveler preceding Columbus by two centuries had gone to China via the land route through the Levant in the company of his father Niccolo and his uncle Matteo. In the prison of Genoa his story was committed to posterity by the pen of Rustichello da Pisa, a noted author and probably a knight who had also recorded the Breton cycle and the legend of King Arthur.[15]

Marco Polo's Venetian origin recalls the continuous relationship of Venice with the East—with Constantinople, the "second Rome." A Crusade had defined the latter city, sovereign above all others, with its Golden Horn and its Golden Gate, where legends told of golden lions whose roars caused golden birds to take flight. There, by the sunset-gilded sea, in the place cross-bearing knights had called the arm of St. George, the Polos owned a house—not far from the dwelling of the Zeno brothers, who were also pre-discoverers of America.[16] Once again, the connections grow closer and closer. The Polos lived there between 1260 and 1261.[17]

Subsequently required to flee, swept up in the passage of events in a region of the East that harbored resentment against the Church of Rome, the Polos relocated to Soldaia, not far from Caffa, which would see the expansion of a rich and flourishing Genoese colony in years to come. A Christian outpost in a strategically and economically important area, it was later lost following the advance of the Turks in the mid-fifteenth century. The Franciscan brothers had a monastery at Soldaia.

Although cities, nations, continents, names of places, and names of people may appear or disappear in the passage of years and centuries, persons and things still remain to form indissoluble links between them. In those years, on the western front of Galilee, the Mamluks, who were already in possession of Egypt, defeated the Mongols. The Mamluks were of Turkish origin, the recurrent and common danger for the Far East as well as for the West.

Marco Polo was another Italian and another voyager and is another mystery. Very little is known of him; conjectures outnumber truths. At times it has even been said he may never have existed. His name recalls the author of the second gospel: Mark, the saint of the Serenissima, the first bishop of mythical Alexandria with its library, that great source of knowledge. The first Christian church was founded in Alexandria, and one of St. Mark's attributes, it so happens, is a book. Tradition has given him the name by which we know him today, but in the Acts of the Apostles, he is also called "John, whose surname was Mark." So many Johns in the labyrinth of this hidden story! Polo, speaking of north and south, refers to a geography still incomplete between the two frozen extremes at the ends of the world, names forever oracular.

There is a hypothesis that Marco Polo did not actually reach China, considering that he never mentions tea ceremonies or the Great Wall—a gigantic structure impossible to miss. Such things are in the realm of coincidence, speculation, and supposition, but at least a few firm facts remain: It is certain the Polos had the pope, Christianity, and Jerusalem as their main reference points. Marco formed part of a diplomatic mission sent by Pope Gregory X to Kublai Khan and brought with him the oil of the Holy Sepulchre of Jerusalem to offer to the emperor of the East. In the course of his extended peregrinations ("he spent thirty-six years in those lands," states the Tuscan version of his *Travels*), before heading toward those lands of marvels, he sojourned in St. John of Acre,[18] the Crusader knights' outpost at the heart of the Muslim empire. It was held by the Templars, its last defenders, along with the Hospitalers and other knights—and the constant presence of the Franciscans.

The expedition's stop at Acre was unplanned, the result of the pope's death and the consequent vacancy of St. Peter's throne. Before proceeding, counsel had to be taken with the pontifical legate Tedaldo Visconti da Piacenza—who, soon afterward, became Pope Gregory X. "In the patriarchal palace of Acre, the two [the Polos], accompanied by Marco, prostrated themselves at the feet of the apostle's successor, and received his benediction. The pope ordered the justificatory letters that he had signed to be torn up and entirely different orders given them. Among other things, he demanded that Kublai reawaken the good intentions of Aboga [the khan of Persia], to grant him favorable treatment of Catholics, in order to encourage the anti-Muslim alliance in defense of the realm overseas and the protection of the pilgrimages to the holy places. To the oil from the lamps of Jerusalem were added 'many splendid gifts, of crystals and of every kind.'"[19]

Marco Polo's movements were thus controlled by Rome. Between Piacenza, the pope's city, and Acre, the fortress of the knights, the Templar presence was especially influential. The Pallestrello (Pallestrelli, Perestrello) family came from Piacenza; their daughter, the noble Felipa, was the first and perhaps only wife of Christopher Columbus. Given the alleged difference in social origins between the two it was an unlikely marriage for the times and a union that further illuminates a different truth from what has been told. Columbus knew Felipa from frequenting the circles of the Portuguese Knights of Christ, who had emanated directly from the Order of the Temple—still surviving in those regions facing the Atlantic, across from America.

Through the ups and downs of history, Rome never abandoned the idea of the Outremer, the land across the seas, Jerusalem, the Holy Sepulchre. Popes and friars alike joined Marco Polo's mission from the very beginning, though they dropped out along the way; ambassadors, pontifical legates, churchmen, guides, and advisers were the escorts subtending his parabolic journey.

It is also indubitable that Marco had close connections to the order of the Dominicans.[20] For anyone following Columbus's footsteps, this has the appearance of a story already read and seen, a story that would be read and seen again in a series of parallel revelations on the part of the navigator and his relationship to Rome.

Indeed, Marco Polo's expedition also bears the hallmarks of a religious mission following a different path from that of Columbus: by land instead of by sea. Many of the goals and assumptions appear identical, and both have the same financing, the same politics, and the same missionary Christian spirit. Further, Polo was a man of "typical western Christian background (not lacking the characteristic animus against the Muslims), but without this implying—and this is the exceptional fact— a filter excluding the comprehension of the different, which is thus told of with impartiality and, in some cases, with distinct admiration."[21]

Before the Polos, at least four similar journeys were taken, but the number grows considerably if we take into account the many other official expeditions into the lands of the Mongols and the travels of men of the faith, the Franciscans and Dominicans, in their effort to mend the world. They were especially encouraged by Innocent IV, the Genoese Fieschi, the predecessor who inspired Innocent VIII by way of a spiritual union and probably also a blood tie.

It was as if the Gordian knot were tied like a noose around the Christian world's consciousness; no one since Alexander the Great had dared venture beyond its confines. Between the Muslim empire to the East and the forbidden Pillars of Hercules to the West, Europe sat in her fortress in a perfect equilibrium of terror. There were monsters on all sides: sea monsters swarming in the Atlantic, land monsters running wild in Asia, together with the bestial peoples of Gog and Magog. Woe betides any who ventured there without permission!

While the ocean remained taboo (if only because it was less accessible), the pressures of business frequently led to commerce along the Silk Road and the Spice Route. Incursions along this exotic front were not the prerogative of Christians but were also taken by Muslims and particularly by merchants a good four centuries before Marco Polo. For long years, many of them followed the same route, as related by the Arab writer Abu Zeid.

The merchants traveled in pursuit of the economic mirage. The Church, on the other hand, wished to spread the word of Christ in the name of the universal spiritual dominion and in the name of peace. The Franciscan friar Lawrence of Portugal is said to have traveled through various nations along the path of peace, though it is not certain whether he even left on his journey. The Franciscan Giovanni da Pian del Carpini from Umbria did reach Karakorum, the capital of the Tartars. He had taken on assignments in Europe for St. Francis himself. To balance out the proselytism of the mendicant orders, Innocent IV sent the Dominican Ascelino Lombardo from Cremona on a similar mission. He was accompanied by Andrea di Logumel, later the protagonist of another diplomatic mission. They were followed by William of Rubruk, a Flemish Franciscan.

Despite some conversions, the khans—such as Toqta, khan of the Golden Horde in the early 1300s—did not yield to the popes' desires. They listened, sometimes irritated, to the ambassadors of a far-off and unknown "father" calling upon them to submit to him. The case was different for Kublai due to the influence exercised by numerous Nestorian Christian princesses, beginning with the wife or mother of the Great Khan, Sayor-gatani Baigi, whom Marco met. Completing the list of missionaries, Friar Giovanni da Montecorvino reached China in 1294, sent by Pope Nicholas IV.

Who, then, was Marco Polo? Everything points to an envoy, a messenger, a secret agent sent by Rome—another masked knight. "It seems indubitable that the secret brotherhood to which Marco Polo belonged was of the Temple . . . because it is known that as soon as he was freed from prison, he made a gift of the first copy of his book to the Templar master Thibault de Cepoy in honor and reverence of Monseigneur Charles, son of the king of France and count of Valois; he gave this gift to them in August of 1307. Then there is another and more persuasive reason: Rustichello da Pisa, by whose hand the *Travels* were written, was very probably sent by the Order of the Templars to console Marco Polo in prison."[22]

Was he another knight or a knightly monk? In a miniature from a manuscript in London the Polos are pictured wearing habits similar to those of the Franciscans.[23]

In his moments of desperation and penitence, as well as before his death, Christopher Columbus donned the Franciscan habit. Once again, over the centuries, the plot lines weave together into a single web. The common thread is the fabric of the habit, the fabric of heresy. Was Marco Polo, as Columbus's forerunner, inspired by the "ideology of understanding between peoples"? Is he a personage whose testimonies "can in some ways be linked to the 'new man' of humanism and the Renaissance"?[24]

Columbus was not the only one who read and intensely examined Polo's *Travels*. They were read by the Infante of Portugal, don Pedro, and by the Portuguese prince Henry the Navigator, whose maritime knights, heirs to the Templar legacy, naturally headed for the Atlantic. The Florentine physicist Paolo dal Pozzo Toscanelli also read them. Scientists and navigators read them. What made this text so interesting and so new and what did it conceal or reveal beyond a fascination for exotic things and the marvels of the East? Did these readers hold the lost original in their hands? What version of the story did they read, given that the first version is now lost?

The most widespread transcription to circulate throughout Europe was that of Friar Francesco Pipino, the Dominican from Bologna—who "systematically suppressed, in the Latin version, the passages that might reflect any heretical ideas, heterodoxies favorable to the Christian or pagan sects of Asia."[25]

The ideological broadness and tolerance common to every person in our story has been censored. At this point, legitimate suspicion emerges. Marco Polo's narrative might also have concealed geographical heresies relating to the lost other world, especially if we attentively examine the brief description in the surviving text of a marvelous land: Cipango, presumably Japan. It is a place exceeding all his other descriptions, abounding as they do in fascinating details. Even those who have not read his *Travels* may have some notion of Cipango, the land of golden roofs. Other elements in his narrative merit as much, if not more, attention, but do not receive it. Why would so much curiosity be directed toward Cipango?[26]

Japan, with its golden roofs and statues: El Dorado. Marco Polo and Christopher Columbus were in perfect harmony, with the same destinations and the same fascinations.

Did this legendary place correspond to any in reality? Of what land was Marco Polo speaking? The passage seems to combine elements that somehow then separate and cannot lead to a single common denominator. The incongruences are such that they leave us suspecting this land might actually have nothing to do with Japan.[27]

It is said Cipangu, or Zipangu (there are yet more variations to the name, such as Cinpangu, Xipangu, Sipangu—and according to some, this was indeed Antilla), was the accepted version of the Chinese Jinpen-kuo. Japan, in Columbus's time, was an archipelago with a highly developed and extremely refined culture, and where gold was present in modest quantities. Marco Polo had traveled through some incredible regions, and seen riches and architectural marvels of all types. Why were the most far-fetched and mind-boggling things supposedly found in Japan? Why should the story of the land of golden roofs, which caused such outbursts and provoked such ambitions, necessarily refer to a land of the Asiatic Indies? It is so strikingly different from all the rest of the Indies. On the maps of the time we are studying, the Japanese archipelago "was not present and was unknown to classical antiquity."[28] It would appear only in later times.

Let us now attentively tap into the *Travels*.[29] Here we come to Marco Polo's famous description of the awesome and phantom Japan:

Cipangu is an island toward the east in the high seas, 1,500 miles distant from the Continent [Japan is much closer to China] and a very great island it is [Japan is not very large, relatively speaking]. The people are white [as were many Native Americans], civilized, and well favored [just what Columbus said when he met the American natives]. They are idolaters [as the Native Americans were defined], and recognize no lord as their master. And I can tell you the quantity of gold they have is endless [there was not much gold in Japan]. . . . They have also pearls in abundance [Columbus's America had a natural wealth of pearls] . . . it is their custom, when their dead are buried, to put one of these pearls in the mouth [a custom similar to the Native Americans].[30]

Not only do the oddities multiply, but also they intersect. The reference is always and unequivocally to Cipango; but he speaks of idolaters, eaters of human flesh, an endless ocean, seven thousand islands, and men whose lives "are such a combination of extravagance and devilry."[31]

The distance of this fearful and fabled world, even allowing for a certain margin of error, is such as to exclude the possibility of its being Japan. It is across the open, boundless ocean, and the only ocean meriting that description is the Pacific. This land is "very far from India"—so far indeed, "it takes a whole year to get there." They leave in the winter, then start the return trip in the summer, "For in that sea there are but two winds that blow, the one that carries them outward and the other that brings them homeward; and the one of these winds blows all the winter, and the other all the summer." Oceanic winds, monsoon winds: Such things do not blow upon the shores of China and Japan. A year's voyage! Japan is separated from Asia by a mere channel of water.

Columbus, whose final goal after America was Chinese Asia, brought enough provisions on his first voyage for a yearlong expedition. According to Polo's *Travels*, it took a year to go from China to Cipango. It would have taken Christopher Columbus a year to get from America-Cipango to China.

Cannibalism was certainly not a custom practiced by the proud samurais, but it would become one of the excuses for exterminating the American natives. Many of the habits attributed to the idolaters were part of the cultural baggage of "savages," which bore no resemblance to Japanese customs. The Japanese worshipped kami, not idols. The sanguinary description may not agree with everything we know about the customs of the Native Americans, but the most striking elements, beginning with the exceptional quantity of gold to be found there, the gilded palaces, floors, rooms, and windows, recalls the myth of El Dorado—the Indian-American El Dorado.

Another fundamental story precludes Cipango from being Japan: Marco Polo adds that Kublai, "the Great Khan who now reigns," sent forth "two of his barons" to sail to Cipango and conquer it. They reached the island, went on shore, occupied the plains and "hamlets," but could not take any "city or castle." A sudden great wind blew, threatening to destroy the whole fleet. Just after they set sail to escape it, they were shipwrecked.

Those who had not drowned swam to shore, while others fled in the few ships that had survived the hurricane. Thus, thirty thousand (decidedly too many) Tartars remained on the island and believed themselves doomed, especially when the king of Cipango sent forces to take them prisoner. The strategy of the ensuing battle is not consistent with expert medieval warriors such as the Japanese, who surely would never have acted so naively.

The warriors of Cipango foolishly left no guard on board the captured ships. The more cunning Tartars quickly began fleeing inland and were pursued by the enemy. With a skillful strategy they succeeded in getting on board the enemy's ships and sailing to a larger island. Because they were flying the king's standards and banners, the gates of the city were opened to them. They took the people of Cipango by surprise and conquered the city, sparing only the elderly and the women and taking the more beautiful ones as prisoners.

Lasting seven months, the subsequent siege by the natives led inevitably to defeat. The Tartars tried in vain to send a message to their ruler: "So when they saw they could hold out no longer they gave themselves up on condition that their lives should be spared, but still that they should never quit the island." This occurred in 1281. Japan had never been invaded by China; the Chinese had tried repeatedly, but never succeeded. In 1281, therefore, the Chinese sailed to America before Columbus; and it was surely not the first time they had arrived on that distant shore. Customs and physiognomies speak clearly of those long-ago meetings.

The brief account relating to Cipango concludes: "Now we shall speak no longer of these countries and this island, it being too far from our story, and also because we did not go there." "Too far from our story"! This section of the chronicle is amazing, especially considering how it can be interpreted and how it has been consequently ignored. Here we must consider censorship and probable interpolations; everything must be taken with a pinch of salt, but the fact remains that we are very far from identifying Cipango with the Land of the Rising Sun. The alleged Japan on maps has a shape similar to Antilla, and is next to modern-day Mexico: an Antilla-Cipango in the Atlantic, corresponding to the Antilla-Cipango of Columbus's New World, America. The misunderstanding arises from a kind of three-card monte played with maps, their interpretation clouded by centuries of selective blindness.

Antilla-Cipango could just as easily be an island, a continent, or a peninsula jutting out from a continent. Even after the discovery, America was identified one piece at a time. Little by little, the extent of those lands was established, little by little the continent took form. Antilla-Cipango was not an island but part of America, a fragment of a whole, which even ancient navigators had known.[32] The investigation leads us back to the same ambiguous definition of the word *island*.

Indirect confirmation of a historic falsehood comes from the writing of a Jesuit of mixed origin, Blas Valera. He records Columbus's caravels with the names *Santa Maria, Santa Clara,* and *Santa Giovanna.* To what voyage might this refer? From recently uncovered documents, one story of the conquest of Peru emerges completely different from the distorted common version of the Spanish Dominicans. The great state of Atahualpa, it relates, was exterminated with a poisoned wine prepared by a friar—whom Pizarro then killed with his own hands.[33]

Valera somehow managed to return to Peru in secret and to write his *Nueva cronica e buen Gobierno* (1618). An Italian scholar, Laura Miccinelli, supported by texts of other Jesuits and the reading of Inca *quipu* (the knotted ropes that formed the occult legacy of this civilization), as well as a secret document composed in Arabic numerals, was able to reconstruct a manuscript from 1532 which records the arrival in America, a thousand years earlier, of Tartars and white men with "golden beards" coming from the north:

> Approximately one thousand years before this Year of Our Lord, a group of... brave sages from great Tartary... encountered, in the vast South Sea, or the Pacific, numerous islands.... There they became assimilated with the Pacific peoples of the islands and, over successive generations, reached the continent. There, finding the land occupied by people who were builders of great pyramids, they descended... to the south, where they fought with the warlike people of the coasts, who laid down their weapons only when men came down from the highlands ... with white skin, thick hair, and faces covered in beards the color of gold.... And so it was that white people had reached the continent about a century before... but following a different sea route, that is to say, from the other sea, the People of the North.[34]

Once again, people coming from Asia; once again, blond-bearded men arriving from the north. More landings, a thousand years or more before Columbus, and the Incas must have been the result of their intermarrying. The quipu have preserved the truth through the ages, bringing to light ancient explorers, long-ago navigators lost in time. Also because of this the natives of America might indeed be descended from Indians—and so Columbus may not have been so mistaken in calling them Indian.

Let us proceed from lost writings to maps of the world—such as the one drawn by the Bohemian Martin Behaim in Portugal, the country where Columbus landed after an adventurous shipwreck. Columbus knew and consulted with Behaim, who inspired him. The scientist's globe, dated 1492, is considered the first spherical world map. Behaim had been in Rome, in the caput mundi of Christendom, where he had met the geographer Paolo dal Pozzo Toscanelli,[35] the scientist who encouraged Columbus to take his voyage. He was also a great friend of Cardinal Nicholas of Cusa, another universalistic thinker. The circles of great minds broaden and the network thickens; Rome and certain names are continually present.

On Behaim's original, preserved in Nuremberg, Cipango is situated in the Atlantic Ocean, almost exactly halfway between the Azores and the Asian continent. If we try inserting America into this representation[36]—as has been done[37]—then Behaim's Cipango lines up almost perfectly with the country of Mexico.

There is much more on this globe: a great island in the north forming part of a vast archipelago and called Cathay. It has nothing to do with China, with the Cathay of which Marco Polo spoke. Was it Columbus's Cathay? Other pieces of land of considerable extent are scattered to the north and south of Cipango in this intriguing spherical representation of the world—a great, vanished archipelago of lands identified individually, which Columbus knew must have been a true continent, like a puzzle to be put together into a single shape. Columbus revived the ancient, antediluvian concept (never abandoned) of an isthmus he was sure divided the future Americas. It was an erroneous supposition and it was corrected, but Columbus's certainty of it suggested ancient knowledge supported by the maps and books of Alexandria. This is a hypothesis, indeed, but no worse than any other research, accepting as truth that which might not be true—such as the tracing, without a shadow of doubt, of the name Cipango to the Chinese Jik-pen-kuo.

This last hypothesis was even refuted by a great Dutch geographer of the early sixteenth century, Johannes Ruysch.[38] Ruysch, on whose map Japan does not appear, writes:

M. Polo says that . . . there is a very large island called Cipango, whose inhabitants worship idols and have their own king. . . . They have a great abundance of gold and all kinds of gems. But as the islands discovered by the Spaniards occupy this spot, we do not dare to locate this island here, being of the opinion that what the Spaniards call Spagnola [the modern day Dominican Republic and Haiti] is really Cipango, since the things that are described as of Cipango are also found in Spagnola, besides the idolatry.[39]

✠

So, America was there. It was in the books and on the maps, yet no one had been willing to recognize it. The dogma affirms and will continue to affirm that before 1492 it was known neither to the West nor to the whole world!

A forerunner of Columbus, Marco Polo, brought a lamp with the oil of the Holy Sepulchre from Jerusalem and sought an alliance with the Tartars in order to fight Islam. Christopher Columbus, a bearer of crosses and of Christ, wished to reach those islands and continents, and from thence to set his sails for Asia in order to strengthen an ancient alliance left in suspension—and finally, to go with his army, set in motion by gold, to the reconquest of the Holy Sepulchre of Jerusalem.

These were two people who, centuries later, are still—albeit in a different manner—the protagonists of a single, organic design led by the Church of Rome, a relay in the shadow of the missionaries and knightly orders with an idealistic vision, working persistently toward a project without end. Two explorers, different from all others, were seeking a great khan who, with his power, his generosity, and his aspiration to be a universal monarch, had aroused great interest and exercised an immense fascination. "He had soon become an allegorical figure, a sort of political-eschatological metaphor."[40]

What did Kublai Khan say and what did he tell the Venetian ambassador to pass on? "Asking him about the pope and the Church of Rome and all the agents and states of Christendom . . ." he requested the pope send a great number of priests ("an hundred men skilled in the Christian law") in order to

make clear to the idolaters and to the other kinds of believers that their law was not of divine inspiration, but of an entirely different nature, that all the idols they keep in their houses are diabolical things; to send men, in short, who shall be able to show them clearly, by the force of reason, that the Christian law is superior to theirs . . . and then I will receive baptism; and when I shall have been baptized, then all my barons and chiefs shall be baptized also, and after them the subjects of their lands. And thus in the end there will be more Christians here than exist in your part of the world![41]

Thus Polo, like Columbus, was bringing baptism for the salvation of the world. The plenitude of nations would be realized, the good news spread to all corners of the globe, and the revelation-apocalypse brought to humankind on earth, leading all to the celestial world. Such phrases, concepts, and messages could not have been entrusted to a mere merchant or mariner, especially in a time when public role and social rank were so universally respected. Who was Marco Polo truly? At times, he even shines through as a phantom knight, a layman only in appearance, like Columbus, entrusted with a great mission.

What was written in his lost book besides what we know? What was being pursued in the succession of marvels and accounts that was so famous it has come to epitomize the medieval tendency for hyperbolic exaggeration? Such a tendency has ensured that all of Polo's *Travels* have passed into history as an unreliable fanfaronade in an exclusively literal reading of them—even though signs and symbols were the keys to interpreting the marvelous in those days. This contrasts with the prestige of a text so attentively studied by those interested in exploration, like a geographic bible, modern and revelatory regarding the far-off East and the unknown lands.

A great length of time passed between Marco Polo's expedition and that of Columbus, but this is the kind of consideration that arises from our modern way of thinking. In those days, the years and the centuries flowed along in a kind of stagnation to which change was something foreign. The passage of ideas was slowed down especially due to the many powers that formed obstacles to progress. Parameters were not what they are today; the lengths of voyages and distances in the mind were not the same as we know them. Columbus said that from Spain dry land could be reached in a few days. He was right. A month, for a voyage such as his, was next to nothing. Consider the length of Marco Polo's pilgrimage; a year seems like an eternity to us, but in those days it was a mere trifle. Haste and speedy movements are a modern phenomenon.

The Renaissance was a crucible of revolutionary ideas subject to constant restraints. Everywhere there was a physiological tension warning against change, which required worldwide reform. Once new things could no longer be halted, how and when was change to come? How much longer would it take to defeat those who were blocking the epochal revolutions?

It was enough to wait for the crash that would follow Columbus's discovery. Decades and centuries were required for the New World to be "metabolized." In the prevalent mentality, the two hundred years between Polo and Columbus were a mere heartbeat. Indissolubly linking the two people, beyond the navigator's favorite readings, was the indispensable figure of the pope of Rome, who had at his disposal in various forms missionaries, organizers of pilgrimages, and scientists and geographers gathering information. They were the true secret agents of the times, providing a constant influx of news and reports with no counterparts under any other temporal power, despite the universalistic ambitions of various emperors, sultans, or khans. The only true emperor, sultan, and khan was in Rome.

The Great Khan was calling. When would Rome respond? Only when she was able, when she was certain of not failing. The conflicts of the times, the plagues, famines, and wars, and the precarious equilibrium of the world were among the continuous reasons for postponing a project that may have already been on the launching pad—or, at the least, a problem and a "heresy" to be confronted and resolved. Marco Polo left his account for posterity. The Dominican Francesco Pipino revised it, censoring passages he deemed dangerous or that appeared to be early declarations of intent associated with the enactment of a design that would not be abandoned until the time of Innocent VIII and Columbus.

What did Kublai add that was disturbing enough to be suppressed in the Dominican monk's version? "There are four prophets who are worshipped and to whom all the world does reverence," the Great Khan supposedly said to Polo: The Christians worshipped Jesus, the Saracens Muhammad, the Jews Moses, and the Buddhists Buddha. ". . . And I do honor and reverence to all four so that I may be sure of doing it to him who is greatest and truest; and to him I pray for aid."[42]

A universalistic openness of the mind, which was reduced, in line with the progression of the story, to the three "religions of the book"—a Trinitarian vision with only three great prophets—which was the greatest and truest?

This great theme continues in an uninterrupted stream from the Middle Ages to the Renaissance, and the question also elicits a response from a science that had for some time been advancing to assert its presence and existence. Science calls for the faculty of reason. Faith and the Church, on any level, are afraid of reason, because pure *ratio,* stripped of the sacred, becomes a wild and uncontrollable force. And then what happens? Faith and spirit are nearly suffocated by it.

Kublai embodied the new Alexander of Macedon, one of the recurrent symbols in the High Middle Ages. The nephew of Genghis Khan, with a Christian mother and a Christian wife, he was one of those who could "unite all the world and rule it with royal and just laws, assuring well-being, peace, good trading, and protected passage along well-watched routes . . ." He was a leader inspired by the dream of good government and a universal brotherhood.[43]

Marco Polo and Columbus, in a single relay, are supposed to have been more aware of the songs of material sirens than those of the spirit. They were unique individuals among reigning illiteracy; they were "illiterate" men who dictated and wrote a great amount. What remains, what they wrote or had written, is the result of copies of copies. It might all be true, it might all be false, and many falsehoods may have been added later, adulterating the truth to render it less credible—not to mention the passages completely erased.

Universalism, brotherhoods, utopias, merchants, mariners, traders in gold and precious stones: They looked at things that were different without becoming scandalized and were concerned with religion and evangelization. The doors of all the monarchs of the world were open to them. From Marco Polo[44] to Christopher Columbus, the thread colored by truth continues like an indelible trail. It was enough to know it or seek it without the blinders of prejudice in a material and spiritual tandem completing the periplus of the world, as if tying together the alpha and the omega. Not by coincidence, Polo's epigraph "In the name of Our Lord Jesus Christ Son of God living and true, amen" was addressed[45] to *Seignors emperaor et rois, dux et marquois, cuens, chevaliers et b(o)rg(oi)s et toutes gens* (Lords, emperors, and kings, dukes and marquises, counts, knights, and burgesses, and all people). It is a singular audience for an illiterate merchant. Did it arise from unbridled ambition, vanity, or arrogance? Or was it a message, not even encoded, to be read by those who could and would read beyond the marvelous things decorating the narrative? Was the just moment, the moment of the just, approaching?

Perhaps, but just moments require a series of circumstances as fortuitous as they are favorable. This was not to happen in Marco Polo's time.[46]

The broken thread had to wait until around the mid-fifteenth century to be mended in a new, slow, but inexorable advance following the fall of Constantinople in 1453, when the reveille was sounded for the West and could not be postponed. Who would live or die? East or West? It depended on who would reach for the first time the coasts of the El Dorado, of America-Antilla-Cipango, where the Chinese had landed centuries before.

The countless humanity of the Three Indies had to be led back into the Christian sphere and Islam had to be stopped. The deadline established by God had now arrived. The divine kingdom could not wait. "With the epic crusade," writes the medievalist Franco Cardini, "there was a dimension of *pugna spiritualis*, of psychomachy: On the one side were the Christian warriors, paladins of light at whose front marched the knightly saints and warrior angels—from St. George to St. James to the Archangel Michael—and on the other side, the phalanxes of darkness were lined up, monstrous and demoniacal warriors commanded by leaders with infernal names." Along the path of light, St. George and St. James were joined by the giant saint, St. Christopher, ahead of all the others.

Only Rome knew the other world; only Rome, with her keys, could open its doors. Only Rome was considered to have the right and the duty to establish the ways and means so that the Christian body should not suffer from it. The people, the masses of believers, were prepared slowly. All that changes the course of history requires a progressive incubation without trauma. When the decisive spark is struck, lighting the pyre of the known and revealing the unknown, it is as if the man on the street has known about it for a long time. He is mature, inured to revelations and to an incredible event, which now seems taken for granted, in a sort of liberation from doubt long desired and awaited.

For this to happen, people were needed who would have the qualities and moral solidity to bring about, in complete secrecy, the positive introduction of the unforeseen into the foreseeable. Such persons might be called generational guinea pigs. Marco Polo appears to have been one. Christopher Columbus was another.[47]

TEN

THE ÎNFÎDEL PÎRÎ REÎS'S MAP

CHRISTOPHER COLUMBUS MUST have discovered America before the fateful year 1492. Did he go there more than once? Did he reach it earlier by the northern route? In the Capitulations—the agreement signed by the monarchs of Spain—there is a sentence leaving no shred of doubt regarding the objective to be achieved. The preamble attached to the oldest copy of this document, written in 1495 and considered consistent with the original, reads: *Las cosas suplicadas y que vuestras altezas dan e otorgan a don Cristóbal Colón en alguna satisfacción de lo que ha descubierto en las mares océanas y del viaye que agora con la ayuda de Dios ha de hacer* . . . (The document contains "the things requested that Your Highnesses give and concede to *don* [here he is already called don, a title he would only obtain after the discovery] Christopher Columbus as some compensation for what he has discovered in the ocean seas and for the voyage which, with the aid of God, he is now in the process of making upon the said sea. . . .")[1]

The verb is in the past tense: "for what he has discovered." This is a gratuitously open affirmation. Was this an error, the careless mistake of a copyist—or a plain truth?

There are two truths or two slip-ups (the *don* and "*has* discovered"): Is this a document on which some hand not entirely faithful to the court left its trace, intentionally or not? Or was it from a time after the discovery? Did it serve the interests of the state in camouflaging other pacts signed beforehand in documentation, thereby preserving the "slip-ups," or was it simply the truth?

In 1492 Columbus headed out into the Atlantic as though onto a highway, finding exactly what he had predicted. It was like he was sailing from one tollbooth to the next. Isabella, in fact, had to admit: "All that you told us from the beginning would be found there has mostly emerged with as much certainty as if you had seen it before describing it."[2]

The same thought was expressed by Bartolomeo de Las Casas (1474–1566). According to this priest, one of the first direct chroniclers of the Indies, Columbus spoke of America as if he had kept it in his strongbox. What was Columbus hiding? What has history hidden?

The navigator, during the first expedition, demonstrated knowledge of the systems of the winds, the currents, the seasonal trends of the oceanic calms, the danger of coral reefs. He was certain, as can be seen from signed agreements, that he would obtain gold, silver, pearls, and gems, as well as spices—which, at the time, were extremely valuable. Doubt at the outset turned into certainty during the course of research. The certainty becomes documentary proof in the light of studies whose full consequences have never been drawn but which have remained as resounding as they are silent.

The date of the prediscovery is present in a map from 1513, and has constituted a puzzle for enthusiasts and scholars since the director of the Turkish National Museums discovered it in 1929. It has been removed from academic research and become the territory of vilified conjecture and science fiction. The map is kept among the many jewels of the Topkapi Palace in Istanbul, where it cannot easily be seen or consulted. It is a gem among gems, even appearing on Turkish banknotes.[3]

This is the famous cartographic work of Admiral Piri Reis, a contemporary of Columbus, although slightly younger. The map shows the "unknown" America in the form of long stretches of coast, still unexplored. Regions appear that were discovered (or rediscovered) centuries later. It shows, according to the boldest hypotheses, a section of Antarctic coast identified as Queen Maud Land—reproduced in a preglacial phase, completely free of ice. This must date back to at least ten thousand years before Christ: a far-off time into which the eyes of knowledge peer blindly, an age when Antarctica—the last continent to be discovered, officially in 1818—presumably had a different outline, before the advance of the monumental glaciers.

It is an Antarctica seen as if from above, from the air. This is enough to unleash the interpretations of ufologists and investigators of lost civilizations. This further enigma, unfortunately, contributes to casting a shadow over the document, making it somehow unclean. According to Russian experts, the lands to the south are the promontories of Patagonia and Tierra del Fuego. Even these lands were officially identified by explorations starting only in 1520. From what sources and what predecessors did Piri Reis gain information?

This beautifully colored map, surviving incomplete today, covered with pictures and unique inscriptions, this monument of ink drawing with the fantastic flavor of a fairytale, shows many sections of what became America after Columbus arrived—right to the extremities of the South American continent. There are illustrations of llamas and other animals supposedly unknown at the time of the map's creation. The calculations appear to have been based on the computations of the sphere made by the Greek astronomer Eratosthenes, director of the Library of Alexandria. The longitude is consistent with what was established two centuries later. The contours of the lands are surprising in their precision. In short, it is an absolutely impossible map.[4] Thus the past resurfaced in the twentieth century, through the meanderings of treasure inherited from antiquity.

It is a map about which much is said, but about which official science prefers to remain silent. "These coasts," wrote Piri Reis in one of the long captions that accompany the illustrations, "are called the shores of Antilla. They were discovered in the year 890 of the Muslim era (AD 1485). It is reported that a Genoese called Colombo [note the word *called* rather than *named,* almost as if it were a pseudonym] was the first to discover these territories. It is said a book came into his hands which stated that at the end of the Western Sea, on its western side, were coasts and islands and different kinds of metals and precious gems. . . . Colombo was also a great astronomer *(muneccim)*. The coasts and islands on this map are taken from Colombo's map. . . . No one in the present age possesses a map similar to this, devised and drawn by the humble undersigned *(bu fakir)*. The present map is the product of comparative and deductive studies made of twenty charts and world maps, among which was a first map dating from the era of Alexander the Great comprising all the world, the kind of map that the Arabs call *ca' feriyye* . . . and finally a map by Colombo extended to the Western Hemisphere."[5]

Columbus's maps, Columbus's books, "all the world," a "Western Hemisphere," and "unique" maps as secretive as they were valuable . . . was the true story of the discovery of America hidden in a millennia-long secret that ended up in the navigator's hands? And could this mystery have been part of the spoils of war of some Italian republic—Venice, perhaps?

In its age of maritime splendor, during its occupation of Constantinople in the course of the Fourth Crusade ordered in the early thirteenth century by Innocent III, Venice could have had access to sources similar to those of Piri Reis. The Venetian Zeno brothers, Nicolò and Antonio, used such sources earlier in order to reach the coasts of Greenland and present-day Canada—using knowledge more advanced than we have been led to believe. In fact, a "Venetian map from 1484 simultaneously used the portolan system and the medieval system of orientation according to the twelve winds. Also, this map is of absolutely unbelievable precision, considering the knowledge of the times."[6]

The possibility of information derived from the prediscovery of North America by the Vikings, who also reached Constantinople in their day, would not be sufficient to explain the information possessed by the Turkish geographer. There is also "another map of the world known as the Gloreanus map, preserved at the library of Bonn. Lacking proof to the contrary, historians date this map to 1510; therefore, it would predate Piri Reis's map. [It] shows not only the exact configuration of the Atlantic coast of America, from Canada to Tierra del Fuego, already making it extraordinary, but also the entire Pacific coast, from north to south."[7]

✠

America was discovered before 1492. The maps spoke, but no one listened. Thus our investigation is anything but finished. Far from providing a thorough response, geographers are lacking in an organic and complete vision of the available material. Each country limits itself to studying its own documents without taking into account what remains in hidden archives, libraries, castles, museums, and in unfathomed private collections; without taking into account the enormous amount of evidence that has disappeared, or has been made to disappear.

To refute any contradictions is stubborn and rigid; nothing "new" is ever worthy of consideration, and any prediscovery suggested by the maps is automatically inadmissible. So faith continues to be placed in the established date, the fateful 1492. However much disproved, it has come to be seen as untouchable, while any attempt to trace things further back in time ends up resting upon unacceptable assumptions—because nothing is accepted as an honest truth. It is a strange way of proceeding, a crippled science seemingly inspired by the three famous monkeys: See no evil, hear no evil, speak no evil.

Piri Reis's most important work is the *Kitab-i Bahriye*. It was presented to Suleiman the Magnificent in 1526–1527. Even in the introduction, in verse, to this book, "there is a reference made to Columbus's map . . ." Despite its importance, the work has not yet been "either scientifically edited or translated in its entirety." This further proves that the defense of alleged truth rests above all on omissions. The poetic prologue relates to the desire expressed by Columbus, though never fulfilled, of writing in verse himself.

✠

Of course, very little is known of Piri Reis. Who was this obscure character, more cited than studied? He was a complex personality of immense humanistic and technical learning, a universalist on the Islamic side, a Muslim version of Columbus. He was another *nepos,* the nephew of the great corsair Kemal Reis,[8] probably a renegade, who saw to the youth's education, taking him along on sea voyages—the same thing perhaps happened to Giovanni Battista Cybo and Columbus. The Turkish admiral was also probably of Greek and Christian origin.[9]

He was another many-sided protagonist, hard to classify, living on the borderlines between faiths and civilizations. He spoke perfect Italian, Spanish, Latin, Portuguese, and Greek, a close parallel to the many languages known to Columbus—who may also have had knowledge of Arabic, considering that in an entry dated October 13, 1492, he referred to the Indians' canoes with the Arab term *almadias*. For his part, the Turk was not a simple sailor. He had profound philosophical insights, claiming "the drafting of a geographical map [which Columbus and his brother Bartolomeo drew] required profound learning and unquestionable preparation."[10]

If Columbus was not the man whom history has depicted, then neither was Piri Reis. He was a Sufi, a member of the most tolerant movement of Islam, opposed to fundamentalism. This way of thinking had many intersecting points with Christianity, especially in view of the union of peoples that was hoped for and pursued with all possible power near the end of the fifteenth century—in actions as well as in thought.

Examining the Turk's words in detail, Piri Reis clearly referred to a prediscovery of America by Columbus in an incredible statement never before brought to light. The Hegira year 890, in fact, corresponds to AD 1485! This was during the pontificate of Innocent VIII.[11]

The landing on American shores therefore occurred seven years before the official date of the endeavor. This explains much remaining in the realm of conjecture and puts an end to many of the countless accusations leveled at Columbus: stolen maps, obscure pilots, robbed navigators, that what Columbus failed to do was done by Pinzón, that Columbus never understood what he had found.

Such calumny and lies have been in part refuted but are still inexplicably and regularly reinforced. The new date resurrects the theory of a legendary prediscovery made by Columbus himself. More than one historian has put forward the possibility, but consistent proof has never been found.

According to Piri Reis, the discovery of America—the work begun in 1493 and concluded in 1513—had already occurred. The voyage of 1492 was only a repetition, like those that followed.

The Spanish Capitulations spoke of islands and continents to be discovered, conquered, acquired. Columbus's *armada* sailed to take possession of unknown lands whose existence was already a certainty. At the same time, the navigator was given letters of credential by the foreign monarchs and a passport, making his role under them official. It was also established that Columbus could make all decisions concerning gold, silver, pearls, spices, and other merchandise obtained. He surely could not have expected to plunder with such impunity the natural resources of the Great Khan or those under him. Had he been sailing for Marco Polo's Asia, Columbus could never have helped himself to any such thing.

Of what regions were Columbus, Isabella, and Ferdinand speaking? All we can do is ask questions. The documents always mention islands and continents, but never the Indies or Asia. The answer is obvious: Columbus's Indies were never the Indies his chroniclers have given us to understand (intentionally or otherwise). His Indies were never Asia. And yet, the mistake—the house of cards—remained in place for five hundred years. Now, in the continuation of ever thickening mysteries, we are limited to asking questions that remain unanswered. How did Columbus, following a route never traveled, find the correct way out and back through an unknown ocean? Today, his logs are still used as textbooks by those who choose to sail across the Atlantic. They are the gospels of the solitary mariners.

In 1492 Columbus proceeded as if on an already beaten path, slashing through the darkness as if cutting butter with a sword. How did he never make a mistake? Someone even defined him as a wizard or magician during his time. When the sailors aboard his caravels were preparing mutiny, wishing to turn back from this long voyage into the unknown, Columbus begged and regained the crew's confidence. This was the motive for changing the route to west-southwest. On October 6 Columbus decided to head straight for the terra firma, which he knew was not China, hence for the islands. Had he continued sailing due west, he would have landed in present-day Florida. The continent, which he had seemingly already reached in 1485 and perhaps earlier, could wait. Columbus now needed a place to disembark. His description was thus: "The air is extremely soft, like April in Seville, and is perfumed with delightful sweetness. Fresh herbs appear in abundance; there are many birds of the field, and we caught one, and they fled to the southwest: choughs, ducks, and a cormorant."

Landing on an island was enough to break the tension that had been growing for days: "at this point, the crew held him in great disdain." During the voyage, which took about a month, the crusader-knight cheated daily in the calculation of nautical miles traveled. This was not the first time. Many put this down to his naturally deceitful character, but it is merely confirmation that he knew what others did not. The true calculations of the voyage were written in secret; those divulged were much less than the real figures. It was a way to pacify the crew. Columbus was not insane; he was only certain he would arrive. He allowed for a margin of error in order not to risk the voyage failing.

He knew of the changeable moods of men, especially sailors. He knew how dangerous rising fear could be. Why were the Pinzón brothers—particularly Martín Alonso who, according to many sources, was superior in the art of navigation—unable to make their own calculations? Why did they let him fudge the numbers and keep sailing without opposition, only to sneak off later when they smelled gold? Columbus was the only one who knew exactly where and when and in what regions they would land.

By now all the signs indicated they were near the lands of the antipodes. Sighting a mere rock was enough to assuage the growing tension. The unruliness of his crew forced him to cut things short. Three days after having reassured the sailors, as punctual as clockwork, they sighted San Salvador: the island of the Holy Savior, the promised land.

It was sighted in darkness: "At two hours past midnight, land appeared." It was a Friday, a day particularly beloved by Columbus, his fateful day. He had set sail on a Friday in August. Now, in order to run no risks, knowing the dangers of those seas—the treacherous coral reefs—he decreed that they should wait on board until morning. In the mists of daybreak, the miracle was completed. On another Friday, October 12, 1307, during the pontificate of Clement V, Philip the Fair had set in motion the extermination of the Order of the Templars: a strange coincidence, a strange historical reoccurrence. The first three days spent on American soil were a Friday, Saturday, and Sunday: a trinity of exultation for all the peoples of the world. Friday is the day of worship for the Muslims, Saturday for the Jews, and Sunday for the Christians.

It was Rodrigo de Triana who gave the long-awaited cry "Land, land!" The pension of ten thousand maravedis promised by the king of Spain should have been awarded to him—a further detail used to shame Columbus. He, the admiral and viceroy of all the Indies, the man who would have become founder of a new El Dorado if the monarchs of Spain had respected their side of the signed agreement, supposedly stole the pension due to the humble sailor.[12] It is probably yet another lie.

During the night preceding the landing, Columbus wrote of having glimpsed a light: a flickering in the darkness, as if a candle were appearing and disappearing. Was it a flame, an illusion, or the symbol of something finally lighting up the darkness of the ocean, the gloom of ignorance? Was it a lantern of Diogenes, ignited in search of the new man, forging him in the crucible of the immaculate earth? The candle was "the Divine Light illuminating the darkness of the world, Christ as the Light of the World."[13] From the lantern of Genoa to the lamp of the New World, the path of light was complete.

The thankful words of Columbus upon seeing the New World speak for themselves: "Eternal, omnipotent God, God who with the creative force of thy Word hath generated the heavens and the seas and the land! May Thy name be blessed and glorified everywhere! May Thy mastery and Thy sovereignty be praised through the ages, that Thy sacred name may be known and diffused in 'this half' as yet hidden from Thy empire!"[14]

Columbus had only just landed. All of nature around him seemed like Paradise. He had just set foot on virgin sand, between sea and land. And yet he already knew of this other side, the hidden half of the globe—the half not forever hidden but only as yet, the half to which Christo Ferens was chosen to point his sails. The simple fact that Columbus spoke of his being in another hemisphere is enough to make us suspect that, if nothing else, he was not talking about the known Indies but about a new world—a world quite apart from Ptolemy's closed world and Marco Polo's China.

✠

The medieval vision of the globe is like an apple split with disquieting precision. From the dark ocean to the unknown lands, the earth depicted is a perfect hemisphere, as if Ptolemy's work had cut it exactly in half. Was it cut in half deliberately? Even Piri Reis, as we have seen, wrote that it was possible to assemble his world with "a map of Alexander the Great comprising all the world . . . and a map of Colombo drawn with the Western Hemisphere." This was the half of the world Ptolemy was missing.

Both cases confirm the existence of the hemisphere hitherto hidden, on the basis of a geographical *summa* that transcended the known horizons. The plot thickens when we learn that Alexander, who attempted for the first time in history to unite East and West, was the founder of Alexandria, for many centuries a center for Hellenistic culture and great mysteries. Euclid and Archimedes worked there, as did Aristarchus of Samos, Apollonius of Rhodes, Origen, and Clement. In this cosmopolitan center—which over time recorded the presence of Christians, Jews, and Muslims—religions mixed with Hermetism and faith and science intermingled.

There, on the shores of the Mediterranean in great Africa, the mother of humanity, the library was born from which it all began. Eratosthenes (275–195 BC), who calculated the circumference of the earth, was the director of this mine of knowledge. There, Ptolemy wrote his *Almagest* in the second century AD, forcing the earth and the universe into a geocentric view, blocking the path of humanity for more than a thousand years. Of him we also know all too little. Strangely, he did not take Eratosthenes' measurements into consideration. Despite this calculation, he left posterity with a world split in two down to the inch.

Often, during the course of this investigation—in which we wish, as far as possible, to avoid guesswork—questions keep resurfacing: How, where, when, why, and by whom were the Americas made to disappear? And if this was done, taking advantage of Ptolemy's half sphere (or halved sphere), then was it a matter of intent, of a deliberate obscuring by calculation, or merely of knowledge accidentally lost? Was it a temporary secret somehow converted into an age-long secret, either for higher reasons or just by mistake?

The discovery made by Columbus, the envoy of the pope of Rome who had the maps of Alexandria in the Vatican, was intended to reassemble the terraqueous globe in its natural entirety, as in the time of the ancients, reclaiming pagan culture and places in line with the universalism the Renaissance proclaimed and pursued. Columbus, with his ciphered name, was the predestined man, chosen to fulfill the grand design of the reclaimed sphere. Would the admiral have offered to the descendents of the Great Khan glass trinkets, beads, mirrors, knife blades, red caps, or other objects of common use and little value? Such gifts would have been taken as an insult, and Columbus would have risked being killed. Moreover, why was he not surprised or perturbed when confronted with something so different as the American natives? They were not what he should have expected, if he really thought he was landing on the far eastern shore of the already known East Indies.

There are only two possible explanations: (1) Columbus had been there before, and (2) the Indians, the savages, were simply the kind of people he expected to encounter in a hemisphere where Christendom was still unknown.

Columbus had read Marco Polo and knew of the level of civilization and culture in the Asian Indies. Now he found himself facing people more like the Guanches of the Canary Islands: exactly what he had expected. If these lands were even the farthest outposts of some Great Khan's territory, Columbus would never have dared to take possession of them in the name of Spain. The ultimate goal of the expedition—circumnavigating the earth after having revealed the bridgehead of that new world, whose gold was so indispensable for the Crusade and the Great Work—was to reach those ultimate lands of Prester John and the Tartar kings, at the heart of the Oriental Indies.

They were the recurring mythical sovereigns willing to ally themselves with Christendom for the subjugation or definitive defeat of the infidels, taking them by surprise on their eastern flank. If Columbus had landed in China or Japan, his attitude would not have been that of a conqueror—not in an area inhabited by people whose help was to guarantee Christian victory and the long-awaited return to Jerusalem. The ceremonies upon landing, so legalistic, were equivalent to a declaration of war. We can take possession only of what is not known to belong to others. Unfortunately, the natives' ancestral possession of their own land was not recognized—at least, not until they joined the Lord's fold through baptism.

The expropriation was not Columbus's doing; it was not his conquest. It was the prevalent *forma mentis* (thought) of the times—which would later mutate into genocide through the greed and ferocity of the aspiring *hidalgos* (lower Spanish nobility) in an action for which a pope has recently had the courage to beg forgiveness. Of those who landed in that long-ago happy paradise, bringing to it an unexpected tragedy, Columbus remains the best—in the most Christian sense.

Piri Reis's document leaves no room for doubt, especially because it is the work of a famous seaman and a great geographer who, at the time, was definitely on the adversary side—on the Islamic front which the Christian West, if all attempts at reconciliation failed,[15] would have to fight for world domination.

The Turk, referring to Columbus, is also cited as a confirmation of the Genoese origin of the navigator—who, in my view, still remains

Italian in the greater part of his lineage and upbringing. The question of his birth is one we have posed often but in which we are no longer so interested. It has given rise, more than anything else, to a war among his possible hometowns, guilty of drawing yet another veil over the already blurred history of his origins.

The Muslim admiral's testimony is a brainteaser, opening a number of exploratory possibilities that become even more intriguing when we learn that Piri Reis visited the coastal cities of Spain in his youth—namely in 1486, shortly after Columbus's presumed first landing of 1485, and therefore with a knowledge of events possibly verified firsthand. This was precisely the time Columbus was sojourning in those same places—as a guest at the Franciscan monastery of La Rábida, which had once been a pagan temple dedicated to Proserpine, then a Christian church, then a Muslim mosque. The friars who followed Joachim of Fiore and Ramon Llull had prayed there, and before them, the Templars![16]

It was a stronghold of coexistence, a monastery in which people lived through the ages, united in diversity. In this hermitage, Sufis and Christian mystics may have met to sign a blood pact that history would shatter.

For seven years, Piri Reis, with his uncle Kemal Reis, transported Spanish Muslims to northern Africa as an independent corsair, not yet officially an admiral in the service of the Ottoman empire. He was practically a colleague of Columbus. It was a time when East and West were confronting and battling each other but were also open to a peaceful solution to the old conflict: a genuine agreement, a sort of negotiated surrender after the series of battles and treaties signaled the end of the Spanish war against the Moors and the surrender of Granada, with Isabella and Ferdinand as monarchs and Innocent VIII as pope.

At this point, nothing prevents us from imagining—especially given the singular homage paid to the "infidel" Columbus by a man who should have been his rival—that these two knights of the sea entered into negotiations with each other, negotiations between corsairs who were in adverse camps but who did not necessarily duel, following a vision originating from a superior ethic of chivalry. Piri Reis's words sound less like those of a bitter enemy and more like those of an admirer—or even a friend. This is in line with Columbus's "heretical" side (among the many accusations and calumnies leveled at him was one, recorded by the navigator himself, of wishing to offer the New World to the Moors), as well as that of his pope.[17]

It was a view toward universal peace that necessarily passed through the currents of a mystic thought reemerging on both fronts. The design fit perfectly into the mentality of certain Crusading knights—and not just Christian ones. This was especially true in Spain, which was fighting the Moors but was also heir to the mythical Sepharad—the Spain made up of a civil and harmonious coexistence of Christians, Jews, and Muslims, thereby forming a precedent and a model that even today might have inspired humanity, torn between East and West. At the time, this dream was not completely lost. Perhaps it was deferred, waiting for a better time when it could rise up from the ashes of the funeral pyres.

This syncretism emphasized persuasion by love and a mutual understanding between the two sides, under Franciscan direction and following the path of their founder St. Francis, who had even gone in person to the sultan's court to convert to Christianity the "dragon," the head of the infidels. It was a final expedient which, in order to fulfill the project—the Great Work—did not exclude using the cross as a sword. Columbus had all the stigmata of a knight, a Crusader; he was ready for the holy and just Crusade, once all attempts at reconciliation had been exhausted.

Not by chance, assistance in Spain came to him from the noblest families such as the dukes of Medinaceli and those of Medina Sidonia. They were willing to host the humble stranger for a long time, and to finance his endeavor. Medina[18] is the name of the second Muslim holy city after Mecca. The very surnames of the two great families recall the myth of the lost Sepharad, the Spain-Pharos of the three religions.

It was the Spain where the Kabbalah reemerged, according to which "the elements of nature, man, and all other creatures are testimonies and reflections of the divine presence. Man must spend his life preparing for the great departure toward the Last Judgment, the moment of ecstasy and fulfillment of time when all souls will have reached the Infinite. Joseph ha-Kohen of Soria . . . [and] Abraham Abulafia of Tudela were among the most prolific kabbalists whose writings were based on meditation upon the prophecy (something which somewhat disgusted their contemporaries, who preferred "easier" doctrines). [T]hey were all mystics, and some contemporary historians compare them to the Cathars and to Christian mystics such as Joachim of Fiore and Meister Eckhart."[19]

✠

Prophecy, mysticism, and the church of the just, the pure, and the perfect formed the bond between the truths of the three great books of the faith. The mysticisms of the two captains, the Christian Columbus and the Muslim Reis, might have found many common points in this environment. In fact, Columbus even met the requirements for a kabbalist and was a prophet in his time. He wrote a *Book of Prophecies,* almost completely ignored until recently. The text was long considered a fake because it does not seem to fit inside the straightjacket in which the navigator has been confined. Columbus was certainly a mystic; one of the islands he baptized was given the name Cata.[20]

Such names are rich in suggestive echoes, in this story so replete with echoes! If Columbus was thinking of China, he knew China-Cathay was a continental land already present in Ptolemy's hemisphere (though not under that name) and in Marco Polo's *Travels,* a great region of the immense Chinese continent. Columbus's Cata was therefore not the Cathay already known. For him, it was an island. Was it the Cathay we have encountered on Martin Behaim's world map? Was this part of the tangled web of toponyms that was put in place to protect the secrets that generated confusion and supported the great mystification? Perhaps Columbus—who had read the texts of many religions and who was an attentive and devout follower of Joachim of Fiore, waiting for the end of time—was thinking of the Cathars, the martyred Christians who had proclaimed themselves pure and perfect.

Piri Reis's map shows the coastlines of the Americas with remarkable accuracy, reaching much farther than Antilla (according to some, the anti-India, but also Atlantis). Thus, the Turks were in possession of the exact coordinates used for the discovery. Even the Byzantine crown had taken an interest in the New World! Perhaps a voyage there had been planned in Istanbul. Who would first reach the virgin coast, bringing the banners of their faith?

Piri Reis makes reference to between twenty and thirty various charts and documents. Eight are Ptolemy's, four are Portuguese, one is Arabic, and the one relating to the new lands is Columbus's map. The maps studied in Istanbul were surely the same maps kept in the Vatican all along, preserved by Christendom since time immemorial. To these were added the maps taken first in the capture and then in the fall of Constantinople. They were the maps that Pinzón hurried to examine when he went to Rome in the spring of 1492.

The Spanish seaman went there to sell a cargo of sardines (here the historical reconstruction borders on the ridiculous). Yet following secret channels—which may have led back to Rodrigo Borgia—he went to the pope's library to examine the routes to be taken through the stormy ocean. Perhaps it was Innocent himself who consented to the intrusion in order to finally convince Isabella. Pinzón, Ferdinand's pawn in this muddled game, thus consulted books and world maps: the sources of secrets. He became persuaded, it is said, that the mad foreigner's voyage was possible—and then did everything possible to betray him and strip him of all merit.

From the bonfire of the Library of Alexandria some documents and maps had evidently been saved—perhaps simply because they had been kept in other locations. Similar events tend to happen in such circumstances, especially when it is a matter of occult notions, initiatory knowledge, state secrets, or things that could upset revealed truths. What surviving books and maps had been found in the excavations carried out by the Templar knights in the Temple of Solomon? Did they reemerge during the Crusades and end up in Christian hands, in Constantinople? Or had they always been in the possession of the delegates of the Church, waiting for the time when their revelation would be appropriate? Thus, the world was already complete.

Ptolemy had drastically reduced the circumference of the globe, an error perpetuated by the Middle Ages and early Renaissance and one Columbus is said to have inherited, despite his admiration for Marinus of Tyre. Marinus's geography espouses the oceanic hypothesis, giving an insular form to the terraqueous globe in contrast to Ptolemy's continental hypothesis. In addition, Ptolemy's works have not survived in their original versions but have been handed down via medieval documents—yet another demonstration of how history mutates and is always full of gaps. All we have are remnants of knowledge: "I have no certain grounds for stating that Ptolemy himself drew the charts, nor would I be in a position to say—even if I wished to attribute all of them to the author of *Geography*—to what extent the charts contained in the documents are faithful to the originals."[21]

This is all the more shown by the fact that "the first complete version of Ptolemy's work was done by Jacopo Angelo, who carried out his task at the Roman Curia, where he had been employed as an apostolic scribe since 1401. Jacopo finished the translation in 1406 and subsequently dedicated it to Alexander V, who was pope from 1409 to 1410."[22]

The shadow of the Church and the hands of the popes, from the denial of the antipodes to their discovery, form a constant theme of exclusive rights to the other world. In the divided world, the terra incognita was also indicated to the south and the extreme east ended in a vast region *extra Gangem* (beyond the Ganges), which became lost in the unknown. And was there still more? It was a question remaining unanswered for Christianity, in which the existence of other lands was not possible on the basis of sacred texts. To speak of the other was equivalent to blasphemy, defying the Church itself.

Columbus, according to what the Turk wrote, evidently took note—albeit amid excusable errors—of the very part of the world that had never appeared—or had disappeared. The certainty of the sentences and the succession of words emphasize it: "The coasts and islands on this map are taken from Colombo's map.... No one in the present age possesses a map similar to this . . ."[23]

"The coasts and islands" are equivalent to the islands and continents promised by Columbus, shores upon which Spain could plant its flags with impunity. Considering it is from around 1500, the map contains unknown and astonishing elements. The revolutionary matrix came from the Christian's notions. This was a unique map coming from an era in which the earth was whole, with a Western Hemisphere lying opposite the eastern one in the recovery of a lost harmony. It was as if Columbus alone had finally taken possession of the dark side of the moon.

Piri Reis's testimony is incontrovertible. What reason would he have had to mention the Christian Columbus and attribute merits to him? Maintaining that the earth was believed to be flat would entail completely ignoring the meaning of the words, which are there, written as they were five hundred years ago. Piri Reis also wrote of two caravels. There were three on the first voyage. Perhaps he was referring to a previous voyage—but even according to some scholars, there were only two caravels on the first voyage, and there is no consensus on the names of the vessels. What voyage might this refer to, considering one or more voyages remain secret?

There is a further detail on which chroniclers agree: that the proposal was made to the nobles of Genoa. The Cybos probably tried to involve the city to which they belonged. Not succeeding there, they did the best they could along with their allies and waited for a better time: the ascent of Giovanni Battista to Peter's throne.

The greatest infamy continuing to pursue Columbus in the most colossal project of historical disinformation is the claim that he never knew what land he had reached and died believing it was Asia. The Christian admiral had a vision of the world going back to ancient times, when Asia and America were joined at the extreme north to form a single, enormous India, while a sea strait divided the two Americas at their midpoint, somewhere in present-day Central America. It was Columbus's obsession on his last, despairing voyage to search for this sea passage between the two American continents: a passage leading, after many more months of sailing, to Chinese Asia, and from there to Mount Zion. Evidently, everything lined up perfectly with the maps of the ancient sea kings.

It should be added, as evidence that Columbus's notions were correct, that the Bering Strait had not yet been discovered and that there was a frozen sea to the north under which a stretch of land was presumed to exist, uniting the Asian continent to the "new" one. This very ice formed a kind of umbilical cord linking what were known, for a long time, as the East Indies and the West Indies—like the two sides of a coin in an irreproachable vision that avoided shattering antiquated geographical ideas and the Trinitarian geographic dogma of the three floating continents and respected the sacredness of the known world. Furthermore, "a Turkish map from 1559 [at which time the extreme north was still unexplored], that of Hadji Ahmed, shows Antarctica and the Pacific coast of the United States with extreme precision. But it gets better: This map also shows an unknown land, forming a bridge between Siberia and Alaska across the Bering Strait!"[24]

Columbus knew perfectly well the shores he reached were not those of the traditional Indies but instead were those of a composite continent divided into various regions. They were the farthest promontories and shores of an infinite and indistinct territory, forming part of what were known as the Three Indies. The pieces of evidence are innumerable—and finally, albeit with some justifiable errors, Columbus's calculations were almost perfect.

Word of the maps Columbus possessed and his prediscovery—if the Turkish admiral did not learn of them directly from the navigator in Spain—may have come from a Spanish sailor who, it is said, was taken prisoner on the Iberian coast before 1498. In May of that year Columbus set sail on his third official expedition. The sailor, however, told of having already gone on *three* expeditions with the caravels. Surely he must have participated in a hidden voyage with the navigator.

The truth resurfaces, one word at a time. Not by chance, he related: "We first arrived at the straits of Gibraltar; then, having sailed four thousand miles . . ."[25]

In 1492, the caravels sailed from Palos, a port that is beyond the Pillars of Hercules, past Gibraltar, facing the ocean. But the sailor told of a departure from somewhere within the Mediterranean. Once again, the details do not line up with those of the official expedition. According to some, the Spanish sailor was none other than Rodrigo de Triana, the first to sight the New World, whom Columbus then supposedly dispossessed of the ten thousand maravedis promised by the Spanish crown, a man who, made desperate to the point of insanity by the robbery he had suffered, had defected to the enemy side.

If the stool pigeon was Rodrigo, he should have hated Columbus, which would not explain such flattering statements accompanying Piri Reis's map—unless the sailor was an apostate Muslim, in line with a diverse crew that included at least two Jews, starting with the interpreter and the physician, and had himself formed part of some failed utopian plan. Then, with his tip-off he might have wished to avenge himself on someone other than the navigator.

Piri Reis writes of Columbus as a great astronomer, a great man of science. This is a singular compliment from a man of great Muslim science, especially in a time when, after Innocent VIII and Columbus had died, Christianity and Islam were fighting with no holds barred to rule the world. It was a different time in which the Turkish admiral was condemned to death (another heretic?) "officially for having raised the siege from the fortress of Ormuz, but someone asserted that his condemnation was desired by the old keepers of those secret archives, who accused him of having removed ancient documents—the same ones that allowed him to draw his famous map on gazelle skin . . ."[26]

Even his "golden fleece" came back to bite him. The parables of the two admirals, amid secret archives and ancient documents, are incredibly similar; two lives leading from the altar to ashes. Were they great traitors or great men betrayed?

Yet what if this Arabic date was incorrect? A zero (890 is the same

as AD 1485) in old and faded calligraphic evidence can easily be confused with a 6. With good reason some transcribe the year as 896. Paolo
Emilio Taviani, the great Italian scholar of Columbus, speaks of the year
896 of the Arabic calendar. Would this, then, be a colossal mistake? Not
really, because the Muslim year 896 corresponds to 1490–1491 in the
Christian era. It changes the order of events, but we can still speak of a
prediscovery.[27]

Interestingly, on Innocent VIII's tomb in St. Peter's, on Pollaiolo's
beautiful mausoleum, the third line of the epigraph reads: *Novi orbis suo
aevo inventi gloria* (In the time of his pontificate, the glory of the discovery of the New World). In addition, Panvinio states that the greatest
event recorded by human memory occurred toward the end of Innocent's
pontificate. Giovanni Battista Cybo was pope from 1484 until July 25,
1492. The circle is complete: the discovery (whether 1485 or 1490–91)
would indeed have occurred during his pontificate.

In the Christian Temple of Truth that carving could speak only the
truth: the truth history has erased. Pastor defined Pope Innocent VIII
as the sailor pope. Again, why? What has already been written is enough
to explain it. At this point, however, research may lead us elsewhere in a
game of mirrors between the Father and the Son: father and son together,
in the vessel of the Church, driven by the wind of the Holy Spirit so that
the Spirit might breathe upon a world finally made complete. Just as
Columbus would take his young son on board, so the future sailor pope
brought his own son with him, into a world yet to be discovered—and
his name was the Dove *(Colombo)*.

The architecture of the tomb, as we have seen, was inverted from its
original structure. At first, the living pope was at the bottom looking
up, with the dead pope above, but now the dead pope is on the lower
level. It is as if his death (according to history) has prevailed over his
life. Such changes would not have occurred by chance in the Temple
of Christ. The statue of the pope above, with the lance of Longinus
in his hands, has the face of Columbus. His shoulders and his gaze
are oriented perfectly in a north–south direction. "Midnight corresponds to the north, and therefore to the gate of the Gods, while

midday corresponds to summer and therefore to the gate of men. It is no coincidence [that] in the first degree of the apprentice Mason, the work of the adept lasts from midday to midnight. In other words, the initiatory path leaves from the gate of men to arrive at that of the gods."[28] It was the path of the "divine" man.

ELEVEN

Three-Map Monte

THE CARDS OF the great game were dealt slowly over the centuries in a ceaseless dance of maps, a continuous "now you see it, now you don't," a scientific progress extremely rich in astonishing results in the eastern regions and in the parts of Europe where Muslims, Jews, and Christians were to be found often working together to give a face to the new world that was appearing and disappearing, in a truth hard to reconstruct. Such things occurred, for example, on an island in the middle of the Mediterranean where one of the most renowned cartographical schools was established. Its protagonist was a Jew. The island was Majorca, homeland of the Franciscan Ramon Llull, who had prophesied the other world; the Jew was Abraham Cresques. Among his most trusted collaborators was his son Jehuda, who would become geographer to Prince Henry the Navigator of Portugal. Secret knowledge was passed on from father to son.

Cresques, like many others, was inspired by Marco Polo's *Travels,* and so in his Catalan Atlas of 1375 there appears, perhaps for the first time, the peninsular form of India, a Far East at last no longer confined to the unknown far-off lands, but outlined against the azure sea. The Gordian knot of Alexander the Great, roping off the world, was loosening. The design was completed most perfectly and artistically in the remarkable world map of the Venetian monk Fra Mauro from 1459.

Outwardly, Fra Mauro was a silent man of the Church who worked near the Venetian lagoon, in the Camaldolite monastery of San Michele. He was also in contact with Portugal, by the Atlantic, and was the drawer of maps for King Alfonso V. For lack of concrete proof we can only guess that for some of his youth he must have lived in Genoa, one of the centers for ideas in our history. What ideas did the friar have? He was a seeker of the truth for whom faith—as far as possible in those times—was not a set of blinders.[1]

And his Africa is surrounded by the sea—many decades before Bartolomeo Diaz sailed to the tempestuous cape at the southernmost point of the continent, christening it the Cape of Good Hope, and rounding it, proving India could be reached by the southern route.

Cresques was an erudite Jew raised on a Mediterranean island in a multiethnic atmosphere. Mauro was a friar, observant and devout yet somewhat universalistic and tolerant, studying in the islands of the Venetian lagoon. Both men were in search of more islands, the islands of dreams and mystery. Their globe began to resemble reality, and they were as fascinating as an oracle.

Fra Mauro's spherical world is more than six feet in diameter, a work as colossal as it is beautiful. Scholars have detected a probable Islamic influence based on the upside-down orientation of the map. Following the multicultural current of thought running through those minds most open to change, the friar wrote that he had drawn extensively upon Marco Polo's text for the depiction of Asia. "This great map is both the ultimate artifact of medieval cartography and a prime example of the transition to early modern mapping."[2]

Unfortunately, this conception of two opposing spheres has caused us to view our modern era as more enlightened in contrast to the darkness of earlier centuries. Thus errors become set in stone and knowledge divides into two irreconcilable categories: the *before* that was not capable of knowing and the *after* that can explain everything.

Yet people were moving, cautiously but continuously, first receiving new things and then accepting them, in a series of small steps and giant leaps (like those of the first man on the moon, or those of possible extraterrestrial beings), toward the completeness of the terrestrial globe.

They even placed Paradise within it! That place was believed at the time to be the earthly reflection of the celestial world. It was a belief that presented no problems as long as it remained confined within the mystery of an abstract empire, but eventually, its geographic location would have had to be revealed through the exploration of the East. Such were the problems to be overcome. By now, humankind was in motion and resuming its interrupted path.

✠

There was one scientist especially, in the second half of the fifteenth century, who can be considered another inspirer of Columbus's voyage—and who might somehow bring resolution to many aspects of the ancient controversies: Henricus Martellus. Ptolemy had confined the waters between known and unknown shores, making the oceans into closed basins and thus making the Mare Indicum (Indian Ocean) south of Asia an eastern replica of the Mediterranean. Yet that layout was obsolete by now, as we have seen, and had already been torn apart. The world of the German Henricus Martellus was another step toward the truth. In his map the waters of the world, as in the maps by Cresques and Fra Mauro, swell like a flood and surround the land in a turquoise ring. One last step needed to be taken.

Namely, the East had to expand to include a vast space of blue water, beyond the Ganges and the Indicum, populated by countless islands of greater or lesser size. From the coast of Spain to China this extension represents a true ocean: the mythical Ouroboros, in the medieval imagination the serpent that encircled the globe and devoured its tail, a sign of the eternal return between East and West. At the northeast extremity of the map, far from the shores of farthest India, is the usual island—the island that cannot be Japan but might be part of America. It is not the only puzzle in this cartographical depiction.[3]

Martellus was probably from Nuremberg and probably knew Cardinal Nicholas of Cusa. He was in Italy from 1480 to 1496 and had dealings with the Medici, with Lorenzo the Magnificent, and with Pope Innocent VIII, for whom he produced a world map.

It is evident that the Florentine map must have had counterparts jealously guarded in the Vatican. The distances are deceptive, appearing not to reflect those in reality, but the method of projection may correspond to rules we do not know. Nor does the map claim to show the exact location of lands yet to be discovered. An intense war of espionage centered on cartography, and copying or distributing the contents of maps was punishable by death.

In 1489 Martellus drew another version of his Florentine world map but less up to date. This other map is much less explicit regarding the eastern ocean, almost as if one map were partly to reveal things, the other to hide them. In this latter map Asia reaches to the edge, with a tiny strip of sea continuing to the east. Yet both maps are of fundamental importance—because, besides showing an Africa entirely navigable to the extreme south, before the official discovery of that route, they also show an India that is larger and more different than in all previous representations.

What was the novelty? With respect to the dominant *Geography* of Ptolemy, all people now "agree that his numerical data, were corrupted over the centuries through the transcription of manuscripts."[4]

In Martellus's map besides reaffirming the idea of a circumnavigable globe, with the ocean reaching past Asia beyond the River Ganges, there is a mysterious Asiatic "fourth peninsula." It is part of a continent, added to the Ptolemaic view, although in a reconstruction it is stretched to the southwest, just as Africa is shown stretched toward the southeast in the other hemisphere, in a convergence presumably resulting from cartographical requirements. The shape of this unknown fourth peninsula is all too familiar, however; its form suggests definite déjà vu.

A simple test is enough: If you hold Martellus's planisphere in front of a mirror, as if by magic, North America appears more or less as we know it today—an America reaching down to the Central American isthmus, with the hump of present-day Honduras and Nicaragua, ending exactly where Columbus believed he would find the passage through to the Indies.

A New World materializes to reconcile ancient beliefs while respecting Trinitarian geography; Asia and America would thus form a single "body." The unknown land to which voyagers would sail is there but is simply an appendage of the Indies already known. The Pacific is completely abolished, and every doubt appears to be resolved.[5]

Yet it is not understood why some scholars see South America in this peninsular mass depicted by Martellus—a part of the world surely known to the Portuguese and almost surely to Christopher Columbus himself. South America was the only novelty to which Columbus, when he encountered it, would show a certain surprise (whether real or feigned). If the fourth peninsula on Martellus's map were real, then the Spanish caravels reaching it in the direction from which they must have come could easily have rounded it at its southernmost point. Although the shape is distorted, the coastlines drawn by Martellus leave no room for doubt: For him, North America was simply a further projection of the Indies, changing from east into west, and thus the first shore reached by anyone who sailed west from Europe.[6]

From there, it seemed as if the crossing to the (already known) near Indies would be easy and fairly quick. This was what the navigator had professed, according to what we have always been told and given to understand.

This would be the easiest way to answer the age-old question. Columbus was mistaken only regarding the distances, which were wrong even on the maps of more accredited scientists. The factions for and against the navigator's actual geographical knowledge might reach a Solomonic point of disagreement, but it is an unsatisfactory conclusion. It only confirms the cloak of deception that has since shrouded Columbus.

✠

Attentively examining many of these documents and others, we note the presence of a small peninsula with an unmistakable form, Florida. The "flowery land" is just another small mystery within the great mystery. It is stated "that it is perhaps the greatest unresolved cartographic enigma of the period," and the complexity and dimension of the enigmas are underestimated. Officially, this peninsula was reached only in 1513, and yet it appears earlier, on the planisphere of Juan de la Cosa (1500), one of Columbus's companions on the first voyage and later his adversary. The Spaniard places an image of St. Christopher precisely in the place, between north and south, where Columbus believed the passage to be. The strait supposed to separate the Americas is Solomonically divided by the image of the giant saint, the bearer of the Christ child, the new man. La Cosa was not the only one to predict Florida. The land of eternal youth, where the fountain of the elixir of long life was believed to exist, is depicted in numerous other maps, including the green one by Cantino.[7]

Cantino was a diplomatic agent from the Estensi family of Ferrara and an enthusiast for geographical mysteries. He also lived in Lisbon, where he purchased the invaluable map. Returning to Italy, he stopped in Genoa, where he sold a copy of it to Francesco Catanio (the surname is a nearly perfect anagram of Cantino). He finally handed it over to Ercole d'Este in Ferrara. The hunt for the true face of the world fascinated all those in power at the time. Cantino's planisphere is very beautiful. The land indicated as Isabella is Cuba, shown unequivocally as an island, despite the fact that Columbus never knew this, and believed it to be the mainland for the rest of his life. A little farther on, there is Florida, and this is from 1502!

There are similar "errors" in Nicolo Caveri's map from 1504–1505, which bears the signature of a Genoese cartographer. Once again, there is no doubt: The Gulf of Mexico is there, along with the Yucatán and Florida. The list continues with a series of geographers, all showing that they knew much more than they are supposed to have known—now in Genoa, now in Portugal, but various other locations in Italy could also be named. Others, as we have seen, belonged to circles located around Palma in Majorca. Between truth and legend, these places almost always lead us back to the restless peregrinations and many homelands of Christopher Columbus.

North America, with the insular Cuba and the Florida peninsula, was evidently territory already known with a mathematical precision. Since when? It is difficult to answer with absolute surety. One thing is sure: History has continually discounted any possibility that Columbus may have reached the mainland. When earlier studies force scholars to acknowledge this, they try to reinforce the black legend of a man who, however great he may have been, was incapable of understanding anything and made a sensational, though completely unconscious, discovery.

Yet on Wednesday, November 21, 1492, his ship log reads: "He was moved to believe, he says, that the quadrant was correct by seeing that the North Star was as high as in Castile, and if this is true, he had drawn very near to, and was as high as, the coast of Florida. But where, then, are these islands which he had under consideration?" The admiral adds that the great heat there led him to express his doubt once again; but "it is clear that if he was on the coast of Florida it would not be warm but cold." The log mentions Florida.[8]

Considering the weather conditions, we are led to think that Columbus's Florida, known from previous voyages, extended farther to the north than present-day Florida.[9]

November 21 was also the day of Martín Alonso Pinzón's desertion. He left suddenly, in plain sight of Columbus's other ships. The Spaniard may have been aiming for the mainland, but he did not find it. He, and only he, was looking for nothing but gold.

The admiral was therefore near to the mainland and knew it consciously during the first official expedition and the prediscovery. Yet out of ignorance he missed reaching the most important shore. Even though he was hardly mistaken about anything, history has seen to it that Columbus was always wrong. The interests of Spain allow for no acknowledgment whatsoever. Thus, Columbus couldn't, and above all shouldn't, have landed on the American mainland. The final landing must remain an eternally elusive mirage for him. His landing would have cost the state coffers too much—namely, the agreed recompense.

It was not only a case of claiming that Columbus missed the target out of simple foolishness, despite the ease and favorable possibility of running into the New World, a predecessor would have to be created for this eventuality. Amerigo Vespucci was chosen as a convenience, a mercenary, a hired man—only for it to be discovered, centuries later, that his flaunted primacy in landing on the mainland was nothing but a great lie. It was believed this Florentine explorer reached Florida in 1497. Subsequent studies would demonstrate this was not true, but by then it was too late. The fraud (for whose benefit if not for Spain's?) had already overturned Columbus's primogeniture and a false name would forever be given to the new lands. The destiny of the two Italian explorers, who had even been friends, was separated forever.

Did not the well-read courtier Pietro Martire d'Anghiera, a friend of Columbus, write referring to the navigator's voyages to the New World before Columbus's name was known to Vespucci? Pietro Martire had received news from Columbus himself at the Spanish court. The proof, however, has been crushed under the weight of the five-century deception, suppressing truth and justice. Columbus, all things considered, has already had enough glory as compensation for the wickedness attributed to him!

It is true that cartography was muddled, and it has certainly reached us today incomplete and full of holes. It could also be said the ideas were close to the truth, but absolute truths were out of the question. Yet Columbus and his son, amid certainties and intuitions, were stumbling toward a precise reconstitution of the truth. They were approaching it by degrees, by way of superior knowledge and experience. Their fundamental sin was in being strangers in a strange land, aspiring to monopolize El Dorado. They were the messengers of a dream whose mandators would be made to disappear in an incredible sequence of suspicious deaths affecting Rome, Florence, and the representatives of the Neoplatonic academies—precisely at the moment of the dream's realization and the attainment of the cornucopia and the secrets of the world.

Many maps have been rediscovered in recent times, and an organized study of the questions they provoke has not yet been accomplished. Who, in the scientific world, would dare challenge five hundred years of science? But this science has inherited, reinforced, and perpetrated errors and was therefore born under the sign of an unconfessable original sin. It is preferable to leave Columbus in his limbo, or better, in his hell. It is preferable to interpret maps and writings as a medieval legacy, as junk left over from the Dark Ages. It is preferable if we amuse ourselves with the question fit for a game show: Was Columbus a man of the Middle Ages or the Renaissance?

✠

Everyone—Jews, Muslims, and Christians, not to mention the Chinese and Japanese—possessed charts and world maps. Most of these have been lost. Some are surely still to be rediscovered. The subject of the disappearance of countless charts and world maps would require a whole separate chapter. Many more of them existed than is believed, and their distribution was much more widespread than is thought. The illustrated charts, bringing bulletins of new discoveries, were from Portugal, Spain, Germany, and the Vatican—but only the Vatican had at its disposal a constant influx of ideas superior to all other earthly powers. Among the greatest keepers and propagators of geography, only the Muslims could have beaten Christianity to the finish of the competition. Perhaps, indeed, this is the greatest merit of Columbus's endeavor: He planted the cross in a place where we might otherwise have knelt, swaying in prayer and facing Mecca.

From everywhere, more or less in unison, people ventured upon the world's highways. The Arabs in the fourteenth century had their Muslim counterpart to the Christian Marco Polo in Abu Abdallah ibn Battuta, another universal pilgrim whose travels lasted twenty-nine years. "He visited not only the central regions of Islam, but also its remote frontiers in India, Indonesia, Central Asia, East Africa, and Western Sudan."[10]

Ibn Battuta was as brave an explorer as Marco Polo, "risking his life to discover terra incognita and bring knowledge of it to public attention."[11] He made a stop in the Holy Land, where he mingled with Crusaders and visited, among other places, Acre, the knights' epicenter for meetings and knowledge and for friendships that might also be interpreted as treason. He expounds at length upon the lives of religious men, especially the Sufis, of whom he was evidently one himself. Sufism was the form of Muslim mysticism closest to the secret and esoteric vein of the Templars in particular and of Crusaders in general. It professed tolerance and predicted the coming of a single God, a providential God common to all the earth's peoples. Sufism was the secret link to Islam for a universal embrace between enemy faiths. Ibn Battuta's original text has been lost, and little is known of his life other than his own version of events. He had no "experience as a writer of geography, history, or ethnography, but he was . . . 'the supreme example of *le géographe malgré lui*,' ('the geographer in spite of himself')."[12]

The more we proceed with the investigation along the path of knowledge, the more we meet with a series of vocations that were accidental, or were interpreted as such. Yet these people picked the locks of knowledge in a triumphant learned ignorance.

One historical fact remains: In the thirteenth century Mongols coming from central Asia and allied with the Turks conquered China, Russia, and a large part of the Middle East. In the eternal confrontation between East and West, Islam also threatened to prevail in this case. How great was the danger of a discovery of America by the Muslims? The answer remains hidden in the unknown and in vanished documents.[13]

The West—with the exception of a few solitary courageous scientists whose meetings were always held at risk of heresy—was torn apart by territorial and theological disputes, and dogma formed a barrier against anything new. Meanwhile, Islam was involved in the study of mathematics, astronomy, medicine, and physics thanks to the recovery of Greek texts and its proximity to the Far East. On the one side, there were barren disputes and stony censorship; on the other, science was already in motion. The Muslims looked not only at the stars, but also beyond the confines of Ptolemy's world.[14]

✠

Were the Muslims then the first to leave a new footprint upon the world? Did they mentally rediscover America? Were they the real progenitors of the "empire of Satan" that today some of them wish to destroy?

As early as the year 1000, the Neoplatonist Avicenna wrote the most famous medical work of all time, disputing the *Corpus Hippocraticum*. It was drawn from Greek sources. He was accused of being a Jew by maternal descent, and he was irritated by Aristotle's *Metaphysics*. He had grown up within an Islam that had prevailed over Zoroastrians, Manicheans, Buddhists, and Nestorians. He had imbibed information from magical sources, and his healings were even miraculous. A fortune-teller predicted to him: "You will reach the stars. You will approach them as rarely happens to men. You will also be cursed for this. You will be immortal but will pay for your immortality with eternal vagabondage." There is a suspicion he died by being poisoned. Poison, over the course of the centuries, has always been the great custodian of lies and injustice. It would be used unsparingly by Rodrigo Borgia, the successor of Innocent VIII.

The Qur'an and the canonical traditions spoke of knowledge above all else as the instrument of salvation, urging believers to study nature.[15] Medicine involved the related study of plants, and of alchemy. All the elements to ignite the Renaissance were already present embryonically in Islam—but in a syncretism that would not be all-inclusive, provoking endless conflict. A great part of this knowledge migrated to the western courts, beginning with Spanish Andalusia, Al Andalus to the Muslims. Sephardic Spain gathered it and then struck the spark in Europe to bring the Renaissance to life. What swung the scales in favor of the Christian world—right up to the present day—was the subsequent decline of Islam, and surely also Gutenberg's invention. The first Qur'an was printed in Muslim territory only in 1874; the race had already been lost.

Nascent publishing also naturally reproduced maps, such as the Florentine world map of 1506 by Giovanni Matteo Contarini (perhaps a Venetian), which is believed to be the earliest printed map known today. Printed maps meant works could be multiplied indefinitely. Their disappearances occurred undercover. Only one example of it is known, preserved in London. The scientist Contarini's work (rediscovered in 1922) was completed in 1506, the year Columbus died. The mapmaker was totally ignored, even to the point that no news was given of his death. Despite the oblivion already surrounding the figure of the navigator of the two worlds, Contarini wrote, regarding the West Indies, that they had been discovered by "Master Christopher Columbus."[16]

It is obvious the statements in those original chronicles, often contradicting each other, cannot be taken as the truth. Why should a single truth be sustained simply by repetition over the centuries? In Contarini's work, however, the most surprising thing is the appellative "Master" used for Columbus. The Masters were holders of the highest offices in knightly orders. Once again, a knight of the sea rides forth and will sign his name with the esoteric cryptogram of a grand master, never definitively interpreted in five hundred years. The trail of knights is endless, a cavalcade leading back to Innocent VIII and St. Peter's throne.

The revelation of the Americas was the final point in a confrontation between religions, civilizations, and currents of thought. There were then, just as there are today, three great world religions, three expressions of interpreting the human path. Would they be united by prayer and by the cross or divided by the sword? This was, and is, the great question uniting all the believers of the world, a question especially pressing in the Spain of three religions. Meanwhile, all eyes were turned toward Jerusalem, which was also Al Quds, the holy, for the Muslims.

Another Marco Polo came from that same Spain: not a Christian, not a Muslim, but a Jewish rabbi, Benjamin. In the twelfth century, he "left from Tudela on a long voyage, comparable to those undertaken by Marco Polo and ibn Battuta. . . . [H]e decided to go in search of Jewish communities, wherever they might be . . ."[17]

✠

Amid political and religious entanglement and unresolved geography, all the faiths sent their Marco Polos upon the highways of the world: Muslims, Jews, and Christians. Merchants and pilgrims alike—indeed, there was sometimes little difference between the two—advanced along the unknown paths of the globe.[18]

All were seeking the East, a bridgehead to advance into the unknown. Only one of them reached it and baptized it as definitively Christian. We have not yet reflected sufficiently upon this three-player contest, which could even have signaled the final armistice for the world.

The fall of Constantinople in 1453 was, as we have seen, a definite turning point. Retaliation was necessary. Nicholas V, the Ligurian pope from Sarzana who died in 1455, issued a bull to summon Christendom together, denouncing Mehmed as the precursor to the Antichrist, the red dragon of the Apocalypse. The Christians needed a qualitative leap. They needed successors to St. Peter who would free them from their anguish and broaden the horizons of the Crusade. They needed popes who were also scientists and knights. They needed seekers of the Grail, and gold from a Christ-Ophir. In 1454, Enea Silvio Piccolomini announced: "We must admit it: No greater shame has ever assailed the Christians; in the past we have only been defeated in Asia and in Africa, therefore in foreign lands. But now a blow has been struck in Europe, in our homeland, in our house where we must live, and it has been a hard blow."[19]

The future Pius II—whose writings Columbus read attentively, along with the works of Cardinal Pierre d'Ailly—had studied in Byzantium, and probably had knowledge of many secrets. He was a scholar of geography and had been to the East himself. In the moment of peril, a pope was immediately chosen who appeared to have many things in common with the man who would be, some decades later, Innocent VIII. New geography and supreme economic and spiritual power were now hand in hand. The Church was always first in line.[20]

Relations between Rome, Florence, Venice, and Byzantium thicken the plot. In the city of the Medici, a humanist cenacle gathered at the Convento degli Angeli. Besides Enea Silvio Piccolomini and Cosimo de' Medici, members included the friar of St. Mark; Giorgio Antonio Vespucci, uncle of Amerigo; and Paolo dal Pozzo Toscanelli, librarian of St. Mark's. The brother of Henry the Navigator, the great keeper of the Atlantic route, arrived in Venice and Florence in 1428 in order to gather maps and documents, which he brought to the Academy of Sagres, in Portugal, facing the Atlantic. Learned men from all over the world gathered there to study the ocean's puzzles. There, the setting sun descended into a world of mystery in the region where the young Columbus had swum to shore, having apparently survived a naval battle.

People unanimously believed in God, and in the designs of Providence. According to interpretations often verging on the ridiculous, it would always be chance that guided the destinies of the century that would change the world. On the contrary, the hidden framework of this story reinforces the existence of a sort of multinationality of ideas that moved in concert for the achievement of a single end—until rivalry divided them.

When another pilgrim of the East, Niccolò da Conti, returned to Italy, the Venetian Pope Eugenius IV, the predecessor of Nicholas V, who sought a reconciliation between the Romans and the Easterners, obliged him "to give the complete account of his peregrinations in Asia to the pontifical secretary Poggio Bracciolini. Niccolò's account is important because it confirms that of Marco Polo point by point."[21]

The truth was in Marco Polo's original! The truth, known since the time of the Vikings, was already in the hands of the Church. The young Venetian Niccolò da Conti, like the most classic of infiltrators, had married an Arab woman, converted to Islam, and moved to Calicut. This city was a Nestorian center, home of the Holy Apostolic Catholic Assyrian Church of the East. He had traveled there on Chinese junks that had almost certainly reached America and Australia in 1421.[22]

✠

Voyagers, missionaries, pilgrims, merchants, secret meetings of scholars, schools of geography, crowned monarchs and lords, states sovereign or otherwise: A continuous procession moved along in search of the lands to be revealed. The procession combined the will for expansion and domination, economic interests promising immense riches with little effort, the sincere desire to acquire knowledge and expand the confines of human learning, the vow to spread the Christian word to unknown peoples and to save the idolaters, the hope of being able to found a New World and create the new man, and the quest for the Grail and the truth. There was not a single ruler or lord in the second half of the fifteenth century who did not conform to this portrait of a prince.

Temporal powers brought with them the shortcomings of the transient. One place and one role remained central and eternal in the passing of the ages: that of Rome and her pope.[23] Only the Church had the complete vision of what was new and the nearest attainable synthesis of reality, calling into question the origin of Adam and the structure of the world. Only the Church could preside over a traumatic development of consciousness to put at risk its own credibility and that of the Fathers. Galileo Galilei would also suffer for this.

Destination: America. After the anesthesia of ignorance nothing remained but to proceed with the awakening. The time of quibbling and sophistry was over. Like the devastating approach of an immense asteroid, the other half of the terrestrial globe was looming. If the impact could not be predicted and cushioned, then among the many powers, only the survival of Rome was at risk. Governing geography meant governing the world—the old as well as the new—and gaining possession of the future.

Should we laugh or cry? Such are the expressions of the two philosophers, Heraclitus and Democritus, positioned on either side of the terrestrial globe in the 1487 fresco by Donato Bramante, the great artist from Urbino.[24] The globe that appears in this work is singular; it shows the Indian Ocean continuing endlessly to the East, beyond the mythical island of Tabropana, present-day Sri Lanka.

In the moment of truth and need, Providence, which according to faith looks much farther ahead than humans can see, brought forth geographer popes: a geographer Pope Pius II; a geographer cardinal, d'Ailly; and another cardinal, Bessarion, who came from the East and had a map of his own. His learned comrade Nicholas of Cusa also drew maps. Surely the connection includes many others? Columbus, as far as we know, was particularly attentive in reading the works of the first two. He left copious notes to accompany these texts.

Columbus read widely. He had no religious or theological inhibition about preparing himself with the most diverse literature. His problem and aspiration was to reconcile texts of one sort with another without causing damage to the Christian body. He sought the optimum way to gather into a final solution the many scattered and disorganized clues that were already in the relatively public domain of educated circles.

The study of impossible maps could continue; the list was endless. No research is easier than that committed to finding a map with "impossible" characteristics.[25]

As part of his universalistic chimera, the Sienese Pius II had Giro-lamo Bellavista illuminate a colored globe in both large and small scale to serve as an example of his work. More important, "he had another world map designed by Antonio Leonardi, a Venetian churchman and cosmographer upon whom all writers on geographical matters are silent. At the pope's death, the map was left to his nephew and adopted son Francesco, the future Pope Pius III, who mentioned it in his will. These two world maps were studied by Pinzón when he came to Rome in 1491."[26]

Let us return to Tuscany, Siena, the sword in the stone, and the Piccolomini family, a Round Table of omnipresent knights, and to the two Franciscan popes and the ubiquitous world maps Pinzón researched on behalf of Ferdinand. The swift current flowing into the greater waters of the Tiber leads ever on to Christian Rome. The problem, as we have seen, was so pressing as to force Enea Silvio to write to Mehmed II, his alter ego ruling the East. Meanwhile, the past was merging with the present.[27] Now that the conjunction was in process, the future could only belong to Christ. A Christ said to be the one God, a Christ risen to restore peace on earth.[28]

"No one," the pope wrote, "sufficiently knew the exact measure-ment of the earth," but he considered Eratosthenes the most diligent in the calculation of the entire sphere. Taking account of the prestige the task would give him, Columbus read what the pope had written. He could only share Pius II's appreciation of Eratosthenes, especially as he was a student of Marinus of Tyre, with whom Ptolemy had disagreed in defining the limits of the earth. Columbus therefore knew exactly the circumference of the earth.

Even today, history accuses him of having erred in even his simplest calculations. Centuries of injustice have reduced the man who enlarged the world to someone ignorant who was limited to making it smaller. How has the belief persisted for five hundred years that he thought he had arrived in China when he knew he must seek a mythical land—especially considering the Indies used to refer to the Eastern lands, but not those that formed the Chinese empire?[29]

Top left: the most famous portrait of Christopher Columbus, attributed to Ridolfo del Ghirlandaio. Top right: the red pastel drawing of Innocent VIII attributed to Antonio Pollaiolo, which served as a study for the pope's tomb in St. Peter's. Left: another portrait of the navigator, attributed to Tobias Stimmer, from an engraving in a book by Paolo Giovio. The resemblance between the three figures is striking (see below).

Top left: Columbus, with flowing hair, by Aliprando Caprioli (1596), inspired by the model in Paolo Giovio's book. Top right: a recent and controversial discovery: Columbus in his later years, painted by the Spanish artist Pedro Berruguete. Left: Arano-Aronne Cybo, father of Giovanni Battista Cybo, Pope Innocent VIII. Here also there is a notable resemblance to the other two figures (see below).

ARANO CIBO

A RANO Cibò, Figliuolo di Mauritio : fu non men prudente, che forte ; e benche nato d'antica Famiglia , il valore in lui accrebbe honore alla nobiltà. Dalla Republica di Genoua fu con armata di mare mandato al soccorso di Napoli per la parte di Renato, che con Alfonso, del Regno contendeua.

Top left: the statue of Innocent VIII on the upper part of the tomb by Pollaiolo in St. Peter's. In his hand he holds the miraculous Lance of Longinus. Top right: detail of the face of Innocent VIII: once again, the resemblance to Christopher Columbus is surprising. Below: the revealing epitaph, with the third line reading "Novi orbis suo aevo inventi gloria" (the glory of the new world discovered in his time).

D   O   M
INNOCENTIO VIII CYBO PONT MAX
ITALIGAE PACIS PERPETVO CVSTODI
NOVI ORBIS SVO AEVO INVENTI GLORIA
REGI HISPANIARVM CATHOLICI NOMINE IMPOSITO
CRVCIS SACRO SANCTAE REPERTO TITVLO
LANCEA OVAE CHRISTI HAVSIT LATVS
A BAIAZETE TVRCARVM TYRANNO DONO MISSA
AETERNVM INSIGNI
MONVMENTVM E VETERE BASILICA HVC TRANSLATVM
ALBERICVS CYBO MALASPINA
PRINCEPS MASSAE
FERENTILLI DVX MARCHIO CARRARIAE ETC
PRONEPOS
ORNATIVS AVGVSTIVSQ POSVIT ANNO DOM MDCXII

Columbus's shield (left) and that of the Cybo family (right). The colors of the navigator's original arms are almost exactly the same as those of the pope.

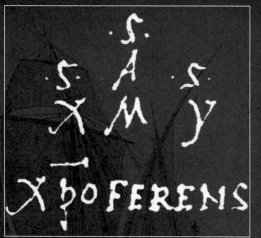

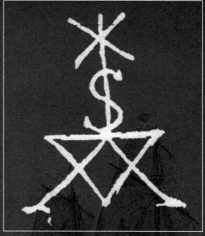

Christopher Columbus's esoteric cryptogram (left) and the signature of the ceramicist and alchemist Mastro Giorgio (right). Many of the letters are the same.

The statue of Boniface IX in the basilica of St. Paul in Rome. On the book it reads: "Stirpe Thomacellus genere Cibo."

The Crusader cross with eight points, like the cross on Columbus's sails in an engraving from 1493. Curiously, on the newly discovered islands, there are already buildings with spires that look like church towers.

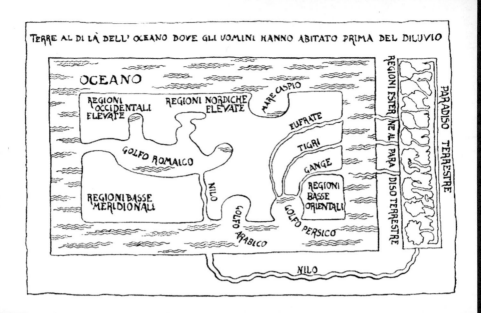

Modern Italian copy of Cosmas Indicopleustes' map: to the right the Earthly Paradise (Columbus's other world) is identified at the top as "The lands beyond the ocean where men lived before the Flood."

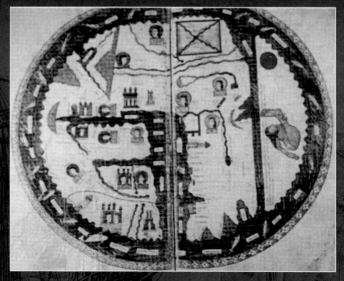

The Mappa Mundi in the cathedral of El Burgo de Osma (1086). To the right there is a fourth "continent" inhabited by a monopod.

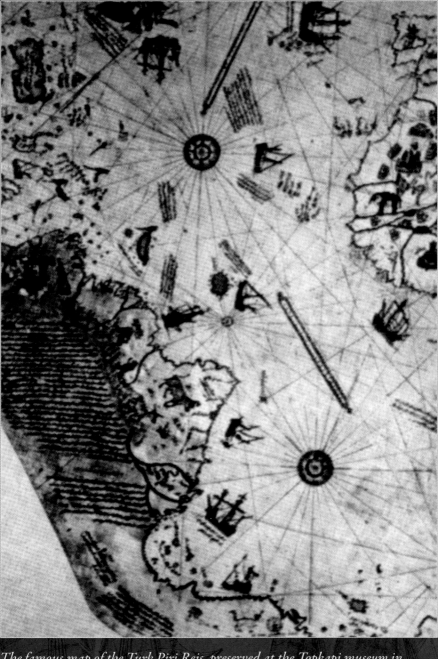

The famous map of the Turk Piri Reis, preserved at the Topkapi museum in Istanbul. The extent of land in South America is far greater than what had been discovered at the time.

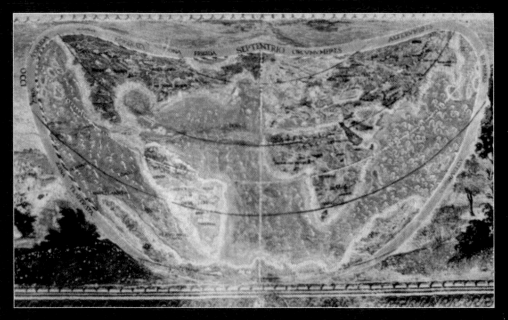

The map at the Palazzo Besta in Teglio shows a green land to the south, tangent to the Americas, "not yet entirely known."

The great map in the Palazzo di Caprarola, upon which there is another portrait of Columbus. As in many other maps, an immense land appears to the south.

Thus, Eratosthenes and Marinus of Tyre, along with books and maps, were the admiral's guides. They may have been imprecise, but they did not invalidate his calculations, which were almost perfect despite the limited technical resources of the scientists who had gone before. These sages had used their minds, not sterile machinery, and their guide was the harmony of the heavens and the stars, forever constant.

After Pius II's death and failed Crusade, a period of apparent quiet ensued: "When it was clear that the Turkish cannons in Constantinople had not announced the end of the world, even the prophecies and the interpretations of the future came to be seen through different eyes. Mehmed II's soldiers may have been the sour cherries of Methodius, but they were evidently not the Gog and Magog of the Last Battle. In Joachimite doctrine, too, the third age of the Holy Spirit prevailed, putting the images of collapse in the shade. Slowly, the Westerners recognized that the Ottomans were indeed a dangerous and foreign people, but that they needed to be fought by human means."[30]

Peace through reconciliation was sought above all else, in hope of a golden age, the return of the Kingdom of God. But further sudden defeats, the imminent year 1500, and other mishaps brought to center stage the final, unavoidable approach of an ultimate challenge. Otranto and the advancing Turkish horde rekindled the fear. How should the Saracens be fought? Would the loving peace of the Franciscans or the peace of the bloody Crusade prevail?[31]

Times change, but in the paths of opposing civilizations, the same questions are always posed at intervals of centuries and millennia. The settings change, but the confrontation between East and West will never, on both sides, lose its connotation of a holy and just war. Meanwhile, the supporters of peace at all cost and respect for the different were quickly shoved aside. From Columbus to the new millennium, little or nothing has changed.

The Renaissance did nothing but intensify the anticipation, in light of various interpretations, sometimes in total contradiction of one another. It was an incandescent centrifuge of science, philosophy, theology, faith, and heresy, a furnace fueled increasingly by events, an alchemy waiting for its philosopher's stone. Man the maker, the God on Earth, forged himself like a new Prometheus. Would he know how to imitate the Father, the Demiurge, the great architect, or would he turn away from him?[32]

✠

In its meandering streets and ancient palaces, Rome, the city of so many mysteries, hides and guards the paths to be retraced—such as in the grandiose residence that the Venetian Pope Paul II, Pietro Barbo, began building in the year 1455, next to the St. Mark's Basilica, of which he was cardinal. Today it is the Palazzo Venezia. Inside there were a number of frescoed rooms, some more beautiful than others: the room of the vestments, the room of the consistory, the royal room. There was also a parrot room—a bird that recalls the Indies—and another Mappamondo room. It contained "a world map of the earth painted on the wall."[33]

This is the room overlooking the Piazza Venezia: the room with the balcony, famous for other historical reasons. This was where Mussolini appeared in the garb of Il Duce.

Johannes Burchard, the chronicler of Vatican events, wrote in 1495 of *ille pulcherrimus Mappamundus* (that beautiful world map). Further on, he wrote of the "beautiful and famous world map, great and hanging high on the wall," *Aula, in qua est cosmografia orbis maxima et ornatissime picta* (the room in which that enormous world cosmography is most ornately painted). It was an immense, spectacular work, a true geographic colossus leading viewers to suppose it was the greatest ever in existence. The room in question is sixty-eight feet long, forty-one feet wide, and forty-two feet high.

Paul II was a Venetian who had taken sea voyages and also had a passion for studying geography.[34] The true author and patron of the colossal map in the Palazzo Venezia are unknown. The author is thought to have been the familiar Bellavista. The model is similar to those of Antonio Leonardi and Fra Mauro, but it surpasses them by a great measure. The Mappamondo room has undergone a number of renovations over time; only the decorative elements, considered innocuous, have remained intact. The room is still there, with much more to reveal than has yet been said. It is augmented by marvelous decorations by Andrea Mantegna, fashioned during the pontificate of Innocent VIII. On the wall where the vanished globe should be, between the central columns, there still are the large colorful arms of Pope Innocent, an imprint none has had the impertinence to obliterate. To the sides of the arms are those of his family and those of Marco Barbo, nephew of Paul II.

Scholars have found traces of this work up to 1683—and after that, nothing, as if it had just vanished. Hardly anyone could have even had access to this room, and what survived at first was made to disappear later.[35] Despite everything, some details in the Mappamondo room still bear the unmistakable signature of Innocent VIII, Giovanni Battista Cybo. Before him, with Callixtus III and Alexander VI, the two Spanish Borgias, as well as Nicholas V of Sarzana, the pontificate had been passed from a Tuscan to a Venetian to two Ligurians. From Florence, the new Athens, to the cities that best represented the maritime republics, popes were sent forth who appeared to play with the world—even if the comparison may seem irreverent—as in the marvelous sequence of Charlie Chaplin in *The Great Dictator*. They were popes whose families boasted fortunes hingeing on the development of commerce and finance, in a flow compromised by closing the borders with the East due to the presence of the Turks in Constantinople.

Every epoch's discovery of new places opens up new dreams for humanity, but it also mingles and muddles economic and territorial aspects in a traumatic and irreversible manner. The dream of those long-ago times vanished in a flash, just as the world maps were lost: "It was the fate of the majority of Europe's many world maps—especially those of large size, and those painted on walls—to disappear with the passage of time . . ."[36]

Who knows how Cipango, Columbus's Indies, the other world, was painted on the spectacular world map in the Palazzo Venezia—on Innocent VIII's map? Perhaps if some vestige of a design still remains beneath the successive layers of plaster, modern technology may one day yield an answer to this question—if the world map really was a fresco.

Even on this point, sources are uncertain; it could have been on board, on vellum, or an enormous inlay.

The Venetian Marco Barbo was a knight of the sea, as was the Genoese Giovanni Battista Cybo. There was a Venetian branch in Innocent VIII's family. If there was no direct link, there was surely an ideal link.

Thus these popes sailed ever farther into the great beyond, painting the world. They were mariners and geographers. The books, charts, and maps of the Vatican were also in the Palazzo Venezia with all their secrets and mysteries. In those rooms, on a hot day—July 25, 1492— Innocent VIII expired. Every July 25 the Church celebrated the feast of St. Christopher [St. Christopher was de-canonized in 1969 due to a lack of historical evidence that he existed and lived a holy life—Editor's note]. Innocent died with his eyes upon the world map, upon the new world soon to come. Seven days later, with the winds of Rome blowing in his sails, emblazoned with the eight-pointed cross of the Crusade, an unwitting beloved son set forth from Spain—on the most fascinating earthly adventure any human being has ever undertaken.

TWELVE

Columbus's Esoteric Signature

Columbus had only to present himself, needed only to knock, and the doors of the most influential palaces and courts of Europe were opened wide to him. He was in close contact with the most advanced thinkers of his time living between Florence and Rome with geographers and scientists, including the Florentine Paolo dal Pozzo Toscanelli (1397–1482), one of the lesser-known but more prestigious representatives of the Italian Renaissance. For a long time correspondence between the two men was not accepted by critics, but historians have since been forced to acknowledge it, even though interpretations are usually in some way oriented toward disgracing the admiral. Some view the allegedly false correspondence as a retroactive attempt by Columbus to give a scientific front to his voyage, while others present the studious Toscanelli as the true source of Columbus's knowledge. Thus, Paolo Fisico is considered a direct influence on the Columbian enterprise, if not a true precursor—and thus, once again, Columbus supposedly profited from Toscanelli's knowledge, which thereby appropriates the discovery. Such is the familiar mangled truth.

Even before Columbus, Toscanelli had written to a man of the Church, the Portuguese canon Fernam Martins (or Martinez, or Martini in Italian), his confidant, a friend and familiar of the king of Portugal. Toscanelli had sent a map to his master Martins, drawn by his own hand, on which is depicted the end of the West, from Ireland south to Guinea with all the islands that lie all along this route, straight to the West of which lies the beginning of the Indies with the islands and places to which one might go. And from the Arctic pole one might move along the equinoctial line, so many leagues as to reach those fertile places with all manner of spices, gems, and precious stones. And do not marvel at my calling *west* the lands from whence these spices come, which are commonly said to arrive from the East, for those who sail to the west will eventually find those aforesaid lands in the East. The straight lines that lie along this map show the distance from west to east; and the others, which are oblique, show the distance from north to south."[1]

From Toscanelli's hand, "seeking the East by way of the West" materializes as a certainty rather than as a vision. This phrase would remain the slogan of the endeavor and the discovery throughout the centuries. He writes of islands and the "beginning of the Indies." Strangely, there is no mention of the mythical Antilla or Cipango, which were also present on Toscanelli's map.

The map was masterfully marked with horizontal and vertical lines, like those of latitude and longitude. Longitude, it is claimed, was not discovered until the eighteenth century; much of what was known earlier was discovered later. Another Florentine, Amerigo Vespucci, had already noted: "Longitude is something more difficult, which can be little known save to those who predict and observe the conjunctions of the moon with the planets. . . . By reason of this said longitude, I have lost much sleep, and shortened my life by ten years . . . all my labors are addressed to your holy service."

For Vespucci, just as for Columbus, the route over the waters was an initiatory path in the service of God. Like Columbus, he peered into the dark night sky, risking his eyes and his health, gazing at a lunar path leading to the other world after crossing the land of shadows. Unquestionably, the stars dictated the routes of these explorers, guiding their navigation. Even the Virgin Mary was interpreted as a stellar image. Columbus himself copied the famous words of Albumasar: "In the first aspect of the constellation of the Virgin, there arises a maiden full of grace, honesty, and purity, of long hair and beautiful face; and in her hands there are two ears of corn, and she sits . . . and nurses a child . . ."

> *Ut Albumasar testatur*
> *Inter stellas declaratur*
> *Virgo lactans puerum . . .*

The mystic song of the Stella Maris consecrates a "spiritual astrology" connecting "the properties of the constellations in precise correspondence" with the Virgin.[2] "If it is absurd to separate medicine from astrology in the fifteenth century, then it is even more absurd to separate geography and astronomy from astrology."[3] Further, we might add that it is equally absurd to separate the divine language of the stars from that of faith, even with all the risks such equivalences might have posed. The stars were speaking, and the Renaissance listened.

Maps and letters were also sent to Christopher Columbus, whose "splendid and lofty desire to travel to where the spices come from" was appreciated by Toscanelli. The scientist wrote from Florence on June 25, 1474, preceding his missive with these words: "Paolo Fisico salutes Christopher Columbus."[4]

The tone is intimate and familiar, that of men who worked together and knew each other well. Toscanelli wrote, among other things, that he had copious experience and practice even before receiving this information. Had he also gone on voyages? When, and with whom? The suspicions grow, especially considering his close connections to Portugal and to the Knights of Christ, the heirs of the Templars. Columbus was called a great heart. The earth was round, and the Christians of the East were still waiting, ready for a mutual exchange of faith and knowledge.

In the letter sent to Martins there is a certain air of secrecy: "Many other things could be said; but as I have already said them by word of mouth, and you are prudent and of good judgment, I shall assume that nothing more remains to be understood, and therefore I will not go on any longer." An operation waitlisted for years is hinted at, as if all Christendom were waiting only for the completion of this voyage. At the court of Rome, where Paolo Fisico evidently was, all the elements necessary for the success of the enterprise had been gathered for some time. From the reports of envoys sent to the East, Rome had accumulated all possible knowledge about Asia, the various (and too many!) Indies and the unknown lands. The lid of Pandora's box was about to be opened, or better, the Holy Grail was within reach.

Two hundred years had passed since Marco Polo's pilgrimage, during which, as Toscanelli noted, the khan had requested "many sages and doctors who would teach him our faith. . . . [A]nd also, an ambassador came to Pope Eugenius IV and told him of the great love the princes and their people had for the Christians, and I spoke at length with him of many things . . ." The voices of the lands of marvels had been heard in many ways over the centuries, calling for baptism. Might they still be waiting for a response, especially now that Islam was advancing menacingly upon Europe beneath the pennants of victory?

Toscanelli's letters and maps are no more; they vanished quickly and, as usual, we must be content with copies in differing versions that resurfaced at various times. In the version preserved at the Columbina Library in Seville, accompanied by a planisphere made by the admiral's hand, the letter is preceded by the *sello de la puridad* (stamp of purity): an unmistakable sign of the cross, even if the passage of time has rendered it almost invisible. It is a symbol with which Columbus signed some of his writings—a ciphered signature.

Toscanelli's map prematurely showed the Antilles, which also appeared on Martin Behaim's globe. Toscanelli, it is said, identified Antilla (the Antilles) as the legendary Island of the Seven Cities reached by Christians fleeing persecution. He placed it in the Atlantic Ocean, between China and Europe, like Cipango (Cippangu), long conjectured to be Japan.[5]

We do not know the exact position he ascribed to it. It was the stepping stone for reaching Asia, the farthest lands of perfumes and spices, goods valued on par with gold or silver, goods in which the Toscanelli family was particularly interested, because their fortune came from trading in medicines—a trade that passed into Arab hands with the victorious advance of the Turks. The evangelization of unknown lands went hand in hand with monetary profit.

Paolo Fisico resided in Florence, his long life lasting close to a century. He was a member of those knowledgeable intellectual cenacles we continually encounter. A great scientist, he was a remarkable character on the borderline between reality and fantasy. Extremely religious, a vegetarian, and abstemious in his habits, he observed a strict vow of chastity, and died a virgin, without "knowing woman." If all of this was true, it seems he led the life of a saint—certainly the life of a mystic. A little-known portrait by Stradanus from the early sixteenth century shows him intent on his researches in a study strewn with symbols. It looks like an alchemist's secret hideaway.

In Padua, at the university where the future Innocent VIII would be educated, Paolo studied medicine, geometry, and mathematics—the same subjects as Columbus. The Padua of his youth is visible in his connections and friendships, which lead inevitably to humanism in its most universalistic and revolutionary sense. It is almost unthinkable that Toscanelli and Innocent VIII could not have known each other and met and spoken of the New World. They may have met again at the court of Rome. Padua was truly different from the Florence of the Medici.[6]

And yet, the Tuscan city also had "a 'central' role as the laboratory of cartographic production near the end of the fifteenth century and the beginning of the next century, as demonstrated by the drawings and works of Francesco Rosselli [whose planisphere of 1488–1489 is almost identical to that of Henricus Martellus] and Leonardo da Vinci."[7]

Thus, the mysterious genius Leonardo joins our indefinite and indefinable Round Table. He was another Johannite prophet and the phantasmal grand master of the equally phantasmal Priory of Sion, a secret order par excellence, which was raved about in many esoteric writings. The axis of Rome and Florence would function perfectly when worked by Lorenzo the Magnificent and Innocent VIII. The new Athens was blooming in

Tuscany and the New Jerusalem blossomed in Rome, identified as the symbol of ancient Latin values and the modern Christian faith.

Toscanelli was an astronomer gazing into the darkness of the firmament. He had a passion for comets and also studied geography, seeking possible answers to the many questions of humanity in the corresponding charts of heaven and Earth. In Padua, he was closely connected with Nicholas of Cusa, a friendship ended only by Nicholas's death at Todi. A minor work (so often the most precious to the earnest seeker) whose author would have had no benefit in writing a lie—an Umbrian canon from the homeland of St. Francis—includes: "And here we must speak of the famous cardinal Nicholas of Cusa, who died in our city. As acknowledged by many, he was the most well-read cardinal that the sacred robe ever honored, the dearest friend of the great Pius II. . . . At his deathbed were Toscanelli, Bussi, and Martinez, witnesses to his testament. Columbus was discussed, and the discovery of the New World."[8]

History, as yet, knew nothing of Columbus. But here he is, spoken of at a secret meeting among Toscanelli; Cardinal Nicholas of Cusa, theorist of the *coincidentia oppositorum;* and the Portuguese canon Martinez. This meeting was surely determinative for the geographic knowledge and letters Columbus exchanged with Toscanelli and probably also for Columbus's marriage. As if this were not enough, Bishop Giovanni Andrea Bussi held office in the Corsica of the Doria and Malaspina families, who were related to the Cybos at various points. Bussi was a refined humanist and librarian of the Vatican. It was a council of the wise around a deathbed, a testament that could be only one of truth.

The most surprising thing about this meeting at the bedside of the German cardinal, who died in 1464, is that it anticipated the New World—whose discovery would occur almost thirty years later—and the existence of Columbus, who should have been still unknown, as if they were already familiar. At this time Christopher, according to the most recent calculations (which are certainly not definitive), would have been only thirteen years old. This was a conference among close friends, confidants, and possibly initiates, taking place in the presence of a dying man. A kind of spiritual legacy was entrusted in the only piece of information leaked from this conversation. They all already knew about the New World—while the reference to Columbus remains hanging in the balance between a person already incarnate and a person somehow to be manifested. If the former is true, he was already well known within a certain church. If the latter is the case, then he was to be prepared and created secretly within that same church in the name of the perfect art.

Nicholas of Cusa used Paolo Fisico as an interlocutor in his dialogue on the quadrature of the circle. Another circle, an earthly circle, was waiting for its final quadrature. Circle and square were the two basic forms of the world in medieval symbolism, which saw the circle as divine perfection and the square as human perfection. The Jerusalem in the Apocalypse is cubic but was also represented in round form. "The circle is the figure of the transcendent, of eternity, of the created nothing or the creation from nothing; the square, on the other hand, is the figure of the created, the cornerstone, the solid foundation. . . . Does not Matthew say in the gospel that at the end of time the Lord will send his angels with the trumpet to call people together 'from the four corners of the earth'?"[9] Cybo (or Cubo) was the cube; Columbus was to perfect the circle, and thus heaven and earth would embrace.

Returning to Florence, Toscanelli assumed the function of judiciary astrologer. Apparently, he was later mocked for reaching the age of eighty-five years even though the stars had predicted a short life for him.[10]

Life in the Tuscan Athens was

agitated amid stellar prophecies and voices of the Lord, between subtle calculations and remainders of ancient superstitions, between the heights of sublime metaphysics and corpulent earthly interests. . . . Leonardo drew and saw imminent cataclysms, Savonarola announced the age of the apocalypse on awful pages, Toscanelli saw the comet as a grave warning of changes in laws and empires, and Columbus sought in Joachim of Fiore and Albumasar the certainty of a new age for the world for which he felt himself called to be the initiator.[11]

In this enlightened climate, which also spread to Rome, ideas and interests were seething, changing, and clashing from one day to the next, making enemies of those who had always been friends and comrades, even within families. Such divergences must even have affected the Medici.[12]

In Florence, Toscanelli collaborated with Brunelleschi, to whom he taught the mathematics necessary for that architectural marvel, Santa Maria del Fiore, and especially its magnificent cupola, a stone ladder to heaven, upon which he placed the highest gnomon known at the time. Toscanelli studied the movements of the sun intensely and built solar clocks; time and space were changing. He was a friend to enthusiasts of geography, and he collected maps. He was also a friend to Leon Battista Alberti, Marsilio Ficino, Cristoforo Landino, the Vespuccis, and Regiomontano and is believed to have been Martin Behaim's teacher. With Cosimo de' Medici, precursory to Lorenzo the Magnificent's Platonic Academy, he attended meetings held in the Camaldolite monastery of Santa Maria degli Angeli. Discussions on life and humankind sometimes went on for four nights in their search for a meaning for existence and for the universe.

✠

At this time a great voyager returned to Florence after many years of traveling in Asia: the Venetian Niccolò da Conti, whom we have already encountered. More than just a solitary explorer, Niccolò da Conti appears to have been yet another agent. He was readmitted to the Christian family after his (pragmatic?) conversion to Islam.

He may, in fact, have sailed with a Chinese fleet from India to Australia and then to China.[13] It is certain he sailed on a junk and encountered a great scholar, Ma Huan, at a time when unparalleled libraries and encyclopedias existed in Peking, where all of humanity's knowledge was preserved. Niccolò also studied maps.[14]

All the news was transmitted to the Portuguese monarchs. Before the rise of the Borgias, the Church of Rome authorized them with the appropriate bulls to advance into the oceans. Their caravels were marked with the red eight-pointed Templar cross inherited by the Knights of

Christ. Yet it has been forgotten that every word spoken by those long-ago voyagers was punctiliously recorded in Rome.

Only Rome knew the complete story of their adventures. Although times and protagonists changed in this labyrinth, Rome remained the one fixed point in the progress of knowledge through the centuries.

Niccolò da Conti, it is said, also reached Japan. Was it really Japan? The globe was beginning to change. Everybody wanted to be the artificer of the great epochal turning point. Niccolò was not the only informer about the route to the East: "At the end of Poggio's book, we learn that a few months after [Niccolò] da Conti, there arrived in Florence the envoy of an unspecified Christian-Nestorian kingdom—situated to the north of India and twenty days' journey from Cathay."[15]

The pieces of information accumulated into a full-fledged torrent, opening up the sluices of geography. The maps were transforming in a slow, evolutionary procession. Jerusalem gradually lost its function as the center of centers and the navel of the world.[16]

Meanwhile, from east to west the moment was approaching for rebuilding "the human and Christian body." In 1439, a true global summit opened in Florence with the transfer of the council begun at Ferrara. This was an incredible concentration of knowledgeable people, an influx of information coming from all the corners of the earth.[17]

In this same period, Toscanelli frequently exchanged ideas with Niccolò da Conti. He met the emissary of the Great Khan and Emperor John VII Palaeologus and kept company with Cardinal Bessarion, the Aristotelian scholar Giovanni Argiropulo, and the Platonic scholar George Gemistos Plethon, further promoters of a universal religion. There was discussion, debate, and deliberation; they dreamed of a reunion between the East and the West, between the Church of Rome and the Greek Church. The Great Work was nearly realized. How much longer could Ptolemy's restricted vision of the world remain? To whom would universal sovereignty fall? What dove's wings would reunite the globe? "Thus, thanks to contacts with Toscanelli, Bessarion, and Plethon, a synthesis was slowly developed of the best that classical geography had to offer," especially taking account of the fresh memories of those who had plunged into the depths of the territories and the knowledge of the unknown East.

✠

Trinitarian dogma, however, could not be simply uprooted. Even Toscanelli, "following the most intransigent and obtuse fathers of the Church, calls the Antipodes 'fabulous.' Elsewhere, repeating almost verbatim the words of St. Isidore and those found on the famous twelfth-century world map of Turin, he lets himself get carried away to believing this most remarkable vision of things to come: *Extra tres partes orbis quarta est pars trans Oceanum interiorem in media zona terre posita, que solis ardoribus nobis, incognita est: in cuius finibus antipodes fabulose abitare dicuntur* (Beyond the three parts of the world there is a fourth part, situated across the inner ocean in the median zone of the earth, which is unknown to us because of the heat of the sun; within its bounds, the fabulous antipodeans are said to dwell).[18]

Toscanelli sometimes showed great knowledge and other times a surprising lack of knowledge. At the bedside of Nicholas of Cusa, he *knew.* The scientist in him sometimes speaks, and is sometimes strangely silent. Besides, the words of St. Isidore of Seville had been confirmed by another man of the Church: the pious St. Antoninus, archbishop of Florence, who appears in the painting by Ghirlandaio, the artist who immortalized the Vespuccis and also painted Columbus's portrait. The world could no longer be a Trinity. The fourth part, lying incomplete beneath the sun's rays, was sending messages that could no longer be left to fall into the abyss at the edge of a flat earth.

Paolo Fisico, furthermore, had heard several incredible accounts. In 1441, he began to design and patiently reconstruct the puzzle of the sphere. According to many, he used the ideas of Marinus of Tyre, thanks to original calculations of longitude.

Toscanelli's conclusion was that the world is small—but is it much smaller than had been thought? These words recall Columbus's writings. Did Columbus therefore believe, like Toscanelli, that the distance between Europe and Asia was short and the ocean between them could be crossed in a small amount of time? By copying, did he err in all his calculations, saving himself from failure by accidentally landing in America? This was not quite the case. Toscanelli and Columbus exchanged opinions, and Columbus was cheered by the scientist's encouragement, yet he remained faithful to a differing idea regarding the earth's circumference. This was his own search for the truth.

He knew that before reaching Asia, he must reach other islands and continents that had nothing to do with the Asiatic landmass. His son Ferdinand, in fact, wrote: "This letter [Toscanelli's letter], as was said before, filled the admiral with even greater zeal for discovery, though its writer was mistaken in his belief that the first lands to which one would come would be Cathay and the empire of the Great Khan, and in the other things that he wrote; for experience has shown that the distance from our Indies to those lands is much greater than the distance from here to our Indies."[19]

Ferdinand Columbus, in the certainty that the Indies he referred to were not Asia, allowed himself to say Toscanelli was mistaken, because he knew the distance was great from the new Indies to the Indies of Asia. He therefore had an almost perfect idea of the vastness of the one great ocean, the Pacific—and in a few words, the lies spread about the admiral's relationship to Toscanelli and his reliance on him, came crashing down like so many sand castles. It was an intellectual bond, closer than has ever been thought. In his translation of the *Sphere* published in Florence (1571), Father Ignazio Danti states that Columbus had written a letter to Toscanelli from Seville mentioning a voyage apparently taken in 1491. On this voyage the navigator claimed he had reached regions beyond the equatorial zone.[20]

This may be yet another remarkable piece of evidence of the pre-discovery during the course of Innocent VIII's pontificate. The voyages prior to the discovery keep increasing in number and the protagonists are varied, but Columbus is always the constant. It is now certain that for many years he navigated and roamed from one side of the world to the other in absolute secret, in order to prepare for his role as the revealer of the globe, perfecting and completing his mission as Christo Ferens, inspired by the pope of Rome.

The chain of connections is once again complex. For what reasons was Toscanelli in Rome? Perhaps his principal motive was his familiarity with the della Rovere family. Anna dal Pozzo had married Giovanni della Rovere, brother of Pope Sixtus IV.[21]

Finally, in 1528, the dal Pozzo and della Rovere families were incorporated into the Cybo house and were definitively introduced into the exclusive circles of the greatest families of Genoa. Did this confirm a single bloodline?

Toscanelli and Columbus were connected through the Florentine Lorenzo Giraldi. The names vary, being written in different ways in different chronicles: According to some, Giraldi was none other than a Berardi, a member of the family of Giannotto, who would be Christopher's friend to the death and later a friend of Vespucci and one of the financiers of the discovery voyages. Giraldi also recalls the Geraldinis of Amelia. As usual, the intrigue of surnames and personages, relationships and kinships, grows ever thicker. The Portuguese canon Martins was present with Toscanelli to hear the last words of the dying cardinal Nicholas of Cusa. They were said to have discussed a virtual Columbus. Another proponent of the Eastern Crusade, Andrea Bussi, was there with them. They spoke of Columbus, and of the lands to be reached. At this point, nothing remains but to find the final link. And this is soon done: Bartolomeo Perestrello, the admiral's father-in-law, Felipa's father, and a Knight of Christ. He was married three times; his second marriage was to Margarita Calvaleiro Martins.[22]

Perestrello, Martins, Toscanelli, Columbus: The plot is reconstructed, leading to an exchange of letters, entirely logical and natural at this point, between Paolo Fisico and Christopher Columbus. This is the final discovery of a reality crushed over the course of time, myriad rivulets apparently without connection, while there was always only one river, the river of truth. To complete the picture, we must also add that Felipa's mother, Isabella Moñiz, was almost surely of Jewish origin, while Columbus's sisters-in-law Isabella and Bianca (another recurring feminine name) Perestrello were both favorites of the great archbishop of Lisbon, Pedro de Noroñha, who fathered a good number of offspring. By marrying the daughter of a noble Knight of Christ and navigator, the obviously noble Columbus was granted complete access to the main port of Portugal, always the front line for voyages into the Atlantic Ocean.

✠

Toscanelli drew maps while lords, princes, kings, emperors, and popes had the walls of their palaces frescoed with incredible world maps. These were installed in Siena, Venice, and Rome; Pius II wanted one, as did Innocent VIII for a background in the Palazzo Venezia. How many others existed? We shall never know. How many still exist? Nor do we know this. The game of three-map monte has lasted for centuries. There will be no lack of surprises for those in search of the maps' colored worlds, and all told, it is still easy enough to find an almost unknown or at least negligently undervalued, impossible map. Fortunately, the facades and walls of manors and castles still speak; their messages only await someone who will pay attention.

For example, there is a remote building in Valtellina with a stone gate and a series of carved figures. Top center among these is a trigram of Christ of San Bernardino of Siena, the Franciscan who long ago stirred this place with his preaching of peace between the Guelphs and the Ghibellines. On the sides are a phoenix and a pelican. The phoenix is the legendary bird reborn from its own ashes, the symbol of death and resurrection through the triumph of eternal life; the pelican was believed to nourish its young with its own blood, symbolizing the sacrifice made by Christ to redeem humankind. There is also a cross inscribed in a circle with a smaller circle upon it and a small hole at the center: a Celtic wheel. Roses are carved on both sides at the bottom.

On the architrave is a phrase sounding like a warning to all who enter: *Novit paucos secura quies* (Tranquillity knows few): a kind of ideological and esoteric motto of the lords of this palace. On the facade, a decorative frieze makes a liaison between the entrance and the entire front of the building. The motif is composed of lozenge-shaped panels alternating between light and dark. More than fake rustication, they resemble a chessboard, recalling the eternal game between white and black, the eternal struggle between light and darkness. This rebus is in a mountainous enclave, seemingly off the main paths of communication. The balcony faces the Rhaetian Alps, their peaks reaching toward the skies of Orobia.

Half a mile below, the Adda River runs through lands passed over: lands of religious battles, lands of invasions from the north— Switzerland, Austria, and Germany. The river valley forms the line joining Venice and Milan and is also not far from Como, Piacenza, Pavia, Ferrara, and Padua. It was once a junction presided over by soldiers, paladins, and Christian knights. At nearby Grosio is a church dedicated to St. George, with his red cross like the one he is depicted wearing in Genoa. This is Valtellina, the land of many Grails carved in stone and many red crosses left in churches. Oral tradition tells of infants and women with Eastern-looking eyes, the result of interbreeding with the Saracens, whose buckwheat (*grano saraceno* in Italian) is still cultivated there, the legacy of blood mingled long ago.

At Teglio a remarkable piece of work raises a number of questions, presenting itself as an entity contained within other entities, like a matryoshka doll. It is a sort of pocket guide of comic strips condensing Middle Ages and Renaissance, present and past, science and faith, esotericism and magic, orthodoxy and heresy. Who were the lords of this small court hidden in the clouds, somehow far removed from any place and any time? Who were the promoters and guardians of this exclusive cenacle accessible to so few? Unfortunately, it is no simple task to reconstruct this history. The dates of the works, especially those of the completion of the pictorial cycles, are not precisely known; nor are the names of the artists and commissioners. The questions merely multiply.

"Tranquillity knows few" is the motto inscribed at the entrance, a welcome to a place consecrated by arcane knowledge.[23] Let us begin with the courtyard, with the recurring use of the numeral 16, a symbol of wholeness and perfection—the sum of 6, the perfect numeral of the Greeks, and 10, the perfect numeral of the Romans. We then proceed into a *horror vacui* that leaves no free space on the walls and ceilings, where there appear figures and inscriptions that are almost always didactic and ethical, but sometimes are downright riddles.

The lords of the place were the Bestas, who originated from an early branch of the Azones. They were knights, "fierce defenders"[24] of the Catholic faith. They were also open to new ideas, especially Andrea Guicciardi, who, legend tells us, is a possible descendant of Robert Guiscard. It was this same Andrea, possessor of an overtly humanistic spirit, who became part of the Alberti family when he married Ippolita degli Alberti, possibly related to the Genoese-Florentine family of Leon Battista Alberti. On his tomb he is remembered as *artium et medicinae doctor* (Doctor of Arts and Medicine),[25] and in 1498 he was also rector of the University of Pavia. His coffin is placed high up in the ancient family church dedicated to St. Lawrence and flanked by two bearded characters watching over the sepulchre. One of them is pointing upward with his right arm, while his left hand holds an armillary sphere; the other has an hourglass in one hand.[26]

Science, medicine, art, an armillary sphere, and geography come together in a person worth investigating. At the time, studies of this kind often led to alchemy and to white magic, which sought the triumph of light, opposing the black magic of the necromancers. On the original cross vault of the small church, there is a "unique stellar wheel with eight divisions and a sun at the center, formed by the face of Christ in relief, crowned by four flaming stars." It is a vision already in line with the Copernican revolution to come. On the crucifix behind the altar, two angels catch the blood of Christ in versions of the Grail. It is an expression of faith with interwoven variations that is not exactly in line with orthodoxy. We find this multiplied along the frescoed walls inside the palace.[27]

It is as if this cultural horizon makes the Bestas and probably the Guicciardis the custodians of knowledge reserved for a select few—as explicitly stated above the castle gate.[28] This is a painted "library," showing a universalistic, courageous, enlightened knowledge and vision of the things of the world. The most captivating part of the palace, a part that raises the most important, neglected, and unresolved questions, is the room of the creation. The cycle covers the entire space of the large room with a depiction of the book of Genesis proceeding in a kind of elliptical sequence from Eden lost to Eden regained.

Above the hearth are shown the creation of the stars, the animals, and the trees; the birth of Adam and Eve; the sin and their banishment; Noah's ark; the Deluge; the tower of Babel; and the dispersion of the peoples in an ensemble forming a large athanor, or alchemical furnace. Opposite Babel and chaos is a white obelisk, an esoteric symbol like a hyphen joining heaven and Earth. The depiction of the Creator is not anthropomorphic, consisting only of rays of light, which represent the Holy Spirit.

Finally, there is a painted map of the New World, the most remarkable thing in the entire palace. It is difficult to explain and is especially hard to understand why such geographical information,[29] reserved for those few adepts of the work and forever a state secret, should be kept (perhaps guarded?) at Teglio in an almost inaccessible place. It appears that the map was reserved for scientists in the service of the close circles of religious or secular powers.

The world map of Teglio, on the high ceiling where it is difficult to see the details, shows the whole of the two Americas presented as the new land revealed after the apocalyptic deluge. It demonstrates remarkable cartographic precision, superior to many maps used as models for research, and reveals disquieting aspects. It is impossible to determine the exact date of its execution because archival references are lacking. The America depicted corresponds to what was known in the second half of the sixteenth century, so the painting should be dated to that time. Other elements lead us to think—considering the construction stages of the palace and a graffito in the Sala dalla Volta ad Ombrello bearing the date September 21, 1519 or 1529—that the map may have been painted during the first three decades of the sixteenth century. Also, as we have seen, the scientific and humanist thinker of this family was Guicciardi, rector of the University of Pavia.[30]

We can now recall Christopher Columbus's son writing that his father studied at this same university. The times, the subjects of study, and the presence of the two persons at Pavia could be entirely coincidental, and there is no surviving proof Columbus actually did study there. Still, the map at Teglio poses unanswered questions and reaffirms the membership of the Bestas in the clan of *illuminati,* if not indeed among the initiatory enthusiasts of the ancient golden age. They were not unusual persons for the times, although certainly they were unusual in such a small and isolated place.

Evidently, the reformist and universal dream of a communion among peoples was cultivated secretly there. (In another room, albeit from later on, there is a fresco of the meeting between King Solomon and the Queen of Sheba.) It was a dream of a return to the primordial golden age of innocence, a movement from the nakedness of Adam and Eve to the finding of a New World, a newfound Paradise placed so as to rival the original. Such were the islands and continents unveiled by Columbus.

More questions exist, for beneath the world map is a date interpreted variously as 1459, 1559, 1469, 1569, and 1499. This last also appears in an inscription in majolica letters at the bottom, reading: *Terra australis* ~~South~~ *anno 1499 sed nondum plene cognita* (Austral land in the year 1499 but not yet fully known).[31]

This was the end of the 1400s. To what expedition does it refer? As shown in other maps of the times, like the one at Teglio, here is an immense austral land—which people have preferred to dismiss, sometimes with disarmingly banal arguments—located in the far south in a rectilinear direction. To what imaginary continent, vanished or current, might this refer? On this map, unlike on others, the region is depicted in a luxuriant green, as if it were perfectly habitable.[32]

On this map America is a land unto itself and is complete, right down to its southernmost extreme. Thus it is evident that not only the New World but also another continent is being displayed here. Australia and Antarctica, according to the chronology of official discoveries—which is more political than historical—had yet to appear. Could this be yet another travel accident of a geography forming its tireless defense against dogma, of a science founded on commonplaces? At Teglio it seems to trip up once again over this green southern land, which looks nothing like the frigid zones of Antarctica. Was it another incredible discovery?[33]

The frescoed walls with the southern land depicted: if it had been reached but not yet entirely explored, this may confirm a prediscovery including Australia, already visited by the Chinese.

✠

On the alpine range across from here, not far from Genoa and Monferrato in a region important in other ways for Columbus's background,[34] there is another castle—Manta a Saluzzo, a few miles from Cuneo—with a Renaissance room containing another puzzle. On the vault is a small globe with the American coasts—including the Pacific—well drawn. Also here, past the tip of South America, there is a stretch of green and mysterious land, the north coast of Antarctica. The painting is supposedly from the second half of the sixteenth century. The globe is ringed by an inscription that reads: The spirit breathes within. It is an esoteric reference to the Holy Ghost, uniting all the peoples of the world in an ecumenical breath.

From the north of Italy to the center, the message does not change, and the mystery is repeated. The centuries have perpetuated the puzzles awaiting solution. This time we find ourselves near Viterbo, not far from Rome. In the ancient territory of Tuscia stands an imposing and little-known structure, rare in its magnificence and suggestiveness, with a path leading from the majestic edifice into an enchanted garden. As Elémire Zolla said, it is a garden that can be read only with an alchemical key. This is the fortress of Caprarola. The ground plan of the central structure is a pentagon, or a pentacle, like a great star or a great rose. The monumental complex, austere and elegant at the same time, is mainly the product of the activity of Alessandro Farnese. Ordained cardinal at the tender age of fifteen, he was the nephew of Paul III, elected in 1534. The Farnese were in possession of Piacentino, the home town of Columbus's father-in-law and first wife. Alessandro was the son of Gerolama Orsini. Clarice Orsini had been the wife of Lorenzo the Magnificent, father-in-law of Innocent VIII's son. Thus more connections emerge.

The architectural harmony and boldness,[35] the beauty of the rooms, the bright colors of the frescoes and their artistic merit leave the viewer gaping in amazement. This was the highest level of artistic expression of the time. The magnificent cycles, always including allegories, alternate between ornamentation and grotesques. "It is probable the patron himself suggested the themes to be treated, while it is certain the choice of contents fell to the famous literary men of the times, such as Annibal Caro, Fulvio Orsini, and Onofrio Panvinio."[36]

We start on the ground floor with the papal historian Panvinio, who wrote in his early sixteenth-century history of St. Peter's throne the discovery of America occurred during the pontificate of Innocent VIII. His words contribute to rebuilding the truth right from the start: "Great things occurred, and among others, almost at the end of his pontificate, the greatest that has ever taken place in the memory of man, in which Christopher Columbus discovered the New World, and not without mystery it came to pass that while a Genoese man was ruling the Christian world, another Genoese man found another world in which to plant the Christian religion." Another link is added to the chain.

By the sixteenth century Columbus's voyage and his image had become submerged in silence. Yet Panvinio defended him, preserving his memory, along with others. Among the battles painted in fresco on the walls is the siege of Malta at the hands of Suleiman III. Among the saints we find St. James the Great, the Moor-slayer, and among the deities we cannot miss Hercules, the hero of the Islands of Hesperides and their golden apples, and the mysterious Hermes, joined with Athena in a single body, forming a perfect esoteric hermaphrodite. The Farnesian deeds proceed with the marriage between Ottavio Farnese and Margaret of Austria, daughter of Emperor Charles V. With the portrait of Philip II of Spain, brother-in-law of Ottavio Farnese, we find a continuous intersection between the descendents and depositories of occult history.

In dimensions decidedly more spectacular and prestigious than those of Teglio, the background of events immortalized on the walls forms an omnipresent hermetic web. The twelve (a fatidic number) rooms of the *piano nobile,* connected to the ground floor by a beautiful spiral staircase, successively form a visual symphony that culminates in the Mappamondo room, the beauty of which is breathtaking. There, an astounding collection of zodiacal signs on the ceiling—the geography of the stars, which guided the course of the navigators—forms a counterpart to the geography of the earth. Finally, the map on the south wall is more beautiful than any other; astronomy and geography unite in this fresco painted around 1574.

Giovanni Antonio da Varese, who had also worked in the Vatican, painted the maps. Besides the charm of the composition and colors, the viewer will be surprised to see a boundless territory in the Antarctic zone, below South America. It is said this was the fruit of imagination, considering Tierra del Fuego was thought to be immense. Our opinion of the protagonists of those times is too high for us to believe such nonsense. The centuries have eroded many things. It is not possible for the general public to see these walls, but those who gain permission, if they look attentively, will see the figures of animals depicted upon this *terra australis*—to say nothing of the representation of Africa, which was not yet completely explored but is shown in its entirety.

It is not the only unresolved dilemma. Beside the immense canvases of the mural atlas, with the images of various parts of the world, the medallions above the doors and windows contain portraits of five illustrious persons painted by the Zuccari brothers: Amerigo Vespucci, Ferdinand Magellan, Marco Polo, Christopher Columbus, and Hernán Cortés. This is a gallery of the protagonists of the New World who can, in a certain sense, be grouped within a single family, affiliated with a unique brotherhood—almost a Santa Hermandad.

The portrait of Columbus with white hair in modest and almost monastic clothing shows the admiral with the compass and portolan chart in his hands—a fairly atypical image, for the Mappamondo room at Caprarola has been studied only since 1952. Columbus is represented here in his natural state.[37] This is a copy of the portrait located at Como, in the collection of Paolo Giovio (1486–1552), which includes a series of portraits of illustrious men. Columbus's portrait was painted according to "oral descriptions of the admiral given by his contemporaries."[38]

Como is very near to Teglio. Paolo Giovio studied philosophy at Padua and medicine at Pavia[39] and was one of the most erudite men in Rome during the time of Leo X, Lorenzo de Medici's son, who was ordained cardinal at a young age by Innocent VIII.

Leaving war-torn Rome, Giovio retired to Lario, where he created a museum. His pleasant retreat was built on the site of the former residence of Pliny, the Roman admiral whose writings were among Columbus's favorite. In such intersections of names and places, a golden rule of certain personages appears to emerge. The religious Giovio, who had been a member of the most educated Roman circles, was particularly fascinated by Muslim civilization, as shown in his writings. He displays courageous independence of thought for a bishop living in the age of the Council of Trent. In his *Elogia,* "one reads unheard of memories and judgments" from the moral and theological point of view.[40]

A little more than fifty years had passed since Columbus's death. It was always highly placed representatives of the Church of Rome who preserved his image and his memory and perpetuated his ideas—members of an interdenominational church free of rigid rules. The admiral's story would vanish into oblivion; his countenance would dwindle to nothing until his rediscovery in the nineteenth century, the age of the superman and the heroes of Romanticism.

Besides the connection between the world maps, there is the constant golden thread of friendships leading along a fascinating path. In 1579 Alessandro Farnese acquired what is now the property of the Lincei Academy, for which reason the villa is called the Farnesina. An architectural jewel, its gallery imitates Innocent VIII's Belvedere. One of the artists who worked there was Sebastiano del Piombo, another great painter of Columbus's portrait. Cardinal Farnese was connected by a close friendship and common interests to Alberico Cybo Malaspina, the creator of the "city of the sun" in Massa.[41]

As we have seen, Alberico was the descendent of Innocent VIII who managed, during the time of Paul V (Borghese), to have the carving placed in St. Peter's, where our research began. The marble epigraph on the carving includes its reference to the discovery of America in the time of his ancestor's pontificate. It is an eternal truth carved in stone, an immortal line of thought.

Alberico and Alessandro (the latter's librarian was an Orsini) are also linked to the story of another companion and mysterious character: Pier Francesco Orsini, known as Vicino, who, upon the death of his beloved Giulia Farnese in 1560, set to work on the enigmatic paths of the Sacred Grove of Bomarzo, filled with symbols and allegories. There we find ourselves like knights in search of the Grail or like Dante in a dark wood. It is a magical and ghostly place, a labyrinth amid statues, monsters, and strange buildings. Pier Francesco, a scholar of books and information from the Indies, was a great friend of many cardinals, but liked to define himself as anticlerical and was proud of thinking with his head. He was in contact with the Frenchman Jean Drouet, an expert in distillation and alchemy. The mansion of Bomarzo, located in the Cimini Mountains, is marked by the "gold or red rose with five petals, the symbol of Venus and Platonic love, as well as of the hermetic secret (the truth is said to be *sub rosa*)."[42]

✠

The Ariadne's thread of occult gnosis continues to weave through time. At Bomarzo it unrolls from within to without, from the rooms out to the formal gardens, to the paths and the strange sculptures standing among the greenery of the Italianate gardens. Its prototype remains the original Belvedere of Innocent VIII, its new art inspired by the *Hypnerotomachia poliphili,* apparently written by Francesco Colonna, the ideologist of the chessboard. The same chessboard appears on the Cybo coat of arms, while the dreams—this time those of Poliphilo—continue to be another guiding thread. The decades passed, but beneath the veil of strange things, the ideas survived.

To visit the Bomarzo garden is to dive into a dark and mysterious aquarium, a visionary other world of unbridled fantasy and endless allusions, where the only names of cities recorded are those of Memphis— the city in Egypt that was so long the seat of the art of kingship—and Rhodes, the base of the knights of the sea. It was a place devoted to alchemy, an island of the roses par excellence, a symbol of knowledge and love which, according to the Greek and Latin meaning of the word, guarded the mysteries of initiation. "It was in fact in Rhodes that Count Bernardo Trevisano (1406–1490) obtained the philosopher's stone during the last three years of his life, after having spent all his riches on absurd and vain quests."[43]

In Rhodes, from whence the Cybo family came, Sir George Ripley, the alchemist who was friends with Innocent VIII, allegedly financed the Hospitaler Knights of Jerusalem in the war against the Turks with gold made in his laboratory.

✠

In its initiatory pilgrimage under the tutelage of ancient knowledge, Bomarzo contains a symbolic sampling, proceeding through a series of puzzles watched over by a group of sphinxes. As the young Count Pico della Mirandola wrote: "[I]t was the opinion of the ancient theologians that they must not rashly publicize divine things and mysterious secrets. . . . The Egyptians carved the sphinx in all their temples for no other reason than to declare that divine things, when written, must be covered by enigmatic veiling and poetic dissimulation." Once again, the connections are everywhere.

From the ancient maps to the world maps of the Middle Ages to those frescoed on castle walls, from Teglio to Cuneo, from Caprarola to Bomarzo, from the Alps to the Apennines, from stones to plants, from charts to books to paintings the thread of arcane knowledge, transmitted oracularly and orally, leading back to the dawn of time, is unbroken. It is boldly manifested, even in the second half of the sixteenth century, despite the Counter Reformation. Beneath the veil, it records what has been hidden and helps to unveil truths confined in secret.

Beginning with the discovery of America and the *damnatio memoriae* placed upon a pope of Christian, Jewish, and Muslim blood, a Christ-Ophir Columbus was committed to history beneath a deformed mask. To the controversy of the antipodes is added the myth of an unknown or not yet fully known austral land, another unsolved mystery in the infinite tangle of discoveries and prediscoveries. It is as if, with the rewriting of the discovery of America, with its golden age restored, the Dreamtime of the Australian Aborigines is also awakened, rising to the surface from so many shipwrecks, from the age-old submersion of the truth—truth bubbling from the deep as when waking from a dream. Imagination, from the visions of the mystics to those of ordinary people, has always been the antechamber of truth: the truth blessed by Innocent VIII on August 3, 1492, and impressed upon American soil with Columbus's first footstep. The first wave covered this footprint and washed it away for five hundred long years. Today, an inscription and a seal remain from which a path to lost justice can be forged once more.

The inscription is in St. Peter's, on the tomb of Innocent VIII. The final seal is the mysterious signature Christopher Columbus used:

It is a cryptogram scholars have attempted to interpret for five hundred years, the signature of a grand master more than of a mariner. With seven letters—the perfect number, the number most often recurring at the end of time, according to St. John's Apocalypse—it is the sum of the

Trinity and the four corners of the world, the four cardinal points, the cosmic cross. The universal numeric value of these letters, according to the science of Gematria and sacred geometry, valid for both the Hebrew and Greek alphabets, is 1641. From the moment Columbus emerged, he began using the signature with the value 1641, a date approximately 155 years in the future. According to Columbus, it was the same date St. Augustine had prophesied as the end of time, in a preordained seven-thousand-year cycle.

The interpretative key of the magic triangle in these rebuses recurring among the secrets of knightly orders is always open to more than one solution. Possible meanings within the cryptogram of Columbus can be quadrupled when it is read in all directions, from left to right and from top to bottom. In its specific composition it can be traced to the pyramid, the eye of God, David's shield, and the Trinity: a symbol of spirituality, the form of the Holy Ghost, evoked simply by the triple *S*—which is also synonymous with *shalom,* the word for peace in the Hebrew language.

In alchemical symbolism, the triangle may incorporate the Cybo cube or square, which, like the color white, is the symbol for truth, wisdom, and moral perfection, and also the circle, the chosen and superior sphere. This is the world finally complete in its unity, launched toward perfection. Curiously, the *X* and *Y* also recall the male and female chromosomes, the separate parts of the primordial hermaphrodite, in an eschatological reunion of celestial sphere and earthly sphere—confirmation of the correspondence between macrocosm and microcosm in search of lost harmony, according to the principle "that which is below is identical to that which is above."

✠

The story we have told of Columbus and Pope Innocent VIII is like an infinite labyrinth, an endless hall of mirrors. It is evident at this point that the *A* in the seal, commonly interpreted as *admiral,* is more likely the initial of the word *apocalypse,* understood as a revelation; of Abraham, father of all peoples and all faiths; or the new Adam who would be born in the new world.

The entire configuration bears the mark of a great initiate. The *X, M,* and *Y* in the seal could signify Christ, Mary, and John (the Baptist and the Evangelist or Yacobus, for James), or Christ, Mary, and Jerusalem (Yerusalem), the goal always pursued, even if Columbus never reached it. Finally, the *X, M,* and *Y* are also the unmistakable initials of Christ, Muhammad, and Yahweh—an interpretation never before made. These are the three to whom the Christ bearer would lead, bringing humanity, by means of his voyage, from confusion into fusion with Christ, for the Holy Spirit works in Christians, Moors, and Jews in a perfect Great Work, with a heavenly New Jerusalem in the new Holy Land, with a new Christ set to disembark upon the virginal lands of the New World. This spiritual legacy, a communion of faiths between East and West, continues to be invoked amid futile bloodshed in the tortured world of the new millennium, reaching from the dawning of the great dream on that long ago August 3, 1492, to the dawning of the great American dream and the dream of all humanity—lost over the course of the centuries, until today.

August 3 to October 12, 1492. In this space of time the squaring of the circle was perfected, as we have wished to perfect Columbus's mysterious signature. We conclude with the enigmatic alchemical engraving that shows the marriage between sun and moon, united by a nuptial ring of golden stars and completed by the globe of the earth. East and West are finally joined together, like the parts of a perfect hermaphrodite.

ΠOTES

Chapter One. The Fall of Canstantinople

1. Strictly speaking, there were two caravels and one ship.

2. Annemarie Schimmel and Franz Carl Endres, *The Mystery of Numbers* (Oxford: Oxford University Press, 1993), 58.

3. Ruggero Marino, *Cristoforo Colombo e il papa tradito* (Rome: Newton Compton, 1991). By the same author and under the same title, see the 4th edition, revised and expanded (Rome: RTM, 1997), with a preface by Franco Cardini; "Cristoforo Colombo e Innocenzo VIII," in *La evangelización del Nuevo Mundo* (SER., 1992), 299–307; "Innocenzo VIII, il papa di Cristoforo Colombo," in *Quaderni Ibero-Americani* (72); *Quinto Centernario, Colombo, l'America* (Rome: Bulzoni, 1992), 595–602; "Innocenzo VIII: il papa di Colombo," in *Il letterato tra miti e realtà del Nuovo Mundo: Venezia, il mondo iberico e l'Italia* (Rome: Bulzoni, 1994), 347–62; "Colombo, Innocenzo VIII e la scoperta dell'America," in *Apollinaris LX–VIII* (Rome: Pontificiae Universitatis Lateranensis, 1995), 773–89.

4. The publication of his work was prohibited by the Council of the Indies until the early 1700s owing to numerous historical errors—another case of the purging that happened to all political writings in Columbus's time, even to those in which the "errors" were not so erroneous.

5. Serendipity: the aptitude or good fortune of making important discoveries by chance.

6. The author Mario Puzo has said that if we were to compose a true portrait of

the navigator, it would be best to read nothing, because we might be forced to come to the conclusion that Christopher Columbus never existed.

7. A "Ship's Log" survives from Columbus's first voyage that critics have always claimed was altered and manipulated by the monarchs of Spain. An abridged version of the log, which had remained unknown for some three centuries, was made by Martín Fernandez de Navarrete in 1791 and published in 1825. Only small fragments remain from the other three voyages. The life of Columbus, written by his son Ferdinand (ultimately, it is doubtful that he was the only author), emerged several decades after his death (1571) in an Italian translation by a Spaniard, Alfonso Ulloa. The subsequent Spanish version is a translation of this Italian version. The writings of the Dominican Bartolomeo de Las Casas came to light in 1875; the author had requested, for unknown reasons, that his work not be published until forty years after his death. Many of Columbus's letters have been discovered in the centuries since. Some contain highly important information, even for our times. The integrity of the sources has always been uncontested. Thus Columbus's image has been embalmed in an interminable farcical process by the navigator's successors and the Spanish crown. Everything possible has been written. There is a gaping chasm between the on-site report and successive notions of the events. Meanwhile, history has taken facts molded in clay and carved them in stone, guided by the will of the ruling power. In an age when falsehood and intrigue form a recurring basis for the art of domination, it has taken a long time to develop a standard version of the facts that is not severely contorted.

8. Christopher Columbus, *Gli Scritti* (Turin: Einaudi, 1992). The preface to the first edition reads: "The publication of Columbus's writings appeared an urgent and necessary task. All the aspects of his life and the circumstances of his discovery have been studied with varying success, *but little attention has been paid to his writings* . . . [author's italics]. The majority of these are difficult to refer to, some because they were published in journals of small circulation, others because they were included in publications with a limited printing, many years out of print." It should also be observed that this version of *Gli Scritti* is missing Columbus's most important work: his *Book of Prophecies,* intentionally ignored by too many scholars because of the difficulty of finding a place for it within the navigator's accepted history. Further, as far as we know, there has never been a complete cataloging of the notes Columbus made in his books.

9. Christopher Columbus, *Libro de las profecias,* trans. Delno C. West and August Kling (Gainesville: University of Florida Press, 1991), 104 and 106.

10. Joseph Perez, *Isabella e Ferdinando* (Turin: SEI, 1991), 210.

11. Steven Runciman, *The Fall of Constantinople 1453* (Cambridge: Cambridge University Press, 1965), 15–16.

12. Ibid., 19.

13. Philip Mansel, *Constantinople: City of the World's Desire 1453–1924* (New York: St. Martin's Press, 1995), 1.

14. Paul Herrmann, *Conquest by Man* (New York: Harper and Brothers, 1954), 426–27: "Never had men believed the end of the world so imminent as in the last decades of the fifteenth century. It was an ancient dread that stalked abroad. The sacred prophetesses of the old Teutons had already prophesied the ghastly Last Battle thousands of years ago. These images were now half obscured beneath a Christo-Oriental overlay. The mystic poem on the End of the World written by Methodius of Patara in AD 800 was reprinted in Cologne in 1475. Twenty years earlier, the Turks had overrun Byzantium, the holy city, with fearful slaughter, and Methodius's warning sent a shudder through the listening world: 'The time will come when the Agareni will gather again in German lands and go forth out of the wilderness. They will take possession of the world for eight years. And they will pervert cities and kingdoms; they will strangle the priests in the holy places. They will lie with the women and they will drink from the sacred vessels. And they will tether their beasts to the hallowed graves.' An Apocalyptic note already rang in the mystical letter of Prester John to the three protagonists of the High Middle Ages, the pope and the two emperors. Now fear of the cataclysm rose to a horrifying certainty. And when, in 1485 [while St. Peter's throne was occupied by a Genoese man of Greek origin, Innocent VIII], a total eclipse of the sun visible to all Europe followed the conjunction of two such powerful and baleful planets as Jupiter and Saturn, it was clear to all who possessed understanding: 'The signs and wonders brought by this eclipse and darkness are horrible and almost terrifying. And much more ghastly if any man has experienced and seen them. So much so that horror prevents me from declaring their import.'"

15. Ibid., 4.

16. Ibid., 6.

17. Ibid., 6: "The Ottomans were also inspired by a desire to equal the glory of Alexander the Great. Mehmed II identified himself so strongly with Alexander

that he commissioned a biography of himself in Greek, from a minor Greek official, Michael Kritovoulos, on the same paper and in the same format as the copy of Arrian's life of Alexander in his library, which was read to him 'daily.' A Venetian envoy wrote that Mehmed II 'declares that he will advance from East to West, as in former times the Westerners advanced into the Orient. There must, he says, be only one Empire, one faith and one sovereignty in the world. No place was more deserving than Constantinople for the creation of this unity in the world.'"

18. Vito Salierno, *I musulmani in Puglia e in Basilicata* (Manduria: Lacaita, 2000), 162.

19. Pius II (Enea Silvio Piccolomini), *Lettera a Maometto II*, ed. Giuseppe Toffanin (Naples: Pironti, 1953), xi of the Introduction.

20. Mansel, *Constantinople,* 16.

21. Pius II, 55: "The Father has foretold the future time, for the heavens shall be opened to the elect, and there shall be made ready for man the eternal Kingdom following this life, in the celestial Jerusalem. And the Lord has told of the peace, for with the birth of Christ the age of Janus was ended for the Romans, and there was born a marvelous peace, and the angels sang glory to God in the highest heavens, and peace on earth among men of good will." Pius II added that "the religion of the Saracens is growing increasingly prone to the tolerance of vices: You are permitted to take as many wives as you wish, and then to dismiss them when they no longer please you; to have concubines ad libitum and to submerse yourself in all manner of desires; to fulfill all the caprices of belly and mouth, except for wine; to immerse yourself in all the delights. Fasts are also among your laws, but with the purpose of stimulating pleasure, for the Saracens fast all day only to eat and drink all through the night."

22. Ibid., xxvi of the Introduction.

23. Ibid., 12.

24. Among the conflicts that distressed Pius II, it is interesting to note his defense of the opulence of the court of Rome, which has even been labeled neo-pagan. This was written in response to criticism, which had already led to protests and which may have spurred on the Lutheran schism, another severe internal injury for the Mother Church. Columbus foresaw this impending blow, anticipating it in the writing of his will. On the subject of wealth, the pope wrote: ". . . and those who despise it are damned. They are moved only by envy. Nor do they well understand the things of faith. Those who wish the

ministers of Christ to be poor wish for this not because they want them to live for the good, but because they want to be able to despise them. Christ certainly wished to appear poor and humble, but he did this not in order that we should be poor, but to redeem us by these means. He brought glory to the world, he suffered the torment of the cross, he raised the dead. For our salvation it is now necessary for the prelates of Rome to be rich and powerful" (Pius II, *Lettera a Maometto* II, xxxi–ii).

25. Pius II, *Lettera a Maometto,* XV. It is added later "for him (Pius II), the medieval idea of the Crusade had not vanished beneath the criticism of humanism (a term much used and little understood), but was perpetuated and exalted as humanistic" (Pius II, LVI).

26. Nestorianism was a Christian belief established in the East in the fifth century by Nestor, bishop of Constantinople. Its doctrine views God as two persons: man and God.

27. Robert Silverberg, *The Realm of Prester John* (Garden City, NY: Doubleday, 1972), Prologue, 2. The letter was first printed in 1480. Prester John wrote: "I am a devout Christian and everywhere protect the Christians of our empire, nourishing them with alms. We have made a vow to visit the sepulcher of our Lord with a great army, as befits the glory of our Majesty, to wage war against and chastise the enemies of the cross of Christ, and to exalt his sacred name. Our magnificence dominates the Three Indies, and extends to Farther India, where the body of St. Thomas the apostle rests."

28. Ibid., 37–38.

29. Sinibaldo Fieschi, Innocent IV, was pope from 1243 to 1254. He undertook the Seventh Crusade along with St. Louis IX of France.

30. Silverberg, 164.

31. Mansel, 25.

32. Ibid., 26: "Many Venetians and Genoese hoped to recapture the city, as they had during the Fourth Crusade in 1204. What nineteenth-century statesmen referred to as the 'Eastern Question'—the design of the European powers to conquer Ottoman territory—began in 1453."

33. It should be noted that medieval numerology placed great importance on the numeral 1480, which is the sum of the values corresponding to the Greek letters forming the name *Christos*. Further, there is a curious connection between 1480 and the number of the beast in the Apocalypse, 666. See "Giochi matematici. Il dottor Matrix scopre meraviglie numerologiche nella

Bibbia di re Giacomo," in *Scienze* (99). I do not have the year or number of the publication, and the article in question may even be a hoax.

34. Luigi Paiano, *Otranto e il suo comprensorio* (Naples: Editrice Salentina, 1989), 48.

35. Grazio Gianfreda, *Otranto nella storia* (Lecce: Edizioni del Grifo, 1997), 253.

36. Ibid., 265.

37. Ibid., 273–74.

38. *Annuario Francescano Secolare d'Italia* 4, no. 4 (1992): 46–47. This publication, to which I have often referred, was issued a year after my first book, confirming in substance many fundamental assumptions.

39. Plato, *Timaeus,* trans. Benjamin Jowett (New York: Grammercy, 1995).

40. Scipio was the Roman general who fought, in Africa, Hannibal of Carthage, the Phoenician city that controlled the Pillars of Hercules.

41. M. T. Cicero, *Scipio's Dream,* trans. Andrew P. Peabody.

42. Christopher Columbus, *Gli Scritti,* XIV n.14.

Chapter Two. The Genoa-Padua Matrix

1. It has been over five hundred years since the discovery of America. By now we are far enough removed from the hubbub of the 1992 celebrations, during which we lacked only the posting of signs showing Columbus and reading WANTED, as if he was an outlaw in the Old West. The year 1992 rode on a wave of emotiveness and ignorance amid a clamor of futile and exploitative lawsuits that were devoid of any logic. There is no sense in applying our current measure of justice after the passage of five hundred years. There is also no sense, out of respect for the natives and abhorrence for the suffering they underwent, in making a defendant of Columbus removed from the historical context in which he lived.

2. Ruggero Marino, articles in *Il Tempo* (1990: March 25, April 5, April 29, June 3, July 1, July 23, July 29, and August 15; 1992: January 24, June 8, and October 11; 1993: January 4; and other contributions to various publications.

3. The doctrine of Enrico di Susa, bishop of Ostia, remains valid: The pope was given jurisdiction over the known world as the deputy of Jesus Christ, and because Jesus was Lord of the world, the pope was as well.

4. With the reintroduction of the figure of Innocent VIII into the history of

Columbus and the discovery, the reading becomes simpler, in some ways even elementary. Everything appears smoother and clearer: The gaps are filled and the motivations are clear in the succession of events. Even if the definite proof for Innocent's role—the scientific proof—will never be found, we can still state with certainty that in the absence of a definitive proof of the traditional version of the story, the version set forth in this book appears much more plausible and credible. "It is [t]oo plausible to be true," in the words of Professor Osvaldo Baldacci at the Lincei Academy in Rome.

5. Guido Nathan Zazzu, "Genova e gli ebrei incontro di due culture," in AA.VV., *Colombo nella Genova del suo tempo* (Turin: ERI, 1985), 216 and 219.

6. St. Francis of Paola also had a vision at Genoa, the result of which was that the sanctuary on Paradiso hill was built in 1488, thanks to the Centurione and Doria families of Genoa. *La preghiera del marinaio* (Rome: Istituto Poligrafico e Zecca dello Stato, 1992), 136. As we shall see, these two families had connections to the Cybo and Columbus families.

7. Jacques Heers, *Genova nel '400* (Milan: Jaca Book, 1991), 239.

8. The charge of collecting the funds was given to the Genoese Meliaduce Salvago and Gregorio Giustiniani. The Giustinianis were related to the Cybos. It should be noted that this island has also been suggested as one of Christopher Columbus's many possible homelands. The Greek Yannis Perikos and the American Durlacher Wolper, also building upon earlier work (Canoutas Seraphim, *Christopher Columbus, A Greek Nobleman* [New York: self-published, 1943], state that the name of the navigator—who, according to them, spoke the language of Homer—was of Greek origin, and that the crew of the three caravels included sailors from the Aegean (Stefano Ardito, "Storie senza frontiere," in *Plein Air,* no. 383 [June 2004]. This Greek origin, as we shall see, connects Columbus to the Cybos in an increasingly closer relationship.

9. Heers, *Genova nel '400,* 45.

10. Vittorio Giunciuglio, *I sette anni che cambiarono Genova (1097–1104)* (Genoa: Don Bosco, 1991), 62. The author wrote another book on Columbus in 1993 in which it is stated that "America was not discovered by Isabella, but by Pope Innocent," without making any reference to my work. I am mentioned, however, in connection to other details of lesser importance, and the first edition of my 1991 book appears in the bibliography.

11. Georgio Possini, ed., *La Commenda di Prè* (Rome: Istituto Poligrafico e Zecca

dello Stato, Libreria dello Stato, n.d.), 16: "Finally, one must not forget the importance of Genoa as a strategic port for the Crusader armies of the twelfth and thirteenth centuries. . . . [A] testimony to this was the departure from the Ligurian port of the fleet, which, in 1190 (the same year in which the knightly order of Jerusalem gained great significance), transported the Third Crusade to the Holy Land." The Genoese admiral Benedetto Zaccaria wrote of the *recuperatione Terrae Sanctae* (recovery of the Holy Lands).

12. L. Tettoni and F. Saladini, *La famiglia Cibo e Cybo Malaspina* (Massa: n.p., 1997), 1.

13. In Corsica there was also a Genoese presence in the form of the Doria and Malaspina families, related to the Cybos and distinguished by the checkers on their coats of arms.

14. Esther Fintz Menascé, *Gli ebrei a Rodi* (Milan: Guerini and Associates, 1992), 74: "The rabbi with whom he stayed at Rhodes in 1826, Colonel Rottiers, did not neglect to inform him of the 'dedication' of the Jews of the island 'to the knights, above all during the siege of 1480, in which they shared in all the dangers, along with their women and children.' There was also a Jewish Rhodes in Roman times. Tolerance and neighborliness become lost over time and was eventually revoked. The situation on the island deteriorated in 1502. The suffering of the Jews began under Pope Borgia, in keeping with the politics of Ferdinand and Isabella."

15. Christopher Columbus, *Gli Scritti* (Turin: Einaudi, 1992), 169. It should be added that in 1120, Foulque d'Anjou, on a pilgrimage to Jerusalem, was made a Templar brother around the time when that order is believed to have been formed. René d'Anjou was "a man ahead of his time, anticipating the cultured Italian princes of the Renaissance. An extremely literate person, he wrote prolifically and illuminated his own books. He composed poetry and mystical allegories as well as compendiums of tournament rules. He sought to promote the advancement of knowledge. . . . He was steeped in esoteric tradition, and his court included a Jewish astrologer, kabbalist, and physician known as Jean de Saint-Rémy. According to a number of accounts Jean de Saint-Rémy was the grandfather of Nostradamus, the famous sixteenth-century prophet. . . . René's interests included chivalry and the Arthurian and Grail romances. Indeed, he seems to have had a particular preoccupation with the Grail" (M. Baigent, R. Leigh, and H. Lincoln, *Holy Blood, Holy Grail* [New York: Dell, 1983], 138). According to the same authors, René d'Anjou was the grand master of another

secret organization, connected to the Templars and Cistercians: the mysterious Grand Priory of Sion. Subsequent grand masters of the Priory included Botticelli and Leonardo da Vinci (ibid., 131). This book inspired Dan Brown's *The Da Vinci Code*.

16. In 1455 Aronne Cybo upheld the statutes of the wool trade in the capital. Domenico, historically the father of Columbus, was also a wool merchant (*Dizionario biografico degli italiani* [Rome: Istituto della enciclopedia italiana Treccani, n.d.], 232). Among Aronne Cybo's other achievements was the negotiation of peace between Genoa and Naples.

17. *Dizionario storico portatile di tutte le venete patrizie famiglie,* 1780.

18. In Apulia there is a document in which Pope Innocent leaves some property and possessions to a Cristoforo or Cristofano (two of the many versions of the navigator's name) Columbo. Cristofano was also the name of a son of a cousin of Innocent. The mystery of the surname Columbus ends here. I have in my possession a photocopy of the document, sent to me in a letter by Michele del Vescovo, deputy of the second Legislature, unquestionably the person who has taken the greatest interest in my research. The document is preserved in the archives of the diocese of Molfetta. It relates to ecclesiastic benefices which, in the year 1494, *tenet ac possidet dominus Christoforus* [Christofanus] *Columbus."* The usufructuary benefits are granted to the assignee for the remainder of his natural life, which, according to Vescovo, explains the date 1494.

19. Barreto Augusto Mascareñhas, *O Português Cristovão Colombo, agente segreto do rei Dom João II* (Lisbon: Referendo Ediçoes, 1988), 332.

20. Agapito Colonna was bishop of Lisbon, the city where Columbus lived in his early years. Might Giovanni Battista Cybo have had an affair with a married woman? Could there have been a secret offspring from such relations? Perhaps Christopher's mother had the surname Colonna, as has recently been suggested in Italy. It has even been suggested that this was a case of pedophilia, with the young victim being the future pope.

21. Other chronicles tell of an affair with a lower-class woman, multiple affairs, or an illegitimate son born in Genoa or elsewhere. Accounts of Giovanni Battista Cybo's life are always conflicting. His memory was discredited in the popular *pasquinades,* the product of lampooning as widespread as it was tolerated. The following amounts to calumny:

> *You should give praises, O Romans, to Innocent,*
> *Who himself increases the stock of the exhausted homeland.*
> *Eight bastard sons he has fathered, and just as many daughters:*
> *That he may be called the guilty father of the land.*

The Counter Reformation was enough to bury the record of a pope with many children. "So weak of the flesh"—such was the terse comment made by Cardinal Casaroli during my meeting with him.

22. There was also a continued Dominican and Franciscan presence in Padua.

23. He wrote a *trionfo* in honor of Pope Innocent VIII.

24. Also in Padua, the geographer Regiomontano read the works of Alfragano. In Padua, Prosdocimo de' Beldomandi wrote a *Commentary on the Sphere* based on the *Tractatus de sphaera* by Giovanni Sacrobosco, a thinker whom Galileo Galilei also studied during his sojourn in Padua.

Pawel Wlodkowic, rector of the University of Krakow, also came to Padua. He pointed out the presence of natural laws among the pagans, the immorality of war, and the need for Europeans to accept the pagans and schismatics among them. Jacques Le Goff, *Il cielo sceso in terra, le radici medioevali dell'Europa* (Bari: Laterza, 2004), 30.

25. Francesco Bottin, *Scienza e filosofia all'università di Padova nel Quattrocento*, ed. Antonino Poppi (Padua: LINT, 1983), 96. This, along with other subjects, is discussed in the cited volume, which does not mention—unlike the biographies of the pope—that Giovanni Battista Cybo was connected with the university. It should be noted that Columbus's son Ferdinand wrote that his father studied at the University of Pavia—where, however, there is no record of him. This was another of the great universities of the epoch, where the new culture of humanism solidified. Might Pavia have been an erroneous contraction of Pataviae (Padua)? Such oversights as these were common enough in the copying of texts; there are many of them in Columbus's works.

26. Giancarlo Zanier, *Scienza e filosofia all'università di Padova nel Quattrocento* (Padua: LINT, 1983), 267.

27. Ibid., 347.

28. Ibid., 360.

29. Ibid., 361. According to the surgeon Leonardo da Bertipaglia, who taught at Padua, "the sign of the cross [which Columbus planted everywhere], under a certain and, let us not forget, unrepeatable stellar position [which would be confirmed in the New World] would have a power, or rather, would be the sign that

the mysterious virtue of the sage plant, of obviously sidereal provenance, had been revealed by the forces of good."

30. Ibid., 364.

31. Columbus, *Gli Scritti,* 8. This is a peculiar recipe, which perhaps should not be taken literally and may conceal a different meaning.

32. Zanier, 372.

33. Painters such as Cosmé Tura, Carlo Crivelli, and Francesco del Cossa worked there: "Everyone went to Padua, just as in the 1960s everyone went to Trento to study sociology" (Sgarbi Vittorio, *Panorama* and *L'Espresso* [November 23, 2000]).

34. Maria Mannu, *I Francescani sulle orme di Cristoforo Colombo: il tempo dei pionieri* (Rome: Centro Nazionale di Cultura Francescana, 1992), v of the preface.

35. Artists hired to do portraits would interpret and translate the message and the idea of the commissioner, beyond just painting the physiognomy. They went to and fro between the courts of princes and popes. But the greatest commissions came from or were offered to the churches.

36. Today, Leonardo da Vinci is the most exalted and respected phenomenon of this long-ago era, not only for his divine art (this adjective is used even in his case), but also for his technological insight. In a twenty-first century founded on machines and the triumph of technology, the love of his ideas can only grow. Those willing and able to understand the fifteenth century to its core will surely find a great number of replicants of Leonardo, albeit from various angles. In some ways, they are as fascinating as Leonardo himself in their search for the eternal mysteries of the world and existence.

37. Francesco M. Serdonati, *Vita e fatti di Innocenzo VIII* (Milan: Vincenzo Ferrario, 1829), 1.

38. Guido Cybo was in the ranks of Emperor Otto I, as "captain of nobles." In the time of Lamberto Cybo, the Tuscan archipelago, including the islands of Gorgona and Capraia, became *Cybei de insulis*. The Cybos took possession of the marquisate of Ancona, which Columbus noted during the course of his first voyage. The navigator decreed that someone from the crew must go as a pilgrim to Loreto, in Ancona, to give thanks for being saved from a storm. In fact, they drew lots to decide who would go. At one time, the Cybos were dukes of Orvieto and Spoleto and later of Massa and Carrara. They obtained the fiefdom of Carafanello and became counts of Sora, Ferentillo, Anguillara, and Cerveteri. Lanfranco Cybo governed Genoa with seven other nobles, and was the sovereign

magistrate of the city, "for which he is honorably remembered in San Francesco of Genoa." (Might Columbus have attended this church?) The ensemble is completed by Guglielmo, who, having become an ambassador, was "an armed knight of Louis of France, the saint." Carlo Cybo was a member of the council, and became captain of the city of Naples in the time of Robert of Naples. Around 1366, Tedizio "enjoyed an honorable status with the king of Cyprus," the island that had been the seat of the Templars and was also inhabited by a group of Sufis. Mutio, Daniele, and Antonio were galley captains. Andrea and Prinzivalle were no less accomplished: The latter was a valiant defender of the island in a victorious battle and was the son-in-law of Bernabò Visconti, prince of Lombardy. Arianito fought at length in the Holy Land. About ten members of the Cybo family became cardinals, and their family tree boasts four doges and many merchants. The Cybos always showed a strong aptitude for business and financial activity. Aronne was also a merchant and had dealings in Spain. Giovanni Battista Cybo was in charge of the Dataria in 1471.

39. Serdonati, *Vita e fatti,* 5; Della Monica Nicolò, *Le grandi famiglie di Napoli* (Rome: Newton Compton, 1998), 365.

40. Earlier, in 1318, another Cybo, Federico, had occupied the same position in Savona.

41. Luigi Staffetti, *Gian Battista Cybo, vescovo di Savona* (Genoa: n.p., 1928), 6.

42. Can. Primicerio Francesco Samarelli, *Il tempio dei Crociati dalle origini ad oggi* (Molfetta: Tip. Iris, 1938), 22–23.

43. Ibid., 30.

44. It is not known what year the knightly order acquired the property of San Nicola, but it is probable that the Molfetta church was served and administered by the Templars of Ruvo before becoming a preceptory (Bramato Fulvio, *La storia dell'Ordine dei Templari in Italia. Le fondazioni* [Rome: Atanòr, 1991], 74).

45. Samarelli, *Il tempio,* 42: "From December 1488 our episcopal seat was no longer annexed to the archbishopric of Bari, but was 'subject to the Holy See.'"

46. Frederick's fleet confronted the one headed by the Genoese admiral Ansaldo de Mari, one of a family related to the Cybos (Horst Eberhard, "Federico II di Svevia," supplement to *Famiglia Cristiana* [Bergamo: n.p., 2003]: 266).

47. Horst, 145.

48. Paul O. Pfister, *La rotonda sul Montesiepi* (Siena: Cantagalli, 2001), 109.

49. Not far off, in the district of Istrice (where, according to an established legend,

Columbus spent part of his youth), there is the tomb of Pinturicchio, who painted at the court of Rome for Innocent VIII. It should also be noted that there was a Jewish presence in Siena (Gabriela Jacomella, "E la contrada riscoprì il tesoro del ghetto," in *Corriere della Sera* [September 4, 2004]) going back to the 800s. In the 1300s they were summoned to manage the pawnshops.

50. Claudio Spagnol, *Templari* 2, no. 3 (2002), 32: "For centuries there was an intense popular veneration of St. Galgano, but a veneration suspected of heresy, as many modern authors have remarked. In fact, according to some, he was actually a heresiarch—perhaps of the Cathar religion, a doctrine that had found favorable acceptance among the affluent bourgeoisie of the time—or else a Waldensian or Dulcinian, or something else."

51. One of the cards of the Garampi file in the Vatican secret archives, in the "Vescovi" volume, reads: *1472 16 Sept. Joannes Baptista, Saonem Episcopus transfertur ad ecclesiam Melphitam.* Transferred?

52. Corrado Natalicchio, *Il Vescovo di Molfetta diventa papa* (Molfetta: Mezzina, 1998), 17.

Chapter Three. Columbus, Son of Innocent VIII

1. Ludwig von Pastor, *Storia dei Papi dalla fine del Medio Evo* 3 (Rome: n.p., 1959), 201.

2. Ibid., 224.

3. Corrado Natalicchio, *Il Vescovo di Molfetta diventa papa* (Molfetta: Mezzina, 1998), 40n16.

4. Ibid., 18.

5. Serdonati, *Vita e fatti,* 15–16. This biography is one of only a few lives of Innocent VIII written. It was commissioned by the same descendent of the Cybo family, Alberico, who had the pope's tombstone placed in the ancestral mausoleum in St. Peter's, where the research for this book began in 1990. The biography, although certainly hagiographic, also seems to be based on documentary evidence. It was ready for printing in 1595 but, curiously, it was not published. It was rediscovered accidentally, and came to light only 230 years after its writing. It was miraculously saved from destruction in 1806 in the cathedral of Massa, where the Cybo family archives were housed in one of the rooms. Many other papers were lost.

6. Sandro Carocci, *Il nepotismo nel medioevo* (Rome: Viella, 1999), 150.

7. Ibid., 151.

8. Johannes Burchard, *Alla corte di cinque papi* (Milan: Longanesi, 1988), 23. On the subject of nepotism, Bianchi writes that this was "an inevitable adaptive appeal and to a certain degree necessary for the survival of the Church, the religious institution, and the accompanying territorial monarchy, which lacked a dynastic heritage or future."

9. Carocci, *Il nepotismo nel medioevo,* 201.

10. Burchard, *Alla corte di cinque papi,* 66.

11. Natalicchio, *Il Vescovo di Molfetta diventa papa,* 32–33: "It would be a lengthy business to describe this election, but this is the truth: that it was St. Peter in Vincula [Cardinal Giuliano della Rovere] who made him pope, and Cardinals Aragon and Vesconte [Cardinal Ascanio Maria Sforza] followed him—for otherwise at their hands, Cardinal Giuliano della Rovere would have agreed with the Venetian cardinals, and the lot would fall to Cardinal San Marco [Marco Barbo], who at the first count had more votes than any other. Hence the following night they all changed, so that he became pope and was named Innocent VIII."

12. Von Pastor, *Storia dei Papi,* 204.

13. Burchard, *Alla corte de cinque papi,* 52.

14. Carocci, *Il nepotism nel medioevo,* 87–88: "Since time immemorial, historians have insisted on the great divide existing between an event and the documentary evidence (when such exists) conveying its record. The positivist faith in the objective value of documents, as long as they are authentic, has been replaced by an insistence on so many ideological, pedantic, and cultural filters that a permanent barrier has been formed between any event and its written documentation. This results in an attitude of great caution toward sources, which is joined to the task of picking the semantic locks of every testimony: the meaning of the writing and the ideological system in which it was recorded and of which it is the product. Jacques Le Goff coined a formula of great resonance: 'A document is a monument,' because 'it is the result of the effort on the part of historical societies to impose on the future . . . that given image of itself.'"

We might add that this is especially because in our present case the sources are with rare exceptions unanimous, telling only what the writers wished to leave in writing, and respecting those things that needed to be covered up or erased. As has often been said, a document is a whitewashed sepulchre.

15. Burchard, *Alla corte de cinque papi,* 87–88.

16. It should be noted, for the sake of completeness, that regarding this relationship, Serdonati wrote that Innocent VIII proclaimed "good orders" against the Jews fleeing Spain following Ferdinand's ultimatum, and proceeded with "highly rigorous inquisitions and persecutions." In truth, the expulsion of the Jews occurred after the date recorded as the date of Innocent's death: July 25, 1492. Serdonati's interpretation could also be the result of anti-Semitism, which was widespread at the time.

17. Clemente Fusero, *Giulio II* (Milan: Dall'Oglio), 166.

18. Von Pastor, *Storia del Papi,* 210n4.

19. Natalicchio, *Il Vescovo di Molfetta diventa papa,* 72.

20. *Enciclopedia ecclesiastica* (Milan-Turin: Vallardi-Marietti, 1942), 590–91: "Having a righteous and peaceable nature, he would have excelled in better times. One of Innocent's great glories was his opposition to the Spanish Inquisition, led, at the time by Torquemada, who used that tribunal to ingratiate King Ferdinand by filling the state coffers; to this end he ordered that a single Dominican should take part in it and the others should be laymen. This mode of proceeding had already been condemned by Sixtus IV. Yet further insulting the great inquisitor, Innocent raised his voice against him in a letter of 1485. Because this was not successful, the pope protested it anew, summoning the cases to Rome.

21. *Lettere di Lorenzo il Magnifico al Som. Pont. Innocenzio VIII* (Florence: Magheri, 1830), 5–7. The letter continues thus: ". . . [N]ot least seeing this affair of yours continue so long, it appears I cannot neglect this intercession, nor any other effort on my part for the necessity of Sig. Francesco, who is very content with Maddalena, as I wrote [the marriage, then, was successful, contrary to what is believed]. I must require Your Holiness to act in such a way that I may again remain content and satisfied, as I was when the matters of the aforesaid San Francesco were settled appropriate to the dignity of Your Holiness and to the quieting of my soul. I have never been of the opinion that Your Holiness, in order to benefit Sig. Francesco, should deprive anyone in the world or scandalize anyone. And as this would be a dishonest thing and foreign to Your nature, thus it appears to me alien to Your innate goodness and kindness not to provide him—without harming anyone else—with the means to support his condition. I beseech Your Holiness in all humility to deign to lift the burden from him and from myself and to provide for him in

such a way that I shall no longer have to disturb you with such solicitation. In so doing, you will be acting in a way truly worthy of your clemency and goodness—not merely pious and reasonable, but also necessary and most pleasing to me, as a good example of all we hope for from Your Holiness, to whom I commend myself." The tone of this letter reveals the true hierarchy that had been established in the relationship between the pope and Lorenzo the Magnificent and contrasts strongly with the entirely different, proud words with which Columbus addressed the monarchs of Spain.

22. This refers to the version printed in Venice in 1715.

23. *Lettere di Lorenzo,* 31–32.

24. Carocci, *Il nepotismo nel medioevo,* 151.

25. Columbus, *Gli Scritti,* 385.

26. *Genova* (Genoa: Costa & Nolan, 1992), 81.

27. *Dizionario di erudizione storico-ecclesiastica, del Cavaliere Gaetano Moroni Romano,* 36 (Venice, 1846): "Although he was a poor cardinal, he supported many honest families, whom he cared for with such delicacy and moderation that he became the object of universal admiration." The story was later haughtily refuted by his descendents. The clarification of the Cybos' wealth, in absence of a standard of comparison, is made on the strength of the inventory.

28. Serdonati, *Vita e fatti,* 74–75. Serdonati continues: "That although it might appear to them that it was more scant than they would have wanted to raise them to higher status, with all this he did not wish to take from the Church in order to enrich or aggrandize his family, and he told them this freely. He was entreated to give a cardinal's hat to Pantaleo Cibo [Cybo], son of Cristofano, the pope's cousin, a youth of the highest expectations, and because the boy was of too tender an age, Innocent did not want to do so . . . and thus the pope must have had greater regard for Christian piety and for Christ than for the benefit of relatives, and therefore could never be induced to give them anything from the ancient estate of the Church. Innocent greatly despised flatterers."

29. A. Baratta in Luigi Grillo, *Elogi di liguri illustri* 1 (Torino: Bocca, 1905) 376.

30. Von Pastor, *Storia del Papi,* 222.

31. Carlo Marcora, *Storia dei Papi* 3 (Milan: Edizioni librarie Italiane), 293.

32. Panvinio's chronicle continues: ". . . which was, in good part, effective and for which he gained much praise and added to the general good will toward him. He had no pride, only infinite humanity and mercy for the poor, so that the

Germans, French, Hungarians, English, and Poles all celebrated him greatly as their benefactor; and he was truly most benign in his dealings, supportive of expeditions, opposed by nature to war, and a great observer of justice. He was gentle, patient before adversity, and judicious in speaking and was always remembered for the benefits received from him. . . ." He always acknowledged those cardinals who had been in favor of his pontificate. This was more a matter of gratitude than of simony. Panvinio adds: "He was also of the most acute cleverness, for as soon as he heard tell of a negotiation, he looked into everything concerning it, courteously receiving the countless ambassadors who came to him from all around, and presented to them all the good that peace brings and the grave damage that war causes and exhorting them to persuade their princes to lay down their weapons in order to point them toward the Turkish enemy. He thereby supported every good work that could further his just desire."

33. Natalicchio, *Il Vescovo di Molfetta diventa papa,* 69–70: Corrado Natalicchio, who has no affection for his bishop of Molfetta, wrote, "Personally, I have spent a large amount of time in search of a definite proof regarding possible 'impure acts' committed by Giovanni Battista Cybo during his life and his pontificate. Although I got hold of a remarkable number of books, ancient and modern, and original documents, carefully analyzed in every archive on the Italian peninsula, it was not possible for me to reconstruct a proof able to supply public opinion with a single event of reproach to Cybo's moral conduct." He was "of irreproachable conduct" (36n6).

34. Melissa Meriam Bullard, "Fortuna della banca medicea a Roma nel tardo Quattrocento," in *Roma Capitale (1447–1527),* ed. Sergio Sensini (Pisa: Pacini, 1994), 245; see also chapter 3, notes 52 and 53. If the story is true, this may have been dictated by exceptional circumstances. Just as likely, it may have been one of the falsehoods created to fuel the *damnatio.*

35. Fr. Pietro Dott, ed., *Enciclopedia ecclesiastica,* 4 (Venice: Pianton, 1858).

36. Ardicino della Porta da Novara, we find, came from a geographic area close to Liguria, near Monferrato (and near to Cuccaro, where, according to some, Columbus was born) and near Piacentino (where others place Columbus's birth). Novara saw the emergence of the heresy of Fra Dolcino, who, having been influenced (like Columbus) by the doctrine of Joachim of Fiore, announced the coming of the fourth and last state in which salvation was imminent and resolved to bring the Church back to radical evangelism. He was burned at the stake. Novara was also the home of Friar Gaspare Gorrizio,

who wrote the *Book of Prophecies* with Columbus and was always the navigator's most trusted alter ego to whom the admiral entrusted his most secret maps. From Arona, on Lake Maggiore in the province of Novara, came the humanist Pietro Martire d'Anghiera, a friend of Columbus and a courtier at the Spanish royal court. He was one of the first chroniclers of the Indies, and even before Amerigo Vespucci, he declared the Americas a New World.

37. Von Pastor, *Storia del Papi*, 284.

38. Panvinio devotes a chapter expressly to "universal peace for all Christendom."

39. Agostino Paravicini Bagliani, *Il corpo del papa* (Turin: Einaudi, 1994), 124.

40. Ibid., 114–15: "In giving an account of the ceremony that occurred on March 28, 1486, in the presence of Innocent VIII, Johannes Burchard dwelled with insistence upon the color white: 'On Easter Tuesday seven great *white baskets* were made ready, full of blessed lambs. . . . [T]hus was prepared a great silver bowl of water, full of *pure water*. . . . [T]he pope immersed them in the water, baptizing them, and the bishops who were around him assisted him. . . . [T]hey took the lambs from the water and carried them in basins to the table prepared for the purpose, covered with *immaculate cloths . . .*' Considered in its entirety, the message of the ritual appears clear: The visibility of the pope's Christ-like function had to be supported by the purity and innocence of life."

41. Ibid., 126.

42. *Enciclopedia del Cristianesimo* (Novara: De Agostini, 1997), 216: "The necessity of the supreme pontiffs to correspond in a more frequent, prompt, and confidential form resulted in the creation of new departments outside of the Apostolic chancellery, such as the Camera Secreta in the time of Martin V and the Secretaria Apostolica for official correspondence in the Latin tongue, established by Innocent VIII in the constitution *Non debet reprehensibile* (31.XII.1487) and comprising twenty-four apostolic secretaries, one of whom bore the title Secretarius Domesticus and held a position of pre-eminence. We can also trace to the Secretaria Apostolica the Chancellery of Briefs, the Secretariat of Briefs to Princes, and the Secretariat of Latin Letters." He also had prepared a new edition of the *Pontificale Romanum*.

43. Innocent first reorganized the Sacra Rota (August 23, 1485), then revised it in 1488. He later set his hand to the Camera Apostolica (December 22, 1485), and finally regulated the Apostolic Chancellery (May 15, 1486).

44. Burchard, *Alla corte di cinque papi*, 22 of the preface.

45. Von Pastor, who often alludes to Innocent's alleged failings of character contradicts himself and writes of the "energetic proceeding of the supreme head of the Church."

46. The letter from Ferdinand to the city of Molfetta of August 30, 1484, gives no foreshadowing of the long conflict with the pope: "Today by the letter of the esteemed Count of Burrello, our ambassador, we have been informed that the Most Reverend Lord Cardinal of Molfetta, yesterday at the thirteenth hour, was canonically created pope with the complete consensus of all . . . for which we give infinite thanks to our Lord God, who has indeed placed the most holy pontiff in governance of the Holy Church and the Christian faith, advising you thereof to your contentment. Make merry and show your joy, as we ourselves have done."

47. Serdonati, *Vita e fatti,* 83.

48. Michaud, *Biographie universelle ancienne et moderne* 20 (Paris: Ch. Delagrave, Libraires-Editeurs), 348.

49. Supplement to *Fotostoria. 7 anni di Guerra* no. 88 (Roma: Rotocolor, n.d.).

50. Professor Osvaldo Baldacci informs us that a priest whose name he did not remember and who took an interest in Innocent's life was amazed at having found a considerable series of concessions allowing priests to marry.

51. Marcora, *Storia dei Papi,* 295.

52. Vittorio Giunciuglio, *I sette anni che cambiarono Genova (1097–1104)* (Genoa: Don Bosco, 1991), 315.

53. *Dizionario biografico degli italiani* 25 (Rome, 1981). If this fact is true, it is the best confirmation that Franceschetto's reputation was the hardest hit by the damning of his father's memory, according to the rule that suggests that the sins of the father are visited upon the son.

54. Nicole Boille, *Il Tempo* (October 15, 1992).

55. Osvaldo Baldacci, *Roma e Cristoforo Colombo* (Florence: Olschki, 1992), 77–79.

56. This is not the only contemporary document of this type. A similar "Columbus *nepos*" appears in a note found in a publication in the possession of the library of Perugia, which reemerged in an exhibition connected with the Quincentenary. On the occasion of one of my lectures at Perugia, I learned of this in an interview with Professor Claudio Finzi, then a contributor to *Il Tempo.* Yet for all my requests for a precise reference to the publication in question, I have received no response.

57. Giampiero Bof, ed., *Dizionario della Bibbia* (Milan: Vallardi, 1993), 174.

58. An encounter with a whale is described in the Book of Jonah, which begins with Jonah fleeing to Tarshish, one of Columbus's mythical shores. The giant creature swallows the prophet in an episode always interpreted as a premonition of the Resurrection of Christ and the dead and is connected with St. Brendan's sailing to other worlds.

59. Robert de la Croix, *Storia segreta degli oceani* (Milan: Mondadori, 1990), 26. This is the only place where I have found, in all my deductions and years of research, any reference to a possible foundling and papal origin. From where did the author draw his assertions? Napoleon plundered the Vatican archive. It is known for certain that maps from the time of Innocent VIII were part of the booty, seeing that documents to this effect were retrieved among the mattresses of the French soldiers. Paris might be an unexplored mine for this history, not to mention that wherever we hunt documents in relation to the discovery of America and to its contorted truth, we find traces of the passage of the shadow of Napoleon, as if the Masonic vein from which this emperor sprang desired to find something, or perhaps erase it—but this is another story.

60. Not by coincidence, more than one researcher has posed the question. The idea of Christopher being the son of Innocent VIII is a theory that I have never wished to champion more than others, lest I be accused by journalists of wanting to make an easy scoop. Attacks from the academy made prudence advisable. For this reason, after the publication of my first book in 1991 and as soon as my first intuitions began, I decided to be silent on the subject of Columbus as a Templar and Cybo descendant. I did, however, discuss it with a cardinal. Also, after finishing my complete reconstruction of events, I was interested above all in the conspiracy devised to alter history. It is a much greater truth to reestablish profaned justice.

   In October 1992, *Il Tempo* ran a headline: "Was Columbus a pope's son?"—that pope being Innocent VIII. I tackled the question by degrees, promising myself I would proceed slowly, as I explained to a professor of mathematics at the University of Perugia in whom I had long confided. He thought he could make use of unpublished information on nascent Templarism and other information in one of his works. (During this time, I was required practically to abandon my research for a few years, for professional and health reasons.) He applied himself to writing the foreword to a book, further discussed below, on the hypothesis of Columbus being the pope's son and presented this notion almost as a novelty. The professor in question was among the first—but not the only one—to be informed specifically regarding the intrigue of the knights Templar, who were beginning to enter the story, and regarding the possibility of a direct blood tie between Innocent VIII and Columbus.

At this time I wished to avoid futile sensationalism over alluring antiquarian gossip. I was thus limited to occasionally planting the news in a series of articles that appeared in various journals, as well as on television and in a long series of lectures. I reasserted it in the 1997 fourth edition of my book, where it appears unequivocally, even on the cover. And I confirmed it in a chapter—planned with the author and written almost entirely by me—in the book *Carovana di lago* by Riccardo Tanturri, who was interviewed by Cinzia Romano (Venice: Marsilio, 1997), 122; see also *La decima isola* by Francesco A. di Maggio (Pavia: n.p., 2000), 194–95. The published interview was in the preceding year.

In 2000 there followed the release of a facsimile (presented by the professor already mentioned, still during a difficult period for me) expanded by over two hundred pages beyond what had already been amply written and published—under a false name (I wondered why). According to the publisher, this concealed a gymnastics teacher who introduced himself ambiguously as "professor," thus succeeding in drawing in university lecturers, journals, and newspapers. This author had approached more than one person already contacted by me, but had never addressed himself to me. Yet he appropriated by literal quotation most of the discoveries and the entire unpublished historical framework depicted in my many articles and books. This copycat writes in the following tone: "I trust, moreover, in the timeliness of the Church, that it may prevent some author, predictably not 'official,' who has reached the implicating truth through his own personal intuition, from being able to bring off a scandalous scoop that could discredit her to the eyes of the world before she could even speak." He dreads the danger "that some biographers of our time, by their intuitive and deductive findings (prematurely with respect to the desires of the Church) might reveal knowledge that is potentially troublesome and disturbing and is perhaps of moral character, if not indeed doctrinal." Knowledge of the person in question reached me, and I wished to meet him. The evasive "historian" said he was the depositary of "some secrets of the Church." He asserted that he would never have published anything in the first place without the Church's consent. It should also be explained that, according to the so-called editor of the book (another person whose behavior is better passed over), many of the points of this research were the fruit of his suggestions and his "visions." The untimely scoop on the pope's son would therefore be the product of nothing less than a collaborative rehashing.

61. Ferdinand Columbus, *The Life of the Admiral Christopher Columbus by his son Ferdinand*, trans. Benjamin Keen (New Brunswick: Rutgers University Press, 1959), 3–4.

Chapter Four. An Epigraph in St. Peter's

1. Von Pastor, *Storia del Papi*, 261.
2. Ibid., 250–51n4.
3. Carli Enzo, "Il Pio umanista. Le libreria Piccolomini," in *FMR*, no. 102 (February 1994): 71. This was depicted in the magnificent fresco cycle created by Pinturicchio (one of Innocent VIII's favorite painters) in the library of Siena Cathedral, where we see Captain Bayezid, the pretender to the Ottoman throne and known as il Turchetto (the little Turk), taking part in a procession in honor of Pius II, who is preparing to leave for the Crusade, by the Church of San Ciriaco in Ancona.
4. Von Pastor, *Storia del Papi*, 257.
5. Ibid., 258.
6. Giacomo E. Carretto, *Gem Sultàn pellegrino d'Oriente* (Treviso: Pagus, 1991), 59: "In the Arab lands in which Jem traveled, he was called al-Junjum, a word meaning "skull" or "goblet," and pronounced "jamjama" . . . it also meant "stuttering." . . . Jem or Jem-scid is the name of an ancient king of Persia whose goblet, Jam-i-Jem, was a miraculous mirror that reflected the world; only by drinking the forbidden wine could a person look into its depths to find every secret revealed. This again recalls the Holy Grail, and the name of Jem was certainly a name gifted with power, a name also used by Alexander the Great and by Solomon. Jem's brother Bayezid had been called Jemgiah, a powerful name like Jem, once again ambiguously uniting the two contenders."
7. Ibid., 185–86. The book's author, who alternates between reality and fantasy, explains in the bibliographic conclusion that the "lesson" is contained in Ismail Hami, ed., *Gurbet-Name-i-Sultan Gem* (Istanbul: Danismend, May 29, 1954).

8. Franco Cardini, "Il Saladino," special edition for *Famiglia cristiana* (2003): 57.

9. Carretto, *Gem Sultàn,* 21.

10. Von Pastor, *Storia del Papi,* 260.

11. Ibid., 259.

12. Gregorovius, *Storia di Roma nel Medioevo* 5 (Rome: Edizioni romane Colosseum, 1988), 167.

13. Johannes Burchard, *Diarium Innocentii VIII,* pars prima (Florence: R. Sercelli, 1896), n116.

14. The lance was the basic unit of divisions of Templars and knights.

15. Giacomo E. Carretto, *Gem Sultàn,* 86.

16. Aldo Gallotta and G. Bova, *Studi magrebini* 12 (Naples: Istituto Universitario Orientale, 1980), 191n71.

17. Juan Manzano Manzano, *Cristóbal Colón. Siete años decisivos de su vida. 1485–1492* (Madrid: Cultura Hispanica, 1964), 198.

18. Agostino d'Osimo, *Cristoforo Colombo ed il P. Giovanni Perez di Marchena* (Ascoli, 1861), 87–88.

19. Von Pastor, *Storia del Papi,* 255.

20. Serdonati, *Vita et fatti,* 92–93.

21. There was a strong Genoese, Florentine, Venetian, Sienese, Piacentine, and Piedmontese presence in the Italian settlements of Seville (Varela Consuelo, *Colombo e i fiorentini* [Florence: Vallecchi, 1991], 15).

22. Giancarlo Zanier, ed., "Ricerche sull'occultismo a Padova," in *Scienza e filosofia all'università di Padova nel Quattrocento* (Trieste: LINT, 1983), 361. There is an interesting reference (see note 29) to the presence in Padua of an Umbrian astronomer and physician, Clementino Clementini da Ameria, involving the two Geraldini di Amelia brothers, who were instrumental in the launching of Columbus's first voyage. Though he did not accept astrological predictions blindly, Clementini prophesied great events for 1513, the year in which the Christian Lord would bring about the renewal of European society. This astronomer, who also predicted the Lutheran schism, among other things, would later be in the service of Louis X.

23. Ruggero Marino, *Cristoforo Colombo e il papa tradito* (Rome: Newton Compton, 1991). This and other pieces of the puzzle concerning the Vatican's role in financing and launching the expedition were patiently and meticulously put together for the first time in Columbus's history in that first book. In my work published in 1998, I wrote: "Contrary to what has been believed for centuries

and although the ships sailed under the flag of Catholic Spain under Ferdinand and Isabella, Columbus's endeavor was heavily financed by Pope Innocent VIII (Cybo Malaspina) and by the great Italian banks of the era." The source is then cited in a note referring to an argument that has nothing to do with the subject at hand, in one of those "scientific" oversights that have afflicted more than one scholar, as if by a strange contagion. Some who have attacked me must in fact have read my book with extreme attention, seeing that they have begun to utilize some of its conclusions. Senator Paolo Emilio Taviani himself initially described it tersely as: "Rubbish from a journalist." He then told me in person that the question constituted "a bombshell," adding: "I will give much emphasis to your researches." In *Grande Raccolta Colombiana,* at the end of a chapter titled "Fino a qual punto il Vaticano intervenne per l'impresa di Colombo" (The Extent to which the Vatican Intervened in Columbus's Endeavor), he limited himself to writing: "At the end of this section acknowledgment is due to the journalist of Rome's *Tempo,* Dr. Ruggero Marino, for having been the first to reveal how the various stated arguments are connected to the strange request to the king in Letter 1 of the *Libro Copiador'* [in which Columbus asks for his son to be made a cardinal], and having thus reopened and reassessed the subject of Innocent VIII's participation in Columbian events, which scholarly bibliographies have too long classified as legends."

To my knowledge, there are no legends or studies of this, apart from sporadic and insignificant references to Innocent VIII. On the subject of Vatican financing, Taviani adds: "The first Columbus scholar to credit this theory is Robertson, who, in his famous *History of America* published in 1777, described Luis de Santangel as 'receiver of ecclesiastical revenues,' thus hinting at a direct interest on the part of the Church, and therefore the Vatican, in Columbus's endeavor." In truth, Robertson, whose book was helpful at the beginning of my research and whose definition of Santangel had never been sufficiently noticed, makes no deduction regarding the argument in question, namely the interest or involvement of the pope in Columbus's activities. Innocent is never mentioned, and the question of financing is vaguely brushed over. The same is the case in the detailed study of Francesco Pinelli by the Columbus scholar Luisa D'Arienzo. The importance of Rome in the preparation for the discovery and the link to Columbus remains completely ignored.

Subsequently, in *Cristoforo Colombo,* published by the Italian Geographic Society, still on the same topic, Taviani writes: "The hypotheses whispered among the circles of Roman nobility around the years of the fifth centenary are not even worth taking into consideration: namely, that the pope was of a mind to finance Christopher Columbus's voyage himself." The "Roman nobility" became acquainted with Innocent VIII and his intentions through articles in *Il Tempo* and one of my lectures, which took place in 1992 at the Circolo degli Scacchi (lit.: The Chess Society; cf. the Cybo arms) and was moderated by my colleague Emanuele Bonfiglio. On this occasion, I was invited to the table of the Colonna princes. My interactions with professors, some of whom I at first humbly attempted to engage in the hope that they would shed some light on the matter; my many useless and frustrating contacts with important and learned persons, political, secular, or otherwise; and my contacts with persons influential in the media and journalists of national importance, historians or otherwise, would merit an entire book by itself. I dwell on this phenomenon here in order to show how difficult it is, in my country, to stand out from the mainstream and confront an academia that often takes refuge within its own positions, ready to defend dogma above all, sometimes doing all within its substantial power to obstruct and suppress research. Academia is even capable of blocking televised programs, as has occurred on more than one occasion. It seems we are dealing with a genuine intellectual Tangentopoli, or better, a Columbian intellectual monopoly.

To conclude this lengthy paraacademic digression on a lighter note, I would like to give my cordial thanks to Professors Osvaldo Baldacci and Gaetano Massa, to the foreigners German Arçiniegas and Arnoldo Canclini, and above all to Francesco Perfetti for their helpfulness. Thanks also to Geo Pistarino for an article by him in *Columbus 92,* and also to Aldo Agosto for providing me with the documentary answer to a question I posed regarding the blood tie between Francesco Pinelli and the pope, which I had found in one source. Thanks, finally, to Franco Cardini, who, albeit with legitimate reservations, agreed to write the introduction to my 1997 book—something that Taviani had always refused to do.

24. The Geraldini family's connections with Innocent and Columbus are highly significant. To complete the picture, Battista Geraldini was governor of Corsica and Milan. One of the brothers' uncles, Angelo, had preceded them in Iberia and returned to Rome, having obtained papal dispensation for the marriage of Ferdinand and Isabella. He was elected archbishop of Genoa and

general legate for the Crusades and had studied at Siena and Pavia. Columbus also supposedly studied at Pavia (Frezza Federici Igea, *Cristoforo Colombo e Alessandro Geraldini* [Genoa: ECIG, 1992], 23–25).

The intimacy between the Geraldini and Cybo families is also confirmed by the fact that the remains of the Geraldini family are preserved in a chapel of the church of St. Francis in Amelia. On a sarcophagus made decades before the discovery of the New World, there are carvings of heads decorated with feathers, typical of representations of Native Americans. There is also a Cybo tomb there. The Geraldini family had members in all the places through which our reconstruction passes, including Apulia, Naples, Novara, and Capua, where Giovanni Battista Cybo's father is buried. Unfortunately, Agapito Geraldini was also the secretary for the Borgias, Pope Alexander VI, and the Valentino family. Probably an accomplice, willing or coerced, he joined with the faction that would alter history.

25. Giovanni Berardi, perhaps a relative, known as Cardinal Tarentino, had been a pontifical diplomat and papal legate in the peace treaty between René d'Anjou and Alfonso of Aragon. He was born at Tagliacozzo, which I visited in the summer of 2003. Tagliacozzo is a small town in Abruzzo where the remains of Thomas of Celano, the biographer of St. Francis, are preserved. In the main square a small obelisk has stood since ancient times, and many of the streets are named after members of the Colonna and Orsini families. In one church, the Madonna of the Knights of Malta is revered. In a sanctuary a few miles away, homage is paid to an icon of Mary that came from the East. Once again, the currents in our story flow together.

26. This is a strange name for an age-old militia derived from the confraternities. Perhaps this name also conceals something—a possible overlapping of intents and persons.

27. Ferdinand Columbus, *Le historie della vita e dei fatti di Cristoforo Colombo suo filgio* 2, ed. Rinaldo Caddeo (Milan: Alpes, 1930), 355. At this point, the suspicion arises that Santangel may have even been Italian, considering that in many books his name is written in the Italian version, Luigi di Sant'Angelo, and he is called a count. In Spain, among many Pinelli there was a Luigi, as the historian Alberto Boscolo relates. Interestingly enough, the Pinelli were the guardians of the Castel Sant'Angelo in Rome. Luis de Santangel might therefore be the Spanish version of Luigi Pinelli di Sant'Angelo, as suggested in my first book.

28. Aronne Cybo had been viceroy of Naples and Giovanni Battista Cybo spent some years of his youth there. The political adventures of Lorenzo the Magnificent began in Naples, and Bessarion and Nicholas of Cusa were also there. The Geraldini, Pinelli, and Santangel families, who had business dealings with the Medici, passed through Naples. The Santangel and Cybo families obviously must have known each other, be it directly during their Neapolitan sojourns, through the Medici, or even from much earlier. In fact, a Luis de Santangel (or Sant'Angelo), probably the father of the Luis who aided Columbus, having the same name as his son, wrote to Piero di Cosimo de' Medici in 1469, while in 1480 Lorenzo the Magnificent addressed a letter to "Luigi da Santagnolo, in Valencia" (Marini Dettina Alfonso, "Il contributo di Roma e Firenze ai viaggi di Cristoforo Colombo," in *Aeropago* [May–August 1997]: 4).

29. Marino, *Cristoforo Colombo e il papa tradito,* 127.

30. Luisa D'Arienzo, "Francesco Pinelli banchiere del papa, collettore e nunzio apostolico in Spagna all'epoca di Cristoforo Colombo," in *Atti del IV Convegno internazionale di studi colombiani* 2 (Genoa: Fondazione Colombiana, 1987), 72.

31. Andrea de Mari, a relative of Innocent VIII on the maternal side, worked under him. Francesco Pinelli owned a bank in Seville together with his brother Battista and the Genoese Andrea de Odone. The bank managed the funds for the Crusade in Granada, financing the war against the Turks on behalf of Innocent VIII. The Pinellis were joined by a series of marriages to the Genoese Centurione family, who owned another of the most important banks of the period, which was particularly influential in Portugal. Columbus was one of their agents. Domenico Centurione was a papal nuncio and administrator of the alum trade in Spain (Alonso Justo Fernandez, *Legaciones y Nunciaturas en España de 1466 a 1521*, 1 [Rome: Instituto español de Historia ecclesiastica, 1963], 374 and 459). Orietta Pinelli, daughter of Isabella Centurione, married Nicolò Pinelli Aprosio. Her brother Ludovico was a partner of the Genoese Paolo di Negro, who sent Christopher Columbus from Lisbon to Madeira (Luisa D'Arienzo, *Atti del VI Conuegno,* 63).

The names Negro and Centurione were recorded by Columbus in his will. The fortune of the latter family, related to the Gentile family of Genoa through a double marriage, had been started through a relationship with the Medici. Among the general commissioners of the bull of the Crusade, which financed the war against the Moors, were Archbishop Fernando di

Talavera (a converted Jew), the great theologian Ximenes de Prestamo, and the Genoese Cipriano Gentili (or Gentile), a member of the pope's family lineage who also governed the fortress of Civitavecchia in Rome—the Vatican's gateway, to which all the proceeds of the alum industry were sent, destined to fund the Holy War. Last, Cipriano Gentili may even have been able to impose ecclesiastical penalties in order to raise money to fund the Crusade, exercising a duty assigned to the prior of the monastery of Santa Maria de las Cuevas. This was the monastery of Gaspare Gorrizio di Novara, the monk who was closest to Columbus. As always, the links are completed by the many connections and interwoven families.

32. Andrés Martín Melquiades, *Dinero Cultura y Espiritualidad en torno al Descubrimiento y Evangelización* (Bogotá: n.p., 1990), 12–13; *Archivo Ibero-Americano* 47 (1987): 4. The publications (my thanks to Arnoldo Canclini and Francesco Perfetti) include a reproduction of the most important document: Coming from Spain, it relates to the origin of the sum required by Columbus. It was discovered only in the nineteenth century, and had never before been published in full. Even in this fundamental study, Innocent VIII is not once mentioned because by then everything possible had already been done to disregard and suppress him, to the point that even in the Spanish *Gran Enciclopedia Rialp,* in the sequence of popes, the articles pass from Innocent IV straight to Innocent X. Not a word is written of the pope who made Isabella and Ferdinand "most Catholic," and whose donations made possible the victory over Granada—similar to what occurred in Spain upon Columbus's death. A confirmation of the standards adopted for the administration of the funds of the Church comes from another document, in the possession of Dr. Paolo Pelù in Massa. It is from about a hundred years later and has attached to it a notarial certification. The arms of many of the Cybos of Genoa and Naples appear on it, among them those of Boniface IX and Innocent VIII, as well as the Medici, Pinelli, and Grimaldi families (the Grimaldi escutcheon also bears a checkered pattern). At one point, reference is made to the residue of an annuity of payments for the bull of the Crusade, which, in the last year of Innocent VIII's reign, the pope decided to use in Spain "for pious works." If nothing else, this confirms the dependence of these funds on Rome's decisions.

33. Ibid., 16–17.

34. Clemente Fusero, *The Borgias*, trans. Peter Green (New York: Praeger, 1972), 151: "A month later [in late June], Innocent VIII collapsed under the weight

of that illness which, despite a deceptive improvement at one point, was to prove his last. Its symptoms included agonizing abdominal pains, an old scar in one leg, which broke open again, and persistent high fever. The first person to feel the impact of the pope's sickness was Gem [Jem], who found himself subjected to more rigorous surveillance." Why was Jem treated in this way, considering his excellent relationship with Innocent? Because he was also being poisoned?

35. Von Pastor, *Storia del Papi,* 272–73.

36. Ibid., 203. The split that would divide Christendom was approaching faster than ever. This caused Columbus, in his will, to leave his goods to the service of the Holy Father in the event, "may God forbid," of a schism.

37. Piero Bianucci, *La Stampa,* September 22, 1992.

38. Bagliani, *Il corpo del papa,* 173n34.

39. Lorenzi was a friend of Cardinal Bessarion and the Greek philosopher Demetrius Chalcondyles, who taught in the city of Padua. Lorenzo de' Medici had asked Chalcondyles for an exact translation of a text of Strabo "for the part relating to Asia" (*Archivio Veneto,* series 5, vol. 32–33 [Venice: n.p., 1943]: 122). Lorenzi was one of the many intellectuals welcomed to the court of Rome in a cenacle second to none other which engaged in many cultural exchanges with Florence. When the keeper of the books rose to a higher office, Lorenzo the Magnificent recommended Angelo Poliziano to succeed him.

40. M. Pierre de Nolhac, "Giovanni Lorenzi, bibliothécaire d'Innocent VIII," in *Mélanges d'archéologie et d'histoire* 8 (Paris: n.p. 1888): 5.

41. *Archivio Veneto,* series 5, vol. 32–33 (Venice: n.p., 1943): 137–38.

42. Antonio Di Pierro, *Il sacco di Roma* (Milan: Mondadori, 2003), 29.

43. Christine Shaw, *Giulio II* (Turin: SEI, 1995), 135.

44. Ibid. The book dwells at length upon the relationship between the two popes, and demonstrates extensively that Innocent, after his election, was in no way subservient to della Rovere—rather, he took advantage of him authoritatively on several occasions.

45. Fabio Isman, *Il Messaggero,* October 7, 1993.

46. The correction made in the stone, replacing the word *imperatore* (referring to the Turk) with *tyranno,* shows that the carving was carefully revised. In the original drafting as desired by the pope's descendent Alberico Cybo, this confirms an intimacy with Islam that the Church of Rome, heir to the Counter Reformation, could no longer tolerate. It is also confirmed by the action of

Bayezid, who, upon Innocent's death, fruitlessly recommended to Alexander VI that Niccolò Cybo be made a cardinal (Luigi Staffetti, "Il libro di ricordi della famiglia Cybo," in *Atti della Società Ligure di Storia Patria* [Genoa, 1908–1909], 480n289).

47. In the publication of the letter to Raffaello Sanchez, in the first year of Alexander VI's pontificate, the "93" part of the date is written the same way: M.CCCC.XCIII (Bossi Luigi, *La vita di Cristoforo Colombo* [Bologna: Edison, 1992], 123).

48. Luigi Staffetti, "Il libro de ricordi," 431.

49. Serdonati, *Vita e fatti,* 88.

50. Ibid., 95.

51. At the time of the drafting of the notarial document that I consulted in Massa—the one in the possession of Dr. Pelù (see note 32)—the controversy was already underway. On the document is added, after the confirmation of the fact that the pope died in exemplary mode: "There are scribes who say that in the lifetime of the pope, Columbus found and had certain knowledge of the New World, of the Indies, and others who say that it was during the reign of Alexander VI, of which there is great doubt, as one must doubt the words of the cardinal of St. Peter in Vincola that followed shortly after his creation." What did Giuliano della Rovere say?

Chapter Five. The Witches and Pico della Mirandola

1. It is hard to obtain precise information on the pontificate's finances, the remnants in the Vatican archive and the state archives of Rome being insufficient—speaking of which, a researcher for thestate archives ascertained after my research that some sources for the years in which I was interested had unexpectedly gone missing.

2. Ferdinand Gregorovius, *Storia di Roma nel Medioevo* 5 (Rome: Edizioni romane Colosseum, 1988), 115.

3. Ibid., 115.

4. Jean Delumeau, *L'allume di Roma. XV–XIX secolo* (Rome: COAC, 1990), 17.

5. The members of this trade took the common name of Giustiniani, a surname found among the relatives of the Cybo family. Giustiniani was the name used by the Genoese families of Chios. "It was, in fact, a Paride Giustiniani who, in 1455, had to leave Phocaea in the hands of the Turks" (ibid., 19).

6. Ibid., 22–23 (Giovanni di Castro is addressing Pius II; italics are mine):
"... Each year, [the Turks] extort over three hundred thousand ducats from
the Christians for the alum we require in order to dye fabrics. The island of
Ischia produces only a little of it, and the caves of Lipari have already been
exhausted by the Romans. I have discovered *seven* mountains so rich in alum
that they could supply *seven* worlds. If you give me the order to hire workers,
to set up cauldrons, and to have the stones boiled, you will be able to supply
alum to all of Europe, and take away the Turks' profits. The raw material
and water are abundant. You have a port close enough: Civitavecchia. Now
you can prepare the Crusade against the Turks; the quarries will give you the
necessary finances!"

7. Gregorovius, *Storia di Roma,* 115.

8. Rinaldi, *Le Lumiere,* 14.

9. Gregorovius, *Storia di Roma,* 116.

10. Rinaldi, *Le Lumiere,* 15.

11. Jean Delumeau, *L'allume di Roma,* 90: "It can be ascertained that in the
period from July 1489 to the end of 1490 the Castros produced a total of
52,171 cantari of alum (2,608 metric tons). ... The Gentili did not remain
contractors of the enterprise in Tolfa for long, considering that they were new
contractors in 1489 and that by 1492 their place had already been taken by
the Florentine Paolo Rucellai and Company, who exported 77,221 cantari
(3,681 metric tons) from Civitavecchia between March 5, 1492, and May 5,
1494."

12. Ibid., 62. A book on pyrotechnics reads: "The alum commonly called rock
alum is a substance similar to ice. It is lustrous, of a warm and dry nature
and of sour taste, accompanied by a salty flavor with an astringent and bit-
ing property. It can be obtained through artifice from mineral rocks. ...
Alchemists, and those who separate gold make marvelous use of it."

13. Nicolò Del Re, *La Curia romana* (Rome: Edizioni di storia e letteratura,
1970), 73n2.

14. Paolo Cortesi, *Alla ricerca della Pietra filosofale* (Rome: Newton Compton,
2002), 136.

15. Marco Berberi, *Bomarzo, un giardino alchemico del Cinquecento* (Bologna:
n.p., 1992), 12.

16. Jacques Le Goff, "Il papa e l'alchimista," in *La Repubblica* (March 14, 2003):
"The alchemist is 'not a *magister* devoted to speculation, but a philosopher-

artificer, learned but gifted with the prudent willpower and dexterity of experts and artisans, capable of relating both to the powerful and to simple workmen.'"

17. Johannes Fabricius, *Alchemy* (Copenhagen: n.p., 1976), 7.

18. The peacock is the symbol of the sun. In the Muslim world it symbolizes the cosmos or the great celestial bodies of the sun and moon. Its flesh, believed to be incorruptible (corresponding to the body of Christ risen from the sepulchre), is a symbol of renewal. It was eaten at great banquets. According to tradition, the knights of the time had to swear to carry out their heroic deeds before the corpse of the magnificent bird decorated with its feathers. Philip the Good, duke of Burgundy, took such an oath committing himself to carrying out the Crusade. The peacock sometimes appears in images depicting the grotto of Jerusalem. The "eyes" on its tail were considered to be those of divine omniscience. Rarely seen in heraldry, it symbolizes splendor and resurrection. Knights, crusades, and resurrection are all elements at the basis of Columbus's endeavor.

19. Fabricius, *Alchemy,* 135, fig. 251.

20. Stanislas Klossowski de Rola, *Alchemy, The Secret Art* (London: Thames and Hudson, 1973), 11.

21. Roberto Mussapi, "Stregati da un frammento di cielo," in *Il Giornale* (December 18, 2002).

22. Alexander Roob, *Alchemy and Mysticism* (Cologne: Taschen, 1997), 356.

23. Riccardo Tanturri, "Cristoforo Colombo e il tradimento della Spagna, intervista a Ruggero Marino," in *Libro aperto,* no. 21 (April–June 2000): 58. The interview occurred a few months earlier.

24. Adriano Chicco and Rosino Antonio, *Storia degli scacchi in Italia* (Venice: Marsilio, 1990), 30–31.

25. Donato Masciandaro, "Il mercato sulla scacchiera," in *Il Sole-24 ore* (February 9, 2003), 32. The word *loyalty* was the motto of Innocent VIII. *Reciprocity* might refer to the relationship with the Muslims.

26. Chicco and Antonio, *Storia degli sacchi,* 15: "Colonna, belonging to a noble family of that name, was born in 1433 in Venice and at the age of thirty-one entered the order of the Dominicans at Treviso. He was made master of novices, but dedicated a great part of his time to writing the *Hypnerotomachia poliphili*. He finished it in three years but did not publish it until 1499, accompanying it with splendid illustrations that are generally attributed to Mantegna or one of his disciples. In the meantime, he had become a teacher at the University of Padua." I read Maurizio Calvesi's book on Francesco Colonna Romano

while the original Italian edition was in the proofing stage. Even in this case, and perhaps with a better understanding of the reasons, we can make remarks analogous to what we have said of Francesco Colonna of the Veneto.

27. Emilio Palla, "Il piccolo insediamento ebraico negli Stati Cybei," in *Il tempo di Alberico 1553–1623*, ed. Claudio Giumelli and Olga Raffo Maggini (Archivio di Massa: Ministero dei beni culturali e ambientali, n.d.), 113: ". . . with the idea of being generous in granting favors [to the Jews], and as such hoping that the competition of their industry would result in an advantage, rather than a disadvantage, to the people."

28. Giorgio Viani, *Memorie della famiglia Cybo e delle monete di Massa di Lunigiana* (Massa: n.p., 1971), 122.

29. John 8:59. See Luigi Staffetti, "Il libro dei ricordi."

30. Roberto Ricci, "L'oro del principe," in *Il Tempo di alberico 1533–1623* (Massa: n.p., 1991), 310. Earlier, it reads: "If, on the one hand, the iconography of the temple is identified with the Renaissance esoteric, aristocratic, and cultural archetypes of the period, and the iconography of the stars (coupled with the temple in the same emblem) is identified with other symbolic and universal meanings which are linked to the esoteric-magical world, then these elements together (temple and stars) constitute a particularly striking, if cryptic, framework. The motto alluding to the great star that overtakes the others seems to indicate Alberico's stubborn will in pursuing a single splendid idea—and all this is a reflection of a creative will reforming and organizing the mother state, which shines through even in the first years of government, in the ideological-cultural sphere of enlightened absolutism."

31. Roberto Ricci, *Magia alchimia, essoterismo e farmacopea alla corte di Massa*. I have only a typewritten copy of the document. In the same period a certain Girolamo Ghirlanda (perhaps a member of the family of Ghirlandaio who was one of the painters of Columbus's portrait), secretary to Giulio Cybo, a man of letters, scholar, poet, and philosopher, ended up in the clutches of the Inquisition, even while the Bishop of Luni lamented to Alberico "that in Carrara there are some persons living bad lives, infected by heresy." The prince had to intercede with Pope Pius V on Ghirlanda's behalf.

32. In the eighteenth century the Lunigiana region hosted another Cypriot, Giovanni Battista Diana Paolologo, an educated man who, in his *Sacra universal filosofia dell' Immacolata Concezione di Maria, sempre vergine madre di Dio*, described the deeds of Moses (to whom Columbus compared himself)

and the golden calf. In the *Sacra* he wrote the following: ". . . then it is told that the prophet made this profane gold into powder, and threw this same powder onto the waters. Why was this extra diligence needed? Was it not enough that the calf was consumed or incinerated? His caution was remarkable, for this powdered gold is of such a nature that when thrown over lead or tin, or flowing mercury, it reverts to its specific humidity and is reconstituted in gold as before . . ."

33. Cipriano was buried in a church of St. Francis. He was involved in the fortification of the papal holdings along the Adriatic coast, fearing attacks from the Turks, "the impious ugly monster." He was a knight of the Order of St. George and a member of the Academy of Eccentrics and fell suddenly into disgrace, thus not becoming governor of the fortress of Massa Carrara.

34. Giulio Vada, *Cipriano di Piccolpasso, tra ceramico e alchimia*. The article is available on the Internet. In note 15, the author explains that the Latin word *cabala* became *caballus*, the packhorse that, according to Athorène, "carries the burden of esoteric truth handed down over the centuries."

35. Claudio Palandrani, "E Alberico volle la 'Città del sole,'" in *La Nazione* (March 12, 1998). Even today, proving the power of tradition and symbols, the cultural supplement to the local daily paper is called *Il Mercurio* (The Mercury).

36. "La Profezia di Lincoln," in *Il Nostro Diritto* (Rome: Tumminelli and Co., Città Universitaria, 1941), 11–12.

37. This information comes from an article signed Gruppi Pietromarchi, in an issue of the journal *Gardenia* for which I do not have the reference.

38. *Il giardino magico degli alchimisti* (Milan: Il Polifilo, 2000), lxx–lxxi. Gherardo Cybo corresponded with the scientist Ulisse Aldovrandi.

39. It is easy enough to draw analogies between this and today's practice of televised magicians, with their recurrent scams.

40. Cristoph Daxelmüller, *Magia storia sociale di un'idea* (Milan: Rusconi, 1997), 190.

41. Ibid., 191.

42. Claudio Corvino, "La caccia alle streghe," in *Medioevo Dossier,* De Agostini-Rizzoli Periodici, no. 1 (2003): 53–54; Alfonso M. di Nola, *Il diavolo* (Milan: Newton Compton, 1994), 260: "In effect, the document of 1484 . . . was not the starting point of the persecution, but only one among many acts of papal legislation which, without arriving at any dramatic statement on the problem

or on the reality of the diabolical pact and nocturnal flight, constituted judiciary and inquisitorial power and authority. The importance of the measure lay rather in its widespread and deadly effects, surely more profound than those resulting from analogous acts of pontifical authority."

43. The *Malleus* was reprinted in 1576, having had no further editions since 1520.

44. *Dictionnaire de Théologie Catholique* 7 (Paris: Libraire Letouzey et Ané, 1927), 2004.

45. Maria Luisa Ambrosini, *L'Archivio segreto del Vaticano* (Milan: Mondadori, 1973), 251.

46. Vincenzio d'Avino and P. Antonio Pellicani, eds., *Enciclopedia dell'Ecclesiastico* 2 (Turin: n.p., 1878), 665.

47. Adriano Bernareggi and Vallardi-Marietti, eds., *Enciclopedia ecclesiastica,* 591.

48. Maria Montesano, "Magia," in *Medioevo Dossier, De Agostini-Rizzoli Periodici,* no. 2 (2001): 35.

49. Ibid., 37.

50. Mariateresa Fumagalli Beonio Brocchieri, *Pico della Mirandola* (Casale Monferrato: Piemme, 1999), 19.

51. In 1491 Innocent VIII granted him the Patriarchate of Aquileia.

52. As pointed out by von Pastor, almost no one has written that Marsilio Ficino took his vows in 1473 and that he was an apprentice of Platina and Nicholas of Cusa, among others.

53. Henri De Lubac, *Pico della Mirandola. L'alba incompiuta del Rinascimento* (Milan: Jaca Book, 1997), 11. According to the great scholar Cristoforo Landino, Pico was "the prince of our times in all doctrine and literature." Landino described him as "almost divine."

54. Ibid., 53 and note 25. In 1459 Cardinal Bessarion made a speech on peace in Nuremberg beginning with the same verse.

55. Ibid., 314.

56. Marcella Farioli, *Le religioni misteriche* (Milan: Xenia, 1998), 109.

57. *Enciclopedia ecclesiastica,* 591. Columbus studied the same texts of all the seven cultures.

58. De Lubac, *Pico della Mirandola,* 40.

59. Brocchieri, *Pico della Mirandola,* 131.

60. Ambrosini, *L'Archivo,* 218.

61. A. Martin V. Fliche, *Storia della Cheisa* 15 (Turin: LICE-Berruti, 1972), 291.

62. Brocchieri, *Pico della Mirandola,* 101.

63. De Lubac, *Pico della Mirandola,* 46.

64. Ibid., 450.

65. Brocchieri, *Pico della Mirandola,* 103.

66. Antonio Archi, *Il tramonto dei Principati in Italia* (Bologna: Cappelli, 1962), 85 and 238.

67. De Lubac, *Pico della Mirandola,* 326. Pico della Mirandola was no exception. His name is often associated with that of Ferdinand of Cordova, "a knight in arms and battle," a Spaniard who had preceded him. Like Pico, Ferdinand, in his time, was young, handsome, and charming, a musician, painter, and swordsman, raised in the milieu of the Italian humanists. He debated in "fine Latin, Greek, Hebrew, Chaldean, Arabic." His success was such that the jealous "mandarins" of knowledge in Paris had him arrested. He went to Italy, and in Genoa declared himself ready to take on anyone in discussing various theses in medicine, physics, philosophy, and theology. In Florence he met Cardinal Bessarion, who introduced him to the Platonic Academy and led him to begin a comparative study of Plato and Aristotle. The cardinal made him a subdeacon, and he acquired a position in Rome (where Giovanni Battista Cybo was still a cardinal), in the Tribunal of the Rota. He died in 1485, a year before Giovanni Pico published his theses (De Lubac, *Pico della Mirandola,* 7).

68. Staffetti, *Atti della Società,* 230.

Chapter Six. Santa Croce and the Lance of Longinus

1. The falsity of the act on which the temporal power of Christianity was based was discussed as early as the fifteenth century by Cardinal Nicholas of Cusa and Lorenzo Valla, who, prior to going before the papal court in Rome, confirmed in 1442 in Naples under Alfonso V (where the Cybo family had lived) the manifest falsity of the Donation of Constantine. It was one more rationale for establishing a new Church of Rome, beginning with Constantine.

2. Claudio Varagnoli, *Santa Croce in Gerusalemme* (Rome: Bonsignori, 1995), 16: "The fourth century layout recalls that of the Eastern churches, with the *memoria,* the area containing a relic or sacred object, located at the back of the church for the gathering of the faithful. The positioning of the entrances to the chapel, with two corridors, probably one for the faithful to enter and one for

them to exit, is highly reminiscent of a similar arrangement in the catacombs, but the layout of the Roman churches recalls ... that of the Constantinian Basilica of the Holy Sepulchre in Jerusalem, where the rotunda containing the sepulchre is at the back of the great basilica of the *matryrium*."

3. Ibid., 16–18.

4. Mariano Armellini, *Le chiese di Roma* (Rome: Tipografia Editrice Romana, 1887), 205.

5. Michael Hesemann, *Titulus Crucis* (San Paolo: Cinisello Balsamo, 2000), 298–99. From the sixth century on, "the pope celebrated the Good Friday rite until the Avignon exile (1305–1377). According to the *Ordines Romani*, the liturgical books containing the description of the papal ceremonies, the pope walked barefoot from the Lateran Basilica to the Sessorian Basilica, to pay homage there to the 'banner of salvation.' The popes also celebrated there the fourth Sunday of Lent (Laetare Sunday). From the ninth century, a symbol of this occasion was the golden rose that the pope brought each year from his residence at the Lateran to Santa Croce, where he consecrated it."

Santa Croce was in a secluded and highly sacred location, for a long time fallen into disuse. In a reference in the *Regesto Sublacense* mention is made of a monastery there around the turn of the millennium.

6. Varagnoli, *Santa Croce,* 21–22.

7. Ibid., 24. In a pontifical letter from 1488, at the height of Innocent VIII's reign, when Pedro Gonzales de Mendoza, the "third monarch of Spain," was the Church's cardinal, he called upon the Carthusian monks to contribute to the repair and rebuilding of the *domus sanctae* Crucis de Jerusalem.

8. Cf. Paolo Coen, *Le sette chiese. Le Basiliche giubilari romane* (Rome: Newton, 1999), 63.

9. Varagnoli, *Santa Croce,* 49n83.

10. Ibid., 26.

11. Carsten Peter Thiede and Matthew d'Ancona, *La vera croce* (Milan: Mondadori, 2001), 114.

12. *Enciclopedia del Cristianesimo* (Novara: De Agostini, 1997), 617.

13. Speaking of pineapples, their impossible presence has even been revealed in a Roman mosaic (as well as in Egypt and Pompeii) in an exhibit in the Palazzo Massimo at the Roman Baths (Fulco Pratesi, *Corriere della Sera,* December 3, 1998). Parrots, pineapples, and corn have thrown the authorship of Melozzo's work into a crisis: If America was effectively discovered only after Columbus's

voyage of 1492, such images cannot have been produced in earlier times—unless some knowledge of the New World existed, restricted to the circles of the Vatican and above all to the "sailor pope." This argument is taboo, however, a problem that certainly cannot be solved by art critics or architects' studies. Melozzo da Forli, who for us remains the artist most suspected of painting the pineapple, was close to the Paduan Mantegna and is considered a master of perspective, a technique that made possible revolutionary visions in art. He was one of the greatest fresco painters of the Holy House of Loreto, the Marian sanctuary particularly linked to the figure of the giant saint Christopher; Melozzo's *Entrance into Jerusalem* still remains there, and Innocent VIII, like Columbus, always wished to go there as a pilgrim—a desire that the pope would never realize because of the duties of his office, which required him to remain in Rome. Nor was Columbus able to fulfill his vow.

14. *Melozzo da Forli* (Milan: Leonardo Arte, 1994), 18. The artist still remains little known, described as "esoteric, theorematic . . . almost a Leon Battista Alberti of painting." Before going to Rome for the plans of Sixtus IV's *Renovatio Urbis,* he also worked in Padua. Melozzo is called a "dark star," because of the fate that befell the greater part of his works, which were irrevocably lost—and he was also cursed by a *damnatio memoriae.* His was a creative career in the service of a patron, as was the case for almost all the other artists already mentioned, which unfailingly led to ecclesiastical circles directly involving the pope—another confirmation that the Vatican and humanism were inseparable and proceeded in unison in those times, albeit amid inevitable conflicts arising from differing mentalities, interpretations, and ambitions. It is a difficult history to reconstruct in detail, between the "ideological oppositions that were becoming a way of life, the disputes among groups of intellectuals and oppositions between families disguised beneath political content" (ibid., 51).

15. Ibid., 59. Luca Pacioli, another of the most eminent thinkers of the period, was an aficionado of formulas, Euclidian teachings, and ancient knowledge. He told Melozzo of "a very formidable intersection of proofs and applications—mathematical, geometric, antiquarian, and architectonic in substance—and also of the Roman lapidary alphabet" (ibid., 58).

16. Ibid., 80: "These [solids] are those . . . whose material forms with some adornment were in the very hands of Your Holiness in the supreme palace of the Most Reverend Cardinal our Protector, Lord of St. Peter in Vincula on the

occasion of the visit of Supreme Pontiff Innocent VIII, in the year of our salvation 1489."

17. Otto Mazzuccato, "Una scritta dedicatoria cinquecentesca in ceramica," in *Ceramica per l'architettura,* no. 37 (2000). This publication will be discussed in further notes.

18. The attribution and dating of the two long inscriptions on the wall of the dark corridor are always linked to the coat of arms of the Spanish cardinal Bernardino Carvajal. It was probably he, above all, who sought to divert memory from Innocent VIII many years after the fall of Granada, in the temple where the pope had reclaimed the Titulus of the Cross.

19. Ilaria Toesca, "A Maiolica Inscription in Santa Croce in Gerusalemme," in *Essays in the History of Art presented to Rudolph Wittkower* (London: Phaidon, 1969), 105. The parentheses of the inscription in the text indicate the letters that are now missing.

20. As the text shows, even the number relating to the years of the pontificate shows omissions sufficient to cover tracks. The year 1492, if connected with the eighth year of the pontificate, as in the original inscription, would have created a temporal discordance that would arouse immediate suspicion, leading back inevitably to Innocent VIII. Borgia, who usurped the merit of the former in that same year, 1492, had only just begun his pontificate.

21. Thiede and d'Ancona, *La vera croce,* 87.

22. Michael Hesemann, *Titulus Crucis,* 320. It is not known precisely when the saint's relic became part of the collection of Santa Croce, but "it is said that the finger of St. Thomas was there 'in most ancient times' and that an appropriate altar of Thomas was placed there, which was venerated throughout the Middle Ages."

23. Giovanni Sicari, *Stemmi cardinalizi,* sec. 15–18 (Rome: Alma Roma, 1996), 128–29. The succession of Spaniards goes from Mendoza to Quinones, a Franciscan who became confessor to Charles V, and ends with the omnipresent Carvajal. It was certainly Carvajal, together with others, who had the greatest responsibility in the systematic adulteration of history that took place in Rome. Already an ambassador for the monarchs of Spain, he played a determining role in Alexander VI's election to the pontifical seat. Alexander rewarded him with a cardinal's hat. A man of great ambitions, more a man of power than of faith, more a proponent of a state Church than of ecumenism, he was also the head of the Hispanophile faction in Rome, along with

Charles V. He took sides against Giuliano della Rovere, who became Pope Julius II, and plotted to depose him. For Carvajal, the interests of Spain and the emperor took priority over those of the head of Christianity, to whom he owed obedience. Oral tradition successfully imposed for five centuries attributes to him the commissioning of Melozzo's cycle. The most recent studies, however, attribute it unequivocally to Mendoza, who was the titular cardinal of the Church during the pontificate of Innocent VIII. Carvajal would later be excommunicated but reinstated by Leo X, son of Lorenzo the Magnificent (the father-in-law of Innocent VIII's son). Evidently, in the silent pact that linked the pope and the emperor in the play of battles and alliances, there was an agreement or at least a compromise—also because Spain, faced by recurrent dangers to the Church, had confirmed its role as a most Catholic country, a defender of the faith. To reinforce the Spanish stamp, the chapel of San Giacomo, dedicated to the saint of Compostela, was built on the ground floor of the belfry, to the right of the entrance of Santa Croce.

24. Professor Emilia Stolfi, who manages the archive, informed me that among the files there is a document referring to Christopher Columbus. Unfortunately, due to reorganization, the document is currently not retrievable.

25. Mariano Bizzarri, *Il Mitreo di San Clemente* (Rome: Sydaco, 1997), 6–7.

26. Ibid., 12–13: "Mithraic iconography illustrates how the wheat (which becomes the bread and the body of the Communion) sprouts from the marrow, and how the vine from which the wine (the blood of Christ) is made grows from the blood, wine being the drink that plays the role of a symbolic substitute for the Persian Haoma [a kind of Grail]. The ritual sacrifice of the bull is distinct from the propitiatory act performed toward the deity. The latter is the meaning of the sacrifice of white bulls, which took place in Atlantis and is described in Plato's *Critias*. The slitting of the bull's throat by Mithras, as well as the slaying of the Minotaur in Crete by Theseus, assumes the significance of an initiatory triumph over the taurine element innate in the human being." We might add that the bull (symbol of Pope Borgia), according to some traditions the first creature that was created, corresponds in alchemy to the *prima materia* and that the dramatic battle with Mithras occurs in conjunction with the winter solstice, at a time close to December 25—a time already consecrated to the feast of the Sol invictus, signifying the resurrection of the sun after three days. December 25 became the day of the birth of the infant Jesus, and on December 25, following the shipwreck of Columbus's *Santa Maria,* the first settlement in the Indies was

founded—to begin the Resurrection? The bull's counterpart in Christianity is the ox, which gave life to Jesus the new man, he whom St. Christopher carried on his shoulders on his journey toward the light.

27. Leonard E. Boyle, *Piccola guida di San Clemente* (Rome: Collegio San Clemente, 1989), 4.

28. *Enciclopedia del Cristianesimo,* 165. On the "Letter to the Corinthians," it is stated "to further the restoration of peace, a first exhortation emphasizes the eternally destructive consequences of discord. Thus he expounds the origin and precise significance of the mystery of the leadership of the Christian community. It is a grave misunderstanding to imagine it as a power to be competed for, because it is not a matter of dominion over the Christian community, but of a memory of its origins in the Lord by way of the missions of the apostles. . . . Both the organization of the Church and the believers' way of living are charged with preserving its memory and showing its fruitfulness and ability to renovate the whole web of relationships and obligations."

29. Boyle, *Piccola guida,* 12.

30. Ibid., 30.

31. Without a shadow of doubt, Vasari attributes the work in the nearby chapel of St. Catherine of Alexandria to Masaccio, the forerunner of perspective and the master of so many great painters, who died in 1428. This was before the expeditions to the south of the ocean.

32. Von Pastor, *Storia dei Papi,* 270. The bishop of Foligno, Luca Boriano, once again in Franciscan Umbria, was also confessor to Innocent VIII, who supposedly allowed him to take the surname Cybo. The coats of arms can still be seen in the church of San Giacomo in Foligno, in Umbria.

33. Giovanni Morello and Gerhard Wolf, eds., *Il volto di Cristo* (Milan: Electa, 2000), 216–17.

34. Hesemann, *Titulus Crucis,* 15.

35. Trevor Ravenscroft, *The Spear of Destiny* (New York: G. P. Putnam's Sons, 1973), 16–17.

36. Ibid., 18.

Chapter Seven. Vatican, Campidoglio, and Quirinal

1. Jacques Attali, *1492* (Milan: Sperling and Kupfer, 1992), 95. It was a phenomenon that the historian Giorgio Ruffolo described as an Italian miracle,

capable of creating "a richness that did not transform itself into power, but instead transfigured into beauty," and which, as the French author Braudel wrote, was such that "when night fell on Italy, she lit up all of Europe."

2. Pollaiolo, not being an architect, supposedly passed on the work to others. "It is said that he designed the structure of the Belvedere by order of Innocent and then went on to other projects, not having much practice in building."

3. Eugenio Muntz, "L'architettura a Roma durante il Pontificato d'Innocenzio VIII, in *Archivio storico dell'arte, Nuovi Documenti* 4 (1891): 458. Further notes will refer to this publication. The document records the presence of an assistant of Pollaiolo, a certain Giacomo di Pietrasanta, which leads us back to the area around Carrara and to those who would be called the Cybos of Massa. In one building project there is identified a Tuscan architect named Jacopo di Cristoforo. The acquisition of the land necessary for new construction and the expansion of the Vatican gardens began in 1485.

4. Giovanni Morello, *I Giardini vaticani* (Rome: Logart), 12–13: "A radical action of renewal was attempted in the late Middle Ages during the pontificate of Innocent VIII (1484–1492), with the construction of a casino known as the Belvedere. . . . The casino was surrounded by a garden with cypress trees, and within, a cultivated area was set up with orange trees, watered by a fountain. There some statues were assembled, the initial core of the antiquarian collection that would form the origin of the Vatican Museum . . ."

5. Deoclecio Redig de Campos, *I Palazzi vaticani* (Bologna: Cappelli, 1967), 77.

6. Muntz, "L'architettura a Roma," 458.

7. Ibid., 458. The facade would later be used as a model for Agostino Chigi's famous Villa Farnesina.

8. On a page of the *Codice Atlantico,* kept at the Ambrosian Library in Milan, there is a design for the Belvedere signed by Leonardo da Vinci, another mysterious personality of probable Johannite tendencies, who sojourned in the villa during the time of Julius II, there to find the inspiration for his masterpieces.

9. De Campos, *I Palazzi Vaticani,* 77.

10. Von Pastor, *Storia dei Papi,* 276.

11. Muntz, "L'architettura a Roma," 460. Above the cornices, we "can catch a glimpse of marvelous and insufficiently noted exploits of two *putti* in each lunette, among a thousand other bizarre fantasies, and they are so graceful, of such a charming air and form, that the viewer cannot easily lift his eyes from them."

12. Giorgio Vasari, *The Lives of the Artists,* trans. Julia Conaway Bondanella and Peter Bondanella (Oxford: Oxford University Press, 1991), 253: "Not long afterward—that is, in the year 1484—Pope Innocent VIII of Genoa had him [Pinturicchio] paint several rooms and loggias in the Belvedere Palace, where among other things, as the pope wished, he painted a loggia entirely with landscapes, in which he depicted Rome, Milan, Genoa, Florence, Venice, and Naples in the Flemish style, something which was rarely employed until that time and which was very pleasing. In the same place he painted a Madonna in fresco at the entrance of the main door. At Saint Peter's, in the chapel containing the lance that pierced Christ's side, he painted a panel in tempera with a Madonna larger than life-size for Pope Innocent VIII."

13. Mantegna, *I Classici dell'Arte* (Milan: Rizzoli, 1967), 11. In a manuscript chronicle from 1486, Mantegna is described as "the first man whose designs and paintings can be found throughout the world." The great humanist and poet Battista Mantovano called him the "pride of Italy, glory of our age," writing of "a man of great renown who shows to posterity every rule and type of painting and does not merely surpass everyone in the use of the paintbrush."

14. Carrara and Padua, as always, remind us of the Cybos.

15. Vasari, *The Lives of the Artists,* 247.

16. Ibid., 247.

17. De Campos, *I Palazzi vaticani,* 78. Pastor explains: "Ancient designs show how great was the palace intended for the officials of the Curia, which was to be erected near the atrium of the Basilica of St. Peter." Moreover, "at the Vatican palace, Innocent VIII undertook grandiose works near the portico, begun under Pius II and those who followed him, or more probably on the very foundation of the palace begun under Paul II."

18. Von Pastor, *Storia dei Papi,* 260.

19. Muntz, "L'architettura a Roma," 368. Unfortunately, nothing remains of a Cybo palace either; whatever Borgia spared vanished in the work done in 1610 to make room for the façade of a new basilica. According to one scholar, however, "the portal with its bronze doors that gives access to the Vatican palace, on the right side of the portico that preceded the basilica, originates from the construction of Innocent VIII" (ibid., 370).

20. Von Pastor, *Storia dei Papi,* 282.

21. *I Borgia* (Milan: Electa, 2002), 174–75. Who was Symmachus? There was a Pope Symmachus around the year 500 who became a saint. He freed the slaves

from servitude and proceeded with the construction of the first Vatican palace. This reference appears pertinent. Another Symmachus translated the Bible into Greek in the second century AD. He was a commentator on sacred texts, deviating from the so-called Septuagint Bible. He was probably a member of the Ebionites (the poor ones), the Judeo-Christian sect in Palestine, who were connected to Jesus through their gospel (the *Naziroi*), which combined the new law with the old. Their concept of Jesus the Nazarene, whose teaching they believed had been corrupted (the same went for the Bible), was similar to that of Islam. Their rituals recalled those of Qumran, and the Ebionites must have been the direct continuers of the theories of the Essenes.

22. Rome also boasts a smaller fountain with a pinecone in the Piazza San Marco, behind the Palazzo Venezia, where Innocent VIII died. In Rimini in 1502, Leonardo da Vinci wrote exalting the harmony of the roaring water of the local pinecone fountain, an aqueous musical instrument. A pinecone sometimes appears at the top of Hermes' caduceus, and it can also be seen in Egypt in the Alexandrian catacombs of Kom al Sukkfa and in the Tell el Amana rooms of the Museum of Cairo, where among the votive objects there is an unmistakable pineapple! It is dated to the reign of Pharaoh Akhenaton, 1351–1334 BC.

23. Emilio Venditti, *Il Castello della Magliana* (Rome: n.p., 1994), 21–22: "Around 1471, Count Girolamo Riario, nephew of Sixtus IV (della Rovere) and brother of Cardinal Pietro Riario, obtained from his uncle, the pope, the use of this vast holding, a most delightful place at the time, there to organize hunting parties. . . . A description by Volterrano, a chronicler of the epoch, relates how on April 10, 1480, Count Riario organized a great boar-hunting party in honor of the dukes of Sassonia, guests at Rome." Muratori writes: "The feast was in the open air, near the Magliana springs. . . . The woods and fields all around rang with songs, with joyous voices, with the clamor of trumpets and the ululation of horns." At the accession of Giovanni Battista Cybo, this pastoral property became a "favorite place for the sojourns of the new pope." Innocent VIII commissioned Antonio Graziadeo Prata from Brescia, who had fortified Castel Sant'Angelo and the now destroyed Loggia of the benedictions, to build the Innocentian palace, quadrangular in form and with a crenellated wall, which, in many ways, recalls the austere style of the Belvedere. It could be reached by way of the river. To get to Magliana, the popes, with their followers, would exit through the Porta Santo Spirito or the

Porta Settimiana, crossing the Aurelian Wall or following the Lungara to the gate of Ripagrande, "where, on a heavy barge nobly decorated, they could proceed along the Tiber to the small river landing of the Magliana, a few meters from the castle" (ibid., 108).

24. Ibid., 28–29.

25. Traces of the works undertaken during Innocent VIII's pontificate can be found at Santa Balbina, St. John Lateran, San Giuliano dei Fiamminghi, Santa Maria della Pace, Santa Prassede, San Biagio della Pagnotta, San Sisto in Piscina, and Santa Maria in via Lata, where the remains of an ancient Roman arch were leveled and on the outside of which there is another Cybo shield. Santa Maria del Popolo, with its chapel, was built while the future pope was still a cardinal; Pinturicchio painted a Madonna there. The chapel was successively modified over the course of the centuries.

San Giovanni Battista in Trastevere was naturally connected to the Ligurian colony, which owned land, offices, businesses, shops, and warehouses around the port of Ripa Grande. Innocent VIII established that the rectors must be chosen from among Genoese priests, declaring the establishment national.

Similar work was done on the civic buildings of Rome, from Castel Sant'Angelo to Ponte Mollo and the Palace of the Chancellery, which was built in this period, as well as the Orsini Palace, the Porta Pinciana, the Torre del Soldano, the Tor di Nona, the Campidoglio, the Trevi Fountain, the gates and walls of the city, and the university, for which a project of complete restructuring was intended. Innocent VIII "provided for the stipends of professors to be paid completely and promptly, and only death stayed his hand in the rebuilding of the institution" (von Pastor, *Storia dei Papi*, 286).

The fever of innovation also spread outside the holy city and reached Argnano and Corchiano; the port of Civitavecchia; and the centers of Tolfa, Corneto, Iesi, Mentana, Osimo, Terracina, Viterbo, Perugia, and some nearby places. It reached France at Avignon: "Several works were carried out in this city by order of Innocent VIII, as is demonstrated by his arms, which can be seen on the exterior gate opening onto the bridge" (Muntz, "L'architettura a Roma," 467).

Among the recurring names in the surviving documents, we find a nobleman, Clemente Giovanni Toscanelli, presumably a relative of the Florentine physicist Pier Paolo; the bishop of Aiaccio, who was surely the third person at the bedside of the dying cardinal of Cusa, together with this same Toscanelli; Cardinal Marco Barbo, administrator of the priory of the order of the knights of Rhodes; Cardinal Raffaello Riario with the title San Giorgio; and a certain Hilarius Gentile, *domesticus noster et nepos* (our servant and nephew), who was a member of that great Genoese family—one of those Gentiles who, besides being governors of the fortress of Civitavecchia, were also among the administrators of the fund for the Crusade in the diocese of Badajoz and whose taxes funded the loan that was instrumental for Columbus's departure. Also present were a protonotary, de Nigris, which leads us back to the powerful di Negro family of Genoa; and two Cybos: Leonardo, who worked around Civitavecchia, and Domenico, governor of Terracina.

Among the names of the builders, we find that of the Florentine architect Baccio Pontelli, and almost always those of Giacomo and Lorenzo di Pietrasanta, who come from the marble-producing area of Carrara and who confirm the suspicion that the Cybos were already present in that area, where they would later be united to the Malaspina branch. The web of connections, families, alliances, and faithful friendships points to a patient weaver.

26. Giorgio Vasari, *Le vite* (Rome: Newton Compton, 1991), 490.

27. Upon seeing the statue, a scholar of alchemy, Alvaro Palanga, whom I took to St. Peter's, said: "It looks like the image of a Hopi Indian."

28. Luigi Staffetti, "Il libro di ricordi," 428n189. The same note, on the subject of the documents preserved in the archive of the state of Massa, citing an "autograph" memoir of Alberico Cybo, reads: "Our Pope Innocent died in 1491, and today it is 1621, which is 130 years later, and during the new building in St. Peter's, the place where his bronze sepulchre was has been damaged . . ." Thus Innocent's descendent, who was concerned with the reorganization of the mausoleum, amazingly got the date of the pope's death wrong. The date—1491—differs from the date on the monument and the date recorded in history. Was this Alberico's mistake? A death date of 1491 could eliminate many doubts regarding the phrase *Novi orbis suo aevo inventi gloria*. Moving Innocent's demise back to the year preceding Columbus's departure would nullify many possible claims relating to the origin of the discovery. Thus Alberico Cybo, in his own hand, renounced the very detail that should have been so dear to his heart. On the memoir in question there is written, "by the hand of Alberico," but Staffetti explains that "it is a copy by another hand"—the hand of that mysterious editor who once again endeavored to change the

records and who, referring to a renovation made in 1621, according to him, evidently knew nothing of the fact that the work of reorganizing the tomb had begun in 1606 and that 1621 was merely the year of the final step in the long process. It must have been a laborious negotiation: to gain permission to carve in stone a phrase that would please everyone, in the absence of documents that had disappeared or been hidden. What a triumph of Curial diplomacy!

29. Muntz, "L'architettura a Roma," 367.

30. Morello, *I Giardini vaticani,* 19.

31. Benedetto Grandi, "Memoria storica sull'antico Tuscolo e moderna città di Frascati, Della Chiesa Tuscolana e dei suoi Vescovi," in *Cenni storici intorno alla terra di Monteporzio nell'agro tuscalono,* 41.

    Not far from Monte Porzio, in Grottaferrata, the abbey of San Nilo has stood for some thousand years. The Greek Orthodox rite is still observed there. This is another element that may be connected with the Greek origins of the Cybo family, and thus to the presence of persons from that family in these places. Not by chance, fragments of a stone preserved in the cathedral of Frascati read: *Alderanys Card. Cybo Episcopus Tusculanus.*

32. Signora Maria Fiorelli, who has from the beginning upheld my theories regarding Pope Innocent VIII and Columbus, has reported that while she was still a child, her father, Osea Fiorelli, found in the city archives of Monte Porzio the documentation for what I have asserted, and that the documents were consigned by him to Cardinal Laurenti. Osea Fiorelli told his daughter that history had been changed by the Borgias, the Ricci, some members of the Geraldini family, and perhaps even by Franceschetto Cybo. Though their veracity is confirmed by her nephews and nieces who affirm that their aunt always told these stories, Maria Fiorelli's reminiscences appear somewhat confused with the passage of decades. She asserts that Columbus's relatives, in order to create a complete diversion, changed their name so that the navigator's eventual heirs would not be findable. According to Signora Fiorelli, the carving whose text is transcribed here also contains some intentional errors.

33. Paolo Mascherucci, "Amici di Frascati" in *Monte Porzio Catone* (Tuscolana: Associazione), 68.

34. Piero Ceccopieri Maruffi, *I marmi dei Cybo da Massa al Quirinale* (Modena: Aedes Muratoriana, 1985), 1.

35. Ibid., 7–8: "The vestiges of the Cybos are in the Castello Obertengo, a pallazo in Bagnara that became the governor's palace; Villa Sopra la Rocca or

Villa di Volpigniano, which today bears the name of Villa Massoni (Villa of the Masons!); Villa della Rinchiostra; the more modest Villa della Cuncia; a so-called palazzino, the Palazzo di Santa Elisabetta; and the Palazzo Principesco, today a center for the fine arts."

36. Ibid., 59–62: "It is time to consider the property of the Cybos destined to house the marbles of Massa: Thanks to Camillo's meticulous precision, today we can trace the origin of the acquisition, which in fact leads back to Innocent VIII.... In the garden, which is the most significant and monumental part of the complex, there remain, for the worthy decoration of the new dwelling and mounting guard over the memory of the sovereigns of Massa, six stone eagles bearing upon their breasts the escutcheon of this family, the statues, the obelisks, and the balusters. The Cybo Villa and Palazzo now form part of the complex that gained extraterritorial status in 1929, and constitutes the pontifical villa of Castel Gandolfo. This, with the papal palace and 136 acres of parks and gardens, extends over a territory whose walls and ruins are steeped in Roman history, from the legend of the first Latins up to the historical reality of the Empire. The property of the Holy See, in fact, extends (or we might better say, stretches) from the summit of the hill of Castel Gandolfo, where the Palace of the Popes stands, to what was the *arx albana,* up to the borders of the commune of Albano, along the southwest edge of the crater that contains the lake. The venerable stronghold and later castle of the Gandolfi, as it appears, was the original center of Alba Longa, from whence the first Latin people came to found the city of Rome."

37. Ibid., 70–71. The garden of the Cybos can still be seen in the paintings preserved in the billiard room of the papal palace picturing Clement XIV walking between four compartments of box, cut in arabesques and divided by small intersecting pathways, recalling the villa above la Rocca or that of Rinchiostra. The same principles could also be found at Massa, in what is now the Villa Massoni.

38. Ibid., 95.

39. Ibid., 118.

Chapter Eight. Monks, Knights, and Vikings

1. Christopher Columbus, *Libro delle profezie*, ed. William Melczer (Palermo: Novecento, 1992), 86. The final phrase is from Jeremiah, the rest from Isaiah.

2. Thule was generally identified with the Shetland Islands, to the north of Scotland.

3. Columbus, *Libro delle profezie,* 124.

4. Ibid., 126.

5. Columbus, *Gli Scritti,* 169. The information, according to Luis Ulloa, (*Cristòfor Colom fou catalá* [Barcelona, 1927]), 163, is confirmed by the director of the library of Copenhagen, Sofus Larsen. At the request of Alfonso V of Portugal, King Christian I sent an expedition to the coast of Greenland in which Portuguese sailors took part. Dates and evidence lead us to presume that Columbus joined this expedition. There is also an inscription on Mercator's terrestrial globe relating how the Danish captain Jaon Scolvus arrived in Greenland in 1476. We can conclude that, among other things, there was already talk of a West lying beyond Ptolemy's West.

6. Luca Antonelli, *I Greci oltre Gibilterra* (Rome: n.p., 1997), 12: "With Tartessus, the Phocaeans, in the archaic period, appeared to enter a climate of complete harmony with the Phoenician merchants of the Iberian colonies. Toward Gades [Cádiz], heir to all the riches of Tartessus, went those Greeks who brought Attic pottery to the shores of the Ocean during the fifth and fourth centuries [BC]." We should add that the ancient Iberian city in the Guadalquivir delta was destroyed by the Carthaginians around 500 BC.

7. Christopher Columbus, *Gli Scritti,* 36.

8. Claudio Finzi, *Ai confini del mondo* (La Spezia: Club del libro Fratelli Melita, 1982), 43: "There is no doubt that Libya [in ancient times, Libya was identified with Africa, while Egypt was part of Asia], except for the part bordering Asia, is surrounded by the sea. The first to demonstrate this, as far we know, was Neco, king of Egypt. After ceasing work on digging the canal from the Nile to the Arabian Gulf, he sent Phoenicians aboard merchant ships with the task of returning through the Pillars of Hercules, from thence to reach the northern sea and Egypt. The Phoenicians left from the Red Sea and crossed the South Sea. As autumn approached, they landed and sowed seeds at the places in Libya where they had sometimes voyaged before, and awaited the harvest. They gathered the grain and reembarked. Two years passed, and during the third year they rounded the Pillars of Hercules and returned to Egypt. They told something to which I do not give credence, but perhaps others do: that during the circumnavigation of Libya, they had had the sun to their right."

The episode of the Egyptian Neco is controversial, but we must take into account an anonymous atlas called Medicean, dating from 1351 and kept in the Biblioteca Laurenziana (*La carta perduta, Paolo dal Pozzo Toscanelli* [Florence: Fratelli Alinari, 1992], 72). On this map Africa is completely surrounded by sea long before Vasco da Gama rounded the southernmost point of the continent and christened it the Cape of Good Hope, the Cape of Tempests, thus opening the route to the Indies. I have the book reproducing the Africa drawn in the Medicean atlas. Even in viewing it repeatedly, I had never before noticed this impossible detail—the publication makes not the slightest mention of this obvious anachronism—until one day this same map was displayed and revealed by an enthusiast. This shows just how difficult it is, in the face of established mental patterns, to take account of certain anomalies, even though (or perhaps because) they are right before our eyes. By our notions and our knowledge, we are programmed to the point of becoming blind. "Vision," as someone said, "is prejudiced by the viewer."

9. Umberto Eco, *Segni e sogni della terra* (Novara: De Agostini, 2001), 17.

10. Ibid., 18. The main suspects in the centuries-long imbroglio, according to Eco, are a fourth-century Christian author, Lactantius, and a sixth-century Byzantine geographer, Cosmas Indicopleustes, with his world tabernacle—which, however, "cannot be considered as a representation of the scientific knowledge of the Fathers of the Church." Cosmas Indicopleustes, whose name itself is a statement (literally, "Mr. World Sailing to India"), appears guiltless to us, because his geography is already surprisingly revolutionary. It depicts an earth seen from above in which the earthly Paradise is located to the extreme east, cordoned off by the ocean in a distinct and solitary location. The map is accompanied by an enigmatic inscription: "The lands beyond the ocean where men lived before the Flood." Was this where Noah lived in an upturned history?

Eco continues that in 1896, Andrew Dickson White, in his *History of the Warfare of Science with Theology in Christendom,* wrote: "We cannot hide the fact that Augustine, Albert the Great, and Thomas knew well that the earth was round. One might think that to sustain this, they would have had to struggle against dominant theological thought. But dominant theological thought was represented by Augustine, Thomas, and Albert themselves, and therefore they needed to struggle against no one!"

11. Ibid., 50. An aureus of Augustus shown in a catalog shows the globe according to Craterus, which indeed bears markings that resemble meridians and parallels. Pino dell'Orco is studying this, among many other things.

12. Luciano Lago ("Le carte nautiche medievali e le prime carte geografiche moderne dell'Italia," supplement to *Porto e mare* [July–September 1991]: 5) writes: "A fairly hasty comparison of these maps that have been handed down to us from the second half of the thirteenth century, mostly as hand-drawn copies, so perfect compared to the bizarre illustrations in the world maps, already reveals a complex question with no easy answer."

13. Claudio Finzi, *Ai confini del mondo,* 70: "We must also not forget how the necessity for secrecy always contributed to slowing the disclosure and diffusion of geographic discoveries. A new route, by land or sea, could be counted among the greatest of weapons, a resounding achievement both for economic competition and in armed conflict [as the route to the stars is today]. It is the ancient history of the millennia, always repeating itself. In the eighteenth century the findings of the Pacific voyages of Quiros and Torres were kept secret for about half a century by the Spanish government, and the English dealt similarly with some of the results of Cook's first voyage. Almost two centuries earlier, the Dutch had acted identically, hiding their observations of the routes to be taken across the Indian Ocean. People cunningly spread many legends about the dangers of the seas for the same purpose: to hold potential competitors at bay and keep the routes to themselves! Ptolemy knew well that merchants' reports were purposely highly inaccurate. The Carthaginians were most able masters at defending their own secrets, doing everything possible to protect these and their countrymen. When a Roman ship—writes Strabo—tried to follow a Carthaginian vessel beyond the waters of Cádiz into the route of the Atlantic, the Punic captain would voluntarily drive his own ship into the shallows, dragging with it the pursuing ship, which would be wrecked."

14. Eco, *Segni e sogni della terra,* 65–66. On the first map, from El Burgo de Osma, "as in all the maps from this group, Paradise is represented by four rivers in the upper (eastern) part of the map. The evangelization of the inhabited lands, which is to precede the Last Judgment, is represented by the texts of the apostles, in the places to which they are linked. The discovery of the bones of St. James a short while earlier had led to the construction, in this location, of the church of Santiago de Compostela, and a rapidly spreading devotion to the

saint. . . . The other peculiar characteristic of the Osma map is the depiction of four continents. Derived from the theories of Macrobius and the globe of Crates, this was a problem for the Christians. If, in fact, all creatures that occupied the three continents of the world after the Deluge were descended from the three sons of Noah and their animals, then a fourth continent must necessarily be unreachable and uninhabited. Least of all does this fit the context of a map such as that of Beatus, with its exaltation of the inhabited and evangelized world. While Ryland's map maintains an almost embarrassed silence regarding this question, the Osma map presents a prolix citation and shows a Monopod—belonging to an athletic race living in North Africa, mentioned by Isidore—using his single large foot to shade himself from the sun, which is depicted as a red disk. Despite possible confusion with the race of the Antipodes . . . this map constitutes the first representation known to us of the monsters that would prominently decorate the great planispheres."

15. Ibid., 134. Giacomo Gastaldi, for example, "believed—probably, like many in his circle, for religious reasons—in the existence of a land bridge between Asia and America."

16. *Vado verso la terra nuova* (Perugia: Quattroemme, 1992), 62: "As late as the first decades of the seventeenth century, the Lombard Servite Filippo Ferrari, in his *Lexicon geographicum,* published a year after his death in 1627, denied that America was a new continent. Indeed, we find the word *America* in the index, but not in the text, where we are required to search for Atlantis; Peru is in the index, but in the text we are redirected to Ophir, the gold-bearing biblical land."

17. Claudio Finzi, *Ai confini del mondo,* 10: "Geographical knowledge was never acquired all at once, but was obtained, lost, regained, lost again, in new findings over the course of the centuries and millennia, in an infinity and multiplicity of causes. The only people who knew of a certain route might disappear; or these same people might for so long remain confined to their own territory by pressure from other clans that they would forget what was beyond their borders. The few sailors who had kept a route secret for commercial reasons might die; one state with great capacities and military organization might be replaced by another not gifted with the same qualities. Thus the will for great expeditions was lost. And so things went."

18. Tim Severin, *The Brendan Voyage* (New York: McGraw-Hill, 1978), 80: "Ireland became the grand repository for this intellectual treasure, and the Irish

monks copied and codified this information. They wrote commentaries on it, and handed the knowledge on from one generation to the next. They read Virgil and Solinus and, in translation or original, had access to Greek authors. In their geographical concepts the monks understood that the world was round—'like a well-formed apple' was how it was sometimes put. They understood Ptolemy's concept of geography, and could read how the Romans had sent a fleet around Scotland and found islands lying to the north. The flowering of early Christian culture in Ireland, about which so much has been written, was a process that lasted almost five hundred years. Irish monks were acknowledged to be the best-educated and best-informed men in all of Western Europe; and in due course they set out to carry their knowledge back into the mainland. They... established monasteries from Lombardy to Austria. They and their pupils were regarded as Europe's wandering intelligentsia." The author repeated St. Brendan's voyage in a small boat; we will see further details of this operation.

19. Ibid., 275–76.
20. Ibid., 255.
21. Ibid., 282.
22. Paolo Emilio Taviani, *Cristoforo Colombo, la genesi della grande scoperta* (Novara: De Agostini, 1982), 308. Later, details regarding the Viking expeditions will be taken from this work.
23. Enio Iezzi, *Vinland hit goda* (n.l.: n.p., 1984), 28. The epic of Erik the Red, which includes the story of Leif, can be read "as a missionary story. In fact, King Olaf Tryggvason had given them the task of introducing Christianity into Greenland." The essay in question appears not to have been published.
24. Paul Herrmann, *Sette sono passate e l'ottava sta passando* (Milan: Martello, 1955), 359. A priest, Adam of Bremen, wrote of Vinland in 1070 in the *Ecclesiastical History of Hamburg.* The text relates that the Christians of Greenland made their contribution for the support of a crusade: "Knowledge of Vinland was acquired by Adam of Bremen during a visit to Roeskilde in Denmark, at the court of Sven Estrithson, probably firsthand from the Icelandic notable Gellir Thorkelsson, who spent some time at Roeskilde in 1070 on his return from a pilgrimage to Rome and who was naturally quite well aware of the Viking discoveries beyond the Western Sea. Thus we can rule out the possibility that Vinland was one of the fictional islands."

25. Antonio Angelini, "Scoperta e riscoperta dell'America," *Informazioni della difesa,* bimonthly publication of the Stato Maggiore della Difesa, special number 2, December 1992, 48.

26. In 1153 the region was placed under the archbishopric of Nidaros in Norway, which had become an independent district of the Roman Church in 1152. It is claimed by some that after the second half of the fourteenth century, Greenland had no further contact with Christian Europe, but the historian Humboldt proves that this was not the case.

27. Antonio Angelini, "Scoperta e riscoperta dell'America," 71.

28. Samuel E. Morison, *The European Discovery of America: The Northern Voyages A.D. 500–1600* (Oxford: Oxford University Press 1971), 60–61.

29. Sonia Piloto di Castri, ed., *La saga di Erik il rosso* (Palermo: Sellerio, 1991), 82–83. The letter proceeds: "'. . . and he orders the Benedictine Mathias Knudson to assume the bishopric of Gardar, an office which, however, he seems never to have filled.' Still on the subject of the alleged decline of the faith in Greenland, Alexander VI's brief had a precedent in a notice reported in the *Annals of Iceland*, transcribed by the hand of Bishop Oddson, but concerning the year 1342. It reads: 'Some inhabitants of Greenland are voluntarily deviating from the just faith and from Christianity and, renouncing all the true virtues and good customs, are leaving to join the peoples of America.' It was presumed, in fact, that Greenland was not far off from the western lands . . ." Oddson's lapse in using the word America while transcribing, in the seventeenth century, a chronicle from 1342—long before the time when this toponym would be used—shows how, at least at the bishop's seat of Skalholt, Vinland and America had become synonymous.

30. Iezzi, *Vinland hit goda,* 91. This is a loose translation of the original.

31. Mark Kurlansky, *Cod: A Biography of the Fish that Changed the World* (New York: Walker and Co., 1997), 24–26. A map from 1502 designates Newfoundland as the "land of the King of Portugal."

32. Ibid., 28.

33. Ibid., 52.

34. Jacques de Mahieu, *I Templari in America* (Casale Monferrato: Piemme, 1998), 25.

35. Ibid., 38–39.

36. Christopher Knight and Robert Lomas, *The Hiram Key* (Gloucester, Massachusetts: Fair Winds, 1996), 302.

37. Steven Sora, *The Lost Treasure of the Knights Templar* (Rochester, Vt.: Destiny Books, 1999), 62. It is obviously not easy, in light of our current geography, to reconstruct a geography that changed over the course of time, more than one might believe.

38. Ibid., 51–52.

39. Ibid., 96.

40. One of the better-known presumed portraits of Christopher Columbus— which, in truth, bears no resemblance to him—shows him with the collar of the Golden Fleece.

41. Knight and Lomas, *The Hiram Key,* 305.

42. *Hera,* no. 14 (February 2001): 13.

43. The most recent study conducted on this map, and published in the journal *Analytical Chemistry,* states that it is original ("Quella mappa è dei vichingi," in *Il Messaggero* [November 27, 2003], signed by Emanuele Perugini).

44. *Hera,* no. 13. The studies by Heyerdahl and Lilliestrom bring added validity to facts and interpretations, which though rarely divulged and often purposely ignored, were already known to scholars who persist in turning a deaf ear. In his statements, published in the Oslo newspaper *Aftenposten,* Heyerdahl added that as a geographer, Columbus went along with a nautical expedition in 1477 (to which we have already referred in the words of Columbus himself) that passed through Davis Strait between Greenland and Canada and landed on the North American continent. Once again, Columbus is confirmed as a prediscoverer, going back ever farther in time.

Chapter Nine. Marco Polo and America-Cipango

1. The dilettante Columbus, the flighty do-it-yourselfer, is doubtless more helpful to the passively accepted tradition of the man of little learning. But this is another fabrication. Despite all efforts, Columbus emerges from the few remaining fragments of his library preserved at the cathedral of Seville as an attentive, punctilious, and shrewd intellectual, avid for knowledge. Among the twenty-five hundred annotations that accompany his readings, only two are in the Italian language—the only such traces in his writing, which alternates between Latin and Castilian. On this subject, critics lose themselves amid sterile lucubrations. Many of the annotations, it is claimed, were made by his brother Bartolomeo, whose handwriting was similar to Christopher's,

but don Ferdinand, Columbus's son, wrote that his uncle Bartolomeo "did not have Latin letters."

This is another usual futile attempt to belittle the navigator's role and demolish his achievements—even though the members of the Columbus family are shown, in every circumstance, to have been united solidly as a common body in the pursuit of their objectives, with Christopher always representing the recognized leader of the family clan and placed at the front of Operation America. The volumes naturally have dates, indicating that Columbus's studies of them must have begun after those times. Because some notes refer to events that occurred at certain points in history, the reasoning is analogous. Given that there are no notes made in texts from earlier times, we can conclude that Columbus began to deepen his knowledge during the time of his sojourn in Spain. Yet many volumes that Columbus could have read might well not have been annotated. Though research consists of a continuous study of a single text at completely different times, a simple temporal reference cannot be applied to the entire process.

2. Luis Ulloa, *Cristòfor Colom fou català* (Barcelona: n.p., 1927), 70.

3. Plato, *Tutte le opere* (Rome: Newton Compton, 1997), 14–15. It should be noted that the Greek philosopher apparently visited Egypt, where he may have learned of Atlantis from the priests of Sais. He also spent some time in Taranto (the city in Apulia that later saw the passage of the Crusades), where he came in contact with the Pythagorean school of Archytas, which was flourishing in Magna Graecia. In one of his *Letters,* Plato wrote: "Those who have not the true philosophic temper, but a mere surface coloring of opinions penetrating, like sunburn, only skin deep, when they see how great the range of studies is, how much labor is involved in it, and how necessary to the pursuit it is to have an orderly regulation of the daily life, come to the conclusion that the thing is difficult and impossible for them, and are actually incapable of carrying out the course of study. Yet some of them persuade themselves that they have sufficiently studied the whole matter and have no need of any further effort" (Plato, *Seventh Letter,* trans. John Harward, n.p., 1928). It is a statement that could be applied to many of the bigwigs of so-called scientific research.

4. Alessandro Geraldini, *Viaggio di Alessandro Geraldini, Itinerarium di Alessandro Geraldini* (Turin: Nuova ERI, 1991), 136–37. Geraldini, one of Columbus's friends at the Spanish court, wrote: "This land [America, or Atlantis] is believed

to be greater than Europe and Asia [so the land was no longer considered part of Asia, but something else], even including the eleven thousand islands of which Aristotle speaks in his famous *Cosmographia.* There are more lands in the southern hemisphere than in the northern, as Plato said in his *Critias."* The historian Gomara also confirms that Columbus knew of the myth of Atlantis.

5. Plato, *Timaeus,* trans. Benjamin Jowett, 24–25.

6. Plato, *Critias,* trans. Benjamin Jowett.

7. This masterpiece was recently used by Berlusconi's administration as the background for a European congress that took place in Rome.

8. Maria Luisa Ambrosini, *L'Archivio segreto del Vaticano* (Milan: Mondadori, 1972), 179. Was it then Pinzón who confused or wished to confuse Cipango with Japan? How is this possible, especially if this land was vaster than Africa and Europe?

9. A contemporary director, Ridley Scott, in the excellent film *1492: Conquest of Paradise,* had Pinzón ask Columbus: "But what was a sailor doing in a monastery for seven years with the Franciscans?" The navigator was at the height of his strength, eager for discoveries and for new and daring adventures. Yet he lingered in the company of monks—although, of course, he was awaiting definitive assent from the monarchs—first of all he had to understand the cultural foundations in order to repeat a voyage that could not fail, and he had to wait for the right time.

10. The term *infidel* was applied in both directions; both Christians and Muslims used it when referring to the followers of the other religion.

11. Paul Lunde, "Piri Reis and the Columbus Map," in *Saudi Aramco World* (May/June 1992): 18–25.

12. A. Afetinan, *Life and Works of Piri Reis: The Oldest Map of America* (Ankara: Turkish Historical Society, 1987), xx.

13. Lunde, "Piri Reis and the Columbus Map."

14. John Baldock, *The Elements of Christian Symbolism* (Longmead: Element Books, 1990), 106: "The pearl, concealed beneath the waters of the deep, is made available to man as he emerges from the waters, reborn through the rite of baptism." Columbus gathered pearls and brought baptism. Pearls form the basis for one of the many accusations and robberies leveled at him. His detractors often accuse him of having tried to appropriate funds without informing the monarchs of Spain or of not having understood the real possibilities that the new lands offered. According to them, Columbus became a hero "by acci-

dent" through his voyage to the Indies, and in their widely accepted opinion he amounted to a kind of full-time bungler, almost a complete idiot. He found banks of pearls but did not realize it; the natives spoke of "Cubanacan," and he heard "great khan"; they told of endless expanses of land, and he concluded from this that he must have reached China, besides accepting anything they offered him—which would immediately put him off track. And all this during the course of four separate voyages, spanning a decade of exploration! He who disembarks is considered a dreamer; he who lands on the far shore is considered naïve. Columbus is portrayed as a foreigner and a *loco* (madman) in Spain—more foreign and loco than he ever was in an unknown land where he was ignorant of the language.

15. It would be interesting to know how the rapport developed between a revered man of letters and a merchant, albeit a famous one, apparently imprisoned after his participation in a battle.

16. Many claim that the account of their voyage was a scholarly hoax.

17. Alvise Zorzi, *Vita di Marco Polo veneziano* (Milan: Rusconi, 1982), 10.

18. Loredana Imperio, *Templari* 1, no. 2 (2001), 31–32: "It is interesting to note an unusual document signed with the date 1257, regarding the agricultural production of the diocese of Acre, in which *maize* is mentioned. Maize, a crop from the Americas, became known, it is said, only after Columbus's expedition."

19. Zorzi, *Vita di Marco Polo veneziano*, 87–88.

20. Marco Polo, *Il milione* 1, with notes by Christopher Columbus (Turin: Edizioni Paoline, 1985), 17: "The Dominican Order appropriated Marco Polo when, about seventy years after his voyage, they decided to produce, in Santa Maria Novella in Florence, a great cycle in fresco—the famous Chapel of the Spaniards, the work of Andrea Buonaiuto (1366–1368)—depicting, along with the saints and the deeds of the order, a group of laymen resembling those educated persons so beloved by the order. Among these, besides Petrarch, Boccaccio, and—the identification is uncertain—Cimabue and Giotto, we also find portraits of Nicolò, Matteo, and Marco Polo holding in their arms a great book, obviously the *Travels*."

21. Ibid., 17–18: "Marco Polo's intent to give his voyage a religious missionary character is made known early in the first part of his book. His pious and ecclesiastical motives are abundant from the point where the three Venetians obtain the oil of the lamp of the Holy Sepulchre of Jerusalem, extending to

the account of the Christian sects in Western Asia, the narrative of the miracles of the faith in the struggle against the infidels, and the account of the homage paid by the Three Kings to the infant Jesus . . ."

22. Nicola Pezzella, "Il Templarismo nel Veneto e l'architettura neotemplare," in *Atti del XIX Convegno di Richerche templari* (Latina: Penne e Papiri, 2002), 42–44. The author refers to a study by Cesare Augusto Levi, a "profound expert in Masonic Templarism." The Zenos were also among the Venetian Templar families.

23. Marco Polo, *Il milione* 1:25n25: "The fact that Marco Polo was integrated, consciously or unconsciously, into a series of Catholic missionaries, in particular Franciscans, is further confirmed by the interesting miniature in the manuscript from London B.M. Reg. 19 D.1, 'which contains reports from missionaries, and also the fabulous texts of Alexander the Great.' In fact, it 'depicts the Polo brothers in Franciscan garb before the Great Khan, who gave them the charge of bringing his requests to the pope.'"

24. Ibid., 39.

25. Ibid., 33.

26. Franco Cardini, *Gerusalemme d'oro, di rame, di luce* (Milan: Il Saggiatore, 1991), 89–90: "A decisive stage in the history of the *Travels* corresponds to a passage that is one of the most incredible (to us) and one of the least based on direct observation. Marco spoke of the mysterious Cipangu or Zipangu—Japan, which Kublai Khan attempted to conquer twice, in 1274 and 1281, failing both times (according to legend, there was a *kamikaze,* a divine wind, that rose up furiously, beating back the invaders' ships). He also spoke of the golden lands where every roof was covered with solid gold. The mental process he followed was simple: among the greatest wonders that he had observed in Asia, still none were equal to those marvelous riches described in the legends of Prester John and the romances of Alexander. Reluctant to draw from this the conclusion that these things were mere fantasy, he located them in the island of the Rising Sun, which he did not visit. It was this same optimistic passage that struck Christopher Columbus, egging him on more than anything else to reach the East via the western route. The origins of El Dorado lie in this improbable vision of cities covered in precious metal."

27. Ancient Japan had no official name. After AD 670 it was called Nippon or Nihon.

28. Benedetto Capomazza di Campolattaro, *Affari sociali internazionali,* no. 4

(Milan: n.p., 1986), 11. We have found no further confirmation of this statement, as we have with most other statements. It probably refers to the prevalent but not absolute custom of "the maps of the times." In fact, as we shall see later, the *Dizionario biografico degli italiani* (249) tells of a world map from 1457 attributed to Toscanelli and presented in 1459 to the ambassadors of the king of Portugal on which Japan is already called Japan and not Cipangu. The latter name—Cipangu—was therefore simply America.

29. Marco Polo, *Il milione* 2 (Milan: Mondadori, 1999), 240. It is worth mentioning that in this edition, when he begins to describe Cipango, the text reads: "Here begins the book of the Indies." Why, when up to this point the author has been speaking exclusively of the Indies?

30. Ibid., 242.

31. Ibid., 245–46: "You should know," Marco Polo's text continues, "that when the idolaters of this island take prisoner an enemy who cannot pay the ransom, he who has the prisoner summons all his friends and relations with these words: 'I wish you to come to my house to eat.' And they put to death the man they have captured, cook him, and eat him. They consider human flesh to be the best meat in the world. . . . This sea lies to the east and has, according to what is said by the experienced pilots and mariners who know how to navigate it, seven thousand four hundred and forty-eight islands [Columbus writes in a letter of seven thousand islands, referring to the Caribbean], most of which are inhabited. On these islands grow trees that all have a strong and pleasant scent [just as in Columbus's description] and that are very useful. . . . There are many things of great value, beginning with gold and other precious things; but these islands are so far off that it takes them a whole year to get there [Japan is very close to the coast of China]. . . . These places are very far from India. Though that Sea is called the Sea of China, as I have told you, yet it is part of the Ocean Sea all the same." This can only refer to the boundless expanse of the Pacific.

32. The name ending in *ango,* rather than being of Oriental origin, occurs in the modern language of Latin America—especially, but not only, in reference to predominantly Mexican places (Durango, Quezaltenango, Chimaltenango, Huehuetenango, Chichicastenango, etc.). Even today, near Mexico City, there is a town called Xipangu, and not far from Acapulco there is Chilpancingo. Astounding treasures of gold have been found recently in the northern area of Peru known as Sipan (or Xipan). In a tomb containing the mummified

body of the ruler, a gold rod "had been placed in the mouth of the corpse, perhaps the Andean equivalent of the 'offering to Charon" (*Archeo,* no. 4 [April 2001]: 77). The Chinese had a similar custom to that of the Andeans: The former placed a coin in the mouth of the corpse, the latter placed gold and silver there (Francisco Loayza, *Chinos llegaron antes que Colon* [1948], 160). The author draws numerous proofs of commercial and cultural exchanges between the Chinese and the Native Americans based on common funerary customs. Marco Polo, as we have seen, told of pearls in the mouths of the dead.

33. For his favorable attitude toward the Native Americans, Blas Valera was imprisoned under the false accusation of sexual abuse. Exiled to Spain, he supposedly died before the time of the Company of Jesus—and was thus silenced forever. Through the centuries, all those who have searched for the truth about the Indies have come to a bad end.

34. Antonio Aimi, "Libri e quipos di storia e segreti," in *Il Sole-24 ore* (October 3, 1999). Both the chronicles of ancient Peru and Miccinelli's findings—despite the large amount of evidence in their favor even following careful analysis—have been ignored, and even attacked, by "specialists." This prediscovery would date more or less to the days of Isidore of Seville and Cosmas Indicopleustes.

35. Taviani, *Cristoforo Colombo, la genesi della grande scoperta,* 133. Behaim was a student of Regiomontano, a German astronomer who had studied under Georg Peurbach.

36. We are not in a position to judge the method of projection.

37. Maria Mannu, *I francescani sulle orme di Cristoforo Colombo* (Rome: Centro Nazionale di Cultura Francescana, 1992). This superimposition curiously appears on the cover and on the back of this book.

38. Kenneth Nebenzahl, *Atlas of Columbus and the Great Discoveries* (Chicago: Rand McNally, 1990), 50: "Ptolemy's *Geography* was the most sought-after atlas during the early stage of the Age of Discovery and was reissued repeatedly. The first edition to be published after Columbus's voyage appeared in Rome in 1507. Some copies contained a revolutionary new world map compiled by Johannes Ruysch." The cartographer Ruysch, in the legend that accompanies the illustration, explains that "as far as this, Spanish navigators have come, and they have called this land, on account of its greatness, the New World. In as much as they have not wholly explored it . . . further than the present termination, it must remain thus imperfectly delineated until it is

known in what direction it extends." This is an authoritative confirmation of the idea we have expressed regarding the progressive cataloging of the maps of the new lands—based on the reality that was validated by exploration up to that time.

39. Ibid., 50. Finally, a scientist outside of the norm!

40. Cardini, *Gerusalemme d'oro*, 94.

41. Zorzi, *Vita di Marco Polo*, 57–58.

42. Ibid., 55.

43. Polo, *Il milione* 2:40–41 of the Introduction by Maria Bellonci. According to her, Kublai Khan "placed power above all, even religion, but yet considered power as the moral and the moralizer of that religion. His calm statement that being a friend of every religion and respecting every rite allowed him to govern well, however, would have surprised Niccolò Machiavelli. . . . Marco Polo appears singularly well balanced regarding religion. . . . The 'illiterate' Marco [as Columbus also supposedly was, apparently because he followed a different course of study], alone in the world, through serenely confronting what he did not know, found the poetry of knowledge, the humility of listening to different but equal men. His account breaks the confines of space and time; but even more, it frees us from the limits we see before us and almost makes the utopia of brotherhood real."

44. The Chinese actor who played the Great Khan in the RAI (Italian State Television) production directed by Alberto Lattuada was asked, in an interview, what Marco Polo's message was. He replied: "He had no single message that stands out to me. In truth, he had several. Marco Polo was different from other explorers: He did not travel to discover lands, but to get to know people. Europe at the time was convinced it was the center of the world. The Chinese were convinced they were the same thing. Marco Polo was the inventor, in a certain sense, of the distinction between East and West . . . of understanding between peoples. I might add that a certain philosophy of discovery held by Marco Polo influenced Columbus, who made notes in the *Travels*" (Marco Polo, *Il milione* 1:38). Sometimes actors see more than scholars . . .

45. From the version in a French manuscript kept at the National Library in Paris, and not the more restrictive version of Friar Francesco Pipino.

46. Franco Cardini, *Gerusalemme d'oro*, 45: "The first phase could be said to have begun in the mid-thirteenth century with the first council of Lyon and to have ended in the third quarter of the fourteenth century through a number

of factors: the breaking up of the Mongol empire and the isolation of China within its own borders; the rise of Ottoman power, which—established in the Balkans and the Anatolian peninsula—intervened to block or somehow obstruct most of the routes linking Europe and deepest Asia; the dazzling rise of Tamerlane and the disorder in which he left the regions he overturned; for Europe, the beginning (with the plague of 1347—1350) of a long economic crisis which, to tell the truth, had begun earlier and could not help but influence her commercial prospects; the exhaustion of the first missionary drive in the 1240s, which had begun with St. Francis of Assisi's voyage to Egypt and whose protagonists had been the mendicant orders."

47. Many of the hypotheses in this chapter were published in 2002, in three successive articles in the monthly *Hera* (nos. 27, 28, and 29).

Chapter Ten. The Infindel Piri Reis's Map

1. Taviani, *Cristoforo Colombo, la genesi della grande scoperta,* 450–51.

2. *Pleitos Colombinos* 1 (Seville: n.p., 1967), 163. Thus, the Queen did not consider Columbus to be a braggart, and his discoveries, contrary to popular opinion, provoked no surprise, much less disappointment.

3. Senator Paolo Emilio Taviani himself admitted to me that he had not been allowed to see the map, despite his double prestige as a scholar and a politician. We may add, quite objectively, that had it not been for Taviani and his work—backed up by his influence and reputation—in defending Columbus's Genoese origin, a Spanish Columbus and a holy Queen Isabella would have triumphed, in a "perfect murder" accomplished for the second time, at a distance of five hundred years—despite all justice.

4. The Norwegian explorer Nordenskiold was convinced that it was copied from an original, which he held to be Carthaginian.

5. Alessandro Bausani, "L'Italia nel *Kitab-i Bahriyye* di Piri Reis," ed. Leonardo Capezzone, in *Eurasiatica,* no. 19 (1990): 10–12. We have put the most important concepts in sequence. The translation used is the work of the author of the study, a renowned Islamist whose translation of the Qur'an into the Italian language is considered unsurpassed to date. Bausani's work appears in the *Quaderni del Dipartimento di Studi Eurasiatici* of the University of Venice.

6. Umberto Cordier, *Dizionario dell' Italia misteriosa* (Milan: Sugarco, 1991), 109.

7. Louis Pauwels and Jacques Bergier, *L'uomo eterno* (Milan: Mondadori, 1972), 64.

8. *Reis* was equivalent to chief, captain, or admiral.

9. Antonio Ventura, *L'Italia di Piri Reis* (Lecce: Capone, 2000), 6; Charles H. Hapgood, *Le mappe delle civiltà perdute* (Rome: Mondo Ignoto, 2004), 253.

10. Rosario Mascia, "Piri Reis, la carta dei misteri," in *il Giornale*, 20. The year of publication is missing.

11. Bausani, "L'Italia." The date has been converted, but no one has taken note of it before now. Bausani himself, the greatest Italian Islamist, offers no further precision, hazarding neither explanation nor comment, almost as if he were afraid. Yet he must have been well enough aware that the date handed down by history, marking Columbus's first landing, remains the famous and all-too-well-known October 12, 1492. Regarding what the Turkish admiral wrote, Bausani dismisses the question of the ancient map from Alexandria, tracing it to the usual excuse: Ptolemy's geography. The preexisting maps, according to him, could have been only those by the Alexandrian geographer, which were already known—the maps that depict the Mare Indicum, our Indian Ocean, as a closed basin, with Africa and Asia joined and forming a single continuous continent. In our search for reactions to this date, so sensational yet left to fall into such absolute silence, we discovered that Bausani was by no means the first to report this revolutionary chronology. In a work in French by Yusuf Akçura, *Piri Reis Haritasi* (Istanbul: Deulet Basimexi, 1935), the Arabic date of Columbus's discovery also corresponds to the Hegira year 890. The short essay entitled "Maps of Piri Reis, is signed by the president of the Society for Turkish Historical Studies—who informs us from the first that the essay is not the product of exclusively personal research, but of the latest researches. He goes on to list several professors of various nationalities.

12. In the course of more than fifteen years spent reading about Columbus, I cannot count how many reports I have found of this episode, which certainly does not cast Columbus in a flattering light. No proof has been found of it beyond his having bequeathed an equal sum to Beatrice, his second wife or companion, without further clarification. This sum, if it really applied to the sighting of whoever was first to announce the new land, can only demonstrate the fact that the failure of Isabella and Ferdinand to keep their word forced the admiral, perhaps in a time of particular indigence, to avail himself of this pension and in consequence to act uncharacteristically. This does not fit with the

psychological and intellectual profile of the navigator, which has never been sufficiently or truthfully explored. If the story originates from a testimony given during the course of the *Pleitos Colombinos*, the lengthy lawsuit between Columbus's descendents and the Spanish crown, then in my view it has no value.

13. John Baldock, *The Elements of Christian Symbolism,* 88.

14. Jacques Attali, *1492* (Milan: Sperling and Kupfer, 1992), 223. The words reported by the French author do not correspond to what is written in Columbus's ship's log, but Attali placed them in quotation marks like a citation, and accompanied them with a note number. Unfortunately, in the edition to which I have referred, the note numbers—but not the relevant notes—are there. Nevertheless, the phrase does not lose its validity through this, because as we shall see later, it is confirmed through other declarations made by Columbus.

15. *Via della Conciliazione* (Reconciliation Street) is the name of the street in Rome that leads to St. Peter's Basilica. *Catholic* is equivalent to universal.

16. Arnoldo Canclini, *La Fe del Descubridor* (Buenos Aires: Editorial Plus Ultra, 1992), 204.

17. On this subject it is interesting to note a remarkable report in the *Osservatore romano* ("Un marinaio di Colombo, catturato, rivelò ai turchi la scoperta," by Salvatore Bono [January 15, 1993]): "One of Columbus's sailors, captured, revealed the discovery to the Turks." According to this article, a persistent oral tradition—reported by a nineteenth-century Ottoman scholar, Emin Efendi, and pointed out in the biography of the poet Arif Efendi (1771–1849)—claims that during the time of Sultan Bayezid, a Christian named Kolon presented himself to the sultan's court, requesting of him the technical and financial means for sailing to the discovery of a "new world." Here, among other things, there is already talk of a "new world."

18. At this point, it is worth adding a detail: Recently, overturning history, a final descendent of the Medina Sidonia family has emerged, Duchess Luisa (the Italian travel program *Turisti per caso* by Suzy Blady and Patrizio Roversi has mentioned her). In the library of her palace in Andalusia, in the archives inherited from her ancestors who aided Columbus, there were supposedly books, maps, and documents that made reference to America prior to 1492. The maps, once again, were believed to originate from the time of Alexandria in Egypt. The documents allegedly confirmed the theory that "the American coast was known before the expeditions and was reported as an African territory that was reached after a twenty-day voyage and was rich in gold mines.

In fact, it was Brazil" (Alessandra Coppola, "In una carta abbiamo trovato il segreto di Colombo," in *Corriere della Sera* [January 11, 2001], 24). In this case, according to the duchess, the America reached by the Arabs was passed off—in order that it should not be discovered—as part of Africa, namely the region of Guinea. The gold of Mina was said to come from Guinea, in Africa; and Columbus had also gone to Guinea (an African Guinea or an American Guinea?) before 1492. The warlike duchess of Medina Sidonia wrote a book that was naturally opposed by the Spanish authorities and published in France. Her theories can be found on an Islamic Internet site: a continuous thread leading to that religion, uninterrupted for over five centuries.

19. Beatrice Leroy, *L'avventura sefardita* (Milan: ECIG, 1994), 57.
20. Osvaldo Baldacci, *Roma e Cristoforo Colombo* (Florence: Olschki, 1992), 85. Another island was given the name Monferrato.
21. *Cosmografia, tavole della geografia di Tolomeo,* with an introduction by Lelio Pagani (Milan: Stella Polare, 1990), iv.
22. Ibid., vii. Lelio Pagani's introduction discusses, among other things, a document preserved at the library of Naples and belonging to the Farnese family. The work is attributed to one Nicolò Germano (Nicholas of Cusa?), operating in Padua in the mid fifteenth century—more or less in the period when Innocent VIII studied there.
23. Bausani, "L'Italia," 12.
24. Cordier, *Dizionario dell' Italia misteriosa,* 109.
25. Yusuf Akçura, *Piri Reis Haritasi,* 3.
26. Mascia, *Il Giornale.*
27. Gaetano Uzielli, *La vita e i tempi di Paolo dal Pozzo Toscanelli* (Rome: Ricerche e studi, 1894), 185: "Between 1486 and 1490, according to Pedro Vasquez de la Frontera, Columbus and Pinzón accompanied the Infante of Portugal to the west on a voyage of discovery that was halted by the Sargasso Sea."
28. Mariano Bizzarri, *Il Mitreo di San Clemente* (Rome: Sydaco, 1997), 18n18.

Chapter Eleven. Three-Map Monte

1. James Cowan, *Il sogno di disegnare il mondo* (Milan: Rizzoli, 1998), 16: "For all that his prejudices show through on some occasions (his suspicion toward Islam, for example), the impression still prevails that Fra Mauro was quite inclined to tolerance. Nor does the personal faith of the practicing

Christian gain the upper hand in him. We notice that the monk bore his own Catholicism lightly, out of a desire to prevent the Church and doctrine from coming between him and the truth."

2. Kenneth Nebenzahl, *Atlas of Columbus and the Great Discoveries,* 12. We have drawn further information relative to this map from the same work.

3. Ibid., 15. The illuminated manuscript is dated Florence, 1489, and is kept at Yale University in the United States.

4. Lucchetti Stella Polare, *Cosmografia* (Bergamo: n.p., 1990), xn12. Ptolemy's world faded out to the east with the toponym Sinarum Regio. The farthest of the peninsulas jutting into the Indian Ocean was the golden Chersonesos, and the farthest great gulf was the Sinus Magnus. Beyond these limits were lands still unknown—but only lands, not seas.

5. Roberto Almagià, *Cristoforo Colombo visto da un geografo* (Florence: Olschki, 1992), 167–68: "If, in purely conjectural mode, we change the orientation of this fourth peninsula delineated by Martellus, imagining it reaching to the southwest and enlarged at the south into a greater mass, then we obtain an outline that is not dissimilar to that derived from the sketches attributed to Bartolomeo Columbus. The same peninsula appears drawn in roughly the same way in another famous cartographic document, the globe of Martin Behaim from 1492." Therefore, according to Almagià, the Columbus brothers (if we consider the attribution of these sketches to be truthful) knew the new lands no better or worse than Henricus Martellus. The drawing attributed to Bartolomeo, Christopher's brother, actually shows only a very small extent of land. But Columbus was very careful not to spread his knowledge, except by degrees. He was conscious of how treacherous were the lands to which he was headed, and of the worldwide interests that were involved.

   In another study (*I mappamondi di Enrico Martello e alcuni concetti geografici di Cristoforo Colombo* [Florence: Bibliopolis, 1941], 311), Almagià presents another highly interesting item: the presence, among the maps of the *Insularium illustratum* in the original Laurentian manuscript, of a map of Cipango, excluded from the definitive versions of his work—a singular omission! This map, among others, is ignored by the scholars who study the ancient cartography of Japan. Perhaps Henricus Martellus's Cipango was not Japan?

6. This type of interpretation is supported by the world map of Francesco Rosselli from 1508, in Florence (*Segni e sogni della terra* [Novara: De Agostini, 2001], 147), where America appears separate from Asia but where Beragua (Veragua),

roughly the area of present-day Panama, one of the lands reached by Columbus on the Central American isthmus, appears as the "fourth Asiatic peninsula" together with the place names of Ptolemy's China and those used by Marco Polo. This is evidence of confusion that has not yet been resolved and that perhaps none wish to resolve.

7. The map is now in Modena.

8. It is remarkable that a peninsula yet to be discovered is mentioned in a later revision of the log, which, because it constantly quotes the navigator's original words, probably uses only the original toponyms. In the account of the voyage of 1492, Florida should not have been mentioned at all. If I am not mistaken, there seems to be nothing else like this in the transcription of that first expedition, which is much more detailed and accurate than the others.

9. On the map from 1556 by the Spaniard Girava, on which the two Americas are depicted, Florida is in fact placed much farther to the north, beneath the Tierra de Bacalaos (Land of the Codfish).

10. Ross E. Dunn, *Gli straordinari viaggi di Ibn Battuta* (Milan: Garzanti, 1993), 9.

11. Ross E. Dunn, *The Adventures of Ibn Battuta* (Berkeley: University of California Press, 1986), 6.

12. Ibid., 5.

13. Luca Carra, "Corriere Scienza," in *Corriere della Sera,* 29: "Many Islamic philosophical and scientific thinkers from the golden age [eighth to twelfth centuries] have still not been translated or read by western scholars. 'Islamic science has yet to be discovered.'" The traditional truth, as always, is based on a set of omissions.

14. Ibid.: "Algebra took a leap forward with the school of al-Khwarezmi, and Islamic mathematics derived from Indian mathematics the numeral 0 and the principal elements of trigonometry, such as the sine, which was unknown to the Greeks. It was thanks to the use of these new tools that Islamic astronomy perfected that of Ptolemy."

15. The very word for science, *ilm,* has a double meaning: "Both the investigation of nature and of man, and the study of the Prophet's tradition."

16. Nebenzahl, *Atlas of Columbus,* 44. The text then relates that the admiral, "sailing westward, reached the Spanish islands after many hardships and dangers. Weighing anchor, thence he sailed to the province called Ciamba. Afterward he betook himself to this place which, as Christopher himself, that most diligent investigator of maritime things, asserts, holds a great store of gold."

17. Hermann Schreiber, *Gli arabi in Spagna* (Milan: Garzanti, 1992), 249: "He went to Provence, Italy, the near East, Mesopotamia, Yemen, and Egypt, and perhaps also to India and Tibet. When he returned in the year 1173, he had recorded about three hundred Eastern Jewish communities..."

18. Marina Montesano, ed., "Magia. L'eterno fascino dell'occulto," in *Medioevo Dossier,* no. 2 (2001), 62: "Anthropologically speaking, there was not the difference that might be imagined between merchants and pilgrims. With the proceeds from voyages, the merchants—to atone for their sins—often financed beautiful churches, great frescoes, and splendid stained glass. Meanwhile, the pilgrims very often commercialized the outcomes of their pilgrimages, even with a trade in relics."

19. Gerhard Herm, *I bizantini* (Milan: Garzanti, 1997), 305.

20. Numa Broc, *La geografia del Rinascimento* (Modena: Panini, 1996), 12–13: "At the beginning of the century (1410), Cardinal Pierre d'Ailly composed his *Imago mundi*, drawing upon the ancients (Aristotle, Ptolemy's *Almagest,* Pliny, Seneca), the Arabs, and the doctors of the Church (St. Augustine, Albertus Magnus). Very respectful of authority, Pierre d'Ailly generally avoided taking positions. Thus, speaking of Antichthon and the austral continent, he examined the opinions of his predecessors without giving his own. He did, however, express some original opinions: an 'opening' of the Indian Ocean toward the south, and the extension of Eurasia by 225 degrees, according to the calculations of Marinus of Tyre. We know that Christopher Columbus copiously annotated the *Imago mundi* and underlined some citations from Aristotle, such as: 'The regions of the Pillars of Hercules and India are bathed by the same sea...' In the second half of the century, Enea Silvio Piccolomini wrote a cosmography that was printed in Venice in 1477 with the title *Historia rerum ubique gestarum.* A man of great erudition (he used Strabo extensively), Pius II tried to achieve a synthesis between modern and ancient geography. He seemed to be inspired by Pierre d'Ailly in his general chapters on the earth, the distribution of the continents, and the inhabitability of the tropics and the arctic regions as well as the access to the Indies from the west. He also includes information on Asia taken from Marco Polo and Odoric of Pordenone. Like the *Imago mundi,* Pius II's cosmography was one of Christopher Columbus's favorite books." The pope's secretary, Flavio Biondo, was also a geographer.

21. Ibid., 171.

22. Gavin Menzies, *1421: The Year China Discovered America* (New York: Harper

Collins, 2002), 85: "... as penance for da Conti's renunciation of Christianity, Pope Eugenius IV made him relate the story of his journeys to the papal secretary Poggio Bracciolini." Niccolò da Conti, as has been said, infiltrated the infidels, marrying a Muslim, converting to Islam, and seeking to reach the followers of St. Thomas in the Nestorian church. Bracciolini was a humanist, an apostolic writer, and an enthusiast of ancient books (he read part of the *Argonautica* by Apollonius of Rhodes, in the version of Valerius Flaccus). He was familiar with Cardinal Calandrini, the brother of Pope Nicholas V, the prelate who brought Giovanni Battista Cybo to Rome. "Since [Niccolò da Conti] had spoken with the pope, and seeing that he held the city in reverence, he left without asking for gold or silver, as one who had come to us not from motives of profit, as was the custom of many liars, but because he had been commanded" (Taviani, *Cristoforo Colombo, la genesi della grande scoperta*, 380). The da Contis were a noble family. Sigismondo da Conti from Foligno, a humanist and poet, was a student of Ermolao Barbaro and formed part of the entourage of Innocent VIII. The Roman branch of the da Contis originated from Segni; their family tree includes churchmen and more than one pope. Innocent III, Lotario dei Conti di Segni, had checkers on his shield, like the Cybos.

> Gavin Menzies is a former officer in the British navy. In his detailed and highly fascinating analysis, he limits himself to discussing a voyage taken in the year 1421. Through this single great and lengthy expedition, knowledge emerges that comes to us from a far earlier time, at least from the time of Marco Polo. Moreover, Poggio Bracciolini, in his office of papal secretary, was the intermediary between the court of Rome, the Venetian cartographer Fra Mauro, Peter of Portugal, and Prince Henry the Navigator (ibid., 93).

23. Broc, *La geografia*, 179–80: "Some hotbeds of geographical study saw only a limited and fleeting influence; and some, such as the important centers of Florence or Nuremberg, did not outlast the great discoveries. Rome, on the other hand, had not ceased affirming its role over the course of the two centuries that interest us. The Church's attention to geography may at first seem surprising: Why would an institution with an essentially spiritual function wish to be involved in a discipline good only for sailors and merchants? Should it not rather distrust a science that questioned the system of the world, the placement of lands, and the origin of man?" The question appears legitimate but mistakes the true interests of the Church at the time.

24. *Rinascimento* (Milan: Catalogo Skira, 2001), 122–23: "The two personages are, in fact, representatives of currents of thought radically opposed to each other relating to the ultimate essence of things, to the existence of a higher good, that gives or does not give meaning to things and to the actions of man." The fresco is part of a cycle that represents the perfect state of equilibrium of the elements and the virtues in the concatenation of the four elements: water, air, earth, and fire. In the choice of Heraclitus and Democritus, one scholar detected a theme typical in humanist culture (Edgar Wind, *Pagan Mysteries in the Renaissance* [London: Faber and Faber, 1968], 48–49n50). Incidentally, Bramante worked mostly in Milan, but at the court of Urbino he was in close contact with Melozzo da Forli, one of Innocent VIII's papal painters.

25. The Antilles, for example, were present prematurely on the planispheres of Andrea Bianco (1436), Bartolomeo Pareto (1455), and Grazioso Benincasa (1482), just to name a few.

26. Gaetano Uzielli, *La vita e i tempi di Paolo dal Pozzo Toscanelli* (Rome: Ricerche e studi, 1894), 587–88. The existence of the fantastic world map created by the Venetian churchman and cosmographer (in this case it is explained that it was a *lintea tela depictam in forma rotunda*, "a linen canvas depicting the world in round form") is confirmed in *Storia dei vescovi di Siena,* a history of the bishops of Siena written by Antonio Pecci in 1748. To get some help in my research, I shared this reference to Leonardi with a map enthusiast living in Sondrio, closer to possible Venetian sources. He told me he had found something but has not consented to share it with me. Moreover, the Palazzo Besta in Teglio and especially the relevant impossible map located just a few miles from Sondrio and to be discussed in the next chapter, were altogether unknown to me until I spoke of them to him who, to tell the truth, had at first seemed friendly and cooperative. I would have saved the information for this book, but the bad turn of events following a lecture, together with other unpleasant episodes, led me to anticipate the results of my research in *Hera,* no. 37 (January 2003). Unfortunately, the news that emerged from years of investigation caused a sort of treasure hunter's syndrome in many. Some believed themselves to be in a position to plagiarize my work or convinced themselves that they had known of it all along. It is true that I also encountered people of honest and generous intellect who sought to lend me a hand without asking anything in return. The overall balance, however, remains

decidedly negative, even though I have always been open (perhaps too open) to cooperation and teamwork.

27. Pius II (Enea Silvio Piccolomini), *Lettera a Maometto II* (Naples: Pironti and Figli, 1953), 1 of the introduction by Giuseppe Toffanin. Pius II's remarkable letter, discussed earlier, "represented an abbatial or papal confirmation that the humanists had joined the Fathers of the paganization of the Church, conferring upon the ancient philosophers the same attributes as the prophets."

28. Pius II's letter begins in the name of "the consolation awaited by many people: peace." But there was no lack of controversy regarding the measurement of the spheres, both celestial and terrestrial: "The circumference of the earth, namely of the entire sphere, has been calculated as two hundred and fifty thousand stadia. But the harmonious law that requires the nature of things to be in concordance with each other (by the testimony of Pliny) adds to this measurement seven thousand stadia. Eratosthenes, the most diligent investigator of these things, assigned to the earth's circumference two hundred and fifty thousand stadia. Hipparchus added to this a little less than twenty-five thousand. There are yet more differing hypotheses. Nor do I believe that even today any mortal sufficiently knows this measure of the earth, whose confines are unknown to the north and south." In the pope's text, Ptolemy is cited more as a great astronomer than as a geographer, having calculated the distances of the universe with regard to the moon, the sun, and Mars.

29. Geo Pistarino, *La sede di Roma nell'apertura del Nuovo Mondo* (Milano: Mondadori, 1990), 553. Despite my requests, I have not obtained further information on the study in question.

30. Gerhard Herm, *I Bizantini*, 309.

31. H. A. L. Fisher, *Storia d'Europa* 1 (Rome: Newton Compton, 1995), 333: "In the Vatican, and especially among the Franciscans, whose missions extended all over the world, the oceanic endeavors of Portugal and Spain aroused the most lively interest, with the possibility not only of converting the pagans, but also of launching an attack on the Muslims from the East. It was known that the Negus of Abyssinia was a Christian, and a Christian state was believed to survive still in India, derived from a mission by St. Thomas and governed by a monarch known by the name of the grand khan. It was ardently hoped that Europe would have effective aid from this far-off Eastern prince in a final great Crusade against the infidels. This was the 'plan of the Indies' drawn up in 1454 by Nicholas V in a bull sent to the king of Portugal. And in this

atmosphere of anticipation, Columbus himself moved toward the discovery of the Indies in the west."

32. In this constant thread of studies and passions that preceded Columbus's voyages, there is not the least trace of Innocent VIII—at least, not until the betrayed pope was exhumed in the course of my fifteen years of study. The ax of history impiously struck down the man whom Pastor described as the "sailor pope," and truth and justice were buried with him. In this uninterrupted geographical sequence inevitably leading to the men of the Church and to the popes, Giovanni Battista Cybo would find no place. This is the conclusion drawn from almost all the publications in question: Once again, the pope's portrait is completely obliterated. What could a pope without learning and without character, pliable and weak, have wanted with great universal plans?

33. Ignazio Filippo Dengel, "Sulla '*Mappa Mundi*' di Palazzo Venezia," in *Atti del II Congresso Nazionale di studi Romani* 2 (1931). We will draw further details from this essay.

34. Paul II, Pietro Barbo, had connections with Borso d'Este, the duke of Modena, at whose court cosmographic studies were cultivated. Cantino's map, as we have seen, ended up with the Estes of Ferrara. Nicholas Germanus dedicated his work on Ptolemy to the two of them. At the papal court Franciscus Christianus, another expert, was also present, along with the Venetian Girolamo Bellavista, who has been named as a possible author of Pius II's lost world map. The plot grows ever more complex in an inextricable thicket of maps and authors. The names grow in number, as do the personages described as familiars of the popes. This was the same period during which another Venetian we have mentioned, the almost unknown priest Antonio de' Leonardi, lived in Rome and painted his canvas map for Cardinal Francesco Piccolomini. In his studies of the time of Paul II, Giuseppe Zippel adds that Bellavista belonged to the papal family.

35. Maria Letizia Casanova, *Palazzo Venezia* (Rome: Editalia, 1992), 154: "The painted decoration of the Mappamondo room, completed by Cardinal Lorenzo Cybo around 1491 [when Innocent VIII was still living] constitutes one of the rare fresco complexes surviving from fifteenth-century Rome, along with that of the Sala Greca in the Vatican palace. Planned in the time of Nicholas V, this room probably housed the pope's library, subsequently incorporated by Sixtus IV into the main floor of the Vatican Library. This room . . . with its impressive dimensions, triumphantly atmospheric and pictorial and traceable to Roman

mural paintings but linked to a rigorous linearism, has led to suggesting a conception of Tuscan origin, with attributions ranging from Piero della Francesca to Andrea del Castagno, who were present in Rome in 1454. The Mappamondo room, however, appears as the evocation of a classical hall . . . done on a rigorous perspective grid. The extremely narrow range of archeological selections—the decorative motifs are almost exact depictions of the great themes of Roman architecture, the triumphal arch and the basilica—fixed within the rigid frontal framework in a timeless atmosphere free from any figurative or incidental reference, places this most noteworthy pictorial work within a workshop influenced by Andrea Mantegna, whom Innocent VIII had summoned in 1488 to decorate the chapel of St. John the Baptist in the palace of the Belvedere."

36. Dengel, "Sulla *'Mappa Mundi'* de Palazzo Venezia," 2. As a point of interest, here is the conclusion of the study: "But for the history of cartography, it is important to know that a such a conspicuous monument of the fifteenth century once embellished the enormous palace of St. Mark, now the favored office of a statesman who, from there, draws the 'map' of a greater future for Italy." The reference is clearly to Mussolini. Times may change, but geography always ends up influencing the fates of peoples and being interpreted only through the eyes of politics.

Chapter Twelve. Columbus's Esoteric Signature

1. Luigi Bossi, *La vita di Cristoforo Colombo* (Bologna: Edison, 1992), 109–10. For a version in modern Italian, see Eugenio Garin, *La cultura filosofica del Rinascimento italiano* (Florence: Sansoni, 1992), 332–33. In the text cited by Garin (this is obviously a different version of the letter), it is added: "because those who sail continually to the west, by way of navigating to the antipodes, will reach the said regions."

2. Garin, *La cultura,* 320.

3. Ibid., 332.

4. Bossi, *La vita,* 115–16: "I have received your letters," wrote Toscanelli to Columbus, "with the things that you sent me, which I received as a great favor; and I admired your splendid and lofty desire to sail from the sun's rising to its setting, as is shown by the chart which I sent you; which would be better shown in the shape of a round sphere. I am very pleased that this is intended, and not only is the said voyage possible, but it is sure and certain, and of honor

and countless gain, and of enormous fame in the eyes of all Christians. You cannot know this perfectly save through experience and practice, as I have had in the form of most copious and good and true information from distinguished men of great learning who have come here to this court of Rome from the said places; and from other merchants who have long trafficked in those parts, persons of great authority. Thus, when this voyage is taken, in powerful kingdoms and in cities and in the noblest provinces there will be an abundance of all manner of valuable things that are so necessary to us; there will be all manner of spices in great quantity, and a great store of gems. Furthermore, it will appeal to those kings and princes, who much desire to have dealings and trading with the Christians of these our lands, whether to be a part of those Christians, or in order to have conversation and dealings with men here who are learned and informed, both in religion and in all the other sciences; and this for the great prestige of the empires and realms that they have there. Given these things, and many others that could be added, I cannot wonder that you, great-hearted one, and the whole Portuguese nation, which has always had men distinguished in all actions, should be fired up and greatly desirous of making this voyage."

5. *Dizionario biografico degli italiani,* 249. In a world map from 1457, attributed to Toscanelli (mentioned in a preceding note) and offered in 1459 to the ambassadors of the king of Portugal, Japan is already called Japan and not Cipangu. This is further evidence that Marco Polo's Cipangu was never really Japan. Like Antilla, it was a fourth part of the globe.

6. Garin, *La cultura,* 325: "The Florentine climate, artisanal on the one hand and inclined to the political and moral disciplines on the other, never saw a flourishing of science as free from prejudice—albeit also closed and conservative—as that of aristocratic Padua. The Paduan freedom was mainly that of those daring scholars who crossed the line into heresy."

7. Leonardo Rombai, "Firenze e gli studi geografici e cartografici nel Quattrocento," in *La carta perduta, Paolo dal Pozzo Toscanelli* (Florence: Fratelli Alinari, 1992), 32.

8. Pirro Alvi, *Todi città illustre dell'Umbria. Cenni Storici* (Todi: n.p., 1910), 174.

9. Cardini, "L'immaginario geografico medioevale," 87.

10. Garin, *La cultura,* 316–17: "Paolo must not have taken his art completely seriously, although it is difficult, regarding those men always on the border between a faith in crisis and an uncertain science, to say at what point they were actually being ironic about their certainties. In any case, it is probable

that all things considered, Toscanelli preferred the doctrines of Albumasar on the great conjunctions or the cycles of history to the learned Ficinian dissertations on the souls of the stars. Not by chance, during the same years that the great Marsilio was laying out his *Platonic Theology* and delighting in mysteries roaming among ideal worlds, Christopher Columbus was transcribing the letter already sent from Paolo Toscanelli in 1474 to Canon Martins for the king of Portugal."

11. Ibid., 321.

12. While Lorenzo and Innocent VIII were alive, Christopher Columbus remained the man for Operation America. After they died, with the domination of Spain and the Borgias, the one who prevailed was Amerigo Vespucci: the man of another Medici, Lorenzo di Pier Francesco.

13. Menzies, *1421,* 352. Menzies writes earlier (106) of "a world map the Portuguese dauphin, Dom Pedro, Henry the Navigator's brother, had brought back from Venice in 1428." Was it the map by Leonardi, discussed in the previous chapter, "remaining unknown to all"?

14. Ibid., 93: "Chinese knowledge and Chinese maps passed from da Conti to Fra Mauro, and from him to Dom Pedro of Portugal and Prince Henry the Navigator. The Papal secretary, Poggio Bracciolini, was, as we shall see [and as we saw in the preceding chapter], a key intermediary."

15. *Dizionario biografico degli italiani,* 248. We shall draw further information from this publication, including the life of Toscanelli and the del Pozzo families.

16. Francesco Ammannati, "Toscanelli e Colombo: gli errori della ragione e i dubbi della fede," in *La carta perduta,* 66: "They [the world maps] were produced in a religious ambience, their principal purpose being the illustration of the events of the Holy Scriptures.... The new mystic function was realized by transferring the center of the depiction from Rome to Jerusalem.... The world maps constitute a typical example of ideological cartography, subject to a political and religious vision of the world. Even the Ptolemaic system, whose origin was rational and secular, acquired an ideological value at the time when it was adopted as the superior system, becoming rooted in Western culture starting in the mid-fifteenth century. Its dismantling required much more time than we might legitimately expect."

17. Leonardo Rombai, "Firenze e gli studi geograficie," 43: "These and other foreigners were scrupulously interrogated by ecclesiastical authorities, mediated

by 'an interpreter from the Venetian nation, and it was a remarkable thing to see Latin being translated into such strange languages' (according to the testimony of Vespasiano da Bisticci). It is almost certain that this 'Venetian' was the Chioggia merchant Niccolò da Conti."

18. Gaetano Uzielli, *La vita e i tempi di Paolo dal Pozzo Toscanelli,* 192–93.

19. Ferdinand Columbus, *The Life of the Admiral Christopher Columbus by his son Ferdinand,* trans. Benjamin Keen (New Brunswick: Rutgers University Press, 1959), 23. "Our Indies," wrote Ferdinand, clearly meaning America, which is much farther from Asia than Europe ("here") is from the New World ("those lands").

20. Taviani, *Christoforo Colombo,* 370. This was also reported by Uzielli on page 599 of his cited work on Toscanelli. However, Toscanelli died in 1482, and, if the date of 1491 can be confirmed and has not been interpreted erroneously, the letter may be another fake—in this case, a probable fake in Columbus's favor.

21. Pope Sixtus IV was particularly fond of his nephews born from this union, Cristoforo and Domenico dal Pozzo, his constant protégés. The former was made governor of Sant'Angelo; the latter was made a cardinal when his brother died. He continued to accumulate benefices under Innocent VIII, and between 1482 and 1485, he acted as protector of the Sodalitas viminalis, the Roman Academy of Pomponio Leto. A Franciscan del Pozzo, known as Puteolano (perhaps a brother or relative of Paolo Fisico) was Moro of Milan's ambassador to Innocent VIII, who, appreciating his doctrine, granted him the benefice of the abbey of Tolla in Piacenza, the place of origin of the Pallestrello or Perestrello family—from which came Felipa, Columbus's first wife. Many of the del Pozzos were present at Pavia, where it is said, albeit without proof, that the young Columbus studied.

22. Maria Freitas Treen, *The Admiral and his Lady* (New York: Robert Speller and Sons, 1989), 34.

23. The studies that have been done from the architectonic point of view, with respect to proportions and harmonies, point to a definite Tuscan origin; to the teachings of the Florentine-Genoese Leon Battista Alberti (the wives of some of the lords of the palace also had the surname Alberti, a Genoese name transplanted to Florence); and to references to Vitruvius, Filarete, Bramante, and the Florentine Giuliano di Sangallo. This ensemble leads us to imagine a reconstruction carried out starting in the late fifteenth century in a series of

successive renovations. The first and decidedly most important would have been in the late 1530s, followed by the next one.

24. Gian Luigi Garbellini, *Il Palazzo Besta di Teglio* (Sondrio: Lyasis, 1996), 12.

25. G. Galletti and G. Mulazzani, *Il Palazzo Besta di Teglio* (Sondrio: n.p., 1983), 32.

26. Gian Luigi Garbellini, *La Chiesa di San Lorenzo di Teglio* (Teglio: Poletti Printing, 1993), 21.

27. The high walls of the large courtyard present the cycle of the Aeneid in a monochrome sequence, beginning with Aeneas's flight. It is a reconstruction of the events that has no counterpart from the stylistic point of view and omits the famous scene relating to the fall of Troy and above all the Trojan horse. The chosen theme is centered on the vicissitudes of the hero, in the role of *homo viator* up to his arrival in Italy. To frame it, in the friezes beneath a series of cameos depicts illustrious men and women. Each face should have a name and an explanation, but despite the many inscriptions, which are partly illegible due to the various eroded areas, here as elsewhere, most of the choices remain mysteries. It was a time in which nothing was left to chance, and many works of art were like open books—but only for those who were able to read them. The hidden meaning of the illustrations increases in the knightly cycle inspired by Ariosto's *Orlando furioso* (the first edition of his book was published in 1516), of which an interpretation from the ethical, moralistic, and esoteric point of view has been attempted, in what for us forms the real background for fathoming the building and its many "voices." Unfortunately, the interpretations made (Rajna Giuseppina Mazzoni, *L' "Orlando furioso" in Valtellina* [Sondrio: n.p., 1983]) are limited to a superficial reading in this sense, categorizing Orlando as "resurrected through encouragements to virtue, condemnation of vices, spiritual elevation, and the magical rapport between heaven and earth." But the complexity of the symbols and references that appear in the mottoes, defining the twenty-four scenes as if in a puppet show, would require deeper treatment. It is a true downpour of allusive symbols.

28. In one cycle of frescoes, a pictorial crescendo, we see the "arrogance and violence of the governors, discord, avarice, and the greed of the she-wolf and her killing by a young woman who slays the beast with the lance, while holding a compass in her other hand. This ends with the triumph of the wise man or white magician," a jovial squire who rides upon a tortoise, carrying in his

hand an armillary sphere, the symbol of science and knowledge. There are many other traces at which we can only hint, both in the personages and in the backgrounds, in nature and in the animals and in many other curious details that make us suspect another meaning. Their significance may be completely different from what appears to the eye, serving as an allegory, even by means of an art that is not always first rate.

29. Ruggero Marino, "La cartografia occulta del Palazzo Besta," in *Hera,* no. 37 (January 2003): 58. As noted earlier, the map was completely unknown until I revealed its importance to scholars of this material, including one who lived only a few kilometers from its location.

30. Giorgio Galletti, "Aggiunte al Palazzo Besta di Teglio, nuove ricerche e restauri," in *Bollettino storico della Società Valtellinese* 42 (1989), 140n3.

31. Ibid., 154n27 and 156n32.

32. Could this be the vanished Atlantis, according to hypotheses put forward and elaborated by Admiral Flavio Barbiero, or an Antarctica that the latest research suggests once had a completely different climate? A comparison has been made between the world map at Teglio (some find it similar to that of Henricus Martellus from 1490) and the one by the Spaniard Girava. In truth, the shape of the continents is different, but there is still the statement expressed in the inscription, which reads: *Tierra meridional descubierta el año 1499 pero no se sabe ahun por entero lo que sea* (Southern lands discovered in the year 1499 but not yet entirely known). Girava's map is part of a publication printed in Milan in 1556. What lands and what expeditions were referred to in this case? It is also strange that America is not indicated by the name inspired by Amerigo Vespucci, already widely used to erase Columbus. In the cordiform globe of Oronzio Fineo, dated to 1536, there is also a vanished southern land bearing the caption *"Terra australis nuper inventa sed nondum plene examinata"* (Austral land recently found but not yet fully known). And the argument could be continued with other world maps.

33. Recently, in the Australian seas, at the hands of the scholar Greg Jefferys, a warship and cannonballs have been found, as well as objects made by white men and the men's bones mixed with those of Aborigines. This appears to have been a Portuguese ship predating James Cook's arrival in this area by two hundred years. In this case, history has already been written by the English "victors." Since the days of Columbus, as we have repeatedly seen, the Portuguese were completely certain that there were boundless lands to the

south. For this reason, they did everything possible to move the line drawn by Alexander VI in favor of the Spanish—and they succeeded, recovering Brazil among other areas. The writer Gavin Menzies, already cited repeatedly, has ⟵ shown that Chinese junks reached Australia in 1421. Greg Jefferys, on the occasion of finding the wreck, had thought it might be a Chinese ship. (Once Chinese voyages are inserted into the history of navigation, most, if not all, discoveries in the Pacific must be reconsidered.) The Chinese ventured on the ocean in transatlantic ships compared to which the caravels were mere nut-shells. Professor Jefferys was convinced that a Chinese landing in Australia would have been possible in the fifteenth century, but the timber found beneath the waters was unequivocally of European origin. Unfortunately, the maps of Peking [Beijing] were destroyed by the Chinese themselves, who preferred to enclose themselves in their exclusive world, while the Portuguese maps were lost in a devastating earthquake.

34. Cuccaro in Monferrato, we may remember, has been indicated as one of the possible hometowns of Christopher Columbus. The navigator certainly may have spent some time there in his youth.

35. The earlier work on the huge palace was by the Florentine Antonio da Sangallo, the later by Jacopo Barozzi da Vignola. The coats of arms represent illustrious houses such as Hapsburg, Colonna, Orsini, Aldobrandini, Caetani, Borbone, Piccolomini, Pallavicini, Borromeo, Sforza, and Pecci. Among the painters are famous artists such as the Zuccari brothers, Jacopo Bertoia, Giovanni de' Vecchi, Raffaellino da Reggio, and Antonio Tempesta.

36. Graziella Frezza and Fausto Benedetti, eds., *Il Palazzo Farnese di Caprarola* (Rome: De Luca, 2001), 37.

37. Rosanna Pavoni, *Immagini di un volto sconosciuto* (Genoa: Sagep, 1990), 42.

38. George Kish, "The Caprarola Portrait of Columbus," in *Geographical Journal,* 120 (1954), 483–84.

39. Paolo Giovio, *Ritratti degli uomini illustri,* ed. Carlo Caruso (Palermo: Sellerio, 1999), 11 of the preface.

40. Ibid., 22 of the introduction by Carlo Caruso.

41. Riccardo de Rosa, "Alberico I Cybo Malaspina," in *Atti di un Convegno di Studi* (Massa: Modena, 1995), 75. There was a rich correspondence "occur-ring between Alberico, Lord of Massa, and the Farnese, dukes of Parma and Piacenza, which bears witness to the close relations maintained over the course of time between the two families." The golden age of the relationship between

the two great families ended "with the death of Ottavio and Cardinal Alessandro" (85).

42. Cecilia Maria Paolucci, "Il Sacro Bosco di Bomarzo," in *Bollettino Telematico dell'Arte,* no. 327 (June 24, 2003): 3. In one of the rooms of the Fasti Farnesiani we have already seen Ranuccio Farnese decorated with the golden rose of Eugenius IV.

43. Marco Berberi, *Bomarzo, un giardino alchemico del Cinquecento* (Bologna: n.p., 1999), 12.

Bibliography

Baigent, Michael, Richard Leigh, and Henry Lincoln. *Holy Blood, Holy Grail.* New York: Delacorte Press, 2005.

Baldock, John. *The Elements of Christian Symbolism.* Rockport, Mass.: Element, 1990.

Columbus, Christopher. *Libro de las profecias.* Translated by August Kling and Delno C. West. Gainesville: University of Florida Press, 1991.

Dunn, Ross E. *The Adventures of Ibn Battuta.* Berkeley: University of California Press, 2004.

Endres, Franz Carl, and Annemarie Schimmel. *The Mystery of Numbers.* New York: Oxford University Press, 1993.

Fusero, Clemente. *The Borgias.* Translated by Peter Green. New York: Praeger, 1972.

Herrmann, Paul. *Conquest by Man.* Translated by Michael Bullock. New York: Harper, 1954.

Knight, Christopher, and Robert Lomas. *The Hiram Key.* Boston, Mass.: Element, 1996.

Kurlansky, Mark. *Cod: A Biography of the Fish that Changed the World.* New York: Walker and Co., 1997.

Lunde, Paul. "Piri Reis and the Columbus Map." In *Saudi Aramco World* (May/June 1992): 18–25.

Mansel, Philip. *Constantinople: City of the World's Desire 1453–1924.* New York: St. Martin's Press, 1998.

Menzies, Gavin. *1421: The Year China Discovered America.* New York: Perennial, 2004.

Morison, Samuel E. *The European Discovery of America*. New York: Oxford University Press 1993.

Nebenzahl, Kenneth. *Atlas of Columbus and the Great Discoveries*. Chicago: Rand McNally, 1990

Ravenscroft, Trevor. *The Spear of Destiny*. New York: Putnam, 1973.

Roob, Alexander. *Alchemy & Mysticism*. Translated by Shaun Whiteside. New York: Taschen, 1997.

Severin, Tim. *The Brendan Voyage*. Norwalk, Conn.: Easton Press, 1989.

Silverberg, Robert. *The Realm of Prester John*. Athens: Ohio University Press, 1996.

Sora, Steven. *The Lost Treasure of the Knights Templar*. Rochester, Vt.: Destiny Books, 1999.

Vasari, Giorgio. *The Lives of the Artists*. Translated by Julia Conaway Bondanella and Peter Bondanella. New York: Oxford University Press, 1998.

Index

BOOKS OF RELATED INTEREST

The Templar Pirates
The Secret Alliance to Build the New Jerusalem
by Ernesto Frers

The Knights Templar in the Golden Age of Spain
Their Hidden History on the Iberian Peninsula
by Juan García Atienza

An Illustrated History of the Knights Templar
by James Wasserman

The Templars and the Assassins
by James Wasserman

The Knights Templar in the New World
How Henry Sinclair Brought the Grail to Acadia
by William F. Mann

The Templar Meridians
The Secret Mapping of the New World
by William F. Mann

The Lost Treasure of the Knights Templar
Solving the Oak Island Mystery
by Steven Sora

The Lost Colony of the Templars
Verrazano's Secret Mission to America
by Steven Sora

Inner Traditions • Bear & Company
P.O. Box 388
Rochester, VT 05767
1-800-246-8648
www.InnerTraditions.com

Or contact your local bookseller

p 121   I N R I

"Iesus Nazarenus Rex Iudaeorum"

in Hebrew or Aramaic

also in Greek and Latin written
in reverse, running from
Right to left like Hebrew writing

Christopher - Christ

Colombo - dove - Holy spirit
            descending on Jesus
            at his baptism

p 262   athanor - alchemical furnace

p 246   fatidic

BELIEVE

LIVING THE STORY OF THE BIBLE
TO BECOME LIKE JESUS

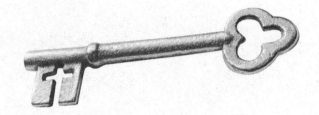

STUDY GUIDE | THIRTY SESSIONS

RANDY FRAZEE

WITH RANDY LARSON

ZONDERVAN

Believe Study Guide
Copyright © 2015 by Randy Frazee

This title is also available as a Zondervan ebook. Visit www.zondervan.com/ebooks.

Requests for information should be addressed to:

Zondervan, 3900 Sparks Dr. SE, Grand Rapids, Michigan 49546

ISBN 978-0-310-82611-8

Cover design: Extra Credit Projects
Interior design: Denise Froehlich

First printing April 2015 / Printed in the United States of America

Contents

How to Use This Guide

SCOPE AND SEQUENCE

The goal of every follower of Jesus Christ is to become more like him, but how do you know where to start? What does it really mean to be a disciple of Jesus? The objective of the *Believe* adult curriculum is to paint a clear picture of what it means to think, act, and be like Jesus. This study guide (and the related video) will help you assess your spiritual life, pinpoint areas that need special attention, and give you tools to help you grow. The first ten sessions focus on the core beliefs of the Christian faith; the next ten sessions focus on foundational practices of the Christian life; and the last ten sessions focus on Christlike virtues. May God bless you as you seek him through this experience.

SESSION OUTLINE

Each of the thirty sessions is divided into three parts. The first is for your own personal study, to be done prior to your group meetings. In this section you will be asked to read one chapter from *Believe* and record your responses to the five questions embedded within the chapter. You will also be given four statements to help you evaluate the alignment of your life with the Key Idea from each session. Then, you will be challenged to take action by memorizing each session's Key Idea and Key Verse.

In the group section of your study guide you will be given a note-taking outline to help you follow along with Randy Frazee's video teaching. There will be an opportunity to discuss your responses to the four self-evaluation statements from your personal study along with other discussion questions. Then, you will be given real-life scenarios of people who struggle with their faith. Using the Key Applications from your study guide, your group will be challenged to think of ways to encourage the people within these case studies.

The last part of each session is a journal. Use this space to take notes from your pastor's or teacher's message or to record your own thoughts from this chapter.

Personal Study

This section helps you connect personally to the Scriptures in the *Believe* chapter and is designed to be completed on your own, before the group meeting.

- **Read:** To help you engage with the *Believe* book as you read, five reflection questions are embedded in the text of each chapter. Space is provided in the study guide for you to record your answers to those questions.

- **Evaluate:** Rate yourself on four belief statements taken from the Christian Life Profile®. These belief statements together help explain the different aspects of the Key Idea.

- **Take Action:** Work on memorizing the Key Verse and the Key Idea, and be prepared to recite them at your group meeting. To help incorporate them into your life, answer the journaling questions related to the Key Idea.

Group Study

This section will facilitate deeper growth that can only be found in a spiritually rich community.

- **Watch:** Your group sessions will begin with a short video teaching from Randy Frazee that will stimulate great discussion in your group. In each session he will give greater insight into the Key Idea and Key Verse along with Key Application points.

- **Discuss:** Each session of the *Believe Study Guide* includes discussion questions that are geared toward the long-time veteran as well as the person completely new to the Christian faith. Group facilitators are encouraged to pick and choose which questions would be best for the maturity of their group.

- **Pray:** The Scriptures found in *Believe* point us to the truth of what it means to think, act, and be like Jesus, but it's prayer that actually empowers us to become all that Jesus created us to be. Each group session concludes with a time of group prayer.

GROUP SIZE

The 30-week *Believe* video curriculum is designed to be experienced in a group setting such as a Bible study, Sunday school class, or any small group gathering. To ensure everyone has enough time to participate in discussions, it is recommended that large groups watch the video together and then break up into smaller groups of four to six people for discussion. Each session can be completed in about an hour.

MATERIALS NEEDED

Each participant should have his or her own study guide, which includes notes for video segments, memorization activities, and discussion questions, as well as a personal study to deepen learning between sessions. Although the course can be fully experienced with just the video and study guide, participants are also encouraged to have a copy of the *Believe* book. Reading the book along with the video sessions provides even deeper insights that make the journey richer and more meaningful.

FACILITATION

Each group should appoint a facilitator who is responsible for starting the video and for keeping track of time during discussions and activities. Facilitators may also read questions aloud and monitor discussions, prompting participants to respond and ensuring that everyone has the opportunity to participate. More thorough instructions are provided in the "Group Facilitator Tips" section that follows.

Group Facilitator Tips

To ensure a successful group experience, read the following information before beginning.

——WHAT MAKES A GROUP DISCUSSION SUCCESSFUL?——

As your group's facilitator, you might be asking yourself, "What am I supposed to accomplish with this study?" Here are few goals you might set for your group:

1. **Discovering truth.** The Bible reveals the truth about who God is and who we are created to be. A successful group wrestles with Scripture in order to find these truths.

2. **Applying truth.** It doesn't do much good to know the truth if we don't act on what we are learning. A successful group seeks to apply the truth to their lives.

3. **Honesty and authenticity.** Many people feel pressure to act "spiritual" when they are in religious environments, masking their true thoughts and feelings. This behavior stunts spiritual growth. Successful groups cultivate a safe place for authenticity and honesty.

4. **Participation.** The person who does the most talking often does the most learning. Therefore, groups that seek to include everyone in the conversation experience the most progress. Successful groups engage all their members in their discussions.

At the end of each group meeting, ask yourself these questions:

- Did we learn something new about God and ourselves?
- Are people actively seeking to apply these truths to their lives?
- Do people feel comfortable talking honestly about their faith?
- Have I engaged all members of the group in the discussion?

If you can answer yes to any of these questions, you are facilitating successfully.

CREATING A SUCCESSFUL ENVIRONMENT

Leading a group can be overwhelming, but it doesn't have to be. Consider these tips to help you create a successful group environment.

Pray: As you prepare for your group meeting, ask God to give you wisdom in choosing discussion questions, courage in creating an authentic environment, and insight into the truths he wants to reveal to your group.

Prime the pump: Your group will be as honest and authentic as you are willing to be. Courageously set the tone for the group by being open about the strengths and weaknesses of your faith. The group will follow your lead. This principle also applies to life application. If you are trying to apply the truth of each lesson to your life, the rest of the group will follow you.

Punctual: Start and stop on time. No matter how long your group meets, it's your job to keep things on track. Make a budget of time for each section of the study and stick to it. It might be uncomfortable to cut people off and move on, but the group will respect you for doing so.

SPECIFICS FOR THIS STUDY

Design your own discussion. Don't feel pressured to use all of the materials found in this study guide; select the modes of lesson engagement that fit your time frame and your group's learning style. This study was written for a vast array of personalities, learning styles, and levels of spiritual maturity. Pick and choose the activities and questions that seem to fit your group the best.

Your group might gravitate to one or two of the discussion segments but not another; that's fine. Choose one or two questions from the segments that your group will benefit from most. Try to vary the discussion by choosing some questions that dig deep into the theology of the belief and others that are more open-ended personal reflection questions. Encourage people to offer insights from their personal study time during your discussion.

The "declaration statements" segment (which revisits the Evaluate section of the personal study) may frequently evoke varying viewpoints. When group members don't believe something exactly the same way, provide a safe place to discuss their differences, questions, and areas of unbelief freely and with grace.

The case studies in each session are based on actual situations. Use them as a creative vehicle to discuss the applications of the session's theme to real life.

God

Personal Study

Every session in *Believe* contains a personal study to help you make meaningful connections between your life and what you're learning each week. Take some time before your group meeting each week to read the assigned chapter from *Believe* and complete the weekly personal study. In total, the personal study should take about one hour to complete. Some people like to spread it out, devoting about ten to fifteen minutes a day. Others choose one larger block of time during the week to work through the entire personal study in one sitting. There's no right or wrong way to do this! Just choose a plan that best fits your needs and schedule from week to week.

This week before your group meeting, read *Believe, Chapter 1: God.* Then spend some time allowing the Scripture to take root in your heart and reflecting on what you personally believe about who God is.

READ

Read Believe, Chapter 1: God *and answer the following questions.*

1. In what ways do you see the invisible qualities of God revealed in nature?

2. What are some of the main points of God's requirements for his people? Why do you think he emphasized these things?

3. Why did God have to prove over and over that he is the one true God?

4. In what ways have you experienced God as Father? As Jesus the Son? As the Holy Spirit?

5. What is meant by the phrase Paul quoted: "For in him we live and move and have our being"? Why do you think this needed to be said to this group of Athenians?

EVALUATE

Based on your reading from Believe, Chapter 1: God, *use a scale of 1 – 6 to rate how strongly you believe the statements below (1 = no belief at all, 6 = complete confidence).*

_____ I believe the God of the Bible is the only true God.

_____ I believe the God of the Bible is one in essence but distinct in person — Father, Son, and Holy Spirit.

_____ I believe Jesus is God in the flesh — who died and rose bodily from the dead.

_____ I believe the Holy Spirit is God and dwells in Christians to empower them to live the Christian life.

---TAKE ACTION---

Memorizing Scripture is a valuable discipline for all believers to exercise. Spend a few minutes each day committing this week's Key Verse to memory.

KEY VERSE: "May the grace of the Lord Jesus Christ, and the love of God, and the fellowship of the Holy Spirit be with you all." (2 Corinthians 13:14)

Recite this week's Key Idea out loud. As you do, ask yourself, "Does my life reflect this statement?"

KEY IDEA: I believe the God of the Bible is the one true God—Father, Son, and Holy Spirit.

Answer the following questions to help you apply this week's Key Idea to your own life.

1. What behaviors help you recognize someone who believes the God of the Bible is the one true God?

2. What, if anything, hinders you from putting your faith solely in the God of the Bible?

3. What is something you can do this week to demonstrate your belief in the one true God?

Group Meeting

Welcome!

Welcome to Session 1 of *Believe*. If this is your first time together as a group, take a moment to introduce yourselves to each other before watching the video. Then, feel free to get started!

---VIDEO TEACHING NOTES---

As you watch the video segment for Session 1, use the following outline to record some of the main points. (The answer key is found at the end of the session.)

- A. W. Tozer wrote, "What comes into our minds when we think about God is the most important thing about us." Why? Because this mind-set—or absence of it—will drive all we _____ and all we _____.

- Key Question: Who is _____?

- "For since the creation of the world God's invisible qualities—his eternal power and divine nature—have been clearly seen, being understood from what has been made, so that people are _____ _____." (Romans 1:20)

- Key Idea: I believe the God of the Bible is the one _____ _____—Father, Son, and Holy Spirit.

- God is three persons who _____ a being.

- "Then God said, _____ _____ make mankind in our image, in our likeness ... So God created mankind in his image, in the image of God he created them; male and female he created them." (Genesis 1:26–27)

- One of the biggest failures for humanity, beginning with the fall of Adam and Eve, is when we try to take over the role of _____ in our lives.

- (Key Application) Because God is God ... I am _____ ... He is in _____ and in control ... I want to know and follow his _____ for my life.

- (Key Application) Because I was created in the image of God and for community ... I recognize others' full _____ and respect boundaries ... I look out for the rights, preferences, and _____ of others ... I _____ and enjoy others.

GETTING STARTED

Begin your discussion by reciting the Key Verse and Key Idea together as a group. On your first attempt, use your notes if you need help. On your second attempt, try to state them completely from memory.

KEY VERSE: "May the grace of the Lord Jesus Christ, and the love of God, and the fellowship of the Holy Spirit be with you all." (2 Corinthians 13:14)

KEY IDEA: I believe the God of the Bible is the one true God—Father, Son, and Holy Spirit.

GROUP DISCUSSION

As a group, discuss your thoughts and feelings about the following declarations. Which statements are easy to declare with certainty? Which are more challenging, and why?

- I believe the God of the Bible is the one true God.
- I believe the God of the Bible is one in essence but distinct in person—Father, Son and Holy Spirit.
- I believe Jesus is God in flesh—who died and rose bodily from the dead.
- I believe the Holy Spirit is God and dwells in Christians to empower them to live the Christian life.

Based on your group's dynamics and spiritual maturity, choose the 2–3 questions that will lead to the best discussion about this week's Key Idea.

1. If you only had two minutes to answer the question, "Who is God?" how would you respond?

2. How does your understanding of God impact your day-to-day decisions?

3. What are the most common reasons people struggle to believe that the God of the Bible is the one true God? What helped you get past these obstacles? Or, what obstacles are you still facing?

Read Luke 3 (see the section "God in Three Persons: Father, Son and Holy Spirit" in Be-lieve) and choose 1 – 2 questions that will lead to the greatest discussion in your group.

1. In what ways is the Trinity a challenging concept to comprehend?

2. If God (the Trinity) is a community within himself, and we are made in his image, what does that tell us about ourselves?

3. How does today's culture help or hinder us from experiencing the community we were created for?

4. What specific actions can this group undertake to create healthy community?

CASE STUDY

Use the following case study as a model for a real-life situation where you might put this week's Key Idea into practice.

Mike is one of your favorite coworkers. He is funny, hardworking, and passionate about life. As a new Christian, he comes to you seeking help, because he and his wife are struggling. They are constantly butting heads, arguing, and simply not getting along. Mike thinks it is just easier to walk away but really wants to know what you think.

Using the Key Applications from this session, what gentle advice would you give him? (If needed, refer to your video notes for a reminder of this session's Key Applications.)

CLOSING PRAYER

Close your time together with prayer. Share your prayer requests with one another. Ask God to help you put this week's Key Idea into practice.

JOURNAL

If your church is doing the *Believe* church-wide campaign, bring this study guide with you to church and use the following space to take notes from the pastor's or teacher's message. If your church provides an outline, consider keeping it with this guide so you will have all of your notes and thoughts from your *Believe* journey in one place.

_____

are, do / God / without excuse / true God / share / Let us / God / not, charge, will / personhood, comforts, value

Personal God

Personal Study

Last week you examined your beliefs about who God is. Perhaps you learned something about God or about yourself that you never knew before. That's great! This week before your group meeting, read *Believe, Chapter 2: Personal God*. Then spend some time allowing the Scripture to take root in your heart and evaluating your feelings about how God is involved in your daily life.

READ

Read Believe, Chapter 2: Personal God *and answer the following questions.*

1. As you read the passage from Genesis 16, look for some ways in which God showed his goodness to Abraham, Sarah, and Hagar. What impact did this have on them?

2. How have you experienced God's personal knowledge of you? When have you known he was searching your heart? What was the result?

3. How did God show the captives in Babylon that he still cared for them and wanted the best for them?

4. Why does Jesus want us to refrain from worry? How does freedom from worry demonstrate confidence in God's provision and care?

---

5. As you read the passage from James 1, ask yourself, "How does God show his care and concern for us when we go through difficult seasons in life?"

EVALUATE

Based on your reading from Believe, Chapter 2: Personal God, *use a scale of 1 – 6 to rate how strongly you believe the statements below (1 = no belief at all, 6 = complete confidence).*

_____ I believe God has a purpose for my life.

_____ I believe pain and suffering can often bring me closer to God.

_____ I believe God is actively involved in my life.

_____ I believe God enables me to do things I could not or would not otherwise do.

TAKE ACTION

Memorizing Scripture is a valuable discipline for all believers to exercise. Spend a few minutes each day committing this week's Key Verse to memory.

KEY VERSE: "I lift up my eyes to the mountains—where does my help come from? My help comes from the LORD, the Maker of heaven and earth." (Psalm 121:1–2)

Recite this week's Key Idea out loud. As you do, ask yourself, "Does my life reflect this statement?"

KEY IDEA: I believe God is involved in and cares about my daily life.

Answer the following questions to help you apply this week's Key Idea to your own life.

1. How would this belief-in-action express itself in your life?

2. What visible attributes can be found in someone who is personally connected to God?

3. What is impeding your ability to experience God in a personal way? How can you overcome these obstacles?

4. What action step can you take this week to increase your awareness of God's involvement in your daily life?

Group Meeting

Welcome!

Welcome to Session 2 of *Believe*. If there are any new members in your group, take a moment to introduce yourselves to each other. Then spend a couple of minutes sharing insights or questions about this session's personal study. Now start the video!

─────VIDEO TEACHING NOTES─────

As you watch the video segment for Session 2, use the following outline to record some of the main points. (The answer key is found at the end of the session.)

- Key Question: Does God _____ about me?

- "The LORD is my shepherd, I lack nothing. He _____ me lie down in green pastures, he _____ me beside quiet waters, he _____ my soul. He _____ me along the right paths for his name's sake. Even though I walk through the darkest valley, I will fear no evil, for you are _____ me; your rod and your staff, they _____ me. You _____ a table before me in the presence of my enemies. You _____ my head with oil; my cup overflows. Surely your goodness and love will follow me all the days of my life, and I will dwell in the house of the LORD forever." (Psalm 23)

- Key Idea: I believe God is _____ in and _____ about my daily life.

- (Key Application) Be _____: God's ways are higher than my ways.

- (Key Application) Don't _____: God, who controls nature and history, cares about me.

- (Key Application) Be _____: God is working out his good plan for my life.

GETTING STARTED

Begin your discussion by reciting the Key Verse and Key Idea together as a group. On your first attempt, use your notes if you need help. On your second attempt, try to state them completely from memory.

KEY VERSE: "I lift up my eyes to the mountains—where does my help come from? My help comes from the LORD, the Maker of heaven and earth." (Psalm 121:1–2)

KEY IDEA: I believe God is involved in and cares about my daily life.

GROUP DISCUSSION

As a group, discuss your thoughts and feelings about the following declarations. Which statements are easy to declare with certainty? Which are more challenging, and why?

- I believe God has a purpose for my life.
- I believe pain and suffering can often bring me closer to God.
- I believe God is actively involved in my life.
- I believe God enables me to do things I could not or would not otherwise do.

Based on your group's dynamics and spiritual maturity, choose the 2–3 questions that will lead to the best discussion about this week's Key Idea.

1. Have you ever asked yourself, "Does God care about me?" If so, what experience or thought helped formulate your answer?

2. Describe the specific ways you experience God in your daily life.

3. What activities or disciplines heighten your awareness of God's activity in your life?

Read Psalm 23 (see the section "God Is Good" in Believe) *and choose 1 – 2 questions that will lead to the greatest discussion in your group.*

1. Psalm 23 describes God as a good shepherd who leads, guides, refreshes, comforts, prepares, and anoints his sheep. Which action best describes your interactions with him?

2. How does freedom from worry demonstrate confidence in God's ability to provide and care for us?

3. Why is it challenging to trust that God's ways are higher than our ways? How can we overcome these obstacles?

4. What thoughts and emotions come to mind when you think about the fact that God has a good plan for your life?

CASE STUDY

Use the following case study as a model for a real-life situation where you might put this week's Key Idea into practice.

Jill has been part of a church community for as long as she can remember. Secretly, she has struggled with doubts about God's will for her life. In a moment of vulnerability, she confesses that she fears she will never get married or have a family of her own. Her questions can be summed up this way:

1. How can I be certain that God's will for me is good?
2. Why would the God of the universe care about the details of my life?

Using the Key Applications from this session, what could you say or do to help Jill find the answers to her questions? (If needed, refer to your video notes for a reminder of this session's Key Applications.)

CLOSING PRAYER

Close your time together with prayer. Share your prayer requests with one another. Ask God to help you put this week's Key Idea into practice.

JOURNAL

If your church is doing the *Believe* church-wide campaign, bring this study guide with you to church and use the following space to take notes from the pastor's or teacher's message. If your church provides an outline, consider keeping it with this guide so you will have all of your notes and thoughts from your *Believe* journey in one place.

VIDEO NOTES ANSWER KEY

care / makes, leads, refreshes, guides, with, comfort, prepare, anoint / involved, cares / mindful / worry / excited

Salvation

Personal Study

Last week you took a look at your beliefs about how God is involved in your daily life. Perhaps you were able to reflect on how God really does care about your daily activities. Maybe you were able to see how God has been at work in your life, even in difficult times. This week before your group meeting, read *Believe, Chapter 3: Salvation*. Then spend some time allowing the Scripture to take root in your heart and considering what salvation through Jesus means to you.

READ

Read Believe, Chapter 3: Salvation *and answer the following questions.*

1. How would you describe Adam and Eve's life in the garden with God before they disobeyed him? What was life with God like for them afterward?

2. What are the similarities between the sacrificed lamb and the sacrifice of Jesus? What type of "Passover" has been caused by Jesus' blood applied to our lives?

3. Look for similarities between Jesus' time on earth and Isaiah's prophecy of the "suffering servant."

4. Why is it important to both believe in our hearts and profess with our mouths that Jesus is Lord?

5. Can you pinpoint a moment or chart a sequence of moments in time when you realized that Christ died for you? How would you describe that process?

EVALUATE

Based on your reading from Believe, *Chapter 3: Salvation, use a scale of 1–6 to rate how strongly you believe the statements below (1 = no belief at all, 6 = complete confidence).*

_____ I believe I will inherit eternal life because of what Jesus has done for me.

_____ I believe nothing I do or have done can earn my salvation.

_____ I believe salvation comes only through Jesus.

_____ I believe people are saved because of what Jesus did, not because of what they do.

TAKE ACTION

Memorizing Scripture is a valuable discipline for all believers to exercise. Spend a few minutes each day committing this week's Key Verse to memory.

KEY VERSE: "For it is by grace you have been saved, through faith—and this is not from yourselves, it is the gift of God—not by works, so that no one can boast." (Ephesians 2:8–9)

Recite this week's Key Idea out loud. As you do, ask yourself, "Does my life reflect this statement?"

KEY IDEA: I believe a person comes into a right relationship with God by God's grace through faith in Jesus Christ.

Answer the following questions to help you apply this week's Key Idea to your own life.

1. How would this belief-in-action express itself in your life?

2. What visible attributes can be found in someone who has received the gift of salvation?

3. If you haven't confessed with your mouth that Jesus is Lord and believed in your heart that he has risen from the dead, what is keeping you from doing so?

4. Is there someone in your life who needs to know about salvation by grace through faith in Jesus? What's stopping you from having that conversation?

Group Meeting

Welcome!

Welcome to Session 3 of *Believe*. If there are any new members in your group, take a moment to introduce yourselves to each other. Then spend a couple of minutes sharing insights or questions about this session's personal study. Now start the video!

—VIDEO TEACHING NOTES—

As you watch the video for Session 3, use the following outline to record some of the main points. (The answer key is found at the end of the session.)

- Key Question: How do I have a _____ with God?

- _____ is found in Jesus.

- Jesus has made the way possible for us to be _____ of our sins and come into a relationship with God. What is our part? How do we take hold of this _____ offer?

- Key Verse: "For it is by _____ you have been saved, through _____—and this is not from yourselves, it is the gift of God—not by works, so that no one can boast." (Ephesians 2:8–9)

- In order for the sacrifice of Christ to be applied to us individually we must reach out and _____ it by faith.

- This is the only way to _____ Adam's decision and restore a right relationship with God.

- (Key Application) No matter what _____ I face in this life, they pale in comparison to my salvation for eternity.

- (Key Application) I need to walk in _____ and _____ grace to others.

GETTING STARTED

Begin your discussion by reciting the Key Verse and Key Idea together as a group. On your first attempt, use your notes if you need help. On your second attempt, try to state them completely from memory.

KEY VERSE: "For it is by grace you have been saved, through faith—and this is not from yourselves, it is the gift of God—not by works, so that no one can boast." (Ephesians 2:8–9)

KEY IDEA: I believe a person comes into a right relationship with God by God's grace through faith in Jesus Christ.

GROUP DISCUSSION

As a group, discuss your thoughts and feelings about the following declarations. Which statements are easy to declare with certainty? Which are more challenging, and why?

- I believe I will inherit eternal life because of what Jesus has done for me.
- I believe nothing I do or have done can earn my salvation.
- I believe salvation comes only through Jesus.
- I believe people are saved because of what Jesus did, not because of what they do.

Based on your group's dynamics and spiritual maturity, choose the 2–3 questions that will lead to the best discussion about this week's Key Idea.

1. How would you define the word "grace"? What is the opposite of grace?

2. What specifically would it look like for us to offer grace to people who don't deserve it, as God did for us?

3. Without naming names, who is someone in your life that doesn't deserve your love and kindness, but you offer it anyway?

4. Many people find it hard to receive something they didn't earn. Discuss how this behavior could hinder someone's spiritual growth.

Read Genesis 3 and Romans 5:12 – 21 (see the sections "The Problem: We Are Not Born into a Relationship with God" and "The Outcome: A Lasting Relationship with Our Loving God" in Believe) *and choose 1 – 2 questions that will lead to the greatest discussion in your group.*

1. How did Adam and Eve's decision to disobey God affect all of mankind?

2. How did Jesus' choices overturn the effect of Adam and Eve's sin in our lives?

3. What do these Scriptures tell you about the character of God and his feelings toward you and all of humanity?

---------CASE STUDY---------

Use the following case study as a model for a real-life situation where you might put this week's Key Idea into practice.

> Rocky is a man's man. It appears as though there's nothing he can't fix. He spends more time tinkering in his garage than in his own house. Luckily, he's your neighbor. So, when you break something, he is always willing to lend a hand. One day in a moment of authenticity, he confesses that he has never quite understood God and religion but knows he needs them. Yet he fears that his past mistakes have disqualified him from ever being what he calls a "religious person."

Using the Key Applications from this session, answer the following questions together as a group. (If needed, refer to your video notes for a reminder of this session's Key Applications.)

1. How can you help Rocky begin a relationship with God?

2. What misconceptions does Rocky have about the character of God, and how can you point him to the truth?

3. In what ways can you relate to Rocky?

---------CLOSING PRAYER---------

Close your time together with prayer. Share your prayer requests with one another. Ask God to help you put this week's Key Idea into practice.

JOURNAL

If your church is doing the *Believe* church-wide campaign, bring this study guide with you to church and use the following space to take notes from the pastor's or teacher's message. If your church provides an outline, consider keeping it with this guide so you will have all of your notes and thoughts from your *Believe* journey in one place.

VIDEO NOTES ANSWER KEY

relationship / Salvation / forgiven, life-changing / grace, faith / receive / overturn / troubles / grace, offer

The Bible

Personal Study

Last week you examined your beliefs about salvation. Did you learn anything new about yourself? About God? Perhaps you've been a Christian for a long time and you're discovering new things about what you believe. Maybe you're new to the faith or simply exploring what it means to be a Christian. If so, feel free to ask questions and connect with your group leader or pastor for help. This week before your group meeting, read *Believe, Chapter 4: The Bible*. Then spend some time praying, asking God to help you recognize the tremendous value of his Word.

──────────────**READ**──────────────

Read Believe, Chapter 4: The Bible *and answer the following questions.*

1. What can we learn about the character of God from the story of Moses and the burning bush? How did Moses react to this direct communication from God? How would you respond in a similar situation?

2. What ways did Jesus use to help his disciples understand who he was and why he came?

3. As you read the passage from 2 Peter 1, think about how God, through Scripture, built a case for the identity and purpose of Jesus.

4. Are the Ten Commandments as relevant today as they were when Moses delivered them to the Israelites? How?

5. In what ways have you experienced the Word of God as "alive and active" in your own spiritual life?

EVALUATE

Based on your reading from Believe, *Chapter 4: The Bible,* use a scale of 1–6 to rate how strongly you believe the statements below (1 = no belief at all, 6 = complete confidence).

_____ I believe the Bible is absolutely true in matters of faith and morals.

_____ I believe the words of the Bible are words from God.

_____ I believe the Bible has decisive authority over what I say and do.

_____ I believe the Bible is relevant to address the needs of contemporary culture.

TAKE ACTION

Memorizing Scripture is a valuable discipline for all believers to exercise. Spend a few minutes each day committing this week's Key Verse to memory.

KEY VERSE: "All Scripture is God-breathed and is useful for teaching, rebuking, correcting and training in righteousness, so that the servant of God may be thoroughly equipped for every good work." (2 Timothy 3:16–17)

Recite this week's Key Idea out loud. As you do, ask yourself, "Does my life reflect this statement?"

KEY IDEA: I believe the Bible is the inspired Word of God that guides my beliefs and actions.

Answer the following questions to help you apply this week's Key Idea to your own life.

1. How would this belief-in-action express itself in your life?

2. What visible attributes can be found in someone who knows and is directed by the Word of God?

3. If you have reservations about the reliability and/or authority of Scripture, what is your plan for finding answers to your questions?

4. What is a reading plan or resource you can implement to deepen your understanding of God's Word?

5. What are some ways you can filter your thoughts and actions through the truth of God's Word?

Group Meeting

Welcome!

Welcome to Session 4 of *Believe*. If there are any new members in your group, take a moment to introduce yourselves to each other. Then spend a couple of minutes sharing insights or questions about this session's personal study. Now start the video!

---VIDEO TEACHING NOTES---

As you watch the video segment for Session 4, use the following outline to record some of the main points. (The answer key is found at the end of the session.)

- Key Question: How does God _____ himself and his truth to us?

- Key Idea: I believe the Bible is the inspired Word of God that guides my beliefs and actions.

- Key Verse: "All Scripture is God-breathed and is useful for _____, _____, _____ and _____ in righteousness, so that the servant of God may be thoroughly equipped for every good work." (2 Timothy 3:16–17)

- The Psalmist writes: "Your word is a _____ for my feet, a _____ on my path." (Psalm 119:105)

- (Key Application) The Bible is the _____ from which I view the world.

- (Key Application) I am motivated to study the Bible to _____ God's will for my life.

- (Key Application) The principles in the Bible must _____ my life even when I don't fully understand or like what it teaches.

GETTING STARTED

Begin your discussion by reciting the Key Verse and Key Idea together as a group. On your first attempt, use your notes if you need help. On your second attempt, try to state them completely from memory.

KEY VERSE: "All Scripture is God-breathed and is useful for teaching, rebuking, correcting and training in righteousness, so that the servant of God may be thoroughly equipped for every good work." (2 Timothy 3:16–17)

KEY IDEA: I believe the Bible is the inspired Word of God that guides my beliefs and actions.

GROUP DISCUSSION

As a group, discuss your thoughts and feelings about the following declarations. Which statements are easy to declare with certainty? Which are more challenging, and why?

- I believe the Bible is absolutely true in matters of faith and morals.
- I believe the words of the Bible are words from God.
- I believe the Bible has decisive authority over what I say and do.
- I believe the Bible is relevant to address the needs of contemporary culture.

Based on your group's dynamics and spiritual maturity, choose the 2–3 questions that will lead to the best discussion about this week's Key Idea.

1. In what ways can the Bible inform and govern your decision making in the areas of business, family life, friendships, and recreation.

2. In what ways have you seen the Bible be specifically useful for teaching, rebuking, correcting, and training?

3. How has understanding the Scriptures changed the way you see the world?

4. Many people are overwhelmed by the Bible, but it doesn't have to be that way. If you have any obstacles that get in the way of you reading and understanding God's Word, honestly confess them. Then, spend some time as a group discussing ways to overcome these challenges.

Read Exodus 20:1 – 21 (see the section "The Authority of Scripture" in Believe) *and choose 1 – 2 questions that will lead to the greatest discussion in your group.*

1. How do the Ten Commandments reveal what is most important to God?

2. How would the world be different if all of humanity were guided by the Word of God?

3. Discuss ways that the Bible has clarified misconceptions you had about God's character.

4. How has the Bible given you a better understanding of who you are and your purpose in this world?

—————————————CASE STUDY—————————————

Use the following case study as a model for a real-life situation where you might put this week's Key Idea into practice.

Suzanne is a college student who attends your Bible study that meets at the local coffee shop on Thursday mornings. As the group discusses prayer requests, Suzanne expresses her need for wisdom in balancing her busy schedule. In the next seven days, she has to study for finals, write a research paper, and work four shifts in the university bookstore.

A few days later, you call to check on her. She still sounds stressed but appreciates the call. "Do you think you will be able to get everything done?" you ask. "Yes, I've already taken two tests that went well, but I have one more that is really important. If I don't do well, I will have to take the class over again next semester. So, I'm thinking about using one of my roommate's research papers from last year. I'll change up the words a little so it sounds like me, but it will allow me more time to study for my test. I know it's kind of dishonest, but I don't see any other way to get everything done."

Using the Key Applications from this session, what could you say or do to help Suzanne see the importance of doing the right thing? (If needed, refer to your video notes for a reminder of this session's Key Applications.)

—————————————CLOSING PRAYER—————————————

Close your time together with prayer. Share your prayer requests with one another. Ask God to help you put this week's Key Idea into practice.

JOURNAL

If your church is doing the *Believe* church-wide campaign, bring this study guide with you to church and use the following space to take notes from the pastor's or teacher's message. If your church provides an outline, consider keeping it with this guide so you will have all of your notes and thoughts from your *Believe* journey in one place.

VIDEO NOTES ANSWER KEY

reveal / teaching, rebuking, correcting, training / lamp, light / lens / understand / govern

Identity in Christ

Personal Study

Last week you considered your beliefs about the Bible. Did you learn anything new about the importance of God's Word in your life? Maybe you even gained a new love of Bible reading. That's great! This week before your group meeting, read *Believe, Chapter 5: Identity in Christ*. Then spend some time allowing the Scripture to take root in your heart and reflecting on who you are as a person.

READ

Read Believe, Chapter 5: Identity in Christ *and answer the following questions.*

1. God gave Abraham and Sarah new names to represent their new identities and their covenant with God. Looking back on the time since you first encountered God, what would your new name be if you could pick one? Why?

2. What are the main points of God's new covenant? What effect does the new covenant have on our identity?

3. As you read the passage from Hebrews 10, compare and contrast the sacrifices made to fulfill the requirements of the old covenant with the sacrifice of Jesus that sealed the new covenant.

4. As you read Romans 8:1 – 25, look for what God gives to those who find their identity in Jesus Christ.

5. Using that same passage, list all the phrases that speak to our new identity in Christ.

EVALUATE

Based on your reading from Believe, Chapter 5: Identity in Christ, *use a scale of 1 – 6 to rate how strongly you believe the statements below (1 = no belief at all, 6 = complete confidence).*

_____ I believe God loves me; therefore my life has value.

_____ I believe that I exist to know, love, and serve God.

_____ I believe God loves me, even when I do not obey him.

_____ I believe I am forgiven and accepted by God.

TAKE ACTION

Memorizing Scripture is a valuable discipline for all believers to exercise. Spend a few minutes each day committing this week's Key Verse to memory.

KEY VERSE: "Yet to all who did receive him, to those who believed in his name, he gave the right to become children of God." (John 1:12)

Recite this week's Key Idea out loud. As you do, ask yourself, "Does my life reflect this statement?"

KEY IDEA: I believe I am significant because of my position as a child of God.

Answer the following questions to help you apply this week's Key Idea to your own life.

1. How would this belief-in-action express itself in your life?

2. What visible attributes can be found in someone who finds his or her identity in Christ?

3. What behaviors or attitudes would change if you found your value in Christ rather than personal achievements?

4. How can you squash the temptation to prove your significance through performance?

Group Meeting

Welcome!

Welcome to Session 5 of *Believe*. If there are any new members in your group, take a moment to introduce yourselves to each other. Then spend a couple of minutes sharing insights or questions about this session's personal study. Now start the video!

VIDEO TEACHING NOTES

As you watch the video for Session 5, use the following outline to record some of the main points. (The answer key is found at the end of the session.)

- One of the most important indicators of your happiness and quality of life will come from the answer to this question: _____?

- Jesus offers us a new _____ when we come to faith in him.

- Key Verse: "Yet to all who did receive him, to those who believed in his name, he gave the right to become _____ of God." (John 1:12)

- Key Idea: I believe I am significant because of my position as a child of God.

- (Key Application) I am free from _____.

- (Key Application) My worth comes from my position in Christ, not my _____.

- (Key Application) I live to _____ who I am in Christ, not to _____ who I am.

- (Key Application) I can focus on _____ others up, not _____ them down.

---GETTING STARTED---

Begin your discussion by reciting the Key Verse and Key Idea together as a group. On your first attempt, use your notes if you need help. On your second attempt, try to state them completely from memory.

KEY VERSE: "Yet to all who did receive him, to those who believed in his name, he gave the right to become children of God." (John 1:12)

KEY IDEA: I believe I am significant because of my position as a child of God.

---GROUP DISCUSSION---

As a group, discuss your thoughts and feelings about the following declarations. Which statements are easy to declare with certainty? Which are more challenging, and why?

- I believe God loves me; therefore my life has value.

- I believe that I exist to know, love, and serve God.
- I believe God loves me, even when I do not obey him.
- I believe I am forgiven and accepted by God.

Based on your group's dynamics and spiritual maturity, choose the 2–3 questions that will lead to the best discussion about this week's Key Idea.

1. Unfortunately, most people find their identity and value in things that don't last (i.e., wealth, power, beauty, influence). Why is it tempting to find our worth in these fading attributes?

2. How has this chapter given you a better understanding of who you are and your purpose in this world?

3. How does understanding our identity in Christ change the way we interact with the people in our lives?

4. What thoughts, feelings, or experiences are keeping you from accepting your identity as a child of God?

Read Luke 19:1 – 9 (see the section "Our Adoption" in Believe) *and choose 1 – 2 questions that will lead to the greatest discussion in your group.*

1. In what ways did Zacchaeus's conduct change when Jesus restored his identity?

2. If you could "start over" with a new identity as Zacchaeus did, what would you leave in your past?

3. Discuss ways that our identity in Christ frees us to live without fear or anxiety.

_____

_____

_____

_____

CASE STUDY

Use the following case study as a model for a real-life situation where you might put this week's Key Idea into practice.

Sam is one of those guys who appear to be good at everything. He's highly educated, frequently promoted, a gourmet cook, and plays the ukulele. He is a model citizen, faithful husband, and coaches his kid's Little League team. You are shocked when Sam's wife asks you to pray for him. She explains that he barely sleeps at night and has been prescribed medication to control panic attacks. He has always been driven to succeed, she says, but never seems to find contentment in his achievements.

Using the Key Applications from this session, answer the following questions together as a group. (If needed, refer to your video notes for a reminder of this session's Key Applications.)

1. What could you say and do to help Sam find peace in his identity in Christ?

2. In what ways do you relate to the pressure Sam feels to succeed?

3. What practical steps can people take to adjust their identity-finding process if it's unhealthy or misguided?

CLOSING PRAYER

Close your time together with prayer. Share your prayer requests with one another. Ask God to help you put this week's Key Idea into practice.

JOURNAL

If your church is doing the *Believe* church-wide campaign, bring this study guide with you to church and use the following space to take notes from the pastor's or teacher's message. If your church provides an outline, consider keeping it with this guide so you will have all of your notes and thoughts from your *Believe* journey in one place.

VIDEO NOTES ANSWER KEY

Who am I / identity / children / condemnation / performance / express, prove / building, tearing

Church

Personal Study

Last week you read about and discussed your identity in Christ. Did you learn anything new about your place in God's kingdom? Perhaps learning about how God sees you changed how you see yourself. This week before your group meeting, read *Believe, Chapter 6: Church*. Then spend some time allowing the Scripture to take root in your heart and considering how you personally can take part in God's plan for the world.

READ

Read Believe, Chapter 6: Church *and answer the following questions.*

1. Look back over the last two stories of Abraham (see Genesis 12:1 – 9; 15:1 – 6, 7 – 21) and Peter (see Matthew 16:13 – 19). What was Abraham's response that was "credited to him as righteousness"? How did Peter respond when Jesus asked, "Who do you say I am?" How are these responses related?

2. How did God equip the the people of the early church to carry out their mission to spread the gospel of Jesus Christ?

3. As you read the story from Acts 8 about the expansion of the church, what are some of the events that show the transformation of a small group of Jesus' Jewish followers into a universal Christian church?

4. Identify some of the ways in which persecution helped the early church in its mission to share the gospel.

5. According to the passages from Ephesians 4 and Revelation 2, what key phrases define the purpose of the Christian church in the world?

EVALUATE

Based on your reading from Believe, Chapter 6: Church, *use a scale of 1–6 to rate how strongly you believe the statements below (1 = no belief at all, 6 = complete confidence).*

_____ I believe God gives spiritual gifts to every Christian for service to the church and the community.

_____ I believe that I cannot grow as a Christian unless I am an active member of a local church.

_____ I believe the community of true believers is Christ's body on earth.

_____ I believe the purpose of the church is to share the gospel and nurture Christians to maturity in Christ.

TAKE ACTION

Memorizing Scripture is a valuable discipline for all believers to exercise. Spend a few minutes each day committing this week's Key Verse to memory.

> **KEY VERSE:** "Instead, speaking the truth in love, we will grow to become in every respect the mature body of him who is the head, that is, Christ. From him the whole body, joined and held together by every supporting ligament, grows and builds itself up in love, as each part does its work." (Ephesians 4:15–16)

Recite this week's Key Idea out loud. As you do, ask yourself, "Does my life reflect this statement?"

> **KEY IDEA:** I believe the church is God's primary way to accomplish his purposes on earth.

Answer the following questions to help you apply this week's Key Idea to your own life.

1. What behaviors help you recognize someone who believes the church is God's primary way to accomplish his purposes on earth?

2. What, if anything, hinders you from fully offering your time and abilities to the mission of the church?

3. What is something you can do this week to demonstrate your belief in the church as God's primary way to accomplish his purposes on earth?

Group Meeting

Welcome!

Welcome to Session 6 of *Believe*. If there are any new members in your group, take a moment to introduce yourselves to each other. Then spend a couple of minutes sharing insights or questions about this session's personal study. Now start the video!

VIDEO TEACHING NOTES

As you watch the video segment for Session 6, use the following outline to record some of the main points. (The answer key is found at the end of the session.)

- Key Question: How will God _____ his plan?

- Key Idea: I believe the church is God's _____ way to accomplish his _____ on earth today.

- "But you will receive power when the Holy Spirit comes on you; and you will be my _____ in Jerusalem, and in all Judea and Samaria, and to the ends of the earth." (Acts 1:8)

- Key Verse: "Instead, speaking the truth in love, we will grow to become in every respect the mature _____ of him who is the head, that is, Christ. From him the whole body, joined and held together by every supporting ligament, grows and builds itself up in love, as each _____ does its work." (Ephesians 4:15–16)

- (Key Application) You belong to the body of Christ; don't go looking for _____ in all the wrong places.

- (Key Application) God will use the church to _____ his purposes in your life.

- (Key Application) God will use _____ to accomplish his purposes in the lives of others and even the world.

GETTING STARTED

Begin your discussion by reciting the Key Verse and Key Idea together as a group. On your first attempt, use your notes if you need help. On your second attempt, try to state them completely from memory.

KEY VERSE: "Instead, speaking the truth in love, we will grow to become in every respect the mature body of him who is the head, that is, Christ. From him the whole body, joined and held together by every supporting ligament, grows and builds itself up in love, as each part does its work." (Ephesians 4:15–16)

KEY IDEA: I believe the church is God's primary way to accomplish his purposes on earth.

GROUP DISCUSSION

As a group, discuss your thoughts and feelings about the following declarations. Which statements are easy to declare with certainty? Which are more challenging, and why?

- I believe God gives spiritual gifts to every Christian for service to the church and the community.

- I believe that I cannot grow as a Christian unless I am an active member of a local church.

- I believe the community of true believers is Christ's body on earth.

- I believe the purpose of the church is to share the gospel and nurture Christians to maturity in Christ.

Based on your group's dynamics and spiritual maturity, choose the 2–3 questions that will lead to the best discussion about this week's Key Idea.

1. Describe specific ways that your local church has helped you grow in spiritual maturity.

2. If it's unhealthy to live life in isolation, why do so many people choose to live that way?

3. Many people seek to find purpose and community outside of the church. In what ways could this harm the church community and hinder an individual's growth?

4. Describe three simple ways that your group could assist your local church in its redemptive mission.

Read Genesis 12:1–3 (see the section "Founding" in Believe) *and choose 1–2 questions that will lead to the greatest discussion in your group.*

1. God's covenantal promise to Abraham and his descendants was to bless them. In turn, they would be a blessing to the world. In what specific ways are these promises displayed in your church today?

2. Brainstorm some simple ways that you, your family, and your church can be a blessing to the world.

3. Discuss the ways you have seen God's blessing on your life.

---CASE STUDY---

Use the following case study as a model for a real-life situation where you might put this week's Key Idea into practice.

> Your friend Jackie has been a principal at her school for nearly two decades. When you run into her at the grocery store, you can tell that she is not her typical cheerful self. So, you ask if she is okay. Her response catches you off guard. "I'm okay, I guess. This school year has been really tough on me. In fact, each year seems to be more challenging. The kids are great! Don't misunderstand me. I'll never get tired of them. I just wish I could do more to help. You see, most of my kids come from families that are struggling on numerous levels. The parents have good intentions, but they are ill-equipped financially, relationally, and emotionally—and there is only so much we can do as educators."

Using the Key Applications from this session, what advice would you give to Jackie? (If needed, refer to your video notes for a reminder of this session's Key Applications.)

---CLOSING PRAYER---

Close your time together with prayer. Share your prayer requests with one another. Ask God to help you put this week's Key Idea into practice.

JOURNAL

If your church is doing the *Believe* church-wide campaign, bring this study guide with you to church and use the following space to take notes from the pastor's or teacher's message. If your church provides an outline, consider keeping it with this guide so you will have all of your notes and thoughts from your *Believe* journey in one place.

VIDEO NOTES ANSWER KEY

accomplish / primary, purposes / witnesses / body, part / community / accomplish / you

Humanity

Personal Study

Last week you took a deeper look at the role of the church in God's great plan. Did you recognize the part that you personally play in that plan? If you are not part of a local church, consider finding a church home — a place where you can get involved in accomplishing God's plan for the world. This week before your group meeting, read *Believe, Chapter 7: Humanity*. Then spend some time allowing the Scripture to take root in your heart and praying that God would reveal to you why it's easier for you to love some people and groups than others.

―――――READ―――――

Read Believe, Chapter 7: Humanity *and answer the following questions.*

1. Describe in your own words God's original intent for the human race.

2. What are some of the results of human sin reflected in the story of Cain and Abel in Genesis 4?

3. How is God our best defense against false teachers?

4. How does the book of Hosea show God's discipline and punishment as well as his compassion and redemption? How do you see his discipline and punishment fitting with your concept of God as a God of love?

5. How do the stories in this chapter highlight God's persistence and compassion in bringing people into a right relationship with him? Which phrases speak to you personally?

EVALUATE

Based on your reading from Believe, Chapter 7: Humanity, *use a scale of 1–6 to rate how strongly you believe the statements below (1 = no belief at all, 6 = complete confidence).*

_____ I believe that each person possesses a sinful nature and is in need of God's forgiveness.

_____ I believe we are created in the image of God and therefore have equal value, regardless of race, religion, or gender.

_____ I believe all people are loved by God; therefore, I too should love them.

_____ I believe the Holy Spirit is God and dwells in Christians to empower them to live the Christian life.

TAKE ACTION

Memorizing Scripture is a valuable discipline for all believers to exercise. Spend a few minutes each day committing this week's Key Verse to memory.

KEY VERSE: "For God so loved the world that he gave his one and only Son, that whoever believes in him shall not perish but have eternal life." (John 3:16)

Recite this week's Key Idea out loud. As you do, ask yourself, "Does my life reflect this statement?"

KEY IDEA: I believe all people are loved by God and need Jesus Christ as their Savior.

Answer the following questions to help you apply this week's Key Idea to your own life.

1. What behaviors help you recognize someone who believes all people are loved by God and need Jesus Christ as their Savior?

2. What, if anything, hinders you from fully loving people the way God loves them?

3. What is something you can do this week to demonstrate this belief?

Group Meeting

Welcome!

Welcome to Session 7 of *Believe*. If there are any new members in your group, take a moment to introduce yourselves to each other. Then spend a couple of minutes sharing insights or questions about this session's personal study. Now start the video!

---VIDEO TEACHING NOTES---

As you watch the video segment for Session 7, use the following outline to record some of the main points. (The answer key is found at the end of the session.)

- Key Question: How does God _____ people?

- Key Idea: I believe _____ people are loved by God and _____ Jesus Christ as their Savior.

- "We all, like sheep, have gone astray, each of us has turned to our own _____." (Isaiah 53:6)

- Key Verse: "For God so loved the world that he _____ his one and only Son, that whoever believes in him shall not _____ but have eternal life." (John 3:16)

- "But God demonstrates his own love for us in this: While we were still _____, Christ died for us." (Romans 5:8)

- (Key Application) I value _____ human life.

- (Key Application) I see and treat all people the way _____ sees and treats them.

- (Key Application) I am compelled to tell all people about _____.

GETTING STARTED

Begin your discussion by reciting the Key Verse and Key Idea together as a group. On your first attempt, use your notes if you need help. On your second attempt, try to state them completely from memory.

KEY VERSE: "For God so loved the world that he gave his one and only Son, that whoever believes in him shall not perish but have eternal life." (John 3:16)

KEY IDEA: I believe all people are loved by God and need Jesus Christ as their Savior.

GROUP DISCUSSION

As a group, discuss your thoughts and feelings about the following declarations. Which statements are easy to declare with certainty? Which are more challenging, and why?

- I believe that each person possesses a sinful nature and is in need of God's forgiveness.

- I believe we are created in the image of God and therefore have equal value, regardless of race, religion, or gender.

- I believe all people are loved by God; therefore, I too should love them.

- I believe God desires all people to have a relationship with Jesus Christ.

Based on your group's dynamics and spiritual maturity, choose the 2–3 questions that will lead to the best discussion of this week's Key Idea.

1. Describe the thoughts and feelings that come to mind when you hear about God's radical love for you.

2. Do you find it difficult to receive God's love and forgiveness? Why or why not?

3. What personal disciplines can we adopt that invite the Holy Spirit to change our hearts toward difficult people?

4. Describe a time when God changed your heart toward a person or people group. What specifically caused the change within you?

Read Romans 1:18 – 32 and Luke 6:27 – 36 (see the sections "The Devastating Human Condition" and "Seeing People as God Sees Them" in Believe) *and choose 1 – 2 questions that will lead to the greatest discussion in your group.*

1. What does Romans 1 reveal about humanity and the human condition?

2. How does loving our enemies show the world that we are children of God?

3. The Bible calls us to love difficult people the way God does. Is this possible? If so, how?

CASE STUDY

Use the following case study as a model for a real-life situation where you might put this week's Key Idea into practice.

Charlie, Jamie, and their two kids have been coming to church with you for the last year and a half. In the beginning they were reluctant, but now they are eagerly seeking to apply God's Word to their lives—and the changes are evident. During a lunch conversation, Charlie mentions a neighbor who has been getting on his nerves. "Honestly, I'm reluctant to say it, but I can't stand the guy. His yard is always a mess, he never makes eye contact, and we couldn't be further apart when it comes to politics. During election times, his yard is filled with signs supporting people and ideas that I think are just plain dangerous. I know we are supposed to love our neighbors as ourselves, but I'm having a hard time finding something lovable about this guy."

Using only the Key Applications from this session, what practical advice would you give to Charlie? (If needed, refer to your video notes for a reminder of this session's Key Applications.)

CLOSING PRAYER

Close your time together with prayer. Share your prayer requests with one another. Ask God to help you put this week's Key Idea into practice.

JOURNAL

If your church is doing the *Believe* church-wide campaign, bring this study guide with you to church and use the following space to take notes from the pastor's or teacher's message. If your church provides an outline, consider keeping it with this guide so you will have all of your notes and thoughts from your *Believe* journey in one place.

VIDEO NOTES ANSWER KEY

see / all, need / way / gave, perish / sinners / all / God / Jesus

Compassion

Personal Study

Last week you explored your beliefs about humanity. Were you able to identify why it's naturally easier for you to love some people more than others? Maybe you learned something about yourself or about God that will help you see others as God sees them. That's great! This week before your group meeting, read *Believe, Chapter 8: Compassion*. Then spend some time allowing the Scripture to take root in your heart and praying that God would help you develop compassion for those around you.

READ

Read Believe, Chapter 8: Compassion *and answer the following questions.*

1. As you read the account from Nehemiah 9, look for some of the ways God showed both compassion and justice to the Israelites.

2. As you read the selected passages from Deuteronomy 24 and 25, look for some of the principles behind the laws Moses gave to govern how the Israelites were to treat others.

3. How did Boaz express his faith when he helped Ruth and Naomi? What was the motivation behind his acts of compassion?

4. In your own words, describe how love for God and love for others are related.

5. What are the attitudes that James advocates? How can you adopt those same attitudes?

EVALUATE

Based on your reading from Believe, Chapter 8: Compassion, *use a scale of 1 – 6 to rate how strongly you believe the statements below (1 = no belief at all, 6 = complete confidence).*

_____ I believe that God calls me to be involved in the lives of the poor and suffering.

_____ I believe I am responsible before God to show compassion to the sick and imprisoned.

_____ I believe that I should stand up for those who cannot stand up for themselves.

_____ I believe that Christians should not purchase everything they can afford, so that their discretionary money might be available to help those in need.

---TAKE ACTION---

Memorizing Scripture is a valuable discipline for all believers to exercise. Spend a few minutes each day committing this week's Key Verse to memory.

KEY VERSE: "Defend the weak and the fatherless; uphold the cause of the poor and the oppressed. Rescue the weak and the needy; deliver them from the hand of the wicked." (Psalm 82:3–4)

Recite this week's Key Idea out loud. As you do, ask yourself, "Does my life reflect this statement?"

KEY IDEA: I believe God calls all Christians to show compassion to people in need.

Answer the following questions to help you apply this week's Key Idea to your own life.

1. What behaviors help you recognize someone who believes he or she is called by God to show compassion to those in need?

2. What, if anything, hinders you from showing compassion to those in need?

3. What is something you can do this week to demonstrate this belief?

Group Meeting

Welcome!

Welcome to Session 8 of *Believe*. If there are any new members in your group, take a moment to introduce yourselves to each other. Then spend a couple of minutes sharing insights or questions about this session's personal study. Now start the video!

---VIDEO TEACHING NOTES---

As you watch the video segment for Session 8, use the following outline to record some of the main points. (The answer key is found at the end of the session.)

- Key Question: What about the poor and _____?

- Key Idea: I believe God calls all Christians to show _____ to people in need.

- Key Verse: "_____ the weak and the fatherless; uphold the cause of the poor and the oppressed. _____ the weak and the needy; _____ them from the hand of the wicked." (Psalm 82:3–4)

- "Religion that God our Father _____ as pure and faultless is this: to look after orphans and widows in their distress." (James 1:27)

- The right question is not "Who is my neighbor?" but "Who _____ to be a neighbor?"

- As a Christian, the plight of the poor, oppressed, abandoned and needy is _____ problem.

- (Key Application) I will do unto others, as I would have _____ do unto me.

- (Key Application) People do not _____ how much I know, until they know how much I care.

- When people cry out, "Where is God when it comes to the poor and injustice on the earth?" the answer should be, "Look at God's people. They are right in the _____ of it."

GETTING STARTED

Begin your discussion by reciting the Key Verse and Key Idea together as a group. On your first attempt, use your notes if you need help. On your second attempt, try to state them completely from memory.

KEY VERSE: "Defend the weak and the fatherless; uphold the cause of the poor and the oppressed. Rescue the weak and the needy; deliver them from the hand of the wicked." (Psalm 82:3–4)

KEY IDEA: I believe God calls all Christians to show compassion to people in need.

GROUP DISCUSSION

As a group, discuss your thoughts and feelings about the following declarations. Which statements are easy to declare with certainty? Which are more challenging, and why?

- I believe that God calls me to be involved in the lives of the poor and suffering.

- I believe I am responsible before God to show compassion to the sick and imprisoned.

- I believe that I should stand up for those who cannot stand up for themselves.

- I believe that Christians should not purchase everything they can afford, so that their discretionary money might be available to help those in need.

Based on your group's dynamics and spiritual maturity, choose the 2–3 questions that will lead to the best discussion of this week's Key Idea.

1. In what ways have you experienced compassion from a family member, friend, or stranger?

2. What is the difference between trying to "fix" poverty and injustice and "suffering with" someone who is experiencing it?

3. In addition to a financial gesture, what other compassionate ways are there to comfort someone in need?

4. In what ways can debt and financial stress hinder compassionate generosity? What would it look like to strategically budget, so that an individual is equipped to act generously in times of need and injustice?

Read Deuteronomy 24:10–15, 17–22 (see the section "Israel: Called to Compassion" in Believe) *and choose 1–2 questions that will lead to the greatest discussion in your group.*

1. Are you aware of any weak, needy, oppressed, or fatherless people in your community? If not, what steps can you take to raise your awareness? If so, discuss what can be done to "defend" and support them.

2. Pick a specific situation (i.e., widow, orphan, refugee, homeless person, addict) and discuss what it would look like to "suffer with" the individual in need.

3. List some reasons why many people choose to ignore the needy and oppressed. Then discuss what it would take to break free from the status quo and be a defender of the weak and oppressed.

CASE STUDY

Use the following case study as a model for a real-life situation where you might put this week's Key Idea into practice.

> Cassandra has worked hard to get where she is in life. She grew up in a big family with a meager income but has found a way to be successful despite her modest beginnings. You have been working out together for two years. Before you leave the gym, you always end your time in prayer together. A few days ago, she told you about her brother who has fallen on hard times. She has been avoiding his calls because she doesn't know what to say or how to "fix" his financial problems.

Using the Key Applications from this session, what practical advice would you give Cassandra? (If needed, refer to your video notes for a reminder of this session's Key Applications.)

CLOSING PRAYER

Close your time together with prayer. Share your prayer requests with one another. Ask God to help you put this week's Key Idea into practice.

JOURNAL

If your church is doing the *Believe* church-wide campaign, bring this study guide with you to church and use the following space to take notes from the pastor's or teacher's message. If your church provides an outline, consider keeping it with this guide so you will have all of your notes and thoughts from your *Believe* journey in one place.

VIDEO NOTES ANSWER KEY

injustice / compassion / Defend, Rescue, deliver / accepts / proved / my / them / care / middle

Stewardship

Personal Study

Last week you took a deeper look at your beliefs about compassion. Did you learn anything new that might make you feel more compassionate toward other people? Maybe you recognized a situation in your own life when someone showed you compassion. This week before your group meeting, read *Believe, Chapter 9: Stewardship*. Then spend some time allowing the Scripture to take root in your heart and identifying some areas in your life where you might become a better steward.

————————————READ————————————

Read Believe, Chapter 9: Stewardship *and answer the following questions.*

1. As you read the passage from Psalm 50, ponder this question: If God is self-sufficient, why do we have to return a portion of our wealth to him?

2. What are the key identifiers of "good stewardship"? How does God reward good stewardship of his resources?

3. Contrast the lifestyle of someone who loves money with that of someone who loves God.

4. Why are we encouraged to practice hospitality? Why is hospitality important to God?

5. List some of the things God has entrusted to you to manage. How are you doing in each of these areas? How can you improve your stewardship of them?

EVALUATE

Based on your reading from Believe, Chapter 9: Stewardship, *use a scale of 1 – 6 to rate how strongly you believe the statements below (1 = no belief at all, 6 = complete confidence).*

_____ I believe that everything I am or own comes from God and belongs to God.

_____ I believe that a Christian should live a sacrificial life, not driven by pursuit of material things.

_____ I believe that Christians should give at least 10 percent of their income to God's work.

_____ I believe God will bless Christians now and in the life to come for their good works.

TAKE ACTION

Memorizing Scripture is a valuable discipline for all believers to exercise. Spend a few minutes each day committing this week's Key Verse to memory.

KEY VERSE: "The earth is the LORD's, and everything in it, the world, and all who live in it; for he founded it on the seas and established it on the waters." (Psalm 24:1-2)

Recite this week's Key Idea out loud. As you do, ask yourself, "Does my life reflect this statement?"

KEY IDEA: I believe that everything I am and everything I own belong to God.

Answer the following questions to help you apply this week's Key Idea to your own life.

1. What behaviors help you recognize someone who believes that everything belongs to God?

2. What, if anything, hinders you from practicing good stewardship?

3. What is something you can do this week to demonstrate this belief?

Group Meeting

Welcome!

Welcome to Session 9 of *Believe*. If there are any new members in your group, take a moment to introduce yourselves to each other. Then spend a couple of minutes sharing insights or questions about this session's personal study. Now start the video!

VIDEO TEACHING NOTES

As you watch the video segment for Session 9, use the following outline to record some of the main points. (The answer key is found at the end of the session.)

- Key Question: What is God's _____ on my life?

- Key Idea: I believe everything I am and everything I own _____ to God.

- Key Verse: "The earth is the LORD's, and _____ in it, the world, and all who live in it; for he founded it on the seas and established it on the waters." (Psalm 24:1-2)

- Everything belongs to and is owned by the Lord, the maker and creator of everything. He has the patent, the intellectual property rights, and the deed to _____.

- Christians recognize they are not _____ who make contributions to God, but rather managers of everything we are and own.

- (Key Application) I move from owner to _____.

- (Key Application) What does God want me to _____ with what he has given me?

- Being a manager is so much more _____ than being an owner.

- I _____ over the deed of my house and life to God.

GETTING STARTED

Begin your discussion by reciting the Key Verse and Key Idea together as a group. On your first attempt, use your notes if you need help. On your second attempt, try to state them completely from memory.

KEY VERSE: "The earth is the LORD's, and everything in it, the world, and all who live in it; for he founded it on the seas and established it on the waters." (Psalm 24:1-2)

KEY IDEA: I believe that everything I am and everything I own belong to God.

GROUP DISCUSSION

As a group, discuss your thoughts and feelings about the following declarations. Which statements are easy to declare with certainty? Which are more challenging, and why?

- I believe that everything I am or own comes from God and belongs to God.
- I believe that a Christian should live a sacrificial life, not driven by pursuit of material things.

- I believe that Christians should give at least 10 percent of their income to God's work.
- I believe God will bless Christians now and in the life to come for their good works.

Based on your group's dynamics and spiritual maturity, choose the 2–3 questions that will lead to the best discussion of this week's Key Idea.

1. Discuss the benefits of good stewardship principles and the ramifications that arise when they are ignored.

2. How would seeing yourself as a manager of God's property, rather than an owner of personal possessions, change the way you approach your daily life?

3. Commonly, one of the first words a child speaks is "mine." What does that tell us about human nature? How does that's-mine thinking hinder good stewardship?

4. In what ways, if any, has good stewardship rewarded you financially, emotionally, or spiritually?

Read Mark 12:41 – 44 (see the section "… Of Their Money" in Believe) *and choose 1 – 2 questions that will lead to the greatest discussion in your group.*

1. Based on what you just read, what seems to be most important to God when it comes to the act of giving?

2. Can the poor widow's example be emulated if you are a person of wealth? If so, how?

3. Who in your life has the poor widow's mentality toward their possessions? What specifically did they do that caught your attention?

---CASE STUDY---

Use the following case study as a model for a real-life situation where you might put this week's Key Idea into practice.

> Financial stress has forced Sophia to sell her house and purchase a small loft in the city. Although she knows this move is the wisest thing for her to do, she admits that having to downsize makes her feel like a failure. Although her new loft only has room for half of her things, she can't seem to let any of her possessions go.

Using the Key Applications of this chapter, what practical advice would you give Sophia? (If needed, refer to your video notes for a reminder of this session's Key Applications.)

---CLOSING PRAYER---

Close your time together with prayer. Share your prayer requests with one another. Ask God to help you put this week's Key Idea into practice.

---JOURNAL---

If your church is doing the *Believe* church-wide campaign, bring this study guide with you to church and use the following space to take notes from the pastor's or teacher's message. If your church provides an outline, consider keeping it with this guide so you will have all of your notes and thoughts from your *Believe* journey in one place.

---VIDEO NOTES ANSWER KEY---

call / belongs / everything / everything / owners / manager / do / freeing / sign

Eternity

Personal Study

Last week you explored ways you can be a good steward of what God has entrusted to you. Did you find any areas in your own life where you could be a better steward? Maybe you recognized for the first time how we are all called to take care of God's creation. This week before your group meeting, read *Believe, Chapter 10: Eternity*. Then spend some time allowing the Scripture to take root in your heart and considering your own beliefs about the life that is to come.

---------------------------------**READ**---------------------------------

Read Believe, Chapter 10: Eternity *and answer the following questions.*

1. Given the fact that the afterlife was not talked about much in the Old Testament, why do you think the prophets insisted on looking for Elijah? How would you have responded if you were there?

2. Having a person come back from the dead to tell you what they experienced on the other side would seem rather compelling. Why did Abraham disagree?

3. How will our resurrected bodies be different from our earthly bodies? How does what the Bible says compare with some of the popular notions of what we'll be like in heaven?

4. As you read the passages from 1 Thessalonians 4 – 5 and 2 Peter 3, look for ways we are encouraged to live our lives today considering Christ's imminent return.

5. As you ponder eternal life in the garden on the new earth without the presence of sin, hatred, strife, war, or death, what do you most look forward to?

——EVALUATE——

Based on your reading from Believe, Chapter 10: Eternity, *use a scale of 1 – 6 to rate how strongly you believe the statements below (1 = no belief at all, 6 = complete confidence).*

_____ I believe it is important to share the gospel with my neighbor because Christ has commanded me to do so.

_____ I believe that people who deliberately reject Jesus Christ as Savior will not inherit eternal life.

_____ I believe that every person is subject to the judgment of God.

_____ I believe all people who place their trust in Jesus Christ will spend eternity in heaven.

---TAKE ACTION---

Memorizing Scripture is a valuable discipline for all believers to exercise. Spend a few minutes each day committing this week's Key Verse to memory.

KEY VERSE: "Do not let your hearts be troubled. You believe in God; believe also in me. My Father's house has many rooms; if that were not so, would I have told you that I am going there to prepare a place for you?" (John 14:1–2)

Recite this week's Key Idea out loud. As you do, ask yourself, "Does my life reflect this statement?"

KEY IDEA: I believe there is a heaven and a hell and that Jesus will return to judge all people and to establish his eternal kingdom.

Answer the following questions to help you apply this week's Key Idea to your own life.

1. What behaviors help you recognize someone who believes Jesus will return to judge all people and to establish his eternal kingdom?

2. What, if anything, hinders you from believing in the afterlife?

3. What is something you can do this week to demonstrate this belief?

Group Meeting

Welcome!

Welcome to Session 10 of *Believe*. If there are any new members in your group, take a moment to introduce yourselves to each other. Then spend a couple of minutes sharing insights or questions about this session's personal study. Now start the video!

—————VIDEO TEACHING NOTES—————

As you watch the video segment for Session 10, use the following outline to record some of the main points. (The answer key is found at the end of the session.)

- Key Question: What happens _____?

- Key Idea: I believe there is a heaven and a hell and that Jesus will return to judge all people and to establish his _____ kingdom.

- "When the LORD was about to take Elijah up to _____ in a whirl-wind, Elijah and Elisha were on their way from Gilgal." (2 Kings 2:1)

- When our body exhales its final breath, our spirit exits the body and goes to one of two places—_____ or _____.

- Key Verse: "Do not let your hearts be troubled. You believe in God; believe also in me. My Father's house has many rooms; if that were not so, would I have told you that I am going there to prepare a _____ for you?" (John 14:1–2)

- (Key Application) Live with _____ every day, regardless of the circum-stances around us. Life can get better here, but even if it doesn't, his home awaits us.

- (Key Application) Love people with freedom and boldness, because our future is _____ in him.

- (Key Application) Lead more people into a relationship with Christ, because we want to _____ this great hope with others.

GETTING STARTED

Begin your discussion by reciting the Key Verse and Key Idea together as a group. On your first attempt, use your notes if you need help. On your second attempt, try to state them completely from memory.

KEY VERSE: "Do not let your hearts be troubled. You believe in God; believe also in me. My Father's house has many rooms; if that were not so, would I have told you that I am going there to prepare a place for you?" (John 14:1–2)

KEY IDEA: I believe there is a heaven and a hell and that Jesus will return to judge all people and to establish his eternal kingdom.

GROUP DISCUSSION

As a group, discuss your thoughts and feelings about the following declarations. Which statements are easy to declare with certainty? Which are more challenging, and why?

- I believe it is important to share the gospel with my neighbor because Christ has commanded me to do so.

- I believe that people who deliberately reject Jesus Christ as Savior will not inherit eternal life.

- I believe that every person is subject to the judgment of God.

- I believe all people who place their trust in Jesus Christ will spend eternity in heaven.

Based on your group's dynamics and spiritual maturity, choose the 2–3 questions that will lead to the best discussion of this week's Key Idea.

1. Describe the moment you became aware of your mortality and pondered what would happen after your death.

2. What is it about heaven that brings you hope? What about it is uncertain? What about it brings you freedom?

3. What is it about the life, death, and resurrection of Jesus that led you to put your faith in him?

4. How does having a secured future in heaven affect the way you live your life in the present?

Read 1 Corinthians 15:1 – 28, 35 – 58 (see the section "The Resurrection" in Believe) *and choose 1 – 2 questions that will lead to the greatest discussion in your group.*

1. Paul seems to be refuting the teachings of other religious leaders in Corinth who claimed there was no resurrection of the dead. In what ways does this belief clash with the gospel of Jesus Christ?

2. Our belief in eternity gives us hope. How would this change if there were no resurrection of the dead?

3. Why do you think Paul (the author of 1 Corinthians) refers to Christians who have died as "those that have fallen asleep"? How does this reflect his belief in eternity?

---CASE STUDY---

Use the following case study as a model for a real-life situation where you might put this week's Key Idea into practice.

> Your neighbor's brother was tragically killed in a recent car accident. Rhonda has always been a great neighbor and good friend. In order to show your condolences, you stop by her house with sympathetic words and a bouquet of flowers. You've never discussed religion before, but this accident has shaken her up. She asks you, "What do you think happens after we die?"

Using the Key Applications of this chapter, how would you answer Rhonda's question? (If needed, refer to your video notes for a reminder of this session's Key Applications.)

---CLOSING PRAYER---

Close your time together with prayer. Share your prayer requests with one another. Ask God to help you put this week's Key Idea into practice.

---JOURNAL---

If your church is doing the *Believe* church-wide campaign, bring this study guide with you to church and use the following space to take notes from the pastor's or teacher's message. If your church provides an outline, consider keeping it with this guide so you will have all of your notes and thoughts from your *Believe* journey in one place.

VIDEO NOTES ANSWER KEY

next / eternal / heaven / heaven, hell / place / hope / secure / share

Worship

Personal Study

Last week you examined your beliefs about eternity. Perhaps you were challenged to share your faith with someone who is far from God. This week we shift our attention from Christian beliefs to spiritual practices. Before your group meeting, read *Believe, Chapter 11: Worship*. Then take some time to prepare your heart for the lessons God wants to teach you.

READ

Read Believe, Chapter 11: Worship *and answer the following questions.*

1. What does the passage from Psalm 95 tell us about how and why we should worship God?

2. As you read the passage from Matthew 23, ponder this question: With what behaviors and attitudes of the Pharisees did Jesus take issue? (Hint: Jesus introduced each one with the words "Woe to you.")

3. What effect did Daniel's bold worship have on the unbelieving King Darius? In what ways do you think our modern-day worship could have that same effect?

4. Why do you think God desires for us to worship him when we are in a difficult situation? When was the last time you worshiped God when it might not have immediately made sense to do so?

5. According to the apostle Paul, what was the centerpiece of New Testament worship? What attitudes and actions constituted proper worship?

---------------------------------------**EVALUATE**---------------------------------------

Based on your reading from Believe, Chapter 11: Worship, *use a scale of 1–6 to rate how well you are living out the statements below (1 = not living out at all, 6 = living out completely).*

_____ I thank God daily for who he is and what he is doing in my life.

_____ I attend religious services and worship with other believers each week.

_____ I give God the credit for all that I am and all that I possess.

_____ I am not ashamed for others to know that I worship God.

TAKE ACTION

Memorizing Scripture is a valuable discipline for all believers to exercise. Spend a few minutes each day committing this week's Key Verse to memory.

KEY VERSE: "Come, let us sing for joy to the LORD; let us shout aloud to the Rock of our salvation. Let us come before him with thanksgiving and extol him with music and song." (Psalm 95:1–2)

Recite this week's Key Idea out loud. As you do, ask yourself, "Does my life reflect this statement?"

KEY IDEA: I worship God for who he is and what he has done for me.

Answer the following questions to help you apply this week's Key Idea to your own life.

1. How could this practice express itself in your life?

2. What visible attributes can be found in someone committed to the practice of worship?

3. What is impeding your ability to make worship part of your everyday activity? How can you overcome this obstacle?

4. What action step can you take this week to give God more honor and praise?

Group Meeting

Welcome!

Welcome to Session 11 of *Believe*. If there are any new members in your group, take a moment to introduce yourselves to each other. Then spend a couple of minutes sharing insights or questions about this session's personal study. Now start the video!

─────VIDEO TEACHING NOTES─────

As you watch the video segment for Session 11, use the following outline to record some of the main points. (The answer key is found at the end of the session.)

- Key Question: How do I honor God in the way he _____?

- Key Idea: I worship God for _____ he is and what he has _____ for me.

- Key Verse: "Come, let us sing for joy to the LORD; let us shout aloud to the Rock of our salvation. Let us come before him with _____ and extol him with music and song." (Psalm 95:1–2)

- (Key Application) I _____ acknowledge God for who he is and what he has done for me.

- (Key Application) I worship God, _____ and _____, with the songs I sing, the words I speak, and the way I live my life.

- (Key Application) When I attribute _____ to God as a child of God, unmerited worth is attributed to me.

GETTING STARTED

Begin your discussion by reciting the Key Verse and Key Idea together as a group. On your first attempt, use your notes if you need help. On your second attempt, try to state them completely from memory.

KEY VERSE: "Come, let us sing for joy to the LORD; let us shout aloud to the Rock of our salvation. Let us come before him with thanksgiving and extol him with music and song." (Psalm 95:1–2)

KEY IDEA: I worship God for who he is and what he has done for me.

GROUP DISCUSSION

As a group, discuss your thoughts and feelings about the following declarations. Which statements are easy to declare with certainty? Which are more challenging, and why?

- I thank God daily for who he is and what he is doing in my life.
- I attend religious services and worship with other believers each week.
- I give God the credit for all that I am and all that I possess.
- I am not ashamed for others to know that I worship God.

Based on your group's dynamics and spiritual maturity, choose the 2–3 questions that will lead to the best discussion about this week's Key Idea.

1. As a group, make a list of different ways that worship can be expressed to God.

2. What about God's character compels you to give him your worship?

3. Discuss which worship song lyrics best describe your thoughts and feelings about God.

4. In what diverse ways do you see your fellow group members expressing worship to God?

Read Matthew 23:1 – 28 (see the section "The Heart's Intent" in Believe) _and choose 1 – 2 questions that will lead to the greatest discussion in your group._

1. In what ways can worship become a heartless ritual?

2. What can we learn from Jesus' rebuke of the Pharisees? How do we keep ourselves from making the same mistake?

3. What has God done in your life that produced a desire to worship him?

CASE STUDY

Use the following case study as a model for a real-life situation where you might put this week's Key Idea into practice.

You became friends with Tiago three years ago when your sons started playing soccer together. As you cheer the boys on, your conversations often lead to serious topics, such as faith, politics, and college football. He describes himself as a spiritual person who keeps his beliefs private. He occasionally says, "I've never felt the need to make my faith public. What's the point?"

Using the Key Applications from this session, what could you say or do to help Tiago? (If needed, refer to your video notes for a reminder of this session's Key Applications.)

CLOSING PRAYER

Close your time together with prayer. Share your prayer requests with one another. Ask God to help you put this week's Key Idea into practice.

JOURNAL

If your church is doing the *Believe* church-wide campaign, bring this study guide with you to church and use the following space to take notes from the pastor's or teacher's message. If your church provides an outline, consider keeping it with this guide so you will have all of your notes and thoughts from your *Believe* journey in one place.

VIDEO NOTES ANSWER KEY

deserves / who, done / thanksgiving / daily / privately, corporately / worth

Prayer

Personal Study

Last week you examined the practice of worship. Perhaps your definition of worship was expanded and enhanced. This week before your group meeting, read *Believe, Chapter 12: Prayer*. Then take some time to allow the Scripture to challenge your thoughts about communication with God.

---READ---

Read Believe, Chapter 12: Prayer *and answer the following questions.*

1. Notice how Jesus prayed before and after each major event in his life. What can we learn from this pattern of prayer Jesus demonstrated?

2. What can we learn about prayer from the psalmist and Solomon?

3. What do Gideon's interactions with God teach us about God's character?

4. In the passage from Luke 11, what are the main points of Jesus' teaching about prayer?

5. How do Paul's words about prayer encourage you? How do they challenge you?

EVALUATE

Based on your reading from Believe, Chapter 12: Prayer, *use a scale of 1 – 6 to rate how well you are living out the statements below (1 = not living out at all, 6 = living out completely).*

_____ I seek God's will through prayer.

_____ I regularly confess my sins to God.

_____ Prayer is a central part of my daily life.

_____ I seek to grow closer to God by listening to him in prayer.

TAKE ACTION

Memorizing Scripture is a valuable discipline for all believers to exercise. Spend a few minutes each day committing this week's Key Verse to memory.

KEY VERSE: "If I had cherished sin in my heart, the Lord would not have listened; but God has surely listened and has heard my prayer. Praise be to God, who has not rejected my prayer or withheld his love from me!" (Psalm 66:18 – 20)

—————————————— 8———★ ——————————————

Recite this week's Key Idea out loud. As you do, ask yourself, "Does my life reflect this statement?"

KEY IDEA: I pray to God to know him, to find direction for my life and to lay my requests before him.

Answer the following questions to help you apply this week's Key Idea to your own life.

1. How could this practice be applied in your life?

2. What visible attributes can be found in someone who regularly connects with God through prayer?

3. What is impeding your ability to communicate with God? How can you overcome these obstacles?

4. What action step can you take this week to develop your connection with God through prayer?

Group Meeting

Welcome!

Welcome to Session 12 of *Believe*. If there are any new members in your group, take a moment to introduce yourselves to each other. Then spend a couple of minutes sharing insights or questions about this session's personal study. Now start the video!

---VIDEO TEACHING NOTES---

As you watch the video segment for Session 12, use the following outline to record some of the main points. (The answer key is found at the end of the session.)

- Key Question: How do I grow by _____ with God?

- Key Idea: I pray to God to _____ him, to _____ direction for my life and to _____ my requests before him.

- "Watch _____ and then simply do what he does."

- It is completely _____ for us to lay our requests before God.

- Like Jesus, we should seek to _____ our lives to God's will, versus asking God to align his life to our will.

- Key Verse: "If I had cherished sin in my heart, the Lord would not have listened; but God has surely listened and has heard my _____. Praise be to God, who has not rejected my prayer or withheld his love from me!" (Psalm 66:18–20)

- (Key Application) I _____ to align my life to God's will.

- (Key Application) I pray to lay my _____ before God to find peace.

- (Key Application) I won't make any major decision in my life without _____ God through prayer.

GETTING STARTED

Begin your discussion by reciting the Key Verse and Key Idea together as a group. On your first attempt, use your notes if you need help. On your second attempt, try to state them completely from memory.

KEY VERSE: "If I had cherished sin in my heart, the Lord would not have listened; but God has surely listened and has heard my prayer. Praise be to God, who has not rejected my prayer or withheld his love from me!" (Psalm 66:18–20)

KEY IDEA: I pray to God to know him, to find direction for my life and to lay my requests before him.

GROUP DISCUSSION

As a group, discuss your thoughts and feelings about the following declarations. Which statements are easy to declare with certainty? Which are more challenging, and why?

- I seek God's will through prayer.
- I regularly confess my sins to God.
- Prayer is a central part of my daily life.
- I seek to grow closer to God by listening to him in prayer.

Based on your group's dynamics and spiritual maturity, choose the 2–3 questions that will lead to the best discussion about this week's Key Idea.

1. What aspect of prayer do you find to be the most challenging? Helpful? Rewarding?

2. How has the act of prayer helped you know and understand God better?

3. In what ways have you seen and experienced the power of prayer at work?

4. As a group, describe the different ways you have seen God answer specific prayer requests.

Read Mark 1:32 – 35, Luke 6:12 – 16, and Matthew 26:36 – 39 (see the section "The Model Prayer Life" in Believe) *and choose 1 – 2 questions that will lead to the greatest discussion in your group.*

1. What specifically inspires you when you examine Jesus' dependence on, confidence in, and commitment to unceasing prayer?

2. In what ways has prayer helped you navigate the tough decisions that life throws at us?

3. What is one aspect of Jesus' prayer life that you would like to emulate?

─────────────── CASE STUDY ───────────────

Use the following case study as a model for a real-life situation where you might put this week's Key Idea into practice.

Gabe has been offered an opportunity to join an exciting start-up company. His existing job pays well and provides great benefits, but he has been bored and uninspired by the mundane tasks he performs. This new opportunity could bring the excitement and creativity he has been longing to find, but it comes with significant financial risk.

Using the Key Applications from this session, what could you say or do to help Gabe? (If needed, refer to your video notes for a reminder of this session's Key Applications.)

CLOSING PRAYER

Close your time together with prayer. Share your prayer requests with one another. Ask God to help you put this week's Key Idea into practice.

JOURNAL

If your church is doing the *Believe* church-wide campaign, bring this study guide with you to church and use the following space to take notes from the pastor's or teacher's message. If your church provides an outline, consider keeping it with this guide so you will have all of your notes and thoughts from your *Believe* journey in one place.

VIDEO NOTES ANSWER KEY

communicating / know, find, lay / Jesus / acceptable / align / prayer / pray / burdens / seeking

Bible Study

Personal Study

Last week you examined the practice of prayer. Perhaps you were challenged to seek God's guidance and wisdom by communicating more frequently with him. This week before your group meeting, read *Believe, Chapter 13: Bible Study*. Then take some time to ask God to speak to you through this session.

READ

Read Believe, Chapter 13: Bible Study *and answer the following questions.*

1. Nehemiah 7 – 9 is a touching account of Israel's return to God's Word. In light of this and your own experiences, what are the benefits of studying God's Word in community?

2. What is the difference between studying God's Word and hiding it in our hearts? What is the difference between reading God's Word and meditating on it day and night?

3. Jesus refers to four types of soil on which the seed of his Word falls. Which type best describes you right now? Was there a time when you would have answered differently?

_____

_____

_____

4. As you read the passages from John 14 and 1 Corinthians 2, look for the ways the Holy Spirit helps us understand Scripture.

_____

_____

_____

5. Reflect on the Key Verse at the beginning of this chapter. According to the author, the Word of God is like a double-edged sword; it gets under our skin and speaks directly to our hearts. In what ways have you experienced this?

_____

_____

_____

—EVALUATE—

Based on your reading from Believe, Chapter 13: Bible Study, *use a scale a 1 – 6 to rate how well you are living out the statements below (1 = not living out at all, 6 = living out completely).*

_____ I read the Bible daily.

_____ I regularly study the Bible to find direction for my life.

_____ I seek to be obedient to God by applying the truth of the Bible to my life.

_____ I have a good understanding of the contents of the Bible.

---TAKE ACTION---

Memorizing Scripture is a valuable discipline for all believers to exercise. Spend a few minutes each day committing this week's Key Verse to memory.

KEY VERSE: "For the word of God is alive and active. Sharper than any double-edged sword, it penetrates even to dividing soul and spirit, joints and marrow; it judges the thoughts and attitudes of the heart." (Hebrews 4:12)

Recite this week's Key Idea out loud. As you do, ask yourself, "Does my life reflect this statement?"

KEY IDEA: I study the Bible to know God and his truth and to find direction for my daily life.

Answer the following questions to help you apply this week's Key Idea to your own life.

1. How could this practice express itself in your life?

2. What visible attributes can be found in someone who regularly engages in Bible study?

3. What is impeding your ability to consistently engage in Bible study? How can you overcome this obstacle?

4. What action step can you take this week to make Bible study a greater part of your daily life?

Group Meeting

Welcome!

Welcome to Session 13 of *Believe*. If there are any new members in your group, take a moment to introduce yourselves to each other. Then spend a couple of minutes sharing insights or questions about this session's personal study. Now start the video!

VIDEO TEACHING NOTES

As you watch the video segment for Session 13, use the following outline to record some of the main points. (The answer key is found at the end of the session.)

- Key Question: _____ do I study God's Word?

- Key Idea: I study the Bible to _____ God and his _____ and to find _____ for my daily life.

- "Whoever has ears to hear, let them _____." (Matthew 13:9)

- Key Verse: "For the word of God is alive and active. Sharper than any double-edged sword, it penetrates even to dividing soul and spirit, joints and marrow; it judges the thoughts and _____ of the heart." (Hebrews 4:12)

- The Bible can go deep if the _____ is willing to receive it.

- (Key Application) Keep your heart soft and _____ to God's Word.

- (Key Application) Understand the one _____ of the Bible.

- (Key Application) Study God's Word in _____.

- (Key Application) _____ God's Word.

GETTING STARTED

Begin your discussion by reciting the Key Verse and Key Idea together as a group. On your first attempt, use your notes if you need help. On your second attempt, try to state them completely from memory.

KEY VERSE: "For the word of God is alive and active. Sharper than any double-edged sword, it penetrates even to dividing soul and spirit, joints and marrow; it judges the thoughts and attitudes of the heart." (Hebrews 4:12)

KEY IDEA: I study the Bible to know God and his truth and to find direction for my daily life.

GROUP DISCUSSION

As a group, discuss your thoughts and feelings about the following declarations. Which statements are easy to declare with certainty? Which are more challenging, and why?

- I read the Bible daily.
- I regularly study the Bible to find direction for my life.
- I seek to be obedient to God by applying the truth of the Bible to my life.
- I have a good understanding of the contents of the Bible.

Based on your group's dynamics and spiritual maturity, choose the 2 – 3 questions that will lead to the best discussion about this week's Key Idea.

1. As a group, make a list of reasons or motivations someone could possess for studying the Bible. Discuss which reasons are most compelling.

2. What obstacles usually hinder a person from practicing consistent Bible study? Discuss ways to overcome these challenges.

3. In what ways has the Bible proven a trustworthy map for navigating decisions in your life?

_____

_____

4. Many tools — devotionals, commentaries, reading plans, etc. — can help people get the most out of their Bible reading. As a group, discuss some of the tools that you have found helpful.

_____

_____

Read Psalm 119:9 – 24 (see the section "The Road Map for Living" in Believe) _and choose 1 – 2 questions that will lead to the greatest discussion in your group._

1. What are some practical ways to "hide God's word in your heart"?

_____

_____

_____

2. In what ways has God's Word been a "lamp for your feet and a light on your path"?

_____

_____

_____

3. The psalmist declares that he loves God's laws and precepts. Why do you think he feels this way?

_____

_____

_____

CASE STUDY

Use the following case study as a model for a real-life situation where you might put this week's Key Idea into practice.

Parker is a promising collegian—smart, talented, and charming. Unfortunately, his compulsive, free-spirited nature often leads him to make foolish decisions. Now that he is entering manhood, the consequences of his actions have become more severe.

He grew up going to church but confesses that he has never been committed to reading the Bible for himself. Because he considers you a role model, he asks, "Can you help me? I don't know what I need to do to get my life on track, but I know that what I'm doing isn't working."

Using the Key Applications from this session, what could you say or do to help Parker find the direction he is looking for in life? (If needed, refer to your video notes for a reminder of this session's Key Applications.)

CLOSING PRAYER

Close your time together with prayer. Share your prayer requests with one another. Ask God to help you put this week's Key Idea into practice.

JOURNAL

If your church is doing the *Believe* church-wide campaign, bring this study guide with you to church and use the following space to take notes from the pastor's or teacher's message. If your church provides an outline, consider keeping it with this guide so you will have all of your notes and thoughts from your *Believe* journey in one place.

VIDEO NOTES ANSWER KEY

How / know, truth, direction / hear / attitudes / heart / receptive / story / community / Memorize

Single-Mindedness

Personal Study

Last week you examined your commitment to the practice of Bible study. Perhaps you learned something about yourself or the Word of God that was new to you. This week before your group meeting, read *Believe, Chapter 14: Single-Mindedness*. Then spend some time allowing the Scripture to take root in your heart and evaluating how much you focus on God in your daily life.

READ

Read Believe, Chapter 14: Single-Mindedness *and answer the following questions.*

1. As you read the passage from Deuteronomy 6, look for what God promised to the Israelites if they obeyed the first commandment and kept their covenant with him.

2. What kind of "treasure" keeps us from being single-minded? How can "unhealthy eyes" keep us from being single-minded? Why isn't it possible to serve two masters?

3. In the passage from 2 Chronicles 20, identify the key beliefs in which Jehoshaphat anchors his prayer. How can these key beliefs instill confidence and guide our decisions?

4. Can you list some of the things that distract you from putting God first in your life? What can you do to become more focused on God?

5. Paul writes, "Whatever you do, whether in word or deed, do it all in the name of the Lord Jesus." What does this admonishment mean to you? Does it change how you prioritize things in your life?

EVALUATE

Based on your reading from Believe, Chapter 14: Single-Mindedness, *use a scale of 1 – 6 to rate how well you are living out the statements below (1 = not living out at all, 6 = living out completely).*

_____ I desire Jesus Christ to be first in my life.

_____ I see every aspect of my life and work as service to God.

_____ I spend time each day reading God's Word and praying.

_____ I value a simple lifestyle over one cluttered with activities and material possessions.

TAKE ACTION

Memorizing Scripture is a valuable discipline for all believers to exercise. Spend a few minutes each day committing this week's Key Verse to memory.

KEY VERSE: "But seek first his kingdom and his righteousness, and all these things will be given to you as well." (Matthew 6:33)

Recite this week's Key Idea out loud. As you do, ask yourself, "Does my life reflect this statement?"

KEY IDEA: I focus on God and his priorities for my life.

Answer the following questions to help you apply this week's Key Idea to your own life.

1. How would this practice express itself in your life?

2. What visible attributes can be found in someone who practices single-mindedness?

3. What is impeding your ability to live single-mindedly? How can you overcome this obstacle?

4. What action step can you take this week to increase your awareness of God's involvement in your daily life?

Group Meeting

Welcome!

Welcome to Session 14 of *Believe*. If there are any new members in your group, take a moment to introduce yourselves to each other. Then spend a couple of minutes sharing insights or questions about this session's personal study. Now start the video!

———VIDEO TEACHING NOTES———

As you watch the video segment for Session 14, use the following outline to record some of the main points. (The answer key is found at the end of the session.)

- Key Question: How do I keep my _____ on Jesus amidst distraction?

- Key Idea: I focus on God and his _____ for my life.

- Key Verse: "But _____ first his kingdom and his righteousness, and all these things will be given to you as well." (Matthew 6:33)

- (Key Application) _____ lay your calendar and decisions before God for direction.

- (Key Application) Make decisions based on Christian _____.

- (Key Application) Try the _____ Day Planner.

- (Key Application) Learn to say "no" to the things you _____ be doing.

---GETTING STARTED---

Begin your discussion by reciting the Key Verse and Key Idea together as a group. On your first attempt, use your notes if you need help. On your second attempt, try to state them completely from memory.

KEY VERSE: "But seek first his kingdom and his righteousness, and all these things will be given to you as well." (Matthew 6:33)

KEY IDEA: I focus on God and his priorities for my life.

---GROUP DISCUSSION---

As a group, discuss your thoughts and feelings about the following declarations. Which statements are easy to declare with certainty? Which are more challenging, and why?

- I desire Jesus Christ to be first in my life.

- I see every aspect of my life and work as service to God.

- I spend time each day reading God's Word and praying.

- I value a simple lifestyle over one cluttered with activities and material possessions.

Based on your group's dynamics and spiritual maturity, choose the 2–3 questions that will lead to the best discussion about this week's Key Idea.

1. Many people are tempted to compartmentalize their faith rather than allow God to influence every aspect of their lives. Discuss some of the reasons for this.

2. In what ways can materialism be the enemy of single-mindedness?

3. Which area of your life (relationships, finances, work, family, etc.) is hardest to submit to God's will and guidance?

4. How have you experienced the benefits of single-mindedness?

_____

_____

Read Matthew 6:19 – 24 (see the section "The Principles of Single-Mindedness" in Be-lieve) and choose 1 – 2 questions that will lead to the greatest discussion in your group.

1. How has seeking and serving God first brought his blessing upon your work, rela-tionships, family, and finances?

_____

_____

2. Discuss why it is tempting to "store up treasures on earth."

_____

_____

3. Discuss what it specifically means to "store up treasures in heaven."

_____

_____

——————CASE STUDY——————

Use the following case study as a model for a real-life situation where you might put this week's Key Idea into practice.

> Your good friend Patty has an internal motor that never stops. She is a mother of three, owns her own business, is president of the PTA, and somehow finds time to work out five days a week. Like clockwork, when you ask her how she is doing, the answer is always, "Busy." Many years ago when you were in a Bible study together, you openly talked to each other about your spiritual lives. These days when you ask her what God is doing in her life, she replies, "Not much. I wish God were more a part of my life, but I just don't have time anymore. I'm barely keeping myself afloat the way things are. I don't know how I could squeeze more into my schedule."

Using the Key Applications from this session, what could you say or do to help Patty? (If needed, refer to your video notes for a reminder of this session's Key Applications.)

CLOSING PRAYER

Close your time together with prayer. Share your prayer requests with one another. Ask God to help you put this week's Key Idea into practice.

JOURNAL

If your church is doing the *Believe* church-wide campaign, bring this study guide with you to church and use the following space to take notes from the pastor's or teacher's message. If your church provides an outline, consider keeping it with this guide so you will have all of your notes and thoughts from your *Believe* journey in one place.

VIDEO NOTES ANSWER KEY

focus / priorities / seek / Daily / values / Hebrew / shouldn't

Total Surrender

Personal Study

Last week you examined the practice of single-mindedness. Perhaps you learned how important it is to fix your focus on God alone. This week before your group meeting, read *Believe, Chapter 15: Total Surrender*. Then spend some time allowing the Scripture to take root in your heart and evaluating your commitment to follow the King of Kings no matter the cost.

READ

Read Believe, Chapter 15: Total Surrender *and answer the following questions.*

1.   Reflect on the Key Verse. What do you think it means to offer ourselves as "living sacrifices"? Recalling our study of the practice of worship in Chapter 11, why do you think offering ourselves as a living sacrifice is the true and proper way to worship God?

2.   The first three of the Ten Commandments govern our relationship with God. Why do you think it is important to get in right relationship with God in order to keep the rest of God's commandments?

3. What did Jesus mean when he instructed his disciples to "take up their cross daily"? Why does Jesus say this is a wise decision to make?

4. Compare and contrast Stephen's story with the story of Shadrach, Meshach, and Abednego. Compare Stephen's death to the death of Christ. Which detail of each story best exemplifies total surrender?

5. Which of the stories you've read inspires you most? Why?

EVALUATE

Based on your reading from Believe, Chapter 15: Total Surrender, *use a scale of 1 – 6 to rate how well you are living out the statements below (1 = not living out at all, 6 = living out completely).*

_____   I am living out God's purposes for my life.

_____   I give up what I want to meet the needs of others.

_____   I give away things I possess when I am so led by God.

_____   I serve God through my daily work.

---TAKE ACTION---

Memorizing Scripture is a valuable discipline for all believers to exercise. Spend a few minutes each day committing this week's Key Verse to memory.

KEY VERSE: "Therefore, I urge you, brothers and sisters, in view of God's mercy, to offer your bodies as a living sacrifice, holy and pleasing to God—this is your true and proper worship." (Romans 12:1)

Recite this week's Key Idea out loud. As you do, ask yourself, "Does my life reflect this statement?"

KEY IDEA: I dedicate my life to God's purposes.

Answer the following questions to help you apply this week's Key Idea to your own life.

1. How would this practice express itself in your life?

2. What visible attributes can be found in someone who is totally surrendered to God?

3. What is impeding your ability fully submit your life to God's purposes? How can you overcome this obstacle?

4. What action step can you take this week to move closer to a life that is entirely surrendered to God?

Group Meeting

Welcome!

Welcome to Session 15 of *Believe*. If there are any new members in your group, take a moment to introduce yourselves to each other. Then spend a couple of minutes sharing insights or questions about this session's personal study. Now start the video!

————————VIDEO TEACHING NOTES————————

As you watch the video segment for Session 15, use the following outline to record some of the main points. (The answer key is found at the end of the session.)

- Jesus is looking for a "_____ faith" from his followers.

- "Whoever wants to be my disciple must _____ themselves and take up their cross and follow me. (Matthew 16:24)

- Key Idea: I _____ my life to God's purposes.

- Key Question: How do I cultivate a life of _____?

- Every time one of Jesus' disciples was martyred or punished, it only _____ the movement of Christ.

- Key Verse: "Therefore, I urge you, brothers and sisters, in view of God's mercy, to _____ your bodies as a living sacrifice, holy and pleasing to God—this is your true and proper worship." (Romans 12:1)

- (Key Application) Constantly remember the _____ Jesus made for you.

- (Key Application) _____ that you are in a no-lose situation.

GETTING STARTED

Begin your discussion by reciting the Key Verse and Key Idea together as a group. On your first attempt, use your notes if you need help. On your second attempt, try to state them completely from memory.

KEY VERSE: "Therefore, I urge you, brothers and sisters, in view of God's mercy, to offer your bodies as a living sacrifice, holy and pleasing to God—this is your true and proper worship." (Romans 12:1)

KEY IDEA: I dedicate my life to God's purposes.

GROUP DISCUSSION

As a group, discuss your thoughts and feelings about the following declarations. Which statements are easy to declare with certainty? Which are more challenging, and why?

- I am living out God's purposes for my life.

- I give up what I want to meet the needs of others.

- I give away things I possess when I am so led by God.

- I serve God through my daily work.

Based on your group's dynamics and spiritual maturity, choose the 2–3 questions that will lead to the best discussion about this week's Key Idea.

1. Discuss what it takes (mentally, spiritually, emotionally) to be a person who is completely surrendered to God's purposes.

2. Not everyone is called to vocational ministry. So, what does total surrender look like for a school teacher, plumber, artist, business owner, or you?

3. The apostle Peter learned that total surrender is easier said than done. In what ways can you relate to his story?

4. As ambassadors of Christ, discuss how acts of sacrifice and surrender can reflect the love of God to people in our daily lives.

_____

_____

_____

Read Daniel 3:1 – 28 (see the section "Profiles of Total Surrender" in Believe) *and choose 1 – 2 questions that will lead to the greatest discussion in your group.*

1. Although the world we live in is drastically different, in what ways can you relate to Shadrach, Meshach, and Abednego?

_____

_____

_____

2. What qualities or virtues, if any, do you see in them that you would like to possess?

_____

_____

_____

3. In this story and many others found in the Bible, people make bold decisions in order to fulfill God's purposes. Discuss the origins of boldness. In other words, where does boldness comes from? Is it a personality trait? Is it generated through willpower? Is it given by God? Or is it developed over time?

_____

_____

_____

CASE STUDY

Use the following case study as a model for a real-life situation where you might put this week's Key Idea into practice.

Duncan's job requires him to travel out of town two or three times a month. For the first time in his life, he is able to put money in the bank rather than live paycheck to paycheck. Unfortunately, his coworkers and supervisor use these out-of-town trips to feed their wild sides and entertain potential clients. Duncan feels stuck. He knows that the activities on these trips are not pleasing to God, but refusing to participate will most likely cost him his job.

Using the Key Applications from this session, what could you say or do to help Duncan? (If needed, refer to your video notes for a reminder of this session's Key Applications.)

CLOSING PRAYER

Close your time together with prayer. Share your prayer requests with one another. Ask God to help you put this week's Key Idea into practice.

JOURNAL

If your church is doing the *Believe* church-wide campaign, bring this study guide with you to church and use the following space to take notes from the pastor's or teacher's message. If your church provides an outline, consider keeping it with this guide so you will have all of your notes and thoughts from your *Believe* journey in one place.

VIDEO NOTES ANSWER KEY

cannonball / deny / dedicate / sacrifice / fueled / offer / sacrifice / Remember

Biblical Community

Personal Study

Last week you examined the practice of total surrender. Perhaps you were challenged to jump in "cannonball" style and actively lay down your life for God's purposes. This week before your group meeting, read *Believe, Chapter 16: Biblical Community*. Then take some time to allow the Scriptures to soak in as you evaluate your personal practice of biblical community.

READ

Read Believe, Chapter 16: Biblical Community *and answer the following questions.*

1. The passage from Ecclesiastes 4 describes a relationship between two people. Why, then, does the Teacher say "a cord of three strands" is not quickly broken?

2. As you read the passage from Ephesians 2, look for the differences between the two dwelling places for God: the temple and the New Testament church. What barriers are there in the two places? Who is allowed into each place? What is the cornerstone of each place?

3. Imagine what it would have been like to be a member of the early church after Pentecost. Would you have wanted to be a part of that community? Why or why not? In what ways should the early church be a model for churches today?

4. As you read the passages from Hebrews 13, Acts 18, 1 Corinthians 16, Romans 16, and 1 John 1 – 3, ponder the emphasis and importance placed on hospitality. Why do you think it was so important to the early church? Is it still important today? Why or why not?

5. God's Word places a high value on Christian fellowship. How important is this value to you right now? What difference is it making in your life?

EVALUATE

Based on your reading from Believe, Chapter 16: Biblical Community, *use a scale of 1 – 6 to rate how well you are living out the statements below (1 = not living out at all, 6 = living out completely).*

_____ I have close relationships with other Christians who have influence on my life's direction.

_____ I participate in a group of Christians who really know me and support me.

_____ I allow other Christians to hold me accountable for my actions.

_____ I daily pray for and support other Christians.

TAKE ACTION

Memorizing Scripture is a valuable discipline for all believers to exercise. Spend a few minutes each day committing this week's Key Verse to memory.

KEY VERSE: "All the believers were together and had everything in common. They sold property and possessions to give to anyone who had need. Every day they continued to meet together in the temple courts. They broke bread in their homes and ate together with glad and sincere hearts, praising God and enjoying the favor of all the people. And the Lord added to their number daily those who were being saved." (Acts 2:44–47)

Recite this week's Key Idea out loud. As you do, ask yourself, "Does my life reflect this statement?"

KEY IDEA: I fellowship with Christians to accomplish God's purposes in my life, in the lives of others, and in the world.

Answer the following questions to help you apply this week's Key Idea to your own life.

1. How would this practice express itself in your life?

2. What visible attributes can be found in someone who practices biblical community?

3. What is impeding your ability to experience biblical community? How can you overcome this obstacle?

4. What action step can you take this week to develop biblical community?

Group Meeting

Welcome!

Welcome to Session 16 of *Believe*. If there are any new members in your group, take a moment to introduce yourselves to each other. Then spend a couple of minutes sharing insights or questions about this session's personal study. Now start the video!

VIDEO TEACHING NOTES

As you watch the video segment for Session 16, use the following outline to record some of the main points. (The answer key is found at the end of the session.)

- In Genesis 2:18, God said, "It is not good for the man to be _____."

- God is a _____—Father, Son, and Holy Spirit.

- We too were created _____ community and _____ a community.

- Key Question: What do I do to develop healthy _____ with others?

- Key Idea: I fellowship with Christians to _____ God's purposes in my life, in the lives of others, and in the world.

- Key Verse: "All the believers were together and had everything in common. They sold property and possessions to _____ to anyone who had need. Every day they continued to _____ together in the temple courts. They broke bread in their homes and _____ together with glad and sincere hearts, praising God and enjoying the favor of all the people. And the Lord added to their number daily those who were being saved." (Acts 2:44–47)

- (Key Application) Fellowship with other believers to keep your relationship with _____ strong.

- (Key Application) Fellowship with other believers to keep your relationships with _____ strong.

- (Key Application) Fellowship with other believers to _____ God's will on earth.

GETTING STARTED

Begin your discussion by reciting the Key Verse and Key Idea together as a group. On your first attempt, use your notes if you need help. On your second attempt, try to state them completely from memory.

KEY VERSE: "All the believers were together and had everything in common. They sold property and possessions to give to anyone who had need. Every day they continued to meet together in the temple courts. They broke bread in their homes and ate together with glad and sincere hearts, praising God and enjoying the favor of all the people. And the Lord added to their number daily those who were being saved." (Acts 2:44–47)

KEY IDEA: I fellowship with Christians to accomplish God's purposes in my life, in the lives of others, and in the world.

GROUP DISCUSSION

As a group, discuss your thoughts and feelings about the following declarations. Which statements are easy to declare with certainty? Which are more challenging, and why?

- I have close relationships with other Christians who have influence on my life's direction.

- I participate in a group of Christians who really know me and support me.

- I allow other Christians to hold me accountable for my actions.

- I daily pray for and support other Christians.

Based on your group's dynamics and spiritual maturity, choose the 2–3 questions that will lead to the best discussion about this week's Key Idea.

1. In what ways is it "not good for man (a person) to be alone"?

2. In a world where people are becoming more isolated and self-centered, what can be done to nurture a vibrant others-focused community?

3. What is or could be an adversary of biblical community? In other words, what in our lives or culture impedes the success of healthy, attractive, faith-based community?

4. What simple steps could this group take to enhance and/or develop more connection with God, each other, and non-believers?

Read Acts 2:42 – 47 (see the section "The New Community" in Believe) *and choose 1 – 2 questions that will lead to the greatest discussion in your group.*

1. In what ways has your church experience been similar to what you just read? How has it been different?

2. Is the type of community you just read about possible today? Discuss why you believe it is or why it is not.

3. If community is something we desperately need, why are so many people of faith content to live lifestyles of isolation?

CASE STUDY

Use the following case study as a model for a real-life situation where you might put this week's Key Idea into practice.

Lauren began to follow Christ as a teenager after a close friend invited her to her church's summer camp. Not growing up in a religious family made her feel far behind in her faith. So, she immediately began to read every Bible study she could find. Lauren's faith soared as she learned more about herself and the character of God.

Ten years have passed and she still reads her Bible daily and attends the worship services at her church, but she feels as if something is missing; that she has hit a spiritual plateau and doesn't know what to do to change it.

Using the Key Applications from this session, what could you say or do to help Lauren? (If needed, refer to your video notes for a reminder of this session's Key Applications.)

CLOSING PRAYER

Close your time together with prayer. Share your prayer requests with one another. Ask God to help you put this week's Key Idea into practice.

JOURNAL

If your church is doing the *Believe* church-wide campaign, bring this study guide with you to church and use the following space to take notes from the pastor's or teacher's message. If your church provides an outline, consider keeping it with this guide so you will have all of your notes and thoughts from your *Believe* journey in one place.

VIDEO NOTES ANSWER KEY

alone / community / for, as / relationships / accomplish / give, meet, ate / God / others / accomplish

Spiritual Gifts

Personal Study

Last week you examined the practice of biblical community. Possibly you learned that community is not just nice to participate in; it's a necessity for a full, healthy lifestyle. This week before your group meeting, read *Believe, Chapter 17: Spiritual Gifts*. Then spend some time allowing the Scripture to take root in your heart and evaluating how God is involved in your daily life.

READ

Read Believe, Chapter 17: Spiritual Gifts *and answer the following questions.*

1. What was Daniel's spiritual gift? Why was it important that Daniel acknowledge his gift was from the Lord?

2. The Holy Spirit now takes up residence in all who believe in Jesus. We are the new temple of God. Jesus called the Holy Spirit our "advocate." What do you think that means to us?

3. As you read the passages from Romans 12 and 1 Corinthians 12, write down which gift(s) you believe you possess. Choose a family member or friend and do

the same for them. Let them know what you think their gift is and how you have been positively impacted by it.

4. What happens when spiritual gifts are exercised without love? (An example of hospitality without love is given by Peter.) Why is it so important to be driven by love when using our spiritual gifts?

5. The Bible compares the church to a body. Collectively, we are the body of Christ. Individual believers are compared to parts of the body that all work together to accomplish what needs to be done. Can you recall a time when one part of your body was injured in some way and how this affected the whole body? How does this analogy work in regard to the church?

EVALUATE

Based on your reading from Believe, Chapter 17: Spiritual Gifts, *use a scale of 1 – 6 to rate how well you are living out the statements below (1 = not living out at all, 6 = living out completely).*

_____ I know my spiritual gift(s).

_____ I regularly use my spiritual gift(s) in ministry to accomplish God's purposes.

_____ I value the spiritual gifts of others to accomplish God's purposes.

_____ Others recognize and affirm my spiritual gift(s) and support my use of them.

---TAKE ACTION---

Memorizing Scripture is a valuable discipline for all believers to exercise. Spend a few minutes each day committing this week's Key Verse to memory.

KEY VERSE: "For just as each of us has one body with many members, and these members do not all have the same function, so in Christ we, though many, form one body, and each member belongs to all the others. We have different gifts, according to the grace given to each of us." (Romans 12:4–6)

Recite this week's Key Idea out loud. As you do, ask yourself, "Does my life reflect this statement?"

KEY IDEA: I know my spiritual gifts and use them to fulfill God's purposes.

Answer the following questions to help you apply this week's Key Idea to your own life.

1. How would this practice express itself in your life?

2. What visible attributes can be found in someone who uses his or her spiritual gifts?

3. What is impeding your ability to know and use your spiritual gifts? How can you overcome this obstacle?

4. What action step can you take this week to discover or better use your spiritual gifts?

Group Meeting

Welcome!

Welcome to Session 17 of *Believe*. If there are any new members in your group, take a moment to introduce yourselves to each other. Then spend a couple of minutes sharing insights or questions about this session's personal study. Now start the video!

———————————VIDEO TEACHING NOTES———————————

As you watch the video segment for Session 17, use the following outline to record some of the main points. (The answer key is found at the end of the session.)

- Key Question: What gifts and skills has God given me to _____ others?

- Key Verse: "For just as each of us has one body with many members, and these members do not all have the same function, so in Christ we, though many, form one body, and each member _____ to all the others. We have different gifts, according to the grace given to each of us." (Romans 12:4–6)

- Key Idea: I know my spiritual gifts and _____ them to fulfill God's purposes.

- (Key Application) As a community, help each other _____ what gift God has given to each of you.

- (Key Application) Know and _____ the gifts of the people God has placed around you.

- (Key Application) _____ your gift(s).

- (Key Application) Acknowledge and give God the _____ for your gift(s).

GETTING STARTED

Begin your discussion by reciting the Key Verse and Key Idea together as a group. On your first attempt, use your notes if you need help. On your second attempt, try to state them completely from memory.

KEY VERSE: "For just as each of us has one body with many members, and these members do not all have the same function, so in Christ we, though many, form one body, and each member belongs to all the others. We have different gifts, according to the grace given to each of us." (Romans 12:4–6)

KEY IDEA: I know my spiritual gifts and use them to fulfill God's purposes.

GROUP DISCUSSION

As a group, discuss your thoughts and feelings about the following declarations. Which statements are easy to declare with certainty? Which are more challenging, and why?

- I know my spiritual gift(s).

- I regularly use my spiritual gift(s) in ministry to accomplish God's purposes.

- I value the spiritual gifts of others to accomplish God's purposes.

- Others recognize and affirm my spiritual gift(s) and support my use of them.

Based on your group's dynamics and spiritual maturity, choose the 2–3 questions that will lead to the best discussion about this week's Key Idea.

1. Take a moment to affirm the specific ways you see members of your group using their spiritual gifts.

2. Discuss the health of your spiritual community. Which parts are thriving and healthy? Which parts are hurting or nonexistent? What action step(s) can the group take to strengthen the body of Christ?

3. If people were unsure of their roles in the body of Christ, how would you advise them to discover their spiritual giftedness?

4. Some gifts get more attention than others, which can cause pride and jealousy within the body of Christ. How can your group safeguard itself from these destructive attitudes?

Read 1 Corinthians 12:4–31 (see the section "Purpose and Function of Spiritual Gifts" in Believe) *and choose 1–2 questions that will lead to the best discussion in your group.*

1. What role does your spiritual gift play in the redemption and restoration of broken people and a broken world?

2. Discuss parts of the human body that are not visible but are incredibly important. Similarly, which gifts within the body of Christ are rarely recognized yet vital to the success of the church's mission?

3. Why is it imperative for us to use our gifts with an attitude of love?

―――――――――――――**CASE STUDY**―――――――――――――

Use the following case study as a model for a real-life situation where you might put this week's Key Idea into practice.

Danny is frustrated. After giving his life to Christ five years ago, he has desperately tried to share the good news with as many people as possible. He has taught Bible studies at work, church, and in his neighborhood, but without the success he had hoped to achieve. Initially he would get a good turnout, but people would gradually lose interest.

A couple of months ago, a coworker invited him to a Bible study on Thursdays during their lunch hour. It started as a small group, but within a few weeks the break room was packed. Danny knew he should be excited, but he was just mad. Why was this guy having so much success, when Danny hadn't? He couldn't understand what he was doing wrong.

Using the Key Applications from this session, what could you say or do to help Danny find the answers to his frustrations? (If needed, refer to your video notes for a reminder of this session's Key Applications.)

―――――――――――――**CLOSING PRAYER**―――――――――――――

Close your time together with prayer. Share your prayer requests with one another. Ask God to help you put this week's Key Idea into practice.

JOURNAL

If your church is doing the *Believe* church-wide campaign, bring this study guide with you to church and use the following space to take notes from the pastor's or teacher's message. If your church provides an outline, consider keeping it with this guide so you will have all of your notes and thoughts from your *Believe* journey in one place.

VIDEO NOTES ANSWER KEY

serve / belongs / use / discover / celebrate / Use / credit

Offering My Time

Personal Study

Last week you examined the practice of spiritual gifts. Perhaps you learned that God has empowered us to work together — as one body — for his purposes. Isn't that incredible! This week before your group meeting, read *Believe, Chapter 18: Offering My Time*. Then allow God's Word to shape your thoughts and feelings toward your use of time.

READ

Read Believe, Chapter 18: Offering My Time *and answer the following questions.*

1. Do you think God still puts people "in the belly of a fish" when they ignore his call?

2. In light of what we have learned about the Old Testament temple from previous chapters, why did God want the returning captives to build his house before they built their own?

3. As you read the passages from Exodus 16, 18, and Proverbs 31, write down any practical principles you find regarding managing time.

4. As you read the passages from Matthew 25, Ephesians 5, and Galatians 6, look for the answer to this question: How does God reward those who do what he has asked them to?

5. What one thing can you do to improve in the key practice of offering your time to God?

─────────────────────── EVALUATE ───────────────────────

Based on your reading from Believe, *Chapter 18: Offering My Time, use a scale of 1 – 6 to rate how well you are living out the statements below (1 = not living out at all, 6 = living out completely).*

_____ I invest my time in others by praying for them.

_____ I spend a good deal of time helping others with physical, emotional, or other kinds of needs.

_____ I give away my time to serve and help others in my community.

_____ I regularly volunteer at my church.

―――――――――――――――TAKE ACTION―――――――――――――――

Memorizing Scripture is a valuable discipline for all believers to exercise. Spend a few minutes each day committing this week's Key Verse to memory.

KEY VERSE: "And whatever you do, whether in word or deed, do it all in the name of the Lord Jesus, giving thanks to God the Father through him." (Colossians 3:17)

―――――――――――――――――― ⌘ ――――――――――――――――

Recite this week's Key Idea out loud. As you do, ask yourself, "Does my life reflect this statement?"

KEY IDEA: I offer my time to fulfill God's purposes.

Answer the following questions to help you apply this week's Key Idea to your own life.

1. How would this practice express itself in your life?

2. What visible attributes can be found in someone who invests his or her time in God's purposes?

3. What is impeding your ability to offer your time to God and others? How can you overcome this obstacle?

4. What action step can you take this week to increase the amount of time you give to God's purposes?

Group Meeting

Welcome!

Welcome to Session 18 of *Believe*. If there are any new members in your group, take a moment to introduce yourselves to each other. Then spend a couple of minutes sharing insights or questions about this session's personal study. Now start the video!

VIDEO TEACHING NOTES

As you watch the video segment for Session 18, use the following outline to record some of the main points. (The answer key is found at the end of the session.)

- Key Question: How does God want us to view the twenty-four _____ we have in a day?

- Key Verse: "And whatever you do, whether in word or deed, do it _____ in the name of the Lord Jesus, giving thanks to God the Father through him." (Colossians 3:17)

- Key Idea: I _____ my time to fulfill God's purposes.

- Give careful thought to your _____.

- (Key Application) Take care of God's _____ and he will take care of yours.

- (Key Application) Do everything as an _____ to God.

GETTING STARTED

Begin your discussion by reciting the Key Verse and Key Idea together as a group. On your first attempt, use your notes if you need help. On your second attempt, try to state them completely from memory.

KEY VERSE: "And whatever you do, whether in word or deed, do it all in the name of the Lord Jesus, giving thanks to God the Father through him." (Colossians 3:17)

KEY IDEA: I offer my time to fulfill God's purposes.

GROUP DISCUSSION

As a group, discuss your thoughts and feelings about the following declarations. Which statements are easy to declare with certainty? Which are more challenging, and why?

- I invest my time in others by praying for them.

- I spend a good deal of time helping others with physical, emotional, or other kinds of needs.

- I give away my time to serve and help others in my community.

- I regularly volunteer at my church.

Based on your group's dynamics and spiritual maturity, choose the 2 – 3 questions that will lead to the best discussion about this week's Key Idea.

1. Make a diverse list of ways time can be used for God's purposes.

2. What challenges make it hard for you to invest time in God's purposes? As a group, discuss ways to overcome them.

3. Often, simple actions such as actively listening to a coworker, helping a neighbor, or coaching Little League are overlooked because they aren't "church related." Discuss simple ways you can offer time to people in your community.

4. In most churches, a small group of people do a majority of the work. Discuss different needs and opportunities you see within your congregation that your group could address.

Read Matthew 25:31 – 46 (see the section "The Rewards of Offering Our Time" in Be-lieve) and choose 1 – 2 questions that will lead to the greatest discussion in your group.

1. Based on what you just read, what activities seem most important to Jesus?

2. The activities Jesus mentions are not usually considered acts done "for God," yet he says, "Whatever you did for one of the least of these brothers and sisters of mine, you did for me." What do you think is Jesus' main point here?

3. Christians tend to narrowly define acts of worship as deeds done within a church building. As a group, redefine what it looks like to worship God with our time.

CASE STUDY

Use the following case study as a model for a real-life situation where you might put this week's Key Idea into practice.

Cici is a busy woman. Her first job involves taking care of her three children and husband. When she isn't kissing boo-boos, refereeing fights between siblings, and looking for ways to encourage her spouse, she designs websites for small businesses.

Recently, a family of five with no mother moved in next door. The dad works long, odd hours. So the kids are left to care for themselves most of the time. She senses that God put them in her life for a reason, but fear has held her back. She worries that spending time with them will force her to neglect other areas of her life.

Using the Key Applications from this session, what could you say or do to help Cici? (If needed, refer to your video notes for a reminder of this session's Key Applications.)

CLOSING PRAYER

Close your time together with prayer. Share your prayer requests with one another. Ask God to help you put this week's Key Idea into practice.

---JOURNAL---

If your church is doing the *Believe* church-wide campaign, bring this study guide with you to church and use the following space to take notes from the pastor's or teacher's message. If your church provides an outline, consider keeping it with this guide so you will have all of your notes and thoughts from your *Believe* journey in one place.

---VIDEO NOTES ANSWER KEY---

hours / all / offer / ways / business / offering

Giving My Resources

Personal Study

Last week you examined the practice of offering your time. Perhaps you were inspired to invest the time God has given you for his purposes. Fantastic! This week before your group meeting, read *Believe, Chapter 19: Giving My Resources*. Then spend some time allowing the Scripture to take root in your heart and evaluating your relationship with money.

―――――――――――――――**READ**――――――――――――――――

Read Believe, Chapter 19: Giving My Resources *and answer the following questions.*

1. Find all the times the word "willing" is used in the passages from Exodus 35 and 36. Why is a willing heart so important to God?

2. As you read the passages from Proverbs 3 and 11, identify the one piece of advice that speaks most to you right now.

3. If someone asked you to summarize what Jesus taught about money and giving, what would you say?

_____

_____

_____

_____

4. As you read the Scripture from 2 Corinthians 8 and 9, look for the process believers should go through to determine what to give.

_____

_____

_____

_____

5. On a scale of 1 – 10, evaluate your level of generosity. What has helped you become more generous? What still causes you to hold back?

_____

_____

_____

_____

_____

----------EVALUATE----------

Based on your reading from Believe, Chapter 19: Giving My Resources, _use a scale of 1 – 6 to rate how well you are living out the statements below (1 = not living out at all, 6 = living out completely)._

_____ I give away 10 percent or more of my income to God's work.

_____ I regularly give money to serve and help others.

_____ My first priority in spending is to support God's work.

_____ My spending habits do not keep me from giving what I feel I should give to God.

TAKE ACTION

Memorizing Scripture is a valuable discipline for all believers to exercise. Spend a few minutes each day committing this week's Key Verse to memory.

KEY VERSE: "But since you excel in everything—in faith, in speech, in knowledge, in complete earnestness and in the love we have kindled in you—see that you also excel in this grace of giving." (2 Corinthians 8:7)

Recite this week's Key Idea out loud. As you do, ask yourself, "Does my life reflect this statement?"

KEY IDEA: I give my resources to fulfill God's purposes.

Answer the following questions to help you apply this week's Key Idea to your own life.

1. How would this practice express itself in your life?

2. What visible attributes can be found in someone who regularly gives away their resources?

3. What is impeding your ability to incorporate this practice into your lifestyle? How can you overcome this obstacle?

4. What action step can you take this week to make this practice a consistent part of your life?

Group Meeting

Welcome!

Welcome to Session 19 of *Believe*. If there are any new members in your group, take a moment to introduce yourselves to each other. Then spend a couple of minutes sharing insights or questions about this session's personal study. Now start the video!

VIDEO TEACHING NOTES

As you watch the video segment for Session 19, use the following outline to record some of the main points. (The answer key is found at the end of the session.)

- Key Question: How do I best use my _____ to serve God and others?

- Key Idea: I give my resources to fulfill God's purposes.

- Key Verse: "But since you excel in everything—in faith, in speech, in knowledge, in complete earnestness and in the love we have kindled in you—see that you also excel in this grace of _____." (2 Corinthians 8:7)

- (Key Application) Your willingness comes from a heart _____ by God's purposes.

- (Key Application) Resources go _____ money.

- (Key Application) Giving to others _____ your intimacy with Christ.

GETTING STARTED

Begin your discussion by reciting the Key Verse and Key Idea together as a group. On your first attempt, use your notes if you need help. On your second attempt, try to state them completely from memory.

KEY VERSE: "But since you excel in everything—in faith, in speech, in knowledge, in complete earnestness and in the love we have kindled in you—see that you also excel in this grace of giving." (2 Corinthians 8:7)

⚷

KEY IDEA: I give my resources to fulfill God's purposes.

GROUP DISCUSSION

As a group, discuss your thoughts and feelings about the following declarations. Which statements are easy to declare with certainty? Which are more challenging, and why?

- I give away 10 percent or more of my income to God's work.

- I regularly give money to serve and help others.

- My first priority in spending is to support God's work.

- My spending habits do not keep me from giving what I feel I should give to God.

Based on your group's dynamics and spiritual maturity, choose the 2 – 3 questions that will lead to the best discussion about this week's Key Idea.

1. Fire can be incredibly beneficial and also terribly dangerous, if not used properly. How are material resources similar?

2. In what ways can money give us a false sense of security, satisfaction, and safety?

3. Why do you think God is more concerned about the intentions of the giver than the size of the gift?

4. What present circumstances in your life provide opportunities to give away your resources for God's purposes?

Read Proverbs 11:24–25, 28 and Ecclesiastes 5:10–20 (see the section "Advice from Wise Men" in Believe) *and choose 1–2 questions that will lead to the greatest discussion in your group.*

1. What truths can be found in the Scripture you just read together?

2. Solomon was one of the wealthiest men to ever walk the earth. In what ways, if any, are you surprised by his comments on wealth and money? Which of his comments do you think are the most insightful?

3. If you could sum up Solomon's advice in one or two sentences, what would you say?

---------------------------------**CASE STUDY**--------------------------------

Use the following case study as a model for a real-life situation where you might put this week's Key Idea into practice.

Karen and Ben were married for twenty-eight years before a year-long battle with cancer took him home to be with Jesus. Left with an abundance of time, money, and a four-bedroom house, Karen ponders what she should do with all of her and Ben's belongings.

Using the Key Applications from this session, what could you say or do to help Karen find the direction she is looking for? (If needed, refer to your video notes for a reminder of this session's Key Applications.)

---------------------------------**CLOSING PRAYER**--------------------------------

Close your time together with prayer. Share your prayer requests with one another. Ask God to help you put this week's Key Idea into practice.

JOURNAL

If your church is doing the *Believe* church-wide campaign, bring this study guide with you to church and use the following space to take notes from the pastor's or teacher's message. If your church provides an outline, consider keeping it with this guide so you will have all of your notes and thoughts from your *Believe* journey in one place.

VIDEO NOTES ANSWER KEY

resources / giving / moved / beyond / strengthens

Sharing My Faith

Personal Study

Last week you examined the practice of giving away your resources. Perhaps you were challenged to loosen your hold on personal possessions, allowing them to be used for God's purposes. This week before your group meeting, read *Believe, Chapter 20: Sharing My Faith*. Then take some time to evaluate your relationship with people outside of the Christian faith.

-----READ-----

Read Believe, Chapter 20: Sharing My Faith *and answer the following questions.*

1. What are some ways in which we can be God's "ambassadors" to the world?

2. What does Paul mean when he writes, "I have become all things to all people so that by all possible means I might save some"? What do you think this does *not* mean?

3. As you read about Philip's divine encounter with the Ethiopian in Acts 8, identify his effective strategies for sharing his faith that you can emulate.

4. What does it mean to "be wise in the way you act toward outsiders"? What does it mean to have our conversation be "full of grace" and "seasoned with salt"?

5. In regard to sharing our faith, what did Jesus mean that some will "sow" the seed and others will "reap" the harvest? Why should we share our faith, even if we think our message could be rejected?

EVALUATE

Based on your reading from Believe, Chapter 20: Sharing My Faith, *use a scale of 1 – 6 to rate how well you are living out the statements below (1 = not living out at all, 6 = living out completely).*

_____ I frequently share my faith with people who are not Christians.

_____ I try to live so that others will see Christ in my life.

_____ I know how to share my faith with non-Christians.

_____ I pray for non-Christians to accept Jesus Christ as their Lord and Savior.

TAKE ACTION

Memorizing Scripture is a valuable discipline for all believers to exercise. Spend a few minutes each day committing this week's Key Verse to memory.

KEY VERSE: "Pray also for me, that whenever I speak, words may be given me so that I will fearlessly make known the mystery of the gospel, for which I am an ambassador in chains. Pray that I may declare it fearlessly, as I should." (Ephesians 6:19–20)

Recite this week's Key Idea out loud. As you do, ask yourself, "Does my life reflect this statement?"

KEY IDEA: I share my faith with others to fulfill God's purposes.

Answer the following questions to help you apply this week's Key Idea to your own life.

1. How would this practice express itself in your life?

2. What visible attributes can be found in someone who regularly shares his or her faith?

3. What is impeding your ability to openly share your faith in Christ? How can you overcome this obstacle?

4. What action step can you take this week to put yourself in a position to share what God has done in your life?

Group Meeting

Welcome!

Welcome to Session 20 of *Believe*. If there are any new members in your group, take a moment to introduce yourselves to each other. Then spend a couple of minutes sharing insights or questions about this session's personal study. Now start the video!

VIDEO TEACHING NOTES

As you watch the video segment for Session 20, use the following outline to record some of the main points. (The answer key is found at the end of the session.)

- Key Question: How do I share my _____ with people I don't know?

- Key Idea: I _____ my faith with others to fulfill God's purposes.

- "The Lord is not slow in keeping his promise, as some understand slowness. Instead he is patient with you, not wanting anyone to perish, but everyone to come to _____." (2 Peter 3:9)

- Key Verse: "Pray also for me, that whenever I speak, words may be given me so that I will fearlessly make known the mystery of the gospel, for which I am an _____ in chains. Pray that I may declare it fearlessly, as I should." (Ephesians 6:19–20)

- (Key Application) Look for divine _____.

- (Key Application) Start with a question and wait for the _____.

- (Key Application) Share your _____.

- (Key Application) Acceptance of the Good News is not your _____.

GETTING STARTED

Begin your discussion by reciting the Key Verse and Key Idea together as a group. On your first attempt, use your notes if you need help. On your second attempt, try to state them completely from memory.

KEY VERSE: "Pray also for me, that whenever I speak, words may be given me so that I will fearlessly make known the mystery of the gospel, for which I am an ambassador in chains. Pray that I may declare it fearlessly, as I should." (Ephesians 6:19–20)

KEY IDEA: I share my faith with others to fulfill God's purposes.

GROUP DISCUSSION

As a group, discuss your thoughts and feelings about the following declarations. Which statements are easy to declare with certainty? Which are more challenging, and why?

- I frequently share my faith with people who are not Christians.
- I try to live so that others will see Christ in my life.
- I know how to share my faith with non-Christians.
- I pray for non-Christians to accept Jesus Christ as their Lord and Savior.

Based on your group's dynamics and spiritual maturity, choose the 2–3 questions that will lead to the best discussion about this week's Key Idea.

1. Is it possible to share your faith without saying a word? If so, how?

2. What present opportunities do you have to share your faith with individuals outside of the faith?

3. If what Jesus did through his death and resurrection is "good news," why do many people hesitate to share it?

4. In what ways are you actively sharing your faith with unbelievers?

Read Genesis 12:1 – 4 and 2 Corinthians 5:14 – 21 (see the section "The Call to Share Our Faith" in Believe) *and choose 1 – 2 questions that will lead to the greatest discussion in your group.*

1. In what ways do you see the world being blessed through God's people? In other words, how is the church positively affecting the world around it?

2. Paul says we have been given a ministry of reconciliation. In your opinion, what does that mean?

3. As ambassadors of Christ, we (the church) represent his character and desires to the world around us. In what ways are we representing him well? In what areas must we improve?

CASE STUDY

Use the following case study as a model for a real-life situation where you might put this week's Key Idea into practice.

Esperanza's story of redemption is powerful. The grace of God radically changed the trajectory of her life from a destination of brokenness and addiction to a place of freedom and hope. Although she has found peace, her family and friends are headed for destruction. She feels a sense of responsibility to share her faith with them, but fear of doing or saying the wrong thing is holding her back.

Using the Key Applications from this session, what could you say or do to help Esperanza? (If needed, refer to your video notes for a reminder of this session's Key Applications.)

———————CLOSING PRAYER———————

Close your time together with prayer. Share your prayer requests with one another. Ask God to help you put this week's Key Idea into practice.

———————JOURNAL———————

If your church is doing the *Believe* church-wide campaign, bring this study guide with you to church and use the following space to take notes from the pastor's or teacher's message. If your church provides an outline, consider keeping it with this guide so you will have all of your notes and thoughts from your *Believe* journey in one place.

———————VIDEO NOTES ANSWER KEY———————

faith / share / repentance / ambassador / appointments / invitation / story / responsibility

Love

Personal Study

Last week you examined the practice of sharing your faith. Perhaps you were inspired to share your story with someone outside the Christian tradition. This week we shift our attention from spiritual practices to Christlike virtues. Before your group meeting, read *Believe, Chapter 21: Love*. Then ask yourself how this virtue manifests itself in your life.

READ

Read Believe, Chapter 21: Love *and answer the following questions.*

1. As you read 1 Corinthians 13, make two lists. What are the characteristics of love in the positive sense (all that love is). What characteristics does love not have?

2. Do you love the Lord your God with all your heart, soul, mind, and strength? How would you describe the amount of love you show for others? Are you satisfied with your answers?

3. Put into your own words what happened in the shift from the Great Commandment of the Old Testament to the new commandment of Jesus.

4. After Paul listed all the qualities of the fruit of the Spirit, why did he then write, "Against such things there is no law"?

5. As you read the story from 1 Samuel 19, write down the ways that Jonathan offered David unconditional and sacrificial love.

―――――――――――――EVALUATE―――――――――――――

Based on your reading from Believe, Chapter 21: Love, *use a scale of 1 – 6 to rate how fully your life demonstrates the statements below (1 = does not demonstrate at all, 6 = demonstrates fully).*

_____ God's grace enables me to forgive people who have hurt me.

_____ I rejoice when good things happen to other people.

_____ I demonstrate love equally toward people of all races.

_____ I frequently give up what I want for the sake of others.

TAKE ACTION

Memorizing Scripture is a valuable discipline for all believers to exercise. Spend a few minutes each day committing this week's Key Verse to memory.

KEY VERSE: "This is love: not that we loved God, but that he loved us and sent his Son as an atoning sacrifice for our sins. Dear friends, since God so loved us, we also ought to love one another. No one has ever seen God; but if we love one another, God lives in us and his love is made complete in us." (1 John 4:10–12)

Recite this week's Key Idea out loud. As you do, ask yourself, "Does my life reflect this statement?"

KEY IDEA: I am committed to loving God and loving others.

Answer the following questions to help you apply this week's Key Idea to your own life.

1. How could this virtue express itself in your life?

2. What visible attributes can be found in someone who embodies the virtue of love?

3. What is impeding your ability to embrace this virtue? How can you overcome this obstacle?

4. What action step can you take this week to love more like Jesus?

Group Meeting

Welcome!

Welcome to Session 21 of *Believe*. If there are any new members in your group, take a moment to introduce yourselves to each other. Then spend a couple of minutes sharing insights or questions about this session's personal study. Now start the video!

────────────────VIDEO TEACHING NOTES────────────────

As you watch the video segment for Session 21, use the following outline to record some of the main points. (The answer key is found at the end of the session.)

- Key Question: What does it mean to sacrificially and unconditionally _____ others?

- Key Verse: "This is love: not that we loved God, but that he loved us and sent his Son as an atoning sacrifice for our sins. Dear friends, since God so loved us, we also ought to love one another. No one has ever seen God; but if we love one another, God lives in us and his love is made _____ in us." (1 John 4:10–12)

- Key Idea: I am _____ to loving God and loving others.

- (Key Application) I am their _____.

- (Key Application) I sacrifice my _____ to see them succeed.

- (Key Application) I help them see God's good _____ for them.

GETTING STARTED

Begin your discussion by reciting the Key Verse and Key Idea together as a group. On your first attempt, use your notes if you need help. On your second attempt, try to state them completely from memory.

KEY VERSE: "This is love: not that we loved God, but that he loved us and sent his Son as an atoning sacrifice for our sins. Dear friends, since God so loved us, we also ought to love one another. No one has ever seen God; but if we love one another, God lives in us and his love is made complete in us." (1 John 4:10–12)

KEY IDEA: I am committed to loving God and loving others.

GROUP DISCUSSION

As a group, discuss your thoughts and feelings about the following declarations. Which statements are easy to declare with certainty? Which are more challenging, and why?

- God's grace enables me to forgive people who have hurt me.
- I rejoice when good things happen to other people.
- I demonstrate love equally toward people of all races.
- I frequently give up what I want for the sake of others.

Based on your group's dynamics and spiritual maturity, choose the 2–3 questions that will lead to the best discussion about this week's Key Idea.

1. Who are the toughest people for you to love? Family members? Coworkers? Strangers? Explain why.

2. It's easy to love someone who meets our needs. Is it possible to genuinely love someone who does nothing for you or even hurts you? If so, how?

3. Outside of Jesus' example, when have you witnessed expressions of Christlike love?

Read John 13:31 – 35, 1 John 4:19 – 21, and Matthew 18:21 – 22 (see the section "The New Commandment" in Believe) *and choose 1 – 2 questions that will lead to the greatest discussion in your group.*

1. Throughout Scripture, love is described as an identifying quality that proves we belong to God. If this is true, why are Christians so frequently described by outsiders as hypocritical and judgmental?

2. Based on what you read, what is the best strategy for developing authentic and genuine love for God and others?

3. Discuss how withholding forgiveness can be an adversary of genuine love.

---CASE STUDY---

Use the following case study as a model for a real-life situation where you might put this week's Key Idea into practice.

Bo's boss is not an easy man to work for. He shovels out criticism by the truckload, talks disrespectfully to his employees, and often takes credit for ideas that are not his own.

Rumors have been circulating around the office that the boss's wife served him divorce papers over the weekend. He has basically locked himself in his office all week. When he does come out, he hardly says a word and looks awful. Most of the employees are reveling in their boss's pain, secretly making jokes and snarky comments.

Bo has never liked his boss, but something in his spirit won't allow him to join in with the other employees. Should he ask his boss if he's okay? Should he give him space? Does he deserve sympathy or is he simply reaping what he sowed?

Using the Key Applications from this session, what could you say or do to help Bo exercise the virtue of love in this situation? (If needed, refer to your video notes for a reminder of this session's Key Applications.)

CLOSING PRAYER

Close your time together with prayer. Share your prayer requests with one another. Ask God to help you put this week's Key Idea into practice.

JOURNAL

If your church is doing the *Believe* church-wide campaign, bring this study guide with you to church and use the following space to take notes from the pastor's or teacher's message. If your church provides an outline, consider keeping it with this guide so you will have all of your notes and thoughts from your *Believe* journey in one place.

VIDEO NOTES ANSWER KEY

love / complete /committed / advocate / rights / vision

Joy

Personal Study

Last week you examined the virtue of love. Perhaps you were challenged to unconditionally love the challenging people in your life. This week before your group meeting, read *Believe, Chapter 22: Joy*. Then take some time to allow the Scripture to enter your mind and to evaluate what truly brings you joy in life.

———— **READ** ————

Read Believe, Chapter 22: Joy *and answer the following questions.*

1. How does keeping God's commands produce joy in our lives?

2. How does acknowledging God's involvement in our lives evoke joy? Israel held annual festivals and traditions to celebrate God's blessings. How do Christians accomplish this today?

3. How can difficult circumstances actually produce joy? What role do our attitudes play in being able to experience joy?

4. Paul said he had to learn how to be content even when he had plenty. Why is it sometimes difficult for people who have plenty to be content?

5. How often do you joyfully acknowledge God's goodness in your life? Identify one good thing God has given to you or done for you in the past week and take a moment to celebrate that with someone else.

EVALUATE

Based on your reading from Believe, Chapter 22: Joy, *use a scale of 1 – 6 to rate how fully your life demonstrates the statements below (1 = does not demonstrate at all, 6 = demonstrates fully).*

_____ I have inner contentment even when things go wrong.

_____ Circumstances do not dictate my mood.

_____ I am excited about the sense of purpose I have for my life.

_____ I can be content with the money and possessions I now have.

---TAKE ACTION---

Memorizing Scripture is a valuable discipline for all believers to exercise. Spend a few minutes each day committing this week's Key Verse to memory.

KEY VERSE: "I have told you this so that my joy may be in you and that your joy may be complete." (John 15:11)

Recite this week's Key Idea out loud. As you do, ask yourself, "Does my life reflect this statement?"

KEY IDEA: Despite my circumstances, I feel inner contentment and understand my purpose in life.

Answer the following questions to help you apply this week's Key Idea to your own life.

1. How would this virtue express itself in your life?

2. What visible attributes can be found in someone who manifests the virtue of joy?

3. What is impeding your ability to choose a lifestyle of joy? How can you overcome this obstacle?

4. What action step can you take this week to increase the presence of joy in your daily life?

Group Meeting

Welcome!

Welcome to Session 22 of *Believe*. If there are any new members in your group, take a moment to introduce yourselves to each other. Then spend a couple of minutes sharing insights or questions about this session's personal study. Now start the video!

VIDEO TEACHING NOTES

As you watch the video segment for Session 22, use the following outline to record some of the main points. (The answer key is found at the end of the session.)

- Key Question: What gives us true happiness and _____ in life?

- Key Verse: "I have told you this so that my joy may be in you and that your joy may be _____." (John 15:11)

- Key Idea: Despite my circumstances, I feel inner contentment and understand my _____ in life.

- (Key Application) Let your _____ help you.

- (Key Application) Saturate your _____ with God's teaching on joy.

- (Key Application) _____ and embrace God's intimate involvement and care in your life.

GETTING STARTED

Begin your discussion by reciting the Key Verse and Key Idea together as a group. On your first attempt, use your notes if you need help. On your second attempt, try to state them completely from memory.

KEY VERSE: "I have told you this so that my joy may be in you and that your joy may be complete." (John 15:11)

KEY IDEA: Despite my circumstances, I feel inner contentment and understand my purpose in life.

GROUP DISCUSSION

As a group, discuss your thoughts and feelings about the following declarations. Which statements are easy to declare with certainty? Which are more challenging, and why?

- I have inner contentment even when things go wrong.

- Circumstances do not dictate my mood.

- I am excited about the sense of purpose I have for my life.

- I can be content with the money and possessions I now have.

Based on your group's dynamics and spiritual maturity, choose the 2 – 3 questions that will lead to the best discussion about this week's Key Idea.

1. In what ways can you relate to Rozanne's story?

2. Discuss practical ways to find joy in the midst of troubling times.

3. Discuss biblical examples of joy that inspire you (i.e., the apostle Paul in prison).

4. Discuss eyewitness examples of joy displayed within your community that motivate you.

Read Psalm 16:1 – 11 and John 15:1 – 11 (see the section "Source of Joy" in Believe) *and choose 1 – 2 questions that will lead to the greatest discussion in your group.*

1. Based on the passages you just read, what practical steps can you glean that will lead to greater joy in your life?

2. Pinpoint unhealthy yet common beliefs and practices that stand in the way of true joy and contentment.

_____

_____

3. How does faith in Christ give us reason to be joyful in all circumstances?

_____

_____

_____

CASE STUDY

Use the following case study as a model for a real-life situation where you might put this week's Key Idea into practice.

Haley joined your book club a few years back. As a group, you usually spend the first fifteen minutes checking in on each other—asking about work, family, health, and hobbies. The discussion is usually uneventful until its Haley's turn to speak. Her life seems to be a chaotic rollercoaster ride. It's either the best week of her life and everything is going as planned, or it's a complete catastrophe. There is no in-between with her. Joy seems to elusively slip through her fingers. Even when things are going well, she seems to be anxious about the future.

As her mentor, she has given you permission to speak honestly when you see areas for improvement in her life.

Using the Key Applications from this session, what could you say or do to help Haley find joy? (If needed, refer to your video notes for a reminder of this session's Key Applications.)

CLOSING PRAYER

Close your time together with prayer. Share your prayer requests with one another. Ask God to help you put this week's Key Idea into practice.

———————————JOURNAL———————————

If your church is doing the *Believe* church-wide campaign, bring this study guide with you to church and use the following space to take notes from the pastor's or teacher's message. If your church provides an outline, consider keeping it with this guide so you will have all of your notes and thoughts from your *Believe* journey in one place.

————————VIDEO NOTES ANSWER KEY————————

contentment / complete / purpose / community / mind / Rehearse

Peace

Personal Study

Last week you examined the virtue of joy. Perhaps you learned that God is the only true source of authentic joy. This week before your group meeting, read *Believe, Chapter 23: Peace*. Then allow the Scripture to enter your mind and release any anxiety that you may be feeling.

READ

Read Believe, Chapter 23: Peace *and answer the following questions.*

1. In the two passages from Romans 5 and Ephesians 2, look for all the references to "peace" and similar terms such as "reconciled," "brought near," and "together." How does Jesus Christ establish peace between us and God and with each other?

2. "Disputable matters" are areas where there is more than one acceptable option or opinion, so we must each decide with conviction and yet respect others who choose differently. What are "disputable matters" for Christians today?

3. After reading Paul's counsel to the church at Colossae and Rome from Romans 12, how would you describe the principles that promote peace in our relationships with each other?

4. How does living at peace with people outside the faith, including government leaders, promote the gospel? How do we achieve this when the government is making decisions and taking actions that conflict with our Christian faith?

5. What is Paul's prescription for anxiety and worry?

EVALUATE

Based on your reading from Believe, Chapter 23: Peace, *use a scale of 1 – 6 to rate how fully your life demonstrates the statements below (1 = does not demonstrate at all, 6 = demonstrates fully).*

_____ I know God has forgiven me because of what Jesus has done.

_____ I am not angry with God, myself, or others.

_____ I forgive people who deeply hurt me.

_____ I have an inner peace from God.

TAKE ACTION

Memorizing Scripture is a valuable discipline for all believers to exercise. Spend a few minutes each day committing this week's Key Verse to memory.

KEY VERSE: "Do not be anxious about anything, but in every situation, by prayer and petition, with thanksgiving, present your requests to God. And the peace of God, which transcends all understanding, will guard your hearts and your minds in Christ Jesus." (Philippians 4:6–7)

Recite this week's Key Idea out loud. As you do, ask yourself, "Does my life reflect this statement?"

KEY IDEA: I am free from anxiety because I have found peace with God, peace with others and peace with myself.

Answer the following questions to help you apply this week's Key Idea to your own life.

1. How would this virtue express itself in your life?

2. What visible attributes can be found in someone who lives at peace?

3. What is impeding your ability to experience true peace? How can you overcome this obstacle?

4. What action step can you take this week to experience greater peace with God, others, and yourself?

Group Meeting

Welcome!

Welcome to Session 23 of *Believe*. If there are any new members in your group, take a moment to introduce yourselves to each other. Then spend a couple of minutes sharing insights or questions about this session's personal study. Now start the video!

VIDEO TEACHING NOTES

As you watch the video segment for Session 23, use the following outline to record some of the main points. (The answer key is found at the end of the session.)

- Key Question: Where do I find _____ to battle anxiety and fear?

- Key Idea: I am free from _____ because I have found peace with God, peace with others, and peace with myself.

- Key Verse: "Do not be anxious about anything, but in every situation, by prayer and petition, with _____, present your requests to God. And the peace of God, which transcends all understanding, will guard your hearts and your minds in Christ Jesus." (Philippians 4:6–7)

- (Key Application) Come to _____ in your relationship with God.

- (Key Application) As much as it is up to you, live at peace with all _____.

- (Key Application) Learn to live at peace with _____.

GETTING STARTED

Begin your discussion by reciting the Key Verse and Key Idea together as a group. On your first attempt, use your notes if you need help. On your second attempt, try to state them completely from memory.

KEY VERSE: "Do not be anxious about anything, but in every situation, by prayer and petition, with thanksgiving, present your requests to God. And the peace of God, which transcends all understanding, will guard your hearts and your minds in Christ Jesus." (Philippians 4:6–7)

KEY IDEA: I am free from anxiety because I have found peace with God, peace with others and peace with myself.

GROUP DISCUSSION

As a group, discuss your thoughts and feelings about the following declarations. Which statements are easy to declare with certainty? Which are more challenging, and why?

- I know God has forgiven me because of what Jesus has done.
- I am not angry with God, myself, or others.
- I forgive people who deeply hurt me.
- I have an inner peace from God.

Based on your group's dynamics and spiritual maturity, choose the 2 – 3 questions that will lead to the best discussion about this week's Key Idea.

1. Although true peace is accessible to all who call Jesus Christ Lord, many continue to live with fear and anxiety. Why do you think this is the case?

2. What are some biblical ways to overcome fear and anxiety? What have you found to be most successful?

3. Who in your life maintains a state of peace even in the most troubling situations? What part does faith play in his or her ability to remain at peace?

4. What thoughts or behaviors feed feelings of fear and anxiety? What boundaries can be set to avoid these pitfalls?

Read Matthew 6:25 – 34 and Philippians 4:4 – 9 (see the section "Peace with Yourself (Inner Peace)" in Believe) *and choose 1 – 2 questions that will lead to the greatest discussion in your group.*

1. Is it possible to give thanks to God in every situation, including the hard times? If so, how?

2. What role does prayer play in combating anxiety? Can you think of an example from your life or someone else's?

3. The apostle Paul writes that the peace of God guards our hearts and minds against anxiety. In what ways have you found this statement to be true?

CASE STUDY

Use the following case study as a model for a real-life situation where you might put this week's Key Idea into practice.

> Your neighbor Kyle has been coming to church with you for about a year now. He was baptized this summer and is attempting to read the Bible on his own. He calls you occasionally when he runs into passages he doesn't understand. During a recent conversation, Kyle admitted, "I'm so grateful for what God has done in my life. I want to make it up to him, but I've done way too many rotten and selfish things. I'm afraid I'll never be able to make things right with him. Honestly, I spend most nights tossing and turning wondering how I can undo the mistakes from my past."

Using the Key Applications from this session, what could you say or do to help Kyle make peace with his past? (If needed, refer to your video notes for a reminder of this session's Key Applications.)

CLOSING PRAYER

Close your time together with prayer. Share your prayer requests with one another. Ask God to help you put this week's Key Idea into practice.

JOURNAL

If your church is doing the *Believe* church-wide campaign, bring this study guide with you to church and use the following space to take notes from the pastor's or teacher's message. If your church provides an outline, consider keeping it with this guide so you will have all of your notes and thoughts from your *Believe* journey in one place.

VIDEO NOTES ANSWER KEY

strength / anxiety / thanksgiving / peace / people / yourself

Self-Control

Personal Study

Last week you examined the virtue of peace. Maybe you were challenged to live at peace in a particular area of struggle — with God, others, or yourself. This week before your group meeting, read *Believe, Chapter 24: Self-Control*. Then allow the Scripture to enter your mind as you evaluate your ability to be self-controlled.

READ

Read Believe, Chapter 24: Self-Control *and answer the following questions.*

1. Note every time the word "self-control" is found in Titus 2:1 – 15. Why do you think self-control is a key virtue required for church leaders?

2. What does the company we keep have to do with our ability to be self-controlled?

3. Why are our tongues so difficult to control?

4. After you read the passage from Peter (see 2 Peter 1:3 – 11) and the passage from Paul (see Galatians 5:16 – 25), describe in your own words how "God-control" works to bring about "self-control" in our lives.

5. In what areas of your life do you struggle with self-control? How do these readings challenge you? How does the knowledge of God's grace comfort you?

EVALUATE

Based on your reading from Believe, Chapter 24: Self-Control, *use a scale of 1 – 6 to rate how fully your life demonstrates the statements below (1 = does not demonstrate at all, 6 = demonstrates fully).*

_____   I am not addicted to any substances — whether food, caffeine, tobacco, alcohol, or chemical.

_____   I do not burst out in anger toward others.

_____   I do not have sexual relationships that are contrary to biblical teaching.

_____   I control my tongue.

TAKE ACTION

Memorizing Scripture is a valuable discipline for all believers to exercise. Spend a few minutes each day committing this week's Key Verse to memory.

KEY VERSE: "For the grace of God has appeared that offers salvation to all people. It teaches us to say 'No' to ungodliness and worldly passions, and to live self-controlled, upright and godly lives in this present age, while we wait for the blessed hope—the appearing of the glory of our great God and Savior, Jesus Christ." (Titus 2:11–13)

Recite this week's Key Idea out loud. As you do, ask yourself, "Does my life reflect this statement?"

KEY IDEA: I have the power through Christ to control myself.

Answer the following questions to help you apply this week's Key Idea to your own life.

1. How would this virtue express itself in your life?

2. What visible attributes can be found in someone who is self-controlled?

3. What is impeding your ability to display self-control? How can you overcome this obstacle?

4. What action step can you take this week to increase your ability to flee from and resist ungodly situations?

Group Meeting

Welcome!

Welcome to Session 24 of *Believe*. If there are any new members in your group, take a moment to introduce yourselves to each other. Then spend a couple of minutes sharing insights or questions about this session's personal study. Now start the video!

VIDEO TEACHING NOTES

As you watch the video segment for Session 24, use the following outline to record some of the main points. (The answer key is found at the end of the session.)

- Key Question: How does God _____ me from addictions and sinful habits?

- Key Idea: I have the power through _____ to control myself.

- Key Verse: "For the grace of God has appeared that offers salvation to all people. It teaches us to say 'No' to ungodliness and worldly passions, and to live _____, upright and godly lives in this present age, while we wait for the blessed hope—the appearing of the glory of our great God and Savior, Jesus Christ." (Titus 2:11–13)

- (Key Application) Self-control is _____ by the grace of God, not the law.

- (Key Application) Self-control is empowered through _____-
_____.

- (Key Application) Self-control is helped along through loving
_____.

---GETTING STARTED---

Begin your discussion by reciting the Key Verse and Key Idea together as a group. On your first attempt, use your notes if you need help. On your second attempt, try to state them completely from memory.

KEY VERSE: "For the grace of God has appeared that offers salvation to all people. It teaches us to say 'No' to ungodliness and worldly passions, and to live self-controlled, upright and godly lives in this present age, while we wait for the blessed hope—the appearing of the glory of our great God and Savior, Jesus Christ." (Titus 2:11–13)

KEY IDEA: I have the power through Christ to control myself.

---GROUP DISCUSSION---

As a group, discuss your thoughts and feelings about the following declarations. Which statements are easy to declare with certainty? Which are more challenging, and why?

- I am not addicted to any substances—whether food, caffeine, tobacco, alcohol, or chemical.

- I do not burst out in anger toward others.

- I do not have sexual relationships that are contrary to biblical teaching.

- I control my tongue.

Based on your group's dynamics and spiritual maturity, choose the 2–3 questions that will lead to the best discussion about this week's Key Idea.

1. When is it most difficult for you to maintain self-control?

2. Describe someone in your life who amazes you with his or her ability to maintain self-control.

3. Often Christians "try harder" to resist sin, but fail. Is there a better way to combat our sinful urges? If so, what is it?

4. What role can biblical community play in building self-control?

Read Titus 2:1 – 15 (see the section "The Call and the Challenge" in Believe) *and choose 1 – 2 questions that will lead to the greatest discussion in your group.*

1. In what way is grace a more effective motivator to resist sin than fear? Can you think of real-life examples?

2. What worldly passions do you have a hard time saying no to?

3. How can focusing on the return of Christ expand our ability to be self-controlled?

CASE STUDY

Use the following case study as a model for a real-life situation where you might put this week's Key Idea into practice.

Molly is one of those people who seems to know everyone. A social butterfly, she is the life of the party wherever she goes. You really enjoy spending time with her, but there are always moments with her that make you feel uncomfortable.

Because of her vast array of friends, she knows the juiciest gossip and loves to share it. Although you know it is wrong, you can't help but get sucked into the conversation. Before you know it, you are openly discussing your coworkers' and friends' darkest moments.

Using the Key Applications from this session, what could you say or do to avoid making this mistake again? (If needed, refer to your video notes for a reminder of this session's Key Applications.)

CLOSING PRAYER

Close your time together with prayer. Share your prayer requests with one another. Ask God to help you put this week's Key Idea into practice.

JOURNAL

If your church is doing the *Believe* church-wide campaign, bring this study guide with you to church and use the following space to take notes from the pastor's or teacher's message. If your church provides an outline, consider keeping it with this guide so you will have all of your notes and thoughts from your *Believe* journey in one place.

VIDEO NOTES ANSWER KEY

free / Christ / self-controlled / motivated / God-control / accountability

Hope

Personal Study

Last week you examined the virtue of self-control. Perhaps you were encouraged to tame your tongue or rein in your temper. This week before your group meeting, read *Believe, Chapter 25: Hope*. Then allow the truths of Scripture to fill your soul with hopefulness.

---READ---

Read Believe, Chapter 25: Hope *and answer the following questions.*

1. Have you ever felt despair like Job did? What questions did you ask of God?

2. As you read about the four sources of false hope, think about which one you are most susceptible to. What made you pick the one you did?

3. What promises of God can you find in the passages from Hebrews 6, Colossians 1, 1 Peter 1, 1 Thessalonians 4, and 1 John 3?

4. What effect did God's promise to Simeon that he would see the first arrival of Christ have on his life? What effect should God's promise to us that we will see the second arrival of Christ have on our lives?

5. According to the writer of Hebrews, what did the biblical heroes endure because they had hope in God? What is the "race marked out" for us? How is hope dependent on faith?

EVALUATE

Based on your reading from Believe, *Chapter 25: Hope, use a scale of 1–6 to rate how fully your life demonstrates the statements below (1 = does not demonstrate at all, 6 = demonstrates fully).*

_____ I think a great deal about heaven and what God is preparing for me as a Christian.

_____ I am confident that God is working everything out for my good, regardless of the circumstances today.

_____ My hope in God increases through my daily pursuit to live like Christ.

_____ My hope for the future is not found in my health or wealth because both are so uncertain, but in God.

---------------------------------TAKE ACTION---------------------------------

Memorizing Scripture is a valuable discipline for all believers to exercise. Spend a few minutes each day committing this week's Key Verse to memory.

KEY VERSE: "We have this hope as an anchor for the soul, firm and secure. It enters the inner sanctuary behind the curtain, where our fore-runner, Jesus, has entered on our behalf." (Hebrews 6:19–20)

--------------------- ---------------------

Recite this week's Key Idea out loud. As you do, ask yourself, "Does my life reflect this statement?"

KEY IDEA: I can cope with the hardships of life because of the hope I have in Jesus Christ.

Answer the following questions to help you apply this week's Key Idea to your own life.

1. How would this virtue express itself in your life?

2. What visible attributes can be found in someone who is filled with hope?

3. What is impeding your ability to experience hopefulness? How can you overcome this obstacle?

4. What action step can you take this week to increase your belief in the promises of God?

Group Meeting

Welcome!

Welcome to Session 25 of *Believe*. If there are any new members in your group, take a moment to introduce yourselves to each other. Then spend a couple of minutes sharing insights or questions about this session's personal study. Now start the video!

————————————VIDEO TEACHING NOTES————————————

As you watch the video segment for Session 25, use the following outline to record some of the main points. (The answer key is found at the end of the session.)

- Key Question: How do I _____ with the hardships and struggles of life?

- Key Idea: I can _____ with the hardships of life because of the hope I have in Jesus Christ.

- The first cause: Believe in the _____. The second cause: Believe in the _____ making the promise.

- Key Verse: "We have this _____ as an anchor for the soul, firm and secure. It enters the inner sanctuary behind the curtain, where our forerunner, Jesus, has entered on our behalf." (Hebrews 6:19–20)

- (Key Application) If you want to increase your hope, get to know and _____ Jesus better.

- (Key Application) If you want to increase your hope, get to know and trust Jesus' _____.

GETTING STARTED

Begin your discussion by reciting the Key Verse and Key Idea together as a group. On your first attempt, use your notes if you need help. On your second attempt, try to state them completely from memory.

> **KEY VERSE:** "We have this hope as an anchor for the soul, firm and secure. It enters the inner sanctuary behind the curtain, where our forerunner, Jesus, has entered on our behalf." (Hebrews 6:19–20)

> **KEY IDEA:** I can cope with the hardships of life because of the hope I have in Jesus Christ.

GROUP DISCUSSION

As a group, discuss your thoughts and feelings about the following declarations. Which statements are easy to declare with certainty? Which are more challenging, and why?

- I think a great deal about heaven and what God is preparing for me as a Christian.

- I am confident that God is working everything out for my good, regardless of the circumstances today.

- My hope in God increases through my daily pursuit to live like Christ.

- My hope for the future is not found in my health or wealth because both are so uncertain, but in God.

Based on your group's dynamics and spiritual maturity, choose the 2–3 questions that will lead to the best discussion about this week's Key Idea.

1. We are all sometimes guilty of placing our faith in false-hopes. Which one (riches, people, idols, human government) is most alluring to you? Why?

2. In what ways have false-hopes let you down in the past?

3. Hope is not an emotion you can make yourself feel with simple willpower. There-fore, what action steps can you take in order to develop a greater sense of hope?

4. What experiences with God have increased your ability to trust him and his promises?

Read Hebrews 11:1 – 12:3 (see the section "Hope Activates Faith, Faith Deepens Hope" in Believe) *and choose 1 – 2 questions that will lead to the greatest discussion in your group.*

1. Faith and hope seem to be the common underlying characteristics of all biblical heroes. In what ways do these characteristics work together?

2. In your opinion, which character's story of faith exhibited the most hope in God's promises?

3. It's easy to "grow weary and lose heart" in the broken world we live in. What does the writer of this passage encourage us to do in order to combat hopelessness?

CASE STUDY

Use the following case study as a model for a real-life situation where you might put this week's Key Idea into practice.

> Your cousin Rob has trust issues, which is understandable. His dad (your uncle) ran out on the family just before Rob's twelfth birthday. Friends and coworkers have continually taken advantage of his generosity and kindness. In an honest moment on your back porch, he confesses that he believes in God but does not trust him. He goes on to explain that he desires to trust God but fears that his past has caused him to be irreversibly jaded.

Using the Key Applications from this session, what could you say or do to help Rob begin to trust in God's character and his promises? (If needed, refer to your video notes for a reminder of this session's Key Applications.)

CLOSING PRAYER

Close your time together with prayer. Share your prayer requests with one another. Ask God to help you put this week's Key Idea into practice.

JOURNAL

If your church is doing the *Believe* church-wide campaign, bring this study guide with you to church and use the following space to take notes from the pastor's or teacher's message. If your church provides an outline, consider keeping it with this guide so you will have all of your notes and thoughts from your *Believe* journey in one place.

VIDEO NOTES ANSWER KEY
---

deal / cope / promise, One / hope / trust / promises

Patience

Personal Study

Last week you examined the virtue of hope. Perhaps you were empowered to better handle the hardships of life. This week before your group meeting, read *Believe, Chapter 26: Patience*. Then open your heart and mind to the lessons God wants to teach you through this session.

READ

Read Believe, Chapter 26: Patience *and answer the following questions.*

1. As you read the passage from Numbers 14, note some examples of God's patience.

2. As you read 1 Samuel 24, look for examples of how David waited on God's timing. Why is this so difficult for many people to do?

3. As you read Proverbs 14:29, 16:32, 19:11, and 25:15, ponder these two questions: How does patience diffuse a conflict? How do impatience and rashness escalate it?

4. Can you discern why God healed the lame man and not Paul? How does trusting in God's goodness give us the strength to live patiently with our pressures?

5. Do you struggle more with being patient with other people or dealing with un-avoidable pressures in your life? What is one thing you learned from this chapter that might help you?

EVALUATE

Based on your reading from Believe, Chapter 26: Patience, *use a scale of 1–6 to rate how fully your life demonstrates the statements below (1 = does not demonstrate at all, 6 = demonstrates fully).*

_____ I do not get angry with God when I have to endure suffering.

_____ I am known to maintain honesty and integrity when under pressure.

_____ I always put matters into God's hands when I am under pressure.

_____ I keep my composure even when people or circumstances irritate me.

---TAKE ACTION---

Memorizing Scripture is a valuable discipline for all believers to exercise. Spend a few minutes each day committing this week's Key Verse to memory.

KEY VERSE: "Whoever is patient has great understanding, but one who is quick-tempered displays folly." (Proverbs 14:29)

Recite this week's Key Idea out loud. As you do, ask yourself, "Does my life reflect this statement?"

KEY IDEA: I am slow to anger and endure patiently under the unavoidable pressures of life.

Answer the following questions to help you apply this week's Key Idea to your own life.

1. How would this virtue express itself in your life?

2. What visible attributes can be found in someone who is slow to anger?

3. What is impeding your ability to respond patiently to life's unexpected pressures? How can you overcome this obstacle?

4. What action step can you take this week to grow in the area of patience?

Group Meeting

Welcome!

Welcome to Session 26 of *Believe*. If there are any new members in your group, take a moment to introduce yourselves to each other. Then spend a couple of minutes sharing insights or questions about this session's personal study. Now start the video!

VIDEO TEACHING NOTES

As you watch the video segment for Session 26, use the following outline to record some of the main points. (The answer key is found at the end of the session.)

- Key Question: How does God provide the help I need to deal with _____?

- Key Verse: "Whoever is _____ has great understanding, but one who is quick-tempered displays folly." (Proverb 14:29)

- Key Idea: I am slow to anger and endure patiently under the unavoidable _____ of life.

- "Consider it pure joy, my brothers and sisters, whenever you face trails of many kinds, because you know that the testing of your faith produces _____. Let perseverance finish its work so that you may be mature and complete, lacking in anything." (James 1:2–4)

- (Key Application) Trust God's timing, his ways, and his _____.

- (Key Application) Don't let unimportant stuff _____ you so much.

- (Key Application) Offer the patience today that you would like to _____ tomorrow.

GETTING STARTED

Begin your discussion by reciting the Key Verse and Key Idea together as a group. On your first attempt, use your notes if you need help. On your second attempt, try to state them completely from memory.

KEY VERSE: "Whoever is patient has great understanding, but one who is quick-tempered displays folly." (Proverbs 14:29)

KEY IDEA: I am slow to anger and endure patiently under the unavoidable pressures of life.

GROUP DISCUSSION

As a group, discuss your thoughts and feelings about the following declarations. Which statements are easy to declare with certainty? Which are more challenging, and why?

- I do not get angry with God when I have to endure suffering.

- I am known to maintain honesty and integrity when under pressure.

- I always put matters into God's hands when I am under pressure.

- I keep my composure even when people or circumstances irritate me.

Based on your group's dynamics and spiritual maturity, choose the 2–3 questions that will lead to the best discussion about this week's Key Idea.

1. What current situations test your patience most? Why?

2. What external forces negatively impact your ability to remain patient?

3. How has your relationship with God impacted your ability to be slow to anger in stressful situations?

4. Describe a challenging time in your life that helped you develop perseverance. How did you grow spiritually during that period?

_____

_____

Read 1 Samuel 26:1 – 25 (see the section "Being Slow to Become Angry" in Believe) *and choose 1 – 2 questions that will lead to the greatest discussion in your group.*

1. How did the years David spent waiting to become king prepare him for the responsibility of the throne?

_____

_____

2. In what ways have periods of waiting developed your character?

_____

_____

3. In what ways have you experienced the foolishness of quick-temperedness?

_____

_____

CASE STUDY

Use the following case study as a model for a real-life situation where you might put this week's Key Idea into practice.

Kelly has been dreaming about creating her own family since she was a little girl. She was engaged soon after college but felt led by God to call it off. Since then, she has tried numerous ways to find a good husband, but nothing has materialized. Anxiety and fear breed within her as each year passes. She is beginning to believe she will always be alone.

Using the Key Applications from this session, what could you say or do to help Kelly? (If needed, refer to your video notes for a reminder of this session's Key Applications.)

CLOSING PRAYER

Close your time together with prayer. Share your prayer requests with one another. Ask God to help you put this week's Key Idea into practice.

---JOURNAL---

If your church is doing the *Believe* church-wide campaign, bring this study guide with you to church and use the following space to take notes from the pastor's or teacher's message. If your church provides an outline, consider keeping it with this guide so you will have all of your notes and thoughts from your *Believe* journey in one place.

---VIDEO NOTES ANSWER KEY---

stress / patient / pressures / perseverance / outcomes / bother / receive

Kindness/Goodness

Personal Study

Last week you examined the virtue of patience. Perhaps you were challenged to endure more patiently under life's hardships. This week before your group meeting, read *Believe, Chapter 27: Kindness/Goodness*. Then take some time to allow the Scripture to enter your mind and prepare your heart to receive the lessons God wants to teach you.

READ

Read Believe, Chapter 27: Kindness/Goodness *and answer the following questions.*

1. Write your own Psalm. Start with the same opening words of Psalm 107: "Give thanks to the LORD, for he is good; his love endures forever. Let the redeemed of the LORD tell their story." Then record an act of kindness and goodness that God has done for you.

2. How do you reconcile Rahab's decision to lie about the spies' whereabouts with her act of kindness?

3. Jesus teaches us to do exactly what David did for Mephibosheth. Why does it matter that we invite people into our lives who cannot reciprocate? Can you think of a way to include someone in your activities who is usually left out?

_____

_____

_____

_____

4. As you read Philemon 1–25, note how Paul models kindness in his appeal to Philemon. Would you have honored Paul's request? Why or why not?

_____

_____

_____

5. Write down a list of every principle you discover from the teachings of Jesus, Peter, and Paul on how to not only do the kind thing but the right thing in our relationships. Which principle speaks to you most? Why?

_____

_____

_____

_____

_____ EVALUATE _____

Based on your reading from Believe, *Chapter 27: Kindness/Goodness, use a scale of 1–6 to rate how fully your life demonstrates the statements below (1 = does not demonstrate at all, 6 = demonstrates fully).*

_____   I would never keep money that didn't belong to me.

_____   I am known as a person who speaks words of kindness to those in need of encouragement.

_____   I give to others expecting nothing in return.

_____   I help those who are in trouble or who cannot help themselves.

TAKE ACTION

Memorizing Scripture is a valuable discipline for all believers to exercise. Spend a few minutes each day committing this week's Key Verse to memory.

KEY VERSE: "Make sure that nobody pays back wrong for wrong, but always strive to do what is good for each other and for everyone else." (1 Thessalonians 5:15)

Recite this week's Key Idea out loud. As you do, ask yourself, "Does my life reflect this statement?"

KEY IDEA: I choose to be kind and good in my relationships with others.

Answer the following questions to help you apply this week's Key Idea to your own life.

1. How could this virtue express itself in your life?

2. What visible attributes can be found in someone who exudes kindness and goodness?

3. What is impeding your ability to embrace this virtue? How can you overcome this obstacle?

4. What action step can you take this week to increase your expressions of kindness and goodness in daily life?

Group Meeting
Welcome!

Welcome to Session 27 of *Believe*. If there are any new members in your group, take a moment to introduce yourselves to each other. Then spend a couple of minutes sharing insights or questions about this session's personal study. Now start the video!

─────────────── **VIDEO TEACHING NOTES** ───────────────

As you watch the video segment for Session 27, use the following outline to record some of the main points. (The answer key is found at the end of the session.)

- Key Idea: I choose to be kind and good in my _____ with others.

- Key Verse: "Make sure that nobody pays back wrong for wrong, but always strive to do what is _____ for each other and for everyone else." (1 Thessalonians 5:15)

- Key Question: What does it mean to do the right thing in my relationships with _____?

- (Key Application) Out of a pure heart ... we do not pay back wrong for _____.

- (Key Application) Out of a pure heart ... seek to _____ others up.

- (Key Application) Out of a pure heart ... do the _____ thing out of love.

─────────────── **GETTING STARTED** ───────────────

Begin your discussion by reciting the Key Verse and Key Idea together as a group. On your first attempt, use your notes if you need help. On your second attempt, try to state them completely from memory.

KEY VERSE: "Make sure that nobody pays back wrong for wrong, but always strive to do what is good for each other and for everyone else." (1 Thessalonians 5:15)

KEY IDEA: I choose to be kind and good in my relationships with others.

GROUP DISCUSSION

As a group, discuss your thoughts and feelings about the following declarations. Which statements are easy to declare with certainty? Which are more challenging, and why?

- I would never keep money that didn't belong to me.
- I am known as a person who speaks words of kindness to those in need of encouragement.
- I give to others expecting nothing in return.
- I help those who are in trouble or who cannot help themselves.

Based on your group's dynamics and spiritual maturity, choose the 2–3 questions that will lead to the best discussion about this week's Key Idea.

1. What are some specific ways you have experienced God's kindness in your life? What impact has it made on you?

2. If the adversary of hope is fear, what would be the enemy of kindness and goodness?

3. How have other people recently shown you genuine kindness? How did you respond?

4. How are the virtues of kindness and goodness different? What are some practical examples of each virtue in action?

Read 1 Samuel 20:13 – 16 and 2 Samuel 9:1 – 13 (see the section "Stories of Kindness: David" in Believe) *and choose 1 – 2 questions that will lead to the greatest discussion in your group.*

1. David's predecessor King Saul was downright evil to him for thirteen years. In what ways would it be tempting for David to use his newly acquired power to exact revenge on Saul and his family?

2. Note specifically how David exhibited kindness and goodness to Jonathan's family, in keeping with his promise to Jonathan. Why was this considered a radical decision?

3. David doesn't appear to have any bitterness or hatred toward Saul's family. After all the hardship Saul caused him, how is this possible? What can we learn from David's example?

CASE STUDY

Use the following case study as a model for a real-life situation where you might put this week's Key Idea into practice.

Jared couldn't believe his eyes. He had read through the lawsuit three times, and with each reading he became more and more shocked. His best friend and former business partner, Cal, was suing him. They had gone into business together right out of college and after five tough, grinding years, their company began to experience incredible success.

After fifteen years of steady growth, they mutually agreed to split their partnership when they couldn't agree on the direction to take the business. Cal took his share of the revenue and tried his luck in the investment world, but risky ventures have left him nearly broke. So he filed a lawsuit filled with false accusations against Jared.

Using the Key Applications from this session, what could you say or do to help Jared? (If needed, refer to your video notes for a reminder of this session's Key Applications.)

CLOSING PRAYER

Close your time together with prayer. Share your prayer requests with one another. Ask God to help you put this week's Key Idea into practice.

JOURNAL

If your church is doing the *Believe* church-wide campaign, bring this study guide with you to church and use the following space to take notes from the pastor's or teacher's message. If your church provides an outline, consider keeping it with this guide so you will have all of your notes and thoughts from your *Believe* journey in one place.

VIDEO NOTES ANSWER KEY

relationships / good / others / wrong / build / hard

Faithfulness

Personal Study

Last week you examined the virtues of kindness and goodness. Perhaps you were challenged to do something good for someone — with no strings attached. This week before your group meeting, read *Believe, Chapter 28: Faithfulness*. Then take some time to allow the Scripture to enter your mind and prepare your heart to receive anything God wants to teach you through this study.

READ

Read Believe, Chapter 28: Faithfulness *and answer the following questions.*

1. As you read the passages from Deuteronomy 32, Psalm 36, and Lamentations 3, note the phrases that best express God's faithfulness to you.

2. Why will a faithful person be richly blessed and a person eager to get rich be punished?

3. As you read Joseph's story, consider this session's Key Verse from Proverbs 3:3 – 4. How did Joseph live out the truth of this passage?

4. Throughout the Bible, God never calls us to be successful. He calls us to be faithful. As we saw in Joseph's life, sometimes success follows faithfulness; sometimes it doesn't. What do you think about this? How are you doing at being faithful?

5. Based on what you have learned about faithfulness, who are some of the most faithful people you know? How have they found honor and a good name in your sight? In the sight of others? If it is possible, let them know.

EVALUATE

Based on your reading from Believe, Chapter 28: Faithfulness, *use a scale of 1 – 6 to rate how fully your life demonstrates the statements below (1 = does not demonstrate at all, 6 = demonstrates fully).*

_____ I take unpopular stands when my faith dictates.

_____ I discipline my thoughts based on my faith in Jesus Christ.

_____ I follow God even when it involves suffering.

_____ I follow through on commitments I have made to God.

-------------------------TAKE ACTION-------------------------

Memorizing Scripture is a valuable discipline for all believers to exercise. Spend a few minutes each day committing this week's Key Verse to memory.

KEY VERSE: "Let love and faithfulness never leave you; bind them around your neck, write them on the tablet of your heart. Then you will win favor and a good name in the sight of God and man." (Proverbs 3:3–4)

Recite this week's Key Idea out loud. As you do, ask yourself, "Does my life reflect this statement?"

KEY IDEA: I have established a good name with God and others based on my loyalty to those relationships.

Answer the following questions to help you apply this week's Key Idea to your own life.

1. How could this virtue express itself in your life?

2. What visible attributes can be found in someone who exhibits faithfulness?

3. What is impeding your ability to be faithful to God and others? How can you overcome this obstacle?

4. What action step can you take this week to increase your faithfulness?

Group Meeting

Welcome!

Welcome to Session 28 of *Believe*. If there are any new members in your group, take a moment to introduce yourselves to each other. Then spend a couple of minutes sharing insights or questions about this session's personal study. Now start the video!

————VIDEO TEACHING NOTES————

As you watch the video segment for Session 28, use the following outline to record some of the main points. (The answer key is found at the end of the session.)

- Key Question: Why is it _____ to be loyal and committed to others?

- Key Verse: "Let love and _____ never leave you; bind them around your neck, write them on the tablet of your heart. Then you will win favor and a good name in the sight of God and man." (Proverbs 3:3–4)

- George MacDonald writes, "To be _____ is a greater compliment than to be loved."

- Key Idea: I have established a good _____ with God and others based on my loyalty to those relationships.

- (Key Application) God's faithfulness to us _____ our faithfulness to him and others.

- (Key Application) God does not call us to be _____ but faithful.

- (Key Application) If we _____ to be faithful, he is faithful and just to forgive us.

GETTING STARTED

Begin your discussion by reciting the Key Verse and Key Idea together as a group. On your first attempt, use your notes if you need help. On your second attempt, try to state them completely from memory.

KEY VERSE: "Let love and faithfulness never leave you; bind them around your neck, write them on the tablet of your heart. Then you will win favor and a good name in the sight of God and man." (Proverbs 3:3–4)

KEY IDEA: I have established a good name with God and others based on my loyalty to those relationships.

GROUP DISCUSSION

As a group, discuss your thoughts and feelings about the following declarations. Which statements are easy to declare with certainty? Which are more challenging, and why?

- I take unpopular stands when my faith dictates.
- I discipline my thoughts based on my faith in Jesus Christ.
- I follow God even when it involves suffering.
- I follow through on commitments I have made to God.

Based on your group's dynamics and spiritual maturity, choose the 2–3 questions that will lead to the best discussion about this week's Key Idea.

1. What do you think is the root or cause of unfaithfulness toward God or others?

2. In a world filled with unfaithfulness, how can we find inspirational examples of faithfulness?

3. In your opinion, what motivates genuine faithfulness?

4. How have you seen suffering test and/or strengthen someone's faithfulness?

_____

_____

Read Ruth 1:1 – 22 (see the section "Stories of Faithfulness: Ruth" in Believe) *and choose 1 – 2 questions that will lead to the greatest discussion in your group.*

1. Life for Naomi and Ruth was much different than the world we live in today. Aside from grieving her loss, why would the death of her husband and sons be so devastating for Naomi? Why did she instruct her daughters-in-law to go back to their families?

_____

_____

2. Why was Ruth's decision stay with her mother-in-law an incredible act of faithfulness?

_____

_____

3. Have you ever witnessed Ruth-like faithfulness in another person? If so, how?

_____

_____

CASE STUDY

Use the following case study as a model for a real-life situation where you might put this week's Key Idea into practice.

Deidre had never stepped foot into a church building until she was well into her twenties. Something about church made her feel anxious. She felt like God was upset or disappointed with her. A year ago, she decided to face her fear and get involved at your church. Although she has been consistently involved in church community, she is reluctant to fully devote herself to Christ because she is sure she will mess up and disappoint God in the long run.

Using the Key Applications from this session, what could you say or do to help Deidre? (If needed, refer to your video notes for a reminder of this session's Key Applications.)

CLOSING PRAYER

Close your time together with prayer. Share your prayer requests with one another. Ask God to help you put this week's Key Idea into practice.

JOURNAL

If your church is doing the *Believe* church-wide campaign, bring this study guide with you to church and use the following space to take notes from the pastor's or teacher's message. If your church provides an outline, consider keeping it with this guide so you will have all of your notes and thoughts from your *Believe* journey in one place.

VIDEO NOTES ANSWER KEY
---

important / faithfulness / trusted / name / inspires / successful / fail

Gentleness

Personal Study

Last week you examined the practice of faithfulness. Perhaps you were challenged to build a trustworthy reputation for yourself. This week before your group meeting, read *Believe, Chapter 29: Gentleness*. Then take some time to allow the Scripture to enter your mind as you evaluate your relationships with people outside of the faith.

READ

Read Believe, Chapter 29: Gentleness *and answer the following questions.*

1. Consider the Key Verse for this session. Why do you think Paul put these two sentences together?

2. Some have suggested that Jesus asked Simon Peter if he loved him three times to help restore him from the three times he denied him. Do you think this was Jesus' intent? Do you think this would have helped you if you were in Peter's sandals?

3. As you read Jesus' pieces of advice on gentleness, identify the one that most speaks to you. Why did you choose this one?

4. Look at Ephesians 4:26 – 28 again. How do we give the devil a foothold in our lives when we let the sun go down while we are still angry?

5. As you read the three stories from 1 Samuel 25, 2 Samuel 16, and 1 Thessalonians 2, find the ways anger is stirred up and look for how gentleness affects tense situations.

EVALUATE

Based on your reading from Believe, *Chapter 29: Gentleness,* use a scale of 1 – 6 to rate how fully your life demonstrates the statements below (1 = does not demonstrate at all, 6 = demonstrates fully).

_____ I consider my own shortcomings when faced with the failures of others.

_____ I am known as a person who is sensitive to the needs of others.

_____ I am known for not raising my voice.

_____ I allow people to make mistakes.

TAKE ACTION

Memorizing Scripture is a valuable discipline for all believers to exercise. Spend a few minutes each day committing this week's Key Verse to memory.

KEY VERSE: "Let your gentleness be evident to all. The Lord is near." (Philippians 4:5)

Recite this week's Key Idea out loud. As you do, ask yourself, "Does my life reflect this statement?"

KEY IDEA: I am thoughtful, considerate and calm in my dealings with others.

Answer the following questions to help you apply this week's Key Idea to your own life.

1. How could this virtue practically express itself in your life?

2. What visible attributes can be found in someone who is consistently gentle?

3. What is impeding your ability to treat people gently? How can you overcome this obstacle?

4. What action step can you take this week to become a gentler person?

Group Meeting
Welcome!

Welcome to Session 29 of *Believe*. If there are any new members in your group, take a moment to introduce yourselves to each other. Then spend a couple of minutes sharing insights or questions about this session's personal study. Now start the video!

―――――――――VIDEO TEACHING NOTES―――――――――

As you watch the video segment for Session 29, use the following outline to record some of the main points. (The answer key is found at the end of the session.)

- Key Idea: I am thoughtful, considerate and calm in my _____ with others.

- Key Verse: "Let your _____ be evident to all. The Lord is near." (Philippians 4:5)

- Key Question: How do I _____ thoughtfulness and consideration?

- "A _____ answer turns away wrath, but a harsh word stirs up anger." (Proverbs 15:1)

- (Key Application) Be _____.

- (Key Application) Be _____.

- (Key Application) Be _____.

―――――――――GETTING STARTED―――――――――

Begin your discussion by reciting the Key Verse and Key Idea together as a group. On your first attempt, use your notes if you need help. On your second attempt, try to state them completely from memory.

KEY VERSE: "Let your gentleness be evident to all. The Lord is near." (Philippians 4:5)

――――――――― 🔑 ―――――――――

KEY IDEA: I am thoughtful, considerate and calm in my dealings with others.

GROUP DISCUSSION

As a group, discuss your thoughts and feelings about the following declarations. Which statements are easy to declare with certainty? Which are more challenging, and why?

- I consider my own shortcomings when faced with the failures of others.
- I am known as a person who is sensitive to the needs of others.
- I am known for not raising my voice.
- I allow people to make mistakes.

Based on your group's dynamics and spiritual maturity, choose the 2–3 questions that will lead to the best discussion about this week's Key Idea.

1. Why do you think the most challenging Christlike virtue for believers to grasp is gentleness?

2. Consider someone in your life who has the ability to be calm and collected in stress-filled moments. How did he or she manage to develop this virtue?

3. Are there certain circumstances in your life that make gentle conduct nearly impossible? How could your relationship with God empower you to alter your reaction to this situation?

4. In what ways can Jesus' life be a guiding example of gentleness for us when we face difficulties of our own?

Read Matthew 7:1–5, 1 Timothy 3:1–4, and James 3:17–18 (see the section "Nuggets on Gentleness" in Believe) *and choose 1–2 questions that will lead to the greatest discussion in your group.*

1. How does judgment choke our ability to be calm, considerate, and thoughtful?

2. Why do you think the Bible specifically instructs authority figures to be gentle with the people under their care?

3. If judgment leads to anger and quarreling, what does gentleness produce?

CASE STUDY

Use the following case study as a model for a real-life situation where you might put this week's Key Idea into practice.

Sean has invested incalculable amounts of time and money into the development of his youngest son, Cade. The results have been infuriating. Cade has flunked out of college twice. Sean has used family and business contacts to help Cade find good jobs, but Cade's work ethic is rotten. Consequently, he lost every job Sean set up for him. As a believer, Sean wants to do what is right, but he can hardly hold back the rage he feels toward his son.

Using the Key Applications from this session, what could you say or do to help Sean? (If needed, refer to your video notes for a reminder of this session's Key Applications.)

CLOSING PRAYER

Close your time together with prayer. Share your prayer requests with one another. Ask God to help you put this week's Key Idea into practice.

JOURNAL

If your church is doing the *Believe* church-wide campaign, bring this study guide with you to church and use the following space to take notes from the pastor's or teacher's message. If your church provides an outline, consider keeping it with this guide so you will have all of your notes and thoughts from your *Believe* journey in one place.

VIDEO NOTES ANSWER KEY

dealings / gentleness / demonstrate / gentle / thoughtful / considerate / calm

Humility

Personal Study

Last week you examined the virtue of gentleness. Perhaps you were challenged to be more calm, thoughtful, and considerate in tough situations. This week before your group meeting, read *Believe, Chapter 30: Humility*. Then take some time to allow the Scripture to enter your mind and open your heart to the lessons God wants to teach you.

READ

Read Believe, Chapter 30: Humility *and answer the following questions.*

1. Servant leadership is what Jesus modeled while on earth. What other ways can we demonstrate this principle besides washing someone's feet?

2. What do you think was involved when it says Jesus "made himself nothing"? What was he before he made himself nothing? Why did he do this?

3. As you read the Scripture passages from Psalms and Proverbs, write down all the ways God opposes the proud and grants favor to the humble.

4. As you read the Scripture passage from Matthew 5, identify all of God's paradoxes (such as, rejoice when people persecute you). Have you seen the truth of any of these paradoxes in your own experience?

5. Micah tells us that God requires us to act justly, love mercy, and walk humbly with God. How are these acts related?

EVALUATE

Based on your reading from Believe, Chapter 30: Humility, *use a scale of 1 – 6 to rate how fully your life demonstrates the statements below (1 = does not demonstrate at all, 6 = demonstrates fully).*

_____ As a child of God, I do not think too highly or too lowly of myself.

_____ I am not known as a person who brags.

_____ I am willing to make any of my faults known to Christians who care for me.

_____ I am not upset when my achievements are not recognized.

─────────────TAKE ACTION─────────────

Memorizing Scripture is a valuable discipline for all believers to exercise. Spend a few minutes each day committing this week's Key Verse to memory.

KEY VERSE: "Do nothing out of selfish ambition or vain conceit. Rather, in humility value others above yourselves, not looking to your own interests but each of you to the interests of the others." (Philippians 2:3–4)

───────────── 🔑 ─────────────

Recite this week's Key Idea out loud. As you do, ask yourself, "Does my life reflect this statement?"

KEY IDEA: I choose to esteem others above myself.

Answer the following questions to help you apply this week's Key Idea to your own life.

1. How could this virtue express itself in your life?

2. What visible attributes can be found in persons who esteem others above themselves?

3. What is impeding your ability to value others above yourself? How can you overcome this obstacle?

4. What action step can you take this week to reject pride and grow in humility?

Group Meeting

Welcome!

Welcome to Session 30 of *Believe*. If there are any new members in your group, take a moment to introduce yourselves to each other. Then spend a couple of minutes sharing insights or questions about this session's personal study. Now start the video!

—VIDEO TEACHING NOTES—

As you watch the video segment for Session 30, use the following outline to record some of the main points. (The answer key is found at the end of the session.)

- Key Idea: I choose to _____ others above myself.

- Key Verse: "Do nothing out of _____ ambition or vain conceit. Rather, in humility value others above yourselves, not looking to your own interests but each of you to the interests of the others." (Philippians 2:3–4)

- Key Question: What does it mean to _____ others before myself?

- What better person to teach us about humility than the person we are passionately seeking to be like— _____ himself.

- "No," said Peter, "you shall never _____ my feet." Jesus answered, "Unless I wash you, you have no part with me." "Then, Lord," Simon Peter replied, "not just my feet but my hands and my head as well!" (John 13:8–9)

- (Key Application) _____ is not the same as humility.

- (Key Application) Christlike humility _____ you up to build others up.

GETTING STARTED

Begin your discussion by reciting the Key Verse and Key Idea together as a group. On your first attempt, use your notes if you need help. On your second attempt, try to state them completely from memory.

> **KEY VERSE:** "Do nothing out of selfish ambition or vain conceit. Rather, in humility value others above yourselves, not looking to your own interests but each of you to the interests of the others." (Philippians 2:3–4)

KEY IDEA: I choose to esteem others above myself.

GROUP DISCUSSION

As a group, discuss your thoughts and feelings about the following declarations. Which statements are easy to declare with certainty? Which are more challenging, and why?

- As a child of God, I do not think too highly or too lowly of myself.

- I am not known as a person who brags.

- I am willing to make any of my faults known to Christians who care for me.

- I am not upset when my achievements are not recognized.

Based on your group's dynamics and spiritual maturity, choose the 2–3 questions that will lead to the best discussion about this week's Key Idea.

1. In what ways are the virtue of humility and our identity in Christ related?

2. How did Jesus teach his disciples the virtue of humility?

3. What do you think are the biggest adversaries of humility? How can we combat them?

4. What spiritual practices help us esteem others above ourselves?

Read Matthew 5:1 – 12, Luke 9:46 – 48, and Mark 10:35 – 45 (see the section "The Paradox of Humility" in Believe) _and choose 1 – 2 questions that will lead to the greatest discussion in your group._

1. What is the difference between what Jesus calls "blessed" and what the world refers to as "success"?

2. In the kingdom of God, Jesus said the last shall be first and the first shall be last. What does this mean for people who desire positions of power and influence in the community of faith?

3. In what ways does Christlike humility set us apart from the rest of the world?

———————————————CASE STUDY———————————————

Use the following case study as a model for a real-life situation where you might put this week's Key Idea into practice.

Les has always felt the need to prove himself to his family. As the youngest of five brothers, he has constantly lived in their shadows. Les was the only one of the boys who didn't excel in sports or make the dean's list growing up. When the other brothers went off to college, he jumped around from one entry-level job to another. Since then, however, he has had some success with a small business he started. At family gatherings Les is continually bragging about his business's success, and it's causing tension because some of the other brothers have fallen on hard times.

Using the Key Applications from this session, what could you say or do to help Les? (If needed, refer to your video notes for a reminder of this session's Key Applications.)

CLOSING PRAYER

Close your time together with prayer. Share your prayer requests with one another. Ask God to help you put this week's Key Idea into practice.

JOURNAL

If your church is doing the *Believe* church-wide campaign, bring this study guide with you to church and use the following space to take notes from the pastor's or teacher's message. If your church provides an outline, consider keeping it with this guide so you will have all of your notes and thoughts from your *Believe* journey in one place.

VIDEO NOTES ANSWER KEY

esteem / selfish / value / Jesus / wash / Humiliation / frees

Christian Life Profile Assessment Workbook Updated Edition

Developing Your Personal Plan to Think, Act, and Be Like Jesus

Randy Frazee

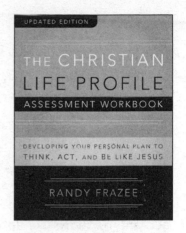

This comprehensive discipleship tool enables churches to assess the Christian beliefs, practices, and virtues of each member to help everyone grow. The assessment is based on the thirty Key Ideas as outlined in the book *Think, Act, Be Like Jesus*, also by Pastor Randy Frazee. These thirty core competencies help churches know when they are making progress in guiding their members toward Christlikeness. Individuals answer 120 questions about their Christian beliefs, practices, and virtues. Three friends also assess them in the virtues area. Using the results, individuals identify areas in which they would like to grow during the upcoming year and create plans to ensure spiritual success.

The Christian Life Profile journey is best experienced in a small group community that seeks to encourage, pray, and hold each other accountable for progress. The goal is to take the profile again, one year later, to monitor the journey.

Available in stores and online!

Believe, NIV

Living the Story of the Bible to Become Like Jesus

Randy Frazee

Grounded in carefully selected Scripture, *Believe, NIV* is a unique spiritual growth experience that takes you on a journey to think, act, and be more like Jesus. General editor and pastor Randy Frazee walks you through the ten key Beliefs of the Christian faith, the ten key Practices of a Jesus-follower, and the ten key Virtues that characterize someone who is becoming more like Jesus. Every believer needs to ask these three questions:

- WHAT DO I BELIEVE?
- WHAT SHOULD I DO?
- WHO AM I BECOMING?

Each chapter uses short topical passages from the New International Version to help you live the story of the Bible. As you journey through this book, whether in a group or on your own, one simple truth will become undeniably clear: what you believe drives everything.

Using this edition of *Believe*, church families around the globe can now embrace a full ministry year through worship services, small group studies, and family activities. Learn more about this church-wide experience at BelieveTheStory.com.

Available in stores and online!

ZONDERVAN®
.com

Think, Act, Be Like Jesus

Becoming a New Person in Christ

Randy Frazee with Robert Noland

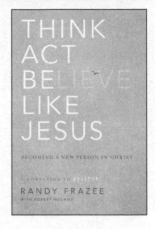

The Bible teaches that the goal of the Christian life is to become like Jesus—for our own personal growth and for the sake of others. Every believer needs to ask three big questions: What do I believe? What should I do? And who am I becoming?

In *Think, Act, Be Like Jesus*, bestselling author and pastor Randy Frazee helps readers grasp the vision of the Christian life and get started on the journey of discipleship. After unfolding the revolutionary dream of Jesus and showing how our lives fit into the big picture of what God is doing in the world, Frazee walks readers through thirty short chapters exploring the ten core beliefs, ten core practices, and ten core virtues that help disciples to think, act, and be more like Jesus Christ.

This compelling new book can be used in conjunction with the 30-week all-church *Believe* campaign or read separately as an individual study. Either way, readers will deepen their understanding of what it means to not just know the Story of God, but to live it.

Available in stores and online!